ROMAN COLONIES
IN THE FIRST CENTURY
OF THEIR FOUNDATION

edited by

Rebecca J. Sweetman

Oxbow Books

Oxford and Oakville

Published by
Oxbow Books, Oxford, UK

© Oxbow Books and the individual authors 2011

ISBN 978-1-84217-974-1

This book is *available* direct from

Oxbow Books, Oxford, UK
(Phone: 01865-241249; Fax: 01865-794449)

and

The David Brown Book Company
PO Box 511, Oakville, CT 06779, USA
(Phone: 860-945-9329; Fax: 860-945-9468)

or from our website
www.oxbowbooks.com

A CIP record is available for this book from the British Library

Library of Congress Cataloging-in-Publication Data

Roman colonies in the first century of their foundation / edited by Rebecca J. Sweetman.
    p. cm.
Papers from a conference held in September 2007 in St. Andrews, Fife, Scotland.
  Includes bibliographical references.
  ISBN 978-1-84217-974-1
1. Rome--Colonies--History--Congresses. 2. Rome--Colonies--Social conditions--Congresses. 3. Rome--Colonies--Social life and customs--Congresses. 4. Cities and towns--Rome--History--Congresses. 5. City and town life--Rome--History--Congresses. 6. Rome--Colonies--History, Local--Congresses. I. Sweetman, Rebecca J. II. Title.

DG87.R64 2011
937--dc22

                    2010052034

Front cover, clockwise from top left:
Corinth, temple D and Archaic temple from the south, photo: R. Sweetman;
Cremna: the baths, photo: A. U. De Giorgi;
Metellinum, 17th-c. bridge and remains of Roman pontooons, photo: J. Edmondson;
Portrait of Augustus from Butrint: Butrint Foundation, photo by J. Barclay-Brown.

Printed in Great Britain by
Short Run Press, Exeter

Contents

Acknowledgements

I am very grateful for the financial support from the School of Classics and the Roman Society.

The conference held in September 2007 was a stimulating and thoroughly enjoyable event thanks to the contributions made by all the speakers and through the work of the organizing team. The event would not have happened without the help of the staff of the School of Classics: those who chaired sessions such as Prof. Christopher Smith, Dr Roger Rees and Prof. Greg Woolf and especially the support staff in the School, Margaret Goudie and Irene Paulton and the Conference team at St Andrews. I was particularly fortunate to have two fine students to help with all manner of organization and coordination and I am very grateful to Alexandra Albury and Jeremy Complin for this. Greg Woolf has been particularly supportive as Head of School, as a colleague and as a contributor.

For the publication I would like to thank all the contributors for their care to their work and I am indebted to the work of the anonymous referees who provided thoughtful and thorough suggestions. I would also like to thank those at Oxbow Books for their hard work on the publication. Finally I would like to thank Brad and Conor for their support and good humour.

List of contributors

Prof. Martha Baldwin Bowsky
University of the Pacific
Stockton
California (USA)

Dr Will Bowden
Department of Archaeology
University of Nottingham

Dr José R. Carrillo
Universidad Pablo de Olavide
Seville

Dr Andrea U. De Giorgi
Visiting Assistant Professor
Classics Dept
Case Western Reserve University

Prof. Jonathan Edmondson
Department of History
York University
Toronto

Dr Inge Lyse Hansen
The Butrint Foundation
John Cabot University

Dr Alicia Jiménez
Consejo Superior de Investigaciones Científicas
Madrid

Dr Kalle Korhonen
Department of World Cultures
University of Helsinki

Prof. Paul Scotton
Program in Classics
California State University, Long Beach
Fellow, Cotsen Institute of Archaeology
UCLA

Dr Rebecca Sweetman
School of Classics
University of St Andrews

Prof. Greg Woolf
School of Classics
University of St Andrews

Abbreviations

AE	*L'Année épigraphique.*
ANRW	*Aufstieg und Niedergang der römischen Welt.*
BE	*Bulletin épigraphique.*
CIL	*Corpus inscriptionum Latinarum.*
HEP	*Hispania Epigraphica*
IG	*Inscriptiones Graecae.*
IGL Lipari	L. Bernabó-Brea – M. Cavalier – L. Campagna, *Meligunìs Lipára* XII: *Le iscrizioni lapidarie greche e latine delle Isole Eolie*, Palermo 2003.
IGL Messina	I. Bitto, *Le iscrizioni greche e latine di Messina* I, Pelorias 7, Messina 2001.
IMC Catania	K. Korhonen, *Le iscrizioni del Museo Civico di Catania. Storia delle collezioni – cultura epigrafica – edizione*, SSF Commentationes humanarum litterarum 121, Helsinki 2004.
IG Mus. Palermo	M. T. Manni Piraino, *Iscrizioni greche lapidarie del Museo di Palermo*, Σικελικά 6, Palermo 1973.
IL Mus. Palermo	L. Bivona, *Iscrizioni latine lapidarie del Museo di Palermo*, Σικελικά 5, Palermo 1970.
IL TermIm	L. Bivona, *Iscrizioni latine lapidarie del Museo Civico di Termini Imerese*, Supplementi a Κώκαλος 9, Palermo 1994.
LGPN	*The Lexicon of Greek Personal Names* I–IV (eds P. M. Fraser, E. Matthews *et al.*), Oxford 1987–2005.
NSA	*Notizie degli scavi di antichità.*
PIR²	(1933–) *Prosopographia Imperii Romani* (2nd ed.). Berlin, de Gruyter.
RE	(1894–) *Paulys Real-encyclopädie der classische Altertumswissenschaft.* Stuttgart, J.B. Metzlerscher Verlag.
SEG	*Supplementum epigraphicum Graecum.*
ZPE	*Zeitschrift für Papyrologie und Epigraphik.*

1. 100 Years of Solitude:
colonies in the first century of their foundation

Rebecca Sweetman

In recent years, great advances have been made on establishing new theories and approaches to studies on the growth of the Roman Empire, particularly by scholars such as Mattingly, Hingley and Hitchner.[1] From these works two major points are clear: that the traditional view of requiring provinces to become part of the Empire without choice or variation, often termed *Romanization,* cannot be sustained; and that a change in methodology, where the process is examined from the perspective of the provinces, facilitates a new understanding. Applications of these theories are still in the early stages[2] and there is still more to be done, particularly in terms of testing the hypotheses on actual sites and provinces, and examining a broader swathe of the community and identity within. Current scholarship is expounding the view that provincial residents had much greater participation in the processes of becoming involved in the Empire, and that the top-down approach needs to be reconsidered. To illustrate this, it is crucial to examine a range of different provinces and periods drawing on diverse evidence. The collection of papers presented here, originating in a conference held in St Andrews in 2007, go some way to achieving these aims by focusing on Roman colonies. In each case, the contributors examine a range of evidence, from literary to ceramic to architecture, to discuss issues of identity, relationship with Rome, and the timescale of change. Consequently, one of key aims of the conference was to bring together scholars working on diverse areas of the Empire spanning a broad range of periods to help to break down some of the perceived differences between provinces. From the West, the colonies of Lusitania (Augusta Emerita (Mérida) and Metellinum (Medellín)) and Baetica (Patricia Augustea (Corduba)) and those of Sicily are included. The colonies from the East include those from Epirus (Buthrotum (Butrint)),

Achaea (Corinth (Laus Iulia Corinthiensis)), Crete and Cyrene (Knossos (Julia Nobilis Cnossus), Syria (Palmyra) and Pisidia (Antioch (Antiochia Caesareia) and Parlais (Iulia Augusta Parlais)). The types of colonies differ too, from the early civilian colony of Corduba[3] to the veteran colonies of Antioch and Mérida and to the civilian (likely) colony of Knossos with a veteran presence. One of the most striking results of the examination of such a divergence of sites and material is that differences between areas and populations of the Empire do not permeate through every aspect of life, and there is more in common than perhaps scholarship has traditionally accounted for.

Issues in evidence and scholarship

Collectively, the papers presented in this volume work to challenge preconceived ideas about the nature and role of Roman colonies through their perspectives on new, as well as previously studied material. While acknowledging that the differences between provinces of the East and West may not be as clear cut as once thought, it is obvious from the range of papers that there is little evidence of a formula for the function or make-up of a colony. A traditional characterization of a colony has been as that of a 'mini-Rome',[4] as defined from the perspective of Rome and the Romans. However, it is now becoming clear that no two colonies are alike, and a blueprint for such a Roman foundation can hardly be defined with any precision. Although the colonies discussed here may appear to have obvious functions for veteran or civilian settlers; economic value; or the preservation of harmony, their functions changed over time and would have been utilized differently by diverse populations at the same time. For example, Mérida was a veteran colony providing land and a central economic hub to local populations, while maintaining direct patronage links to the Imperial family, it was also construed to be seen as a symbol of peace (by some at least). Corduba was a civilian, then veteran, establishment which retained elements of displays of *Romanitas* in the public and private spheres (civic space and houses), while deliberately retaining traditional elements and links with the ancestral past (through the use of the local burial urn type). There are elements within colonies which can be recognized as conscious attempts to emulate or symbolize Rome or *Romanitas* through establishment of cult (Corinth and Butrint), the creation of a version of the Forum of Augustus with the Temple of Mars Ultor (Corduba), the use of a copy of the Aeneas group from the Forum of Augustus (Mérida), or even the use of brick work (*opus reticulatum* in Nikopolis). An issue which lies at the heart of the definition of a colony is the incorporation of multiple-perceptions, for example the variation of impact that symbolic gestures made within the city would have had on the residents or visitors, the local population, landed elite, veterans or other provincials; a theme which is particularly highlighted by Bowden, de Giorgi, and Jiménez and Carillio. Bowden especially notes how it is important to attempt to highlight such a multiplicity of perspectives. But in many cases the evidence of a single urban landscape may not be extensive enough to meet the needs of his approach, hence the importance of contextualization of the colonies in their provincial landscapes and the Empire.

As scholars in this volume approach their material from the standpoint of the provincial evidence, the range of diversity is clear, but surprisingly, so is the commonality of problems involved in discussions of the creation, identity and role of colonies across the Empire. The variety of data used to elucidate such themes makes the point all the stronger. Bowden, Carrillo and Jiménez, Edmondson and Scotton's papers are all strongly archaeological while epigraphic evidence lies at the heart of discussions of the colonies of Butrint (Hansen), Knossos (Baldwin Bowsky) and Pisida (de Giorgi) of the East and Sicily (Korhonen) of the West. Many use onomastic evidence in particular to attempt to define the origins of those who inhabited the colonies (for example, Korhonen illustrates the difference in a range of Sicilian colonies through the distribution of Greek and Latin cognominia with Greek being comparatively stronger in Syracuse and Lipari than in Termini or Palermo). Such a range of material helps to balance the issues of bias concerning purely archaeological or historical studies.

The problems that beset the study of Roman provincial colonies are varied, and include: a dearth of sources for many (including Knossos and Sicily), misleading historical interpretations (Nikopolis and Corduba) and the nature of material evidence retrieval (for example in Knossos where the Roman was sidelined in favour of the Minoan, or in Butrint where many of the buildings were uncovered in a non-stratigraphic fashion). The inconsistency of substantiation has been rectified by some through comparative analysis; for example, Nikopolis, where exploration of Late Antique evidence dominates, is discussed with Butrint. Furthermore, some of the less well explored colonies in Spain (Metellinum and Pisidia (Comama or Parlais) are investigated with the aid of their better known neighbours such as Mérida and Antioch.

From work undertaken on Knossos, an Augustan colony, it was established that the conventional idea of what a Roman colony was could not be harmonized with the archaeological data both in terms of the timescale for change and the nature of the transformation itself.[5] In fact, the archaeological evidence thus far produced in the Knossos valley suggests that there was no major influx of settlers with the establishment of the colony. There is no denying that there was a small number of colonists and that the colony was traditionally and officially run,[6] but evidence suggests that the earliest settlers did not put their *cultural stamp* on Knossos. It was this issue that prioritised the agenda to establish whether other Roman colonies followed similar developments, and the results have been enlightening.

A range of data is used to indicate change. Epigraphic material from Syracuse shows that like Knossos,[7] the public inscriptions were in Latin and the private ones in Greek in the early years of the colony. Architecture may be used as an index for change as seen in the case of Mérida and Medellín, Butrint, Corinth, Palmyra and Knossos.[8] In Corinth, for example, Scotton's architectural analysis supported by the epigraphic and numismatic data, shows that investments were not made in the colony until some 30 years after its original foundation and at this point it may have been a concerted programme. The epigraphic data from the Sicilian colonies shows that the rate of change in these towns is slower than traditionally perceived[9] where Greek inscriptions and names continue to be obvious in the private sphere with Latin operating primarily in the official civic context.[10] For example, local elite make little effort to forsake their use of Greek. Korhonen's exhaustive study shows that this evidence is seen in many of the Sicilian colonies but also across the range of epigraphic contexts, from funerary to religious to civic. In contextualizing the evidence, Korhonen also illustrates that there is little evidence for architectural change with some cities such as Syracuse with the foundation of the colonies. The broad examination of the material allows a more nuanced view of Imperial Sicily where epigraphic changes may be seen in some cities (such as Catania) but so widespread in others (Syracuse) and in many cases, architectural changes are significantly later than the foundation of the colony (Catania and Syracuse). Korhonen's onomastic study further tested the possibility that Greek names fall out of favour through an examination of cognomina of parents and children. The results were varied; it seemed not to be the case in the funerary records of Catania but it was in evidence in Messina. Overall there was no evidence of a systematic avoidance of it.[11] Hansen has pointed out how the nature of the colony at Butrint changes from military to civilian (which is the opposite case for Corduba), as does the focus of its value, from being a strategic location to economic hub. Finally, ceramic material is successfully used by Baldwin Bowsky not only as an index of change in Knossos, where with the foundation of the colony there is a sudden influx of Italian sigillata but after an initial burst of popularity, Eastern sigillatas return to favour. Baldwin Bowsky also successfully illustrates how ceramic data may be used as a means of defining the reasons for that change; certainly in the case of Knossos (and likely the other colonies) the reasons for that change are largely economic.

Many of the scholars highlight unexpectedly slow timescale in which changes occur after a town becomes a colony; in the case of Corduba and Knossos for example, evidence of the effects of the establishment of the colony are not seen until a century after their foundation. Shorter delays are seen in the Sicilian colonies and in Corinth.[12] In the case of Mérida, the latest interpretation as presented here is that the issue of a conscious change in the city is not in doubt; however, it took place over a much longer period of time (nearly 100 years) than the more conventional view of a speedy conversion in the Augustan period. Explanations for such delays and their implications can be addressed through the wide geographical and chronological scope of the papers. The date-range of the papers provides good contrast between the discussions of the early colonies of Sicily (Korhonen) and Corduba (Jiménez and Carrillo), to that of the later imperial foundations of Pisidia (de Giorgi). Given that different contemporary circumstances would have influenced the establishment and growth of the colonies, it is perhaps significant that they

share a number of mutual issues. It is notable that contemporary colonies have more in common with each other sometimes and that often key differences lie within a single colony but in distinct periods. Furthermore, wider issues concerning sources and evidence are as problematic for Sicilian colonies as it they are for Greek or Asian ones.

The study of Roman provinces has been hampered by inconsistent archaeological records,[13] and one of the values in the scope of the papers is that they go some way towards providing a more coherent view. A problem common to all the provinces discussed is the paucity of rural evidence. As such, the relationship between colony and rural space will, in time, need further discussion to advance the investigation into the role of the colony for Rome and the provinces. The continued analysis of survey evidence in relation to written sources (as shown by de Giorgi) and other archaeological evidence (Jiménez and Carrillo) should in time provide fertile ground for discussions of rural activity in the Roman period. In the meantime, the variety of approaches taken by different scholars here also may be used to redress the bias in types of evidence available for different areas; some scholars examine their material at a micro level (for example Baldwin Bowsky with Italian sigillata stamps from Knossos) or at the macro level (Jiménez and Carrillo on the mortuary and other archaeological evidence from Corduba). A theme in all papers is the value of contextualization; be it on the level of putting the data in perspective with other forms of data (Baldwin Bowsky, Korhonen and Bowden), comparisons with other colonies (Hansen) or the broader province-wide framework (Edmondson and de Giorgi). The premise throughout the papers is that the idea of what a Roman colony is can no longer be viewed as a single description. A more useful approach is one which acknowledges that the individual colonies have their own identities which are somewhat fluid over time and diverse in terms of the multiplicity of viewpoints; that Rome requires the colonies as much as the colonies need Rome.

Colonies and Identity

In terms of identity, some papers question what defines a colony in the first place (Jiménez and Carrillo and Baldwin Bowsky), and some deal with the way some within the colony wished it to be perceived (for example, Corinth and Mérida). The papers presented here broadly examine issues of identity in terms of individual groups that make up the population of a colony; for example, the elite of Knossos, or colonists of Butrint, or the local population of Corduba. Individual groups may be defined through direct means such as epigraphic or mortuary evidence, or indirect methods such as ceramic or architectural evidence. For discussions of identity, ideally a range of data should be used and the variety of papers presented helps to realize such a requirement. Bowden stresses the importance of looking at personal elements of material culture (such as domestic contexts) to determine identity, while Jiménez and Carrillo show the possibilities of defining collective identity through architecture. Some, such as Scotton, see cult as an index of identity, Bowden sees the use of cremation as a sign of new populations, whereas Baldwin Bowsky employs ceramic material to indicate the evidence for early Italian settlers in the colony. The strength of the epigraphic record and the value of contextualizing it is clearly shown in the work of Baldwin Bowsky, Edmondson, Hansen and Korhonen but its value is further boosted by any knowledge of the people themselves as seen in the mortuary remains for example (see Jiménez and Carrillo, Bowden and de Giorgi). A salient word of caution is noted by Korhonen who notes that inscriptions found in the funerary context belong with the mortuary assemblages and therefore reflect more the aspirations of the living rather than the real social status of the dead (*e.g.* Greek speaking families may chose Latin epitaphs and vice versa). This emphasises the point that when the material evidence is viewed diachronically it indicates that the colonies do not remain static; colonies, their populations and how they express themselves change over time. In examining the nature of the colonies from the local perspective, it is possible to broadly elucidate the make-up of the population particularly through epigraphic and mortuary data. In the majority of cases presented here, authors note that the evidence for population change (as one would expect with an influx of settlers be they civilian or military), is more of an organic process than a sudden alteration.

While some colonies might distinguish themselves by comparison to other cities (as seen in the case of Medellín, Syracuse and Nikopolis), individual colonies could in part be defined through tangible associations with their historical pasts (for example, Knossos, Corduba and Butrint),. Although new colonial status may be bestowed often the importance of the pre-existing city is well maintained. In Knossos, the image of the labyrinth is used on colonial coinage, Butrint's past is mythicized in the Aeneid, elements of traditional burial practices are retained in Corduba and historically important Greek inscriptions are re-carved in the Imperial

period in the Sicilian towns. In this respect, colonies may consciously use their historical or mythical pasts to help retain the communities' sense of its own previous states and in some ways it may help to maintain its credibility in the eyes of its own population and Rome.

Relationship with Rome

Although it is not always clear who may have been the driving force behind the promotion of colonial identity, the material evidence of Imperial cult at Corinth, the links between Agrippa and political classes as expressed on the coinage of Butrint and the architectural investment in Mérida, is indicative of the importance of patronage and connections with Rome. Moreover, while discussing this evidence from the view of the provinces, it is clear that there is more of a symbiotic and dynamic relationship between Rome and the colonies than one of a dominating power. The reasons for such an association are largely based on the initial interests (overwhelmingly financial), shown either by Rome or the city in becoming part of the Empire.[14] The economic relationship was not a one way process as demonstrated by Baldwin Bowsky's discussion of the movement of Italian sigillata at Knossos. Both Knossos and Butrint have epigraphic substantiation for significant numbers of residents with commercial connections. For many provinces it was of fundamental importance to become part of the Empire and to maintain the attention of those in Rome in order to maximise their economic potential. Moreover, all the colonies discussed here sustain distinct levels of their own identities which further highlight the element of willingness to become part of the Empire. Colonies function as nodes in the Roman network society; there is little to be gained by forcing any particular cultural change on the city as the cities were of value primarily because of their location.

Conclusions

Diachronic views and contextualization lie at the core of many of the papers presented and the role of the colonies in the province and wider Empire is well-illustrated. The variety in character and function of individual cities in the same province as illustrated by Gortyn and Knossos, Merida and Medellín, Syracuse and Taormina,[15] emphasises the value of examining individual cities and provinces, while highlighting the extent of commonality between cities of different provinces (such as slow alterations in the city or desires for links with Rome). Contextualization allows for a broader scope of understanding, for example it is difficult to see how the agricultural potential and historic past of Knossos would have been enough to justify colonial status, but when examined in light of her relationship with Gortyn (as Baldwin Bowsky does), as one end of a trade corridor, her economic potential and usefulness becomes clear.

A key outcome of the presentation of the range of material and approaches here is the realization that the inhabitants of Roman colonies are active players in the roles their cities played in the Empire, and how successful they were as such. Issues of communication as a two way-process are fundamental to the success of a colony; although Rome may have used her provinces for economic strategies, the provinces and, particularly colonies, could equally profit both through a direct communication with Rome, and indirectly as a consequence of having access to the Empire's economic network. When the material is examined without the veil of presumed acculturation, it is possible to see other explanations for change, such as active desires to participate in the Empire and the resulting natural increases in communication channels.[16] The colonies developed as hubs in the network society and the relationships between Rome and the colonies, in particular through the medium of patronage, are the key communication links and control that make these hubs strong. The creation of and investment in colonies appears to be dictated by their usefulness to Rome (investment in Knossos in the 2nd century due to a need for her strategic position) or the desires on the part of the provincials to attract Roman attention (for example at Mérida or Corinth). In the case of the examples here there is little sense of a pressing need for colonization and the range of epigraphic, architectural and mortuary evidence reflects this. Key alterations appear to occur in the colonies when their economic values to Rome are realized but this can come in many forms. For Corinth, Knossos and Butrint it was their geographical potential in terms of trade rather than material resources. For the colonies of Spain it appears to be more to do with the material wealth and maintenance of stability in the region and for Sicily and Pisida the protection of communication links is clear. In all cases, new small population groups can be seen in the early years of the colonies but there is little evidence of widespread and aggressive colonization (such as population or language change). Investments are made (by the Romans and by locals) in the colony if the returns are viable (be they strategic or material), yet at the same time cultural diversity is allowed to prosper (as seen through language, burial and links with historic

past). By the beginning of the 2nd century CE most areas of the Empire share common traits such as substantial public buildings, industries, successful economy and a range of dwellings from lavish to basic with the interior décor to match.

The variety that is seen throughout the colonies is logical, and much depends on the chronological context of their foundation. Although we would not advocate the response-stimulus theory here, it is clear that changes in the city reflect wider but contemporary situations. One of the key results of the collation of the material is that it highlights the extent of diversity of colonies and their occupants, and importantly, it shows that flexibility of approach allows for new interpretations. There are few signs of any kind of cultural process being forced on the local populations. For the regions discussed, there is no evidence of subjugation; for example, little sign of Focault's watched/monitored society or holding back of information that one might see of the oppressed is in evidence.[17] The functions of colonies differ, not just between the East and West but within the same provinces also. But there are similarities between colonies, regardless of the method or date by which they became active in the Empire. Such parallels exist because of the shared commonality of roles, economic, strategic, etc., that the colonies played as network hubs of Rome. While different processes are at play around the Mediterranean, it is possible for them to be understood as well in terms of processes of globalization.[18] The establishment of many of the colonies does not appear to have made a marked impact on the existing populations. Once part of the globalized network the colonies could benefit from the increased trade potential. A consequence of this is a simulation of growth in availability and acquisition of luxury items which would in turn encourage elite classes, patronage and more communication links with Rome. The extent to which this is a natural progression can partly be seen in the broader developments in the Mediterranean and the papers presented here go some way towards the wider contextualization but this is an area that could be usefully explored in the future.

The future

Although this collection contributes to a new perspective on Roman colonies, a number of issues still remain. In terms of the identity of the colony, a more focused examination of the different types of evidence used would be enlightening in terms of defining the diversity, if any, between the public and private identities of the colonies. Further discussions on the relationships between cities and colonies of different status (as discussed by Edmondson) but also of particular interest would be a better understanding of the relationship between city and country (as touched on by Baldwin Bowsky with the case of Knossos) and the importance of this, if at all, to the network society. These issues would in part be elucidated through a more detailed examination of the social make up of the urban in contrast with the rural populations as mentioned by Korhonen where in Sicily early colonists were Latin speaking while in the surrounding countryside they were still predominately Greek. The initial results offered show that for the colonies, it is more useful to conceive a relationship with Rome and the East as one which had the momentum to have cultural affects primarily when it was mutually beneficial. Consequently, perceived differences between the East and Western Empire are not so obvious and in fact there is more commonality between colonies in evidence when viewed together rather than as isolated units.

Bibliography

Barrett, J. C. 1997. 'Romanization: A Critical Comment', in *Dialogues in Roman Imperialism: Power, Discourse, and Discrepant Experience in the Roman Empire*, D. J. Mattingly and S. E. Alcock (eds), *JRA Suppl.* 23 (Portsmouth), 51–64.

Castells, M. 1996. *The Rise of the Network Society* (Oxford).

Foucault, M. 1955. *Discipline and Punish: The Birth of the Prison* (London).

Gosden, C. 2004. *Archaeology and Colonialism. Cultural contact from 5000 BC to the Present* (Cambridge).

Hingley, R. (ed.) 2001. *Images of Rome. Perceptions of ancient Rome in Europe and the United States in the modern age. JRA suppl.* No. 44 (Portsmouth).

Hingley, R. 2005. *Globalizing Roman Culture. Unity, diversity and Empire* (London).

Hitchner, R. 2004. 'Roman Globalization and longevity of Empire', *Archaeological Institute of America 105th Annual Meeting Abstracts*, January 2–5 2004, San Francisco, 83 (Boston).

Hitchner, R. 2008. 'Globalization avant la letter: globalization and the history of the Roman Empire', *New Global Studies*, Vol 2.2, 1–12.

Lechner, F. J. and J. Boli (eds) 2004. *The Globalization Reader* (Oxford).

Le Roux, P. 2004. 'La romanisation en question', *Annales HSS* 59.2, 287–311.

Mattingly, D. 2004. 'Being Roman: expressing identity in a provincial setting', *JRA* 17, 5–25.

Mattingly, D. J. and S. E. Alcock (eds) 1997. *Dialogues in Roman Imperialism: Power, Discourse, and Discrepant Experience in the Roman Empire. JRA Suppl.* 23 (Portsmouth).

Millet, M. 1990. *The Romanization of Britain. An essay in archaeological interpretation* (Cambridge).

Roberston, R. 1992. *Globalization* (London).

Salmeri, G., A. Raggi and A. Baroni (eds) 2004. *Colonie Romane Nel Mondo Greco. Conference proceedings, Pisa November 2000.* Rome: L'Erma di Bretschneider.

Sen, A. 2004. 'How to judge globalism', in *The Globalization Reader,* F. J. Lechner, and J. Boli (ed.), (Oxford), 16–22.

Sweetman, R. J. 2007. 'Roman Knossos. The nature of a globalized city', *AJA* 111.1, 61–81.

Trimble, J. 2001. 'Rethinking 'Romanization' in early imperial Greece: Butrint, Corinth and Nicopolis'. Review of *Die Römische Kolonie von Butrint und die Romanisierung Griechelands* by J. Bergemann. *JRA* 14, 625–28.

Webster, J. 2001. 'Creolizing the Roman Provinces', *AJA* 105, 209–55.

Webster, J., and N. J. Cooper (eds) 1996. *Roman Imperialism: Post-colonial Perspectives. Proceedings of a Symposium Held at Leicester University in November 1994.* Leicester Archaeology Monographs 3 (Leicester).

Witcher, R. E. 2000. 'Globalisation and Roman Imperialism: Perspectives on Identities in Roman Italy', in *The Emergence of State Identities in Italy in the First Millennium BC.* E. Herring and K. Lomas (eds) (London), 213–225.

Woolf, G. 1998. *Becoming Roman: the origins of provincial civilization in Gaul.* (Cambridge).

Notes

1. Mattingly 1997, Hingley 2005, Hitchner 2008, Witcher 2000.
2. See Woolf 1997 on Gaul, Witcher 2000 on Italy and Sweetman 2007 on Knossos.
3. Before becoming *Colonia Patricia*.
4. In part due to the description by Aulus Gellius (*Noctes Atticae* 16.13.8–9).
5. Sweetman 2007.
6. Sanders 1982, 14 names a number of Duviri and also points out that most of the officially inscriptions are in Latin and date from the 1st CE.
7. See Sweetman 2007.
8. Sweetman 2007.
9. Even when taking account of those inscriptions from the religious context which is markedly conservative.
10. A similar deduction is seen in Knossos. Sweetman 2007.
11. Have to bear in mind the bias of survival of evidence when taking account of this.
12. Hence the original title for the conference.
13. As evident in Korhonen's study of the epigraphic record where the material is so easily re-used and therefore prone to significantly inconsistent survival rates.
14. Some such as Butrint are for strategic reasons but even this has economic reasons at its core.
15. In Taormina the local elite are barely visible in the epigraphic record of the early colony with the imperial dedications dominating the material which is the opposite to the situation in Syracuse.
16. As Korhonen points out regarding epigraphic evidence the choice of language in a public inscription may in some cases have more to do with an issue of communication (practicalities) than one of acculturation
17. Foucault 1975.
18. See Sweetman 2007 for discussion of this point pertaining to Knossos.

2. Language and Identity in the Roman Colonies of Sicily

Kalle Korhonen

The purpose of this study

Much is still unclear about acculturation in Sicily in the early imperial period, especially on the linguistic side.[1] Whereas some phenomena of Roman culture, such as gladiatorial entertainment, seem to have spread rapidly to Sicily,[2] it is less easy to make sweeping statements about the spread of the Latin language. Scholars have pointed out the geographical differences and functional distribution of surviving Greek and Latin inscriptions. Latin dominated in the towns of the western and northern coast, Greek on the eastern coast from Taormina to Syracuse, as well as in Lipari. In public epigraphy, especially in honorary and building inscriptions, Latin prevailed; Greek documents were rare, but reappeared in late antiquity. This development appears to be different from the Greek towns of southern Italy, where the manifestations of Greek linguistic identity were most evident during the early Empire, and faded by the end of the 2nd century.[3] In the colonies of the Greek east, Latin had a strong role during the early periods of their existence, but disappeared from the record during the 2nd or 3rd century.[4]

In the social scale, the relation between Greek and Latin was complex. Sicily was in many respects a bilingual society, where the relative status of the languages shifted according to the circumstances; the term "diglossia" has been avoided.[5] Of the literary authors and teachers, some wrote or taught in Greek, others in Latin.[6] Despite the existence of a colonial elite, generalizations like "upper classes used Latin, lower classes Greek" have been considered unfounded.[7]

The purpose of this paper is, on the one hand, to analyze language choice in the epigraphy of the public space and give a more accurate picture of the transformation of the linguistic landscape. On the other hand, I will survey the linguistic identity of the people represented in epitaphs. In my view, with a careful analysis of the epigraphic material in its context, more can be achieved than just new statistics of Greek and Latin documents. I will try to see if the fact that Latin was the dominant language in the forum affected language use in certain other domains, and if there are contexts in which Latin is clearly in a higher position than Greek. The motivations behind language choice in epitaphs will be discussed. One issue that has received relatively little attention in Roman Sicily is onomastics: the prestige of Greek and Latin cognomina and the use of onomastic formulae will be analyzed. Even if such incomplete evidence cannot be used directly to measure the proportions of speech communities, some suggestions about their relative sizes are included. The discussion will focus on questions of linguistic and sometimes cultural identity, as the material allows no access to questions of ethnic identity in Sicily in this period.

The sociolinguistic significance of the founding of the colonies

The majority language in Sicily is likely to have remained Greek throughout the Roman republican period, despite some immigration from the Latin-speaking areas of Italy.[8] Moreover, Punic was used in certain towns of the west, Oscan in some northern areas,[9] and the other indigenous languages were endangered or already extinct. Little changed with the concession of Latin rights to the Sicilian communities in 44, but the turbulent period between 43 and 36, when most Sicilian towns were allied with Sextus Pompeius,[10] was not without demographic consequences. The inhabitants of Lipari are supposed to have been transported to Naples where they were to stay as long as the war continued; it is usually assumed that many returned later.[11]

The situation changed more dramatically in Augustan times, when the number of Latin speakers increased notably across the island. By the year 21, five or six colonies had been founded by Augustus: *Catina* (Catania), *Syracusae* (Syracuse), *Tauromenium* (Taormina), *Thermae* (*Himeraeorum*) (Termini Imerese), and *Tyndaris* (Tindari), possibly also *Panhormus* (Palermo).[12] The founding of the colonies seems to have been meant as a punishment.[13] The colonists were allotted lands confiscated from the supporters of Sextus Pompeius, and the other inhabitants were not necessarily treated much better: at Taormina, says Diodorus, the former inhabitants were expelled.[14] Where they went is not known, but one could guess that most of them remained in Sicily. Even in places where the former inhabitants were not forced to migrate, it is likely that they did not receive the Roman citizenship.[15] On the other hand, there is no evidence of separate administrations, which are known to have existed elsewhere: apparently the whole population in the colonial towns was governed by the colonial administration.

The colonists were veterans, according to Augustus' *Res gestae*,[16] and their number will have been around 3,000 men, at least in Syracuse and Catania.[17] The men who had served in the Roman army in this period must have been mostly Latin-speaking – although some of them or members of their families are likely to have been bilingual in Greek or in an Italic language – and especially Latin-inscribing. On the basis of the inhabited areas in the colonial towns, Wilson has estimated a total population of 28,000 in Syracuse, 13,000 in Catania, and a few thousands in each of the other towns.[18] In the initial phase, then, the colonial towns must have been largely bilingual, with the Latin-speaking colonists and their families, a substantial Greek-speaking group, and smaller linguistic minorities. Especially Syracuse and Catania must have had urban Greek speech communities of notable size, whereas the situation in Thermae was different. The surrounding countryside was divided by the prevalently Latin-speaking settlers and the prevalently Greek-speaking former inhabitants.

It would be important to know more about the social and geographical origin of the colonists, but the surviving evidence does not take us far. In Catania and Syracuse, an accurate analysis is not currently possible. The epigraphic evidence does not allow us to establish which families belong to the colonists, and which had immigrated before or after the Augustan settlement. Many of the gentilicia attested

refer to powerful families of the late republic. Some 90 gentilicia are attested epigraphically at Catania or among Catanians elsewhere.[19] At Syracuse, the number is smaller. Some information can be extracted from the evidence at Termini, analyzed by Bivona: there are certain gentilicia that refer to the northern regions of Roman Italy, but for many families one can only resort to a generic provenance from central Italy.[20] In any case, because the colonies consisted of veterans, there is no reason to assume that a channelized migration took place, in which most of the colonists would have come from a small area.[21]

As Eck has put it, with the advent of the Empire Sicily becomes "geschichtslos",[22] as literary authors pay little attention to it. The rich world of the local elites described in the Verrines disappears from our sight, and freedmen and freedwomen step to the fore. The written sources concerning Sicily are predominantly funerary inscriptions, which separates the early imperial period from the late Hellenistic/republican period.[23] The relative yield of early imperial lapidary inscriptions from Sicily is notably smaller than in Central Italy or in North Africa and can be compared to the southernmost areas of the Italian peninsula. The inscriptions are in general rather modest, regardless of their genre.[24] Languages other than Greek or Latin disappear from the epigraphic record.[25]

Language choice in public epigraphy and the transformation of the linguistic landscape

Syracuse in the 1st century BCE: Latin appears on the stage

In order to find out about the linguistic identity in Sicily from the 1st century BCE to early colonial times it is necessary to look at how the linguistic landscape changed by focusing on the inscriptions produced for public space.[26] I will look at Syracuse in particular, where the transformation can be followed more closely than elsewhere. Because lapidary epigraphy always exists in a context, I will also comment on the monumental transformation of the civic centre in the same period. I will argue that the founding of the colony did bring about changes, but their immediate effect was not as dramatic as might be thought. After Syracuse, a short discussion will be dedicated to the other colonies. Admittedly, only an arbitrary selection of texts that belonged to the linguistic landscape survives, and it is hard to estimate the real amount of texts written on perishable materials and on bronze.[27]

There were evidently many Greek inscriptions visible to the public in late Hellenistic Syracuse.[28] It has even been claimed that the city had a "rather obsessive epigraphic habit" in Ciceronian times.[29] The surviving material from the 1st century comprises five proxeny decrees set up by the evidently powerful guilds of performing artists, possibly in the theatre.[30] Except for the proconsul M. Acilius Caninus (*RE* 'Acilius' 15), who was honoured during his tenure in 46–45, it is not known where the honoured persons originated from; the others may be Sicilians.[31] Moreover, to the 2nd quarter of the 1st century BCE seems to belong a dedication by Masteabar ([βασιλ]εύς Μαστεαβαρ), whose father was the Numidian king known in other sources as Γάος or *Gauda*, and who may be identical to king Mastenizen I.[32] However, the inscription was reused soon afterwards, and most of the text was destroyed.

At the same time, inscriptions were also produced in Latin for display in the public space. The Latin inscriptions *CIL* I² 2224 (= X 7121), 2951 and 3429 belong to the late republic. *CIL* I² 2951, dedicated by the *praetor* C. Norbanus in the early 80's, apparently commemorates the building of a road. The mosaic inscription *CIL* I² 2224, datable either to the late 2nd or the early 1st century, refers to reconstruction work funded by a Cn. Octavius A. f., evidently a fish trader.[33] Even more interesting in terms of language choice is *CIL* I² 3429. The fragmentary text runs: *[- - -]pition [- - -?] / [- - -]sanus·D[- - -?]*. For the second line, the only reasonable interpretation in this context is the ethnic *Syracus(s)anus*, followed by *d(edit)* or *d(ono) d(edit)*.[34] It seems that the inscription was dedicated by a Syracusan with a Greek name who was willing to use Latin in a stone inscription.

Before the founding of the colony, Syracuse evidently became a *municipium* in or shortly before the year 44.[35] There is a published, but previously unrecognized fragment probably from the municipal period: [- - -]ις ἀγορα/[νομ-, - - - δε]κυρεύ/[σας - - - ἐκ τῶ]ν ἑαυτοῦ / [ἀνέθηκε(ν) (?) - - -]. The inscription, which is fully discussed in the Appendix, commemorates a dedication by a member of the local council who had reached the aedileship. Although the fragment could belong to the colonial period, it is more likely that it is from the period when Syracuse was a *municipium*. The language chosen is Greek, as one might expect from a local magistrate in the prevalently Greek-speaking Syracuse, but the text includes the rare verb δεκυρεύω, coined from the Latin term *decurio*. The text could be a religious dedication, and it is difficult to say where the monument stood. The mixture of Greek and Latin administrative terminology in the inscription gives interesting testimony of a pragmatic approach to the Latin language by a member of the local elite.

To the aftermath of Naulochus evidently belong the fragments of a large Greek building inscription in which Achradina is mentioned.[36] It was probably dedicated by Octavian in 30, when he was consul for the fourth time.[37] There is also a Latin fragment that refers to a statue of Octavian, dedicated before he was given the name *Augustus*, *i.e.* between 36 and 27.[38] In this case, the state administration used Greek in communication to the city, and the city responded in Latin. The statue probably stood on the *agora*, given that the inscription was found in the vicinity.

The bilingual civic centre of the colony of Syracuse

The surviving inscriptions set up in the public space of Syracuse from the founding of the colony until the 2nd century CE are regularly in Latin; Greek documents are lacking in the sphere of public administration. Excluding the epitaphs, around 20 Latin inscriptions have been published.[39] This is surprisingly little for a city of this size, but we do not know how much has been lost. Among these inscriptions, some are probably Augustan.[40] If all the Greek evidence from the non-funerary contexts is considered, it is more abundant than has usually been recognized: the evidence of the "philhellenism" that has been missing so far in Syracuse is not totally absent. However, the functional distribution of languages is still there: the Greek evidence refers to the contexts of spectacles, religion and monuments commemorating the past.

From the field of performing arts, a fragment survives with the names of the members of a winning team in a theatrical competition. The titles [διδά]σκαλος and possibly σαλπι(γ)κτής (]ΚΤΗΣ) are given.[41] It is datable to the early colonial period on palaeographical and onomastic grounds. At least two persons have a Latin cognomen: Σεουερ[ος] (*Severus*) and Ἀφρικ[ανός], but this does not imply that they were Latin speakers. The original inscription was probably exhibited in the theatre, as it was found in the Neapolis. Evidence discovered in the Greek east indicates that the guilds of actors mentioned above may have continued to operate in Syracuse in imperial times.[42] Moreover, it is worth pointing out that two Greek epitaphs from early imperial Syracuse contain references to performing arts.[43] On the other hand, it is notable that here, the spectacle can be referred to with the Greek phrase δρόμοι κιρκήσιοι, in which the modifying adjective is a loan-word from Latin.[44]

Religious dedications in Greek by prominent persons also survive from the early colony.[45] Probably the most notable is a limestone altar with an eagle in relief and the inscription Διὶ καὶ / Τύχηι / Μαρκιανός.[46] Even if the dedicator gives only his cognomen, he may well belong to a prominent family.[47] Furthermore, a large marble krater was dedicated by at least two persons, a Theodorus and the son of a Maximus.[48] The name of the divinity has not survived, and the dating is based on onomastics.[49] Finally, one should also mention the Greek inscription *IG* XIV 9 relative to the cult of Dea Syria (Atargatis), of which only a Latin translation survives by the 16th-century scholar Ottavio Gaetani.[50] It is a list of cult officials, the "sacerdos Syriae deae", whose name is transmitted as *Tiberius Tiberii f.*, and the "praesides Syriae deae", five of whom were Roman citizens.[51] The text is difficult to date and may belong either to the late republic or to the early colony.[52] In religious dedications, the full motivations for linguistic and communicative choices can be fairly complicated,[53] but both the linguistic form and the language choice can be more conservative than in other types of documents.[54] In these three cases, the language choice is probably due to the combination of Greek linguistic identity and religious conservatism. But there is also a third possibility: polite or deferential accommodation, well attested in the religious context,[55] which could provide an alternative explanation for the use of Greek on the altar of Zeus and Tyche. At least the relief and the krater are likely to have stood in sanctuaries, probably the list of cult officials as well. The language attested in the extra-urban sanctuaries of the region, such as the one dedicated to Anna and the Παῖδες in Buscemi, or to Demeter in Avola, is predominantly Greek.[56] There is, of course, no reason to think that Latin would have been avoided in the religious sphere: e.g., the evidence of the cult of Serapis contains an interesting but fragmentary inscription dedicated by a [-] Papinius P. f. Fla[- - -], *flamen Serapis*, apparently from the late 1st or early 2nd century CE.[57]

There is also a piece of evidence from yet another context: the monuments that refer to the historical past. To no earlier than the early imperial period belongs an architectural fragment with the Greek words κατὰ Ἀθηναίων, "against the Athenians". The publisher has plausibly suggested that it was part of a monument commemorating events that took place half a millennium earlier.[58] Literary culture provides a parallel: for the literary authors of the imperial period, discussed by Salmeri, Syracuse was a world that had not moved beyond the "heroic" 5th century.[59]

So far, my discussion has focused on inscriptions, not on the whole communicative context. The colonization was followed by building activities in the colonies, and during the imperial period, the civic centres were remodelled.[60] On the other hand, it seems that the restructuring of the former *agora*, at least in Syracuse and Catania, did not begin in Augustan times. Admittedly, the urban developments are not very well known, but in Syracuse, the building activities after the founding of the colony seem to have concentrated in the area of Neapolis, which was monumentalized and where an amphitheatre and a triumphal arch were built.[61] Like the Roman republican officials in Syracuse, the administration of the colony may well have operated in pre-existing structures.[62] There is no reason to think that the inscriptions from earlier periods remaining in the *agora*, which became the *forum*, were systematically removed:[63] inscriptions from between the Hellenistic period and late antiquity have been found in the vicinity.[64] Thus, the overall appearance of the administrative centre in Augustan times was not very different from the pre-colonial period: there may well have been both Greek and Latin inscriptions in sight for enthusiastic readers. However, it is important to keep in mind that the new inscriptions set up in the forum must have been regularly in Latin, which slowly transformed the linguistic landscape.

Greek and Latin in public epigraphy in the other colonies

In the other colonies, nearly all the surviving inscriptions of the public space set up after the colonization are in Latin.[65] In many towns, except in Taormina, there is very little evidence from the period immediately preceding the foundation of the colony: public epigraphy seems to begin with the colonization. Even though this is not the whole truth, as some evidence has been lost, the transformation of the linguistic landscape is likely to have been more dramatic than in Syracuse.

In Catania, where the pre-Roman evidence includes a fragment from the context of the gymnasium (*IMC Catania* 2 = *IG* XIV 456), non-funerary Latin inscriptions make their appearance after the colonization, and are relatively numerous in the early imperial period in comparison with Syracuse.[66] The Greek evidence consists only of small fragments. *IMC Catania* 27, a dedication by the town of Laodicea in Syria, might also have been bilingual.[67] Even if it was only in Greek, the language choice would not be remarkable in a bilingual setting such as Sicily or Rome.[68] Another Greek fragment refers to the activities of the town council (*IMC Catania* 43), containing only the word [ψηφί]σματι, possibly [ψηφί]σματι [βουλῆς] (= *decreto decurionum*). In Italy and Sicily, decrees of the city council in Greek are otherwise rare.[69] However, the expression could well have been of the kind *locus datus decreto decurionum*, and the inscription could refer to a tomb.[70] The linguistic landscape of Catania may have changed more than the built environment in the civic centre. The buildings from the Augustan period include the aqueduct and possibly an early version of the theatre; the structures of the forum are, according to Wilson, datable to the second half of the 1st century CE, at the earliest.[71]

Greek is also attested in Catania in the context mentioned before, religious epigraphy. A well-known bilingual inscription discovered near Acireale commemorates the dedication of a statue of Priapus, with a poem in Greek and a prose part (?) in Latin, and is, in my view, datable to the 1st or early 2nd century.[72] There is also a metric dedication to Apollo, *IMC Catania* 8 (= *IG* XIV 451), which belongs to the late 2nd–3rd century. One or two private dedications that refer to dreams survive.[73]

In Taormina, the texts include fragments of a calendar and consular *fasti*, an exceptional case in the provinces, from the earliest period of the colony.[74] From Tindari, several dedications to persons in high places are known, but mostly from the beginning of the 2nd century on; some fragments might be Augustan.[75] This is also the case in the northwestern "triangle", Marsala, Palermo and Termini, where many more indications of the presence of senatorial families survive than on the eastern coast, partly because this area was well connected with economically important North Africa.[76] The epigraphic culture of politics and administration in these towns is almost exclusively Latin during our period. In effect, because the proportion of imperial dedications is relatively high in these towns, the local elites are not very well known. This is due to the fact that in such inscriptions either the town or the city council is indicated as the dedicator, or no dedicator is mentioned at all. This is not a Sicilian feature, as imperial dedications have similar characteristics all over the Roman world.[77]

As I pointed out, the references to Greek linguistic identity are marginal, but there are exceptions. The famous bilingual stonecutter's advertisement, with the same text in Greek and Latin, now in Palermo, is quite certainly early imperial and Sicilian.[78] The exact provenance is difficult to establish.[79] Alföldy

has convincingly argued that the non-standard grammar in the lower part of the inscription is not due to linguistic incompetence, but rather to irony on the stonecutter's part.[80] There is no reason to interpret it as a manifestation of a linguistic identity that is neither Greek nor Latin. For the purposes of this discussion, the most important detail in the text is that it advertises inscriptions both for "sacred temples and public buildings". This division in two could well indicate how the stonecutter saw the roles of Greek and Latin in the local public space.

In Termini, there is interesting evidence that can be compared to the monument commemorating the historical past from Syracuse, mentioned above on p. 10. Two historically important Greek inscriptions appear to have been reproduced during imperial times.[81] But unlike the inscription from Syracuse, which commemorated the pre-Roman past of the city, the original texts were dedicated by Scipio Africanus Minor after the destruction of Carthage.

In the towns of different status, Greek could have a more visible role.[82] I comment on Lipari and Messina, which never became colonies, but the funerary epigraphy of which will be discussed below. Lipari seems to have been promoted to municipal status in the early imperial period.[83] The chief magistrates are in the early imperial period mentioned in a Greek inscription carved on a block of marble; their title is given as ἄρχοντες.[84] A building inscription dedicated by two former ἀγορανόμοι (ἀγορανομήσαντες) could be early imperial as well (*IGL Lipari* 4), although the publisher Manganaro has suggested an earlier dating.[85] However, the other honorary and building inscriptions from the imperial period are in Latin (*IGL Lipari* 748–757).

To Messina is related some interesting epigraphic material regarding the cult of Asclepius. There are, in particular, two notable altars with Greek inscriptions, one of them with a dedication to Antoninus Pius (*IG* XIV 402 and *IGL Messina* 38). It has been argued by prominent scholars that the altars come from Aigeai in Cilicia,[86] but it has not been explained in a satisfactory way when the transport took place. This must have happened before the early 17th century,[87] *i.e.* before antiquarianism had really started.[88] If the altars were imported in antiquity (2nd–3rd century), the case becomes complicated. If they were produced in Messina, they are of relevance to the cult of Asclepius in Messina, but also to the use of Greek and Latin in the high levels of the local society. In this case, however, the primary targets of the dedications are Asclepius and Hygeia.

Language choice in funerary epigraphy and onomastics

The bilingual context

In order to illustrate problems of linguistic identity in Sicily, it is not sufficient to look at the public spaces only, but also on language choice in epitaphs and in the personal names recorded in them. This material is necessary for a wider sociolinguistic approach. Scholars have been puzzled by the low correlation between the language of the inscription and the ethnic/cultural origin and legal status of the persons commemorated in Roman Sicily, as well as the variation in onomastic formulae,[89] which makes it worthwhile to clarify the issue.

In my discussion I have claimed that Sicily, especially the colonies, was a "bilingual society". This meant that many or most of the people, depending on location, must have been bilingual in the "all-embracing" definition of the term. They had some proficiency in both Greek and Latin, but their abilities ranged, as Adams has put it, "from native fluency on the one hand to imperfect competence verging on incompetence on the other".[90] The sociolinguistic situation in the Sicilian towns must have been rather complex. Unlike in Rome, the native speakers of Greek were not predominantly slaves or libertines.[91] There were Greek-speaking, Latin-speaking and bilingual nuclear families, which in turn belonged to other social groups. The extended family comprised more or less distant relatives; the households (*familiae*) were larger than in contemporary industrialized societies, and not all the members were related, but other dependencies were involved. The Greek and Latin speech communities were intertwined in various ways: a lot of bilingualism must have been present in everyday life.[92] It would be difficult to estimate how many people had native proficiency in only one language: the children simply had more opportunities for learning the two languages "at home".[93]

The surviving manifestations of linguistic identity from Sicily are primarily epitaphs and personal names. Epitaphs were, as elsewhere in the Roman Empire, nearly always written in one language only. Sometimes it is allowed to draw the conclusion that that language was the primary language used in the family, but not always. Funerary inscriptions belonged to the set of funerary or mortuary practices. Such practices belonged, on the one hand, to the sphere of religion and could be very conservative, but on the other hand, they could be used in expressing social status and aspirations. The practices could sometimes be extended to the whole *familia*,[94] but

generally the nuclear families seem to have had the power to decide about their own traditions, conforming at the same time to the habits of the community.

No exact correlation should be assumed between the quality of the funerary monument and the social status, or even wealth, of the family. In effect, the people whose social position was changing, such as libertine families, may have been more inclined towards competition in funerary practices.[95] The epitaphs exhibited for public display – not collocated inside sepulchral chambers – had a communicative role towards the rest of the community. There are likely to have been tendencies for Greek-speaking families to choose Latin epitaphs and vice versa. For those whose position in the society was moving up, such as freedmen with high professional skills, a Latin epitaph could be an indication of status. This is likely to have been so especially in the colonies, in which the Latin-speaking and inscribing elite was visible in the linguistic landscape. In this respect and for certain social groups, the situation resembled a diglossic situation. In addition, there are likely to have been Sicilian families that had changed language, but that for reasons of conservatism or linguistic or cultural identity kept giving names and inscribing epitaphs in their original language. Such Greek families may have existed in towns with a Latin-speaking majority, but also vice versa, and it is difficult to access them in the epigraphic material.

Other factors could also influence the choice of language in epitaphs. The production chain of inscriptions included several participants: the commissioner of the text, the person who composed it and the stonecutter; the roles could overlap.[96] Some practical consequences are visible, which will be seen in the discussion. Finally, I point out that a factor which influenced the language choice of epitaphs in many other areas, the context of the Roman army, was less important in Sicily.[97] In all, we have an interesting combination of potentially conflicting factors.

In personal names, the matters are not less complicated. The evidence entitles us to say that in the Classical and Hellenistic periods Greek speakers in Sicily mostly had a name that reflected Greek linguistic identity. The situation started to change during the late republic. In the Greek east, some Latin cognomina began to be used as personal names, and the phenomenon continued into late antiquity.[98] In Italy, on the other hand, traditional Greek names became an indicator of servile origin during the late republic and were often avoided when freeborn or libertine parents gave names to their children. The importance of this phenomenon diminished significantly only after the 2nd century.[99] Obviously, a Greek cognomen did not always mean that the person was a slave or a freed(wo)man, and slaves, even Greek-speaking slaves could have a Latin cognomen. In any case, in large areas people must have recognized that a name like *Niceros* was in Greek, and *Primus* was in Latin. Moreover, many Greek speakers must, at least in the early imperial period, have perceived that the language of the gentilicium, the indicator of Roman citizenship, was Latin.

The following sections include statistics concerning Greek and Latin pagan epitaphs at Syracuse, Lipari, Catania, Messina, Termini and Palermo. In the other colonies and towns, the number of epitaphs is too small for statistics of this kind. I shall present tables that contain the frequencies of Greek and Latin cognomina (or single names, if only one is indicated) in epitaphs datable to the early Empire, before Christianity. In each case, the numbers of published Greek and Latin epitaphs will be given. In the tables, no distinction has been made between freeborn, freed(wo)men and slaves, because the indications of filiation or of libertine status are rare in general, and almost totally absent from the Greek epitaphs.[100]

The statistics of Greek and Latin epitaphs and names in Syracuse, Lipari, Catania, Messina, Termini and Palermo

I begin with **Syracuse**,[101] where, in published pagan epitaphs, Greek is used more often than Latin (Greek: **70%**, 140; Latin: **30%**, 61). The frequencies of Greek, Latin, and other cognomina are listed in Table 2.1. A gentilicium is shown for 42% of the persons.

There is a substantial group of local epitaphs in which the deceased have the attributes χρηστός (-ά, -ή) or, more often, χρηστὸς καὶ ἄμεμπτος. Such a description could be considered as an indication of servile origin: of all the persons who are described as χρηστός (καὶ ἄμεμπτος), only 33% have a gentilicium, whereas of those who are not given such attributes, 50% have one (total: 68). Furthermore, people of higher social standing seem to avoid these attributes,[102] and the epitaphs in question are often rather modest.[103] I include a similar analysis of the personal names in them (Table 2.2):

The sample is small, but as far as Greek and Latin names are concerned, the percentages are almost the same regardless of whether the persons are given the attributes χρηστός (καὶ ἄμεμπτος) or not.

Lipari is presented next, in Table 2.3. On this small island, the typologies of funerary inscriptions are fairly homogeneous, and it is difficult to distinguish between late Hellenistic / republican and early imperial inscriptions. There may be a small bias in favor of Latin names.[104] The language of epitaphs classified here under early Empire is predominantly Greek (Greek: **92%**, 322; Latin: **8%**, 29). For 34% of the persons, a gentilicium is given.

At **Catania** (Table 2.4),[105] the proportion of Greek and Latin epitaphs is in favour of Latin (Greek: **38%**, 84; Latin, **61%**, 136; bilingual, **1%**, 3). The gentilicium is indicated for the majority of the persons mentioned in epitaphs (61%).

At **Messina**, the count of epitaphs with full onomastic formulae is quite small;[106] the published pagan epitaphs are divided almost exactly in two in terms of language choice (Greek: **52%**, 39; Latin: **48%**, 36). A significant number of immigrants

Table 2.1. The frequencies of Greek and Latin cognomina in onomastic formulas mentioned in the pagan epitaphs from early imperial Syracuse.

Language of cognomen	In Greek inscr.	In Latin inscr.	All inscr.: Person has a gentilicium	All inscr.: Person has only one name	Total (127)
Greek	81% (71)	62% (24)	57% (30)	88% (65)	75% (95)
Latin	15% (13)	33% (13)	38% (20)	8% (6)	20% (26)
Other	5% (4)	5% (2)	6% (3)	4% (3)	5% (6)

Table 2.2. The frequencies of Greek and Latin cognomina in persons with the attributes χρηστός or χρηστὸς καὶ ἄμεμπτος at Syracuse.

Language of cognomen	Person has a gentilicium	Person has only one name	Total (59)
Greek	58% (11)	88% (35)	78% (46)
Latin	37% (7)	10% (4)	19% (11)
Other	5% (1)	3% (1)	3% (2)

Table 2.3. The frequencies of Greek and Latin cognomina in personal names mentioned in the pagan epitaphs from Lipari.

Language of cognomen	In Greek inscr.	In Latin inscr.	All inscr.: Person has a gentilicium	All inscr.: Person has only one name	Total (293)
Greek	80% (213)	56% (15)	64% (65)	85% (163)	78% (228)
Latin	16% (43)	44% (12)	34% (34)	11% (21)	19% (55)
Other[1]	4% (10)	0%	2% (2)	4% (8)	3% (10)

[1] *This category contains the Semitic names, as well as the following: Μυρκειτα (340), Ιεικοκουλα (422), Κοτογια (440), Νουγρα (468); cf. Manganaro, n. 11, 433 and Μαθαλ[- -] (689).*

Table 2.4. The frequencies of Greek and Latin cognomina in personal names mentioned in the pagan epitaphs from Catania.

Language of cognomen	In Greek inscr.	In Latin inscr.	All inscr.: Person has a gentilicium	All inscr.: Person has only one name	Total (240)
Greek	66% (49)	56% (93)	53% (78)	69% (65)	60% (143)
Latin	32% (24)	41% (68)	45% (66)	28% (26)	38% (92)
Other, bilingual	1% (1)	2% (4)	1% (2)	3% (3)	2% (5)

Table 2.5. The frequencies of Greek and Latin cognomina in personal names mentioned in the pagan epitaphs from Messina.

Language of name	In Greek inscr.	In Latin inscr.	All inscr.: Person has a gentilicium	All inscr.: Person has only one name	Total (70)
Greek	54% (14)	64% (28)	52% (28)	88% (14)	60% (42)
Latin	35% (9)	36% (16)	46% (25)	6% (1)	37% (26)
Other	8% (2)	0%	2% (1)	6% (1)	3% (2)

Table 2.6. The frequencies of Greek and Latin cognomina in personal names mentioned in the pagan epitaphs from Termini Imerese.

Language of name	In Greek inscr.	In Latin inscr.	All inscr.: Person has a gentilicium	All inscr.: Person has only one name	Total (187)
Greek	75% (21)	50% (79)	51% (66)	59% (34)	53% (100)
Latin	25% (7)	50% (80)	49% (63)	41% (24)	47% (87)

are commemorated in epitaphs, which shows the importance of Messina as an international port.[107] All of these epitaphs are in Greek, and the persons mentioned have a Greek cognomen. I have excluded them from Table 2.5, in order to be able to focus on which names were given to children in Messina.[108] Of the final sample, the gentilicium of 77% of the people is indicated.

My last table describes the situation in **Termini Imerese** (Table 2.6).[109] Again, the majority have a gentilicium (69%). Latin epitaphs are notably more common than those in Greek (Greek: **18%**, 36; Latin: **82%**, 159).

In **Palermo**, where the provenance of inscriptions in the Regional Museum is in many cases difficult to establish,[110] the majority of published pagan epitaphs are in any case in Latin (at least **73%**). The number of persons known from epitaphs is rather small,

approx. 60, which is why I have not compiled a table. Latin cognomina are more common in all categories except among persons who are commemorated with a Greek inscription and for whom only one name is shown. The statistics are:

Greek cognomina: 37% (22)
Latin cognomina: 63% (38)

Finally, the proportions of Greek and Latin inscriptions and cognomina in the six towns discussed above are shown in Fig. 2.1.[111]

As we can see, there is a correlation between the proportions: where Latin inscriptions are more common, Latin cognomina are as well (although not necessarily in the majority), and vice versa. In every town except Lipari the proportion of Greek cognomina is greater than the proportion of Greek inscriptions.

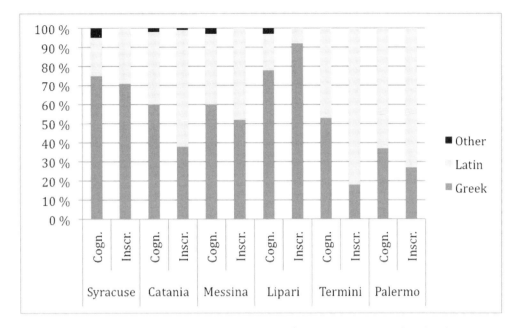

Figure 2.1. Greek and Latin in inscriptions and in cognomina in five Sicilian towns.

Onomastics: the prestige of names and the use of onomastic formulae

The Tables 2.1–2.5 and Fig. 2.1 have shown that, in our material, Greek cognomina are most common in Syracuse and in Lipari (78% and 75% respectively). In Catania and Messina, 60% of the people mentioned have a Greek cognomen. In Termini, the proportions of Greek and Latin cognomina are almost in balance, and in Palermo, with the smallest sample, Latin cognomina outnumber the Greek names. In Latin inscriptions, the proportion of Latin cognomina varies from 33% (Syracuse) to 50% (Termini) and higher (Palermo, 70%). In Termini and Palermo, Latin cognomina are very common even among persons for whom only one name is indicated in the epitaph. Unsurprisingly, the proportion of Greek names is everywhere greater in Greek than in Latin inscriptions. Although the samples are small, the figures at least support the view that the position of Greek was relatively stronger in Syracuse and Lipari than in Termini and Palermo.

In this section, I shall focus on three issues. I shall first try to see if a tendency to avoid Greek cognomina is visible in the Sicilian colonies, and find instances of onomastic acculturation. The discussion will be followed by an analysis of names which seem to have enjoyed a certain prestige. The last part is dedicated to the onomastic formulae used in Syracuse and the apparent omission of the gentilicium.

In Sicily, the funerary epigraphic traditions rarely allow us to compare the cognomina of parents and children because commemorators are often not recorded. Statistically, the most abundant material comes from Catania, where in 23 pagan epitaphs, 17 Latin and 6 Greek, at least one cognomen of a child and one cognomen of a parent are mentioned.[112] In this small sample, no general trend of dropping Greek cognomina can be discerned, as can be seen in Table 7 below:

At Catania, there are instances typical of continental Italy in which parents who seems to be libertine give their freeborn child a Latin cognomen. A nice example is *IMC Catania* 114, dedicated to [T.? Oc]tavius T. f. [- - -] [Co]rnelianus by his *parentes* [T. Octavius - - -]charmo[- - -] and [- - -]

Table 2.7. The language of the cognomina of children compared to their parents in Catania

The number of parents mentioned in the epitaph and their names –>	1 Greek	2 Greek	1 Latin	2 Latin	1 Greek, 1 Latin
child has a Greek cognomen	8	0	3	1	1
child has a Latin cognomen	2	2	4	0	2

Spendu[sa]. But Greek names are certainly not avoided. *CIL* X 7088 was dedicated by [- - -]ntelus (Fonteius?) Seleucus to his homonymous son and to his *nepos*, whose name is transmitted as *Simbolicus*. In *IMC Catania* 142, L. Vibius Niceros mourns his parents L. Vibius Soter and Vibia Lecata.[113] Finally, the lost inscription *IG* XIV 503 evidently belonged to a comely funerary monument with sculptured ornaments. The cognomen of the deceased girl commemorated in the inscription is Χῖα, and her parents are listed as Κούιντος Σόσσις (= *Q. Sos(s)ius*) and Πετρονία (Σοσσία?).[114] The father's cognomen was evidently indicated in other inscriptions of the same monument. We may be dealing with wealthy freedmen of the senatorial family of the Sosii.[115]

The most evident instances of onomastic acculturation in Sicily come from Messina, where a clear effort to get rid of Greek cognomina is visible in the epigraphic evidence of a certain family. I am referring to the tragic case of Claudius Theseus, evidently a freedman, who buried four members of his family possibly within a short period of time. The epitaphs were all discovered in the cemetery of Orti della Maddalena (*IGL Messina* 20–23), but not *in situ*. The two Latin epitaphs, nos. 22 and 23, commemorate Theseus' 38-year-old wife Cartilia Irene and teenage son Ti. Cl(audius) Claudianus, whereas the two Greek epitaphs, nos. 20 and 21, honour young children, Κλ(αυδία) Ῥωμάνιλλα and [Κλ(αύδιος)] Ῥωμανός.[116] There is no way of telling what the chronological order of the documents was, or how many times Theseus was married.[117] It is remarkable that all the children's names are in Latin, and two refer directly to Rome. It is not certain whether this *Rome* is the city or the Empire; probably the latter. It is unlikely that the language is meant, although the Greek words for "Latin language" are derived from the name of the city. A similar onomastic reference to Rome can be seen in a Greek epitaph from Catania (*IMC Catania* 140) that commemorates Urbana, daughter of Urbicus and Nice. I would interpret these names as references to the city of Rome, not to a general difference between *urbanitas* and *rusticitas*.

To sum up, there is no reason to say that Greek names were generally avoided and Latin names preferred in Sicily. The language of the name does not seem to be as relevant as its meaning: some Greek names considered as indications of servile origin may have been avoided, but others, considered prestigious, were transmitted to children. The list below contains some seemingly prestigious Greek and Latin names. They are given here in the Latin form.

1) Names referring to Rome, either to Roman-ness in general or to the city, discussed above.
2) Names derived from other toponyms, which are sometimes difficult to classify as Greek or Latin: *Asiaticus, Atticus, Chia, Himeraeus, Ionius,*[118] *Thermitana/-us, Tyndaris*. Such names can indicate the provenance of the family.
3) Names that refer to famous rulers: *Cleopatra,*[119] *Dionysius, Seleucus*; or to divinities, especially Aphrodite.
4) Latin names derived from Latin gentilicia or cognomina with the endings *-ianus* or *-inus*: *Caecilianus, Catullinus, Claudianus, Cornelianus, Decimianus, Geminianus, Licinianus, Marcianus, Marianus, Nymphidianus, Pudentinus, Titianus, Victorinus*, etc.
5) Other Latin names: *Germanus, Magnus, Pudens,*[120] *Quarta, Severus*.

Some of the names in groups (2)–(3) can be seen as references to Sicilian history and thus as manifestations of cultural identity. *E.g.*, the cognomen *Himeraeus* of [-] Domitius A. f. Quir. Himeraeus from Termini (*IL TermIm* 90) has historical and literary connotations; *Ionius* has many possible frames of reference. In Syracuse, the names referring to the town or to its historical past are not numerous in the early Empire. The name Διονύσιος is attested twice, Φιλιστ- once.[121] If this impression is not just an illusion caused by the loss of crucial evidence, it is in contrast with the situation in Christian Syracuse. Of the most common names attested in the catacombs, some are Christian favourites, such as *Cyriace/-us, Ianuaria/-us, Theodule/-us*, as well as the traditionally popular names derived from ἀγαθός, εὐτυχία or Ἀφροδίτη. But the name Διονύσιος -α is also very common (12 attestations), as well as the names derived from *Syracuse*.[122] It should also be noted that in both pagan and Christian epitaphs of Sicily, cognomina derived from *Sicily* are rare.[123]

In all towns, the frequencies of Greek and Latin names differ in one respect: among the persons for whom only a cognomen is indicated, Greek cognomina are more common than among those who have both a gentilicium and a cognomen. The difference is greatest in Syracuse (88%–57%); Lipari follows, then Catania (69%–53%) and Termini. Why there should be such a difference is obvious: some of the persons with just one name were slaves, *i.e.*, they did not even have a gentilicium, and among slaves, Greek cognomina were more common than among those who were freeborn. The situation must have been similar in most areas of the Empire.

It is however less clear why the difference is greater

in Syracuse than in the other towns. One could think that slaves are better represented in the material from Syracuse, or that not all of the deceased had citizen status; but if that were the case, one wonders why no patronymic is given. In my view, it is more likely that in Syracuse there were more people with Greek names who did not use the full Roman nomenclature in *an epitaph*, even if they were Roman citizens and had a gentilicium. I mentioned above (p. 10) an altar on which the name of the dedicator was shown only as Μαρκιανός: this Marcianus was certainly not a slave, and he may well have been a member of the local elite (although it is impossible to know with certainty if he was a citizen). There seems to be a similar phenomenon in epitaphs: if a person is recorded with a single name, s/he could be either a slave or a freeborn. Evidently there was no risk of confusing the two – the monuments were different. For the relatives of freed(wo)men, however, it may have been more important to show the gentilicium and the fact that the deceased were no longer slaves. In all, one cannot avoid the impression that some Greeks in Syracuse affirmed their linguistic identity by avoiding the Latin onomastic formula.

Epigraphic cultures and speech communities

In Roman imperial times, the funerary epigraphic cultures of Sicily developed into different directions in a way that also reflects linguistic identity. The towns discussed in the previous sections can be split depending on whether the Greek and Latin epigraphic cultures were similar to or different from each other. They were quite different in Termini and in Lipari, Syracuse had an intermediate position, and a contact situation between epigraphic cultures developed in Catania and apparently in Messina.

Separate epigraphic cultures: Termini and Lipari

One of the most important characteristics in which epigraphic cultures differed in Sicily was whether the dedicators of the epitaph were mentioned or not. In the Greek epigraphic culture of pre-Roman Sicily, the tombstone traditionally indicated only the onomastic formula of the deceased, consisting of the name and the patronymic. In many other areas of the western Empire, the indigenous provincials borrowed the habit of inscribing epitaphs from the Romans. This often resulted in Latin epitaphs in which the onomastic formulae were recorded for both the deceased and the commemorator(s).[124]

In the Greek epitaphs from Termini and Lipari the use of the traditional structures was continued into early imperial times. In Termini, the old filiation formula was used, either with or without the word υἱός;[125] it is uncertain whether some of the persons mentioned in such epitaphs were Roman citizens. The commemorators were rarely mentioned in Greek, but often in Latin epitaphs. In Lipari, an epitaph regularly consisted only of the name of the deceased in the genitive, often with filiation, exactly as it had done in Hellenistic times. In the Latin texts, mostly inscribed on stelae similar to their Greek counterparts, invocations to *Dei Manes* were used and the commemorators could be indicated, as well as the age of the deceased. In the two towns, the phenomena that reflect language contact are rare.[126]

In Termini, the group pressure for a Latin epitaph must have been strong. It is difficult to estimate how many of the persons who chose a Latin epitaph were Greek-speaking. The size of such an upwardly mobile group was not necessarily insignificant. It was much more marked to use Greek, but it may not have been less prestigious, at least among the Greek-speaking freeborn. An epitaph in Greek meant that Greek was an important language in the family; it was an affirmation of linguistic identity. All the information gathered here seems to indicate that Latin speakers were in a majority in Termini. In Lipari, the situation seems to have been the opposite, but not in all senses. Greek was the unmarked choice, and the number of Greek-speaking families who chose a Latin epitaph for a deceased in the family may have been minimal. In Lipari, where Greek inscriptions and Greek cognomina dominate, and some onomastic phenomena of the east are attested, I would not hesitate to say that the majority of people were Greek speakers in this period. In Termini and especially in Lipari, I would prefer not to describe the situation in terms of prestige or diglossia, as it does not seem that the prestige of Greek was lower than that of Latin.

Funerary epigraphic cultures in contact: Syracuse, Catania and Messina

The Greek and Latin epigraphic cultures of Syracuse, Catania and Messina are not as disparate as at Termini and Lipari. The Roman onomastic system has been adopted even in the Greek epitaphs; there are only sporadic instances of the traditional filiation. On the other hand, the Roman type of filiation is also rare, even in Latin epitaphs. As I pointed out above, the proportion of persons for whom no gentilicium is indicated is notably greater in Syracuse than in the other colonial towns discussed here. There are more contact-induced phenomena in Greek and Latin epigraphies than in Termini and Lipari, but they are more limited in Syracuse than in Catania (and Messina).

In Syracuse, the earliest Latin epitaphs use a syntactic structure that is clearly based on a Greek one, first attested in the late republic and shown in the following examples (1) and (2):[127]

(**1**) Φιλόξενε / χρηστέ, χαῖρε. (*NSA* 1912, 299 = *NSA* 1915, 203)

(**2**) *Q. Cornifici / Q. lib. Hermes / pie, salve.* (*CIL* X 8314)

It is interesting that this structure is used in one of the rare bilingual epitaphs from Sicily, *CIL* X 7064 = *IG* XIV 472 = *IMC Catania* 74 from Catania, with the same text in Latin and in Greek: *Q. Domitei peie / salve.* / Κόϊντε Δομίτιε / εὐσεβῆ χαῖρε. It is uncertain whether the inscription is slightly earlier or slightly later than the foundation of the colony.

In the epigraphy of Syracuse, the single attribute χρηστός tends to be replaced in the early imperial period by the very common pair χρηστὸς καὶ ἄμεμπτος (cf. above, p. 33). Apparently at the same time or soon afterwards, it becomes customary to indicate the age in epitaphs, both in Greek and in Latin. However, no Latin counterpart for χρηστὸς καὶ ἄμεμπτος is attested. In the same period, the names of the dedicators appear in Latin epitaphs, but not in Greek.[128] In Latin, they are often appended at the end of the epitaph. An example from Syracuse follows:

(**3**) *D(is) M(anibus) s(acrum). / Lollia Irenus / v(ixit) a(nnis) XLIII; / L. Helvius Copria/nus / coniugi b(ene) m(erenti) f(ecit).* (*NSA* 1951, 297)

A structure like the one in (3) becomes almost the "standard" structure for both Latin and Greek

epitaphs in another colony, Catania,[129] but not in Syracuse (see Table 2.8 below).

Moreover, it is interesting that in Syracuse certain families who appear to be immigrants use in their epitaphs structures that are not otherwise attested locally. The following example is the epitaph of a T. Flavius Ganamio, who had received citizenship during the Flavian period:

(**4**) *Dis Manibus. / T. Flavio Gannamali f(ilio) / Ganamioni / Allina uxor viro bene / merenti s(ua) p(ecunia) f(ecit).* (*NSA* 1947, 205)

The epitaph begins with *Dis Manibus*, not abbreviated; the phrase is uncommon in Syracuse, and if it is used, it is abbreviated, with *s(acrum)* (D. M. S.).[130] The closing expression *sua pecunia fecit* is rare in Sicilian epitaphs.[131] The family, who may well have been speaking another language, used an imported Latin structure in the epitaph.[132]

The Greek and Latin funerary epigraphic cultures of Syracuse are not different as far as the overall quality of the epigraphic monuments is concerned. There are fine monuments in both languages. On the Greek side, one must point out in particular the monument of Vulcacia Terentia (*IG* XIV 45), with sculptural decoration and other elements of distinction.[133]

At Catania, the Greek and Latin epigraphic cultures have much more in common, and it is hard to find systematic differences. The commemorators are indicated in Greek epitaphs almost as often as in Latin epitaphs, and the same structural types are common. Unlike at Syracuse, mentioning the dedicators becomes common in both traditions. In *IMC Catania*, I classified the structures used in the epitaphs from Catania. The results of the same categorization, applied in Syracuse, can be seen in Table 2.8 below, in which the differences between Syracuse and Catania become visible.[134] The

Table 2.8. The structures used in the epitaphs from Catania and Syracuse

	Catania		Syracuse	
Structure	Greek epitaphs	Latin epitaphs	Greek epitaphs	Latin epitaphs
1	5%	7%	10%	14%
2	5%	4%	19%	14%
2 + age	7%	–	24%	14%
3	20–21%	22–23%	41%	24%
4	41–43%	33–42%	–	17–21%
5	4%	12–19%	1%	10–14%
6	5%	6%	–	–
7	4%	7%	–	–
other	9%	–	4%	3%

commemorators of the epitaph are not mentioned in categories 1, 2 and 3; they are mentioned in 4, 5 and 6. The situation of Syracuse resembles, to some extent, Athens.[135]

There are some phenomena of contact in the epitaphs from Catania, mostly on the structural-syntactic level,[136] and they have interesting implications for any speculation about the native language of their writers. The influences between Greek and Latin epigraphic cultures worked both ways, although the Latin tradition may have influenced the Greek one more than vice versa. In such situation, there may be various explanations for the influence of Latin in a Greek epitaph.

Code-switching, on the other hand, is uncommon in the material. An illustrative example is *IG* XIV 484, discovered in the countryside some 10 km. to the west from Catania: *D. M. S.* / Κλωδία Βαλεντεῖνα / χαῖρε· ἔζη(σεν) ἔ(τη) *XXXX·* / ἐποίησε ἰδίᾳ γυναι/ κὶ Ἰγνᾶτις Κάρικος / μνή(μης) χάριν.[137] This is an instance of tag- or formula-switching, well attested in ancient epigraphy.[138] If we were dealing with another kind of a document, we might start by presuming that the writer was a Latin speaker. But in this case, a more likely explanation for the initial Latin tag is, in my view, the desire to imitate Latin epigraphy,[139] possibly because Latin was the predominant language in the civic centre of the nearby colony.

A problem relevant for all the colonies is that one could argue that if there were more Greek speakers with Latin epitaphs than the other way around, the influence or interference of Greek should be more visible in the Latin texts than it actually is. However, in the period discussed here, the deviations from the linguistic standard are fairly uncommon, because the texts are short and the production chain involved several participants (see above, p. 12): *IG* XIV 484 is exceptional. Furthermore, many of the (predominantly Greek-speaking) writers of the epitaphs will have had strong proficiencies in Latin, as well.

It is questionable if the linguistic landscape of the civic centre of Catania, which consisted of Latin inscriptions carved by the best stonecutters in town, had an influence on the overall quality of Greek and Latin inscriptions. There is no clear difference between the Greek and Latin epigraphic cultures in this respect. With the exception of some urns, sarcophagi and a monumental altar (in Latin: *CIL* X 7023 = *IMC Catania* 17), the epitaphs are marble slabs that seldom have architectural decoration, regardless of the language. There are examples both in Greek and in Latin in which the quality of lettering is relatively high and the layout of the text is spacious.[140]

Speech communities in Syracuse and Catania

In Syracuse, one could interpret the differences between the Greek and the Latin epigraphic cultures as resistance towards or lack of interest in acculturation. The habit of indicating the commemorators never became common in families that continued inscribing Greek epitaphs; it might have been seen as a sign of Romanization. Some people aspired for a higher social status by using a Latin epitaph, but others used methods such as a more expensive stonecutter or an alternative wording. As a colony, Syracuse was quite different from many colonies of the Greek east. It was no outpost of Roman culture; the colonists formed an important element of population, but probably not even the majority. Because of the high proportion of both Greek epitaphs and Greek cognomina, both in pagan and Christian epitaphs, it still seems that the majority language in Syracuse was Greek in the early Empire. We do not know how this situation changed during the period.

As regards Catania, I think that, in the social classes represented in the epitaphs, the real proportion of Greek and Latin speakers may well have been rather balanced. Latin epitaphs are in the majority, but one must remember the upwardly mobile group hypothesized above, for whom using Latin in an epitaph was important. If what I argue is true, there was a high degree of individual and family bilingualism, and it would have become difficult to classify persons or families under one language. It is again difficult to say if there was a trend of progressive Latinization; four fifths of the Christian funerary inscriptions from Catania are in Greek. In Syracuse and in Catania, neither Greek nor Latin was the more esteemed choice in an epitaph, but there were more or less prestigious ways of producing a funerary monument. A similar situation may well have prevailed in other bilingual cities of the Roman Empire.[141]

Language choice and communicative choice in Messina

The case of Claudius Theseus from Messina, discussed on p. 16 as an example of onomastic acculturation, is also illuminating terms of language choice. I will now tackle the question of why Theseus used both Greek and Latin in the epitaphs of his family members. The Greek epitaphs of Theseus' small children are very similar and must be chronologically close to each other;[142] the two Latin texts, dedicated to his wife and teenage son have affinities, too, but also differences.[143] It is unlikely that both the Greek and the Latin inscriptions were produced by the same stonecutter.[144] The overall quality is higher in the Latin than in the Greek epitaphs: the lettering is more professional and the margins are wider. They must have been more expensive. This is comprehensible, given the high mortality rate of infants in this period. In my view, instead of considering the *language* choice, we should focus on the documents as a whole. Perhaps Claudius Theseus had to choose between a Latin stonecutter who was more expensive, and a cheaper Greek one.

Instead of a language choice, Theseus was making a communicative choice: he chose between a better-looking gravestone and a more modest one, which yet was suitable for the purpose. As he was bilingual, he could produce or at least accept the short text in both languages. Obviously this does not mean that all the Greek stonecutters in Messina produced cheap gravestones: Greek inscriptions by qualified professionals have survived, too. There were stonecutters in Sicily who could produce inscriptions in both languages (see above, p. 11) and the client who could use their services made a language choice, based on family tradition and linguistic identity. Theseus' choice was not so much a manifestation of linguistic identity, but depended on practical factors.

Language, society and identity

Recent studies on ancient Greek identity have reasonably put much emphasis on regional diversification and contacts with other cultures.[145] If we look only at epigraphic material, it is too easy to overlook the regional variation of language. In the Sicilian colonies, the standard variants of the early imperial period are used both in Greek and in Latin epigraphy. In Syracuse, it must be pointed out that the Greek inscriptions from the 1st century BCE discussed above (p. 9) do not have any Doric forms, but the *koiné* is used instead. This is in line with Consani's findings, that in the written sources the "Doric *koiné*" gives way to *koiné* proper in Sicily by the end of the Hellenistic period, leaving behind only some traces.[146] In the Greek east, there were areas in which the local dialect was used as a marker of identity.[147] But in Sicily, whatever the dialectal reality behind the written evidence was, it cannot be labelled simply as "Doric"; the Doric dialect never re-emerged in the written documents.

The kind of Latin spoken in the colonies is likely to have been slightly different in each. After an initial levelling or koineization process, during which the speakers who had come to the colony from various dialectal areas accommodated their speech, the language was influenced by the other languages spoken in the towns.[148] The "urban" language also influenced the language of the surrounding countryside, but the urban centres discussed here were small towns, and the influences probably worked in both directions.[149] The Greek of the colonies, on the other hand, was influenced by the local Latin. However, we cannot access these differences in the spoken languages in this period for reasons which have been explained above; neither is there evidence for mixed languages. In Sicily, the evolution of Greek and Latin becomes more visible in the material from the Christian period.[150] As regards Latin, change is manifested by one of the most famous of the Christian inscriptions, the epitaph of Zoe from the interior of Southern Sicily.[151] It comes from an epoch and an area in which standard orthography was poorly transmitted, and in which innovative phenomena could find their way into an epitaph.

It has not been my intention to squeeze the Sicilian reality into a bilingual framework and neglect the other languages. Throughout the early imperial period, there must have been Sicilian families in which the primary language was neither Greek nor Latin. Some inscriptions in which the onomastics make this probable have been mentioned in the discussion,[152] but the very limited evidence for other speech communities does not take us very far: the surviving inscriptions are in Greek or Latin. The most important of the other languages was probably Punic,[153] but no inscriptions survive from the imperial period. In North Africa, where the linguistic landscape was much more overwhelmingly Latin, Punic stayed alive for centuries,[154] but it is likely that the Punic speech communities in Sicily were much less substantial than in Africa.

Lomas has estimated that the Greek identity in the west was developed through contact with the surrounding peoples towards "a definition of citizenship and an approach to ethnic difference which owes much to the inclusive ethos of their Italian neighbours".[155] She has also discussed the problem of why, during the early Empire, the Sicilian elite chose to Romanize their civic life, but Greek re-emerged in late antiquity. She sees the emergence of Greek in late antiquity as a case of active reinvention of culture, rather than as an indigenous level of Hellenism that diluted the Roman influence with the passing of time.[156]

On the basis of the analyses presented here, it seems to me much more likely that a Greek linguistic identity remained significant throughout the early colonial period. In Syracuse, the linguistic landscape did not suddenly change, but the forum became a place in which the visibility of Latin increased steadily. In the public space, Greek linguistic identity could be manifested in epigraphic contexts that referred to religion, the spectacle, and the past. The use of Greek in these contexts, especially religion, is documented elsewhere in the island as well, and the prestige of Greek must have been high in them. Still, Latin could also be used in the religious context. Brélaz has recently discerned strong ideologically influenced attitudes towards Latin in the east.[157] In Sicily, the evidence from Syracuse as a whole could hint at this direction, although the position of Greek was relatively more marginal than in the east.

Funerary epigraphic evidence has been used here to look at the sociolinguistics and the linguistic identity of the wider population. Although diglossia is difficult to come by in the material from early imperial Sicily discussed here, I have still claimed that there are likely to have been more Greek speakers who had a Latin epitaph than Latin speakers who had a Greek epitaph. This phenomenon must have been especially strong in the colonies, and it was probably due to the significant role of the libertines in the epigraphic material. Among the social groups represented in epitaphs, the real proportion of Greek speakers would then have been higher than the proportion of Greek epitaphs.

More importantly, inscriptions show differences between the colonial towns. In Syracuse, there is some evidence of interaction between the Greek and the Latin tradition, but also of separation. In Catania and Messina, the features of the funerary epigraphic cultures can in my view be due to a close contact between the speech communities and a widespread bilingualism. In Termini, the funerary epigraphy would indicate that the town was prevalently Latin-speaking, but had a Greek speech community, some members of which manifested their linguistic identity in epitaphs. As far as names are concerned, it seems that their prestige depended on meaning and tradition rather than on the language of the name. Some contexts with evidence of the higher prestige of Latin cognomina have been presented, but also material which indicates that Greek cognomina were not categorically stigmatized. Greek cognomina are in general more common in the material discussed here, even in Termini, where the surviving epitaphs are predominantly in Latin.

On the basis of the funerary epigraphic evidence from the early imperial period, it would not be reasonable to assume a strong resistance towards Latin among the Greek-speaking population as a whole. The evidence seems to indicate fairly stable and widespread bilingualism, language maintenance and substantial speech communities for both Greek and Latin on the eastern coast, but a trend of slow Latinization may still have been present. In the colonies of northwestern Sicily, Greek also persisted, but in a relatively weaker position.

Acknowledgements

My thanks are due to Cédric Brélaz, Mika Kajava, Janne Pölönen, Jonathan Prag, Olli Salomies, Heikki Solin, Rebecca Sweetman and especially Giovanni Salmeri.

Appendix: A magistrate of the municipium of Syracuse

In 1895, Paolo Orsi published, with his usual efficiency, numerous inscriptions found the same year in the Christian catacomb of San Giovanni in Syracuse. Among them was a fragment for which no supplements were given (Fig. 2.2).[158] According to Orsi, the height of the text was 9 cm, the width 13 cm. Judging from the drawing, the letters appear to be about 2.5 cm high. The fragment later found its way into a corpus of Christian inscriptions,[159] and has escaped the attention of scholars interested in the earlier periods. However it is quite certainly not a fragment of a Christian epitaph, but was recycled. The letter forms can hardly be later than Augustan. On the basis of the findspot, it is unlikely that the inscription could originate from a Sicilian locality other than Syracuse.

According to Orsi, who did not propose any supplements, the upper side was intact. I propose to read the text as follows:

[---]ις ἀγορα-
[νομ-, --- δε]κυρεύ-
[σας --- ἐκ τῶ]ν ἑαυτοῦ
[ἀνέθηκε(ν) (?) ---].

The supplements are partly based on a dedication of approximately the same size from Centuripe in central-eastern Sicily, *IG* XIV 575: Ἀπόλλωνι / Ἡράκ<λ>ειος / Ἀριστοφύλου / δεκυρεύσας / ἐκ τῶν ἰδίων.[160] The presence of both ΑΓΟΡΑ and ΚΥΡΕΥ make other theoretically possible supplements unlikely.[161] Given the presence of the word ἑαυτοῦ on line 3, the text must refer to one individual. The letters -ις, which can hardly belong to a personal name,[162] may belong to an indication that the dedicator had been ἀγορανόμος several times (δὶς or τρὶς ἀγορανομήσας) or that he had been elected to be one (αἱρεθεὶς or κατασταθεὶς ἀγορανόμος).

Given the presence of the rare verb δεκυρεύω, it is probable that ἀγορανόμος is here the Greek translation of the Latin term *aedilis* and is not used in the more traditional meaning of the term, "supervisor of the market".[163] Two words derived from the Latin noun *decurio* are attested in ancient Greek: (1) the

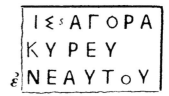

Figure 2.2. Drawing from NSA 1895.

noun δεκουρίων "cavalry officer", "member of the local senate", the earliest attestation of which is in Polybius (6.25.2),[164] and (2) the verb δεκυρεύω "to be a member of the local senate". As far as I can tell, the verb is only attested in the inscription of Centuripe and here, and it may have been used only in the Greek of Sicily (and Italy).

It is now necessary to establish what kind of a town constitution the administrative terms refers to. Centuripe was a *municipium*, and never became a colony. Syracuse became a *municipium* in the mid-40s,[165] and a colony in 21. It is theoretically possible, but unlikely, that Sicilians would have started to use Latin loan-words in local administration before the *municipia* were established because of the prestige of Latin as a language of state administration. The dedicator must then have been a council member in either the *municipium* or the colony of Syracuse.

The modest size of the letters indicates in my view that the fragment belonged to a religious dedication, like the text from Centuripe, rather than a simple building inscription.[166] We cannot tell if the divinity was named in the text; this was not obligatory if the context of the monument made it clear. It would be unwise to argue that the dedicator cannot be a magistrate of the colony of Syracuse only because Greek, and not Latin, was used. In a religious context, the use of Greek would not have been marked in the colony (cf. the discussion in 3.2 above). In any case, given the letter forms, dating our fragment before the founding of the colony seems more likely. The importance of the fragment lies in the fact that it is the only surviving piece of evidence of a magistrate of the short-lived *municipium* of Syracuse.

Bibliography

Abulafia, D. 1986. "The Merchants of Messina: Levant Trade and Domestic Economy", *Papers of the British School in Rome* 54, 196–212.

Adams, J. N. 2003. *Bilingualism and the Latin Language* (Cambridge).

Adams, J. N. 2007. *The Regional Diversification of Latin 200 BC–AD 600* (Cambridge).

Agnello, S. L. 1961. "La catacomba di Vigna Cassia in alcuni appunti inediti dell'Orsi", *Archivio storico siracusano* 7 (1961) 118–31.

Alföldy, G. 1989. "Epigraphische Notizen aus Italien III", *Zeitschrift für Papyrologie und Epigraphik* 77, 155–80.

Aneziri, S. 2002. *Die Vereine der dionysischen Techniten im Kontext der hellenistischen Gesellschaft* (Stuttgart).

Asheri, D. 1982–1983. "Le città della Sicilia fra il III e il IV secolo d.C.", *Kókalos* 28–29, 461–476.

Auer, P. *et al.* (eds) 2005. *Dialect Change: Convergence and Divergence in European Languages* (Cambridge).

Baldwin Bowsky, M. 2004. "Of Two Tongues: Acculturation at Roman Knossos", in Salmeri *et al.* (eds) 2004, 95–150.

Bekker-Nielsen, T. 2007. "The One That Got Away: A Reassessment of the Agoranomos Inscription from Chersonesos", in *The Black Sea in Antiquity. Regional and Interregional Economic Exchanges.* V. Gabrielsen and J. Lund (eds) (Aarhus), 123–31.

Belvedere, O. 1988 "Opere pubbliche ed edifici per lo spettacolo nella Sicilia di età imperiale", *ANRW* II 11.1, 346–413.

Ben-Rafael, E. 2009. "A Sociological Approach to the Study of Linguistic Landscapes", in *Linguistic Landscape*. E. Shohamy and D. Gorter (eds) (New York and London), 40–54.

Bitto, I. 2002. "Testimonianze epigrafiche di Messina romana: iscrizione in onore di Asklepio e di Hygeia", in Gentili and Pinzone (eds) 2002, 127–39.

Bivona, L. 2001. "Brevi considerazioni sulla epigrafia latina di Sicilia", in *Varia epigraphica. Atti del Colloquio Bertinoro 8–10 giugno 2000* (Faenza), 49–61.

Brélaz, C. 2008. "Le recours au Latin dans les documents officiels émis par les cités d'Asie Mineure", in *Bilinguisme gréco-latin et épigraphie. Actes du colloque organisé à l'Université Lumière-Lyon 2, mai 2004.* F. Biville *et al.* (eds) (Lyons), 169–94.

Brugnone, A. 1974. "Iscrizioni greche del Museo Civico di Termini Imerese", *Kókalos* 20, 218–64.

Butler, S. 2002. *The Hand of Cicero* (London – New York).

Coarelli, F. and M. Torelli 1984. *Sicilia* (*Guide archeologiche Laterza*) (Bari).

Consani, C. 1995. "I dialetti greci in età ellenistica e romana: la documentazione epigrafica della Magna Grecia e di Sicilia", in *Studi di linguistica greca. Atti del I Incontro di linguistica greca, Pavia 1993* (Milan), 73–89.

Cordano, F. 1999. "Le istituzioni delle città greche nelle fonti epigrafiche", in Gulletta (ed.) 1999, 149–58.

Croft, W. 2000. *Explaining Language Change* (Harlow).

D'Amore, L. 2007. *Iscrizioni greche d'Italia: Reggio Calabria* (Rome).

Eck, W. 1996a. "Senatorische Familien der Kaiserzeit in der Provinz Sizilien", *Zeitschrift für Papyrologie und Epigraphik* 113, 109–28.

Eck, W. 1996b. "Senatoren und senatorischer Grundbesitz auf Sizilien", in Gentili, B. (ed.) 1996, 231–56.

Eck, W. 2004. "Lateinisch, Griechisch, Germanisch ....? Wie sprach Rom mit seinen Untertanen?", in de Ligt *et al.* (eds) 2004, 3–19.

Felle, A. E. 2005. "Epigrafia pagana e cristiana in Sicilia: consonanze e peculiarità", *Vetera Christianorum* 42, 233–50.

Ferrua, A. 1940. "Nuovi studi nelle catacombe di Siracusa", *Rivista di archeologia cristiana* 17, 43–81.

Ferrua, A. 1941. "Epigrafia sicula pagana e cristiana", *Rivista di archeologia cristiana* 18, 151–243.

Ferrua, A. 1989. *Note e giunte alle iscrizioni cristiane antiche della Sicilia* (Città del Vaticano).

Follet, S. (ed) 2004. *L'Hellénisme d'époque romaine: nouveaux documents, nouvelles approches. Actes du Colloque international à la mémoire de Louis Robert, Paris 2000* (Paris).

Gaetani, O. 1707. *Isagoge ad historiam sacram Siculam* (Palermo).

Gaggiotti, M. 2002. "Nuova luce sull'economia della Sicilia romana da una rilettura dell'iscrizione siracusana *ILLRP* 279", *L'Africa romana* 13, 1053–62.

Gentili, B. (ed) 1996. *Catania antica. Atti del convegno della S.I.S.A.C., Catania 23–24 maggio 1992.* (Pisa and Rome).

Gentili, B. and A. Pinzone (eds) 2002. *Messina e Reggio nell'antichità* (Messina).

Gentili, G. V. 1961. "Nuovi elementi di epigrafia siracusana", *Archivio storico siracusano* 7, 5–25.

Gentili, G. V. 1973. "Studi e ricerche su l'anfiteatro di Siracusa", *Palladio* 23, 3–80.

Giardina, A. 1987. "Palermo in età imperiale romana", *Kókalos* 33, 225–55.

Hall, J. M. 1997. *Ethnic Identity in Greek Antiquity* (Cambridge).

Hodot, R. 2004. "Langue, identité et représentations dans le domaine éolien d'Asie", in Follet (ed.) 2004, 247–54.

Joshel, S. R. 1992. *Work, Identity, and Legal Status at Rome. A Study of the Occupational Inscriptions* (Norman, OK).

Kajanto, I. 1965. *The Latin Cognomina* (Helsinki).

Kajava, M. 2005–2006. "Laodicea al Mare e Catania", *Rendiconti della Pontificia Accademia Romana di Archeologia* 78, 527–41.

Kajava, M. (forthcoming). "Honorific and Other Dedications to Emperors in the Greek East", in: *Royal Cult and Emperor Worship in Classical and Late Antiquity. Proceedings of the Conference organized by the Belgian School at Athens (1–2 November, 2007)*. P. Iossif and A. Chankowski (eds) (Studia Hellenistica, Leuven).

Kerswill, P. and P. Trudgill 2005. "The birth of new dialects", in *Dialect Change: Convergence and Divergence in European Languages*. P. Auer *et al.* (eds) (Cambridge), 196–220.

Korhonen, K. 2001. "Osservazioni sul collezionismo epigrafico siciliano", *Arctos* 35, 85–102.

Korhonen, K. 2002. "Three Cases of Greek / Latin Imbalance in Roman Syracuse", in *Greek Romans and Roman Greeks. Studies in Cultural Interaction*. E. N. Ostenfeld (ed.) (Aarhus), 70–80.

Korhonen, K. 2004. "La cultura epigrafica della colonia di *Catina* nell'Alto Impero", in Salmeri *et al.* (eds) 2004, 233–53.

Korhonen, K. 2007. "Erudite Forgeries or Families Seeking Distinction? Cesare Gaetani's Inscriptions from Syracuse", *Zeitschrift für Papyrologie und Epigraphik* 161, 291–8.

Kruschwitz, P. 2000. "Die sprachlichen Anomalien der Werbeinschrift *CIL* X 7296", *Zeitschrift für Papyrologie und Epigraphik* 130, 239–40.

Labov, W. 2001. *Principles of Linguistic Change* 2: *Social Factors* (Malden, MA and Oxford).

Lazzarini, M. L. 2004. "Sopravvivenze istituzionali e culturali greche nell'Italia romana", in Follet, S. (ed.) 2004, 173–82.

Leiwo, M. 1995. *Neapolitana* (Helsinki).

Levick, B. 1995. "The Latin inscriptions of Asia Minor", in H. Solin *et al.* (eds) (1991) 393–402.

de Ligt, L. *et al.* (eds) 2004. *Roman Rule and Civic Life: Local and Regional Perspectives. Impact of Empire (Roman Empire) 4* (Amsterdam).

Lomas, K. 2000a. "Between Greece and Italy", in *Sicily from Aeneas to Augustus. New Approaches in Archaeology and History*. C. Smith and J. Serrati (eds) (Edinburgh), 161–73.

Lomas, K. 2000b. "The Polis in Italy", in *Alternatives to Athens. Varieties of Political Organization and Community in Ancient Greece*. R. Brock and S. Hodkinson (eds) (Oxford), 167–85.

Lomas, K. 2004. "Funerary Epigraphy and the Impact of Rome in Italy", in de Ligt *et al.* (eds) 2004, 179–97.

Lomas, K. (ed.) 2004. *Greek Identity in the Western Mediterranean. Papers in Honour of Brian Shefton* (Leiden and Boston).

Malfitana, D. 2004. "Anfore e ceramiche fini da mensa orientali nella Sicilia tardo-ellenistica e romana", in *Transport Amphorae and Trade in the Eastern Mediterranean. Acts of the International Colloquium Athens 2002*. J. Eiring and J. Lund (eds) (Athens), 239–50.

Melazzo, L. 1984. "Latino e greco in Sicilia", in *Tre millenni di storia linguistica della Sicilia. Atti del Convegno della Società Italiana di Glottologia, Palermo 1983*. Quattordio A. Moreschini (ed.) (Pisa).

Manganaro, G. 1962. "Graffiti e iscrizioni funerarie della Sicilia Orientale", *Helikon* 2, 485–501.

Manganaro, G. 1963. "Nuove ricerche di epigrafia siceliota", *Siculorum Gymnasium* 16, 51–64.

Manganaro, G. 1964. "Iscrizioni latine e greche dal nuovo edificio termale di Taormina", *Cronache di archeologia e di storia dell'arte* 3, 38–68

Manganaro, G. 1977 [1985]. "Per la storia dei culti nella Sicilia greca", *Cronache di archeologia e di storia dell'arte* 16, 148–64.

Manganaro, G. 1988. "La Sicilia da Sesto Pompeo a Diocleziano", in *ANRW* II 11.1, 3–89.

Manganaro, G. 1989. "Iscrizioni latine nuove e vecchie della Sicilia", *Epigraphica* 51, 161–96.

Manganaro, G. 1992. "Tra epigrafia e numismatica", *Chiron* 22, 385–410.

Manganaro, G. 1993. "Greco nei *pagi* e latino nelle città della Sicilia 'romana' tra I e VI sec. D.C.", in *L'epigrafia del villaggio*. A. Calbi *et al.* (eds) (Faenza), 543–94.

Manganaro, G. 1994. "Iscrizioni, epitaffi ed epigrammi in greco della Sicilia centro-orientale di epoca romana", *Mélanges de l'École française de Rome. Antiquité* 106, 79–118.

Manganaro, G. 1996. "Asklepios e Hygieia 'divinità salvatrici e protettrici della città' a Messina", *Zeitschrift für Papyrologie und Epigraphik* 113, 82–4.

Manganaro, G. 1999a. "Annotazioni sulla epigrafia di Lipara", in *Sicilia epigraphica. Atti del convegno di studi, Erice, 15–18 ottobre 1998*. M. I. Gulletta (ed.) (Pisa), 425–37.

Manganaro, G. 1999b. *Sikelika: Studi di antichità e di epigrafia della Sicilia greca* (Pisa – Rome).

Manganaro, G. 2000. "Fenici, Cartaginesi, Numidi tra i Greci (IV–I sec. a.C.)", *Numismatica e antichità classiche* 29, 255–68.

Meyer, E. A. 1990. "Explaining the Epigraphic Habit in the Roman Empire. The Evidence of Epitaphs", *Journal of Roman Studies* 80, 74–96.

Millar, F. 1968. "Local Cultures in the Roman Empire: Libyan, Punic and Latin in Roman Africa", *Journal of Roman Studies* 58, 125–51 [repr. in *id. et al.* 2004. *Rome, the Greek world, and the East 2: Government, Society and Culture in the Roman Empire* (Chapel Hill), 249–64].

Miranda, E. 1990. *Iscrizioni greche d'Italia 1: Napoli* (Roma).

Moretti, L. 1963. "I technitai di Siracusa", *Rivista di filologia e di istruzione classica* 91, 38–45 [Repr. in *id.* 1990. *Tra epigrafia e storia* (Rome), 189–96].

Mosino, F. 2002. "Profilo culturale di Reggio greca e romana", in Gentili and Pinzone (eds) 2002, 311–19.

Orsi, P. 1900. "Frammenti epigrafici sicelioti", *Rivista di storia antica* 5, 39–66.

Pinzone, A. 1981. "Per la storia di Messana mamertina", *Archivio storico messinese* 32, 5–54 [repr. in *id.* 1999. *Provincia Sicilia* (Catania), 121–72].

Pinzone, A. 1999. "L'immigrazione e i suoi riflessi nella storia economica e sociale della Sicilia del II sec. a. C.", in *Magna Grecia e Sicilia. Stato degli studi e prospettive di ricerca*. M. Barra Bagnasco *et al.* (eds) (Messina), 381–402.

Prag, J. R. W. 2002. "Epigraphy by Numbers. Latin and the Epigraphic Culture in Sicily", in *Becoming Roman, Writing Latin? Literacy and Epigraphy in the Roman West*. A. E. Cooley (ed.) (Portsmouth, RI), 15–31.

Prag, J. R. W. 2003. "Nouveau regard sur les élites locales de la Sicile républicaine", *Histoire et sociétés rurales* 19, 121–31.

Prag, J. R. W. 2006. "*Poenus plane est* – But Who Were the 'Punickes'?", *Papers of the British School in Rome* 74, 1–37.

Prag, J. R. W. 2007a. "Ciceronian Sicily: The Epigraphic Dimension", in *La Sicile de Cicéron: lectures des Verrines. Actes du colloque de Paris, 19–20 mai 2006*. J. Dubouloz and S. Pittia (eds) (Besançon), 245–71.

Prag, J. R. W. 2007b. "*Auxilia* and *Gymnasia*: A Sicilian Model of Roman Imperialism", *Journal of Roman Studies* 97 (2007) 68–100.

Prag, J. R. W. 2008. "Sicilia and Britannia: Epigraphic Evidence for Civic Administration", in *Le quotidien municipal dans l'Occident romain*. C. Berrendonner *et al.* (eds) (Clermont-Ferrand), 67–81.

Reichert, H. 1987. *Lexikon der altgermanischen Namen* (Wien).

Revell, L. 2009. *Roman Imperialism and Local Identities* (Cambridge).

Rizakis, A. D. 1995. "Le grec face au latin. Le paysage linguistique dans la peninsule balkanique sous l'empire", in H. Solin *et al.* (eds) (1991), 373–91.

Rizakis, A. D. 1996. "Anthroponymie et société. Les noms romains dans les provinces hellénophones de l'empire", in *id.* (ed.) *Roman Onomastics in the Greek East. Social and Political Aspects* (Athens), 11–29.

Rizzo, F. P. 1989 [1993]. *La menzione del lavoro nelle epigrafi della Sicilia antica* (Palermo).

Robert, L. 1963. "De Cilicie à Messine et à Plymouth", *Journal des Savants* 1963, 161–211.

Romaine, S. 1995. *Bilingualism*[2] (Oxford).

Ruck, B. 1996. "Die Fasten von Taormina", *Zeitschrift für Papyrologie und Epigraphik* 111, 271–80.

Salmeri, G. 2004. "I caratteri della grecità di Sicilia e la colonizzazione romana", in *Colonie romane nel mondo greco*. G. Salmeri *et al.* (eds) (Rome), 255–307.

Salomies, O. 1987. *Die römischen Vornamen* (Helsinki).

Salomies, O. 1991. "Zu den Fasti consulares von Tauromenium", *Zeitschrift für Papyrologie und Epigraphik* 86, 187–92.

Sfameni Gasparro, G. 2006. "I culti orientali nella Sicilia

ellenistico-romana", in *Ethne e religioni nella Sicilia antica*. P. Anello *et al.* (eds) (Rome), 251–342.

Sgarlata, M. 1993 [1996]. *La raccolta epigrafica e l'epistolario archeologico di Cesare Gaetani Conte della Torre* (Palermo).

Sironen, T. 1995. "Position of Minority Languages in Sicily: Oscan and Elymian", in *Ancient Sicily* (Copenhagen), 185–94.

Solin, H. 1971. *Beiträge zur Kenntnis der griechischen Personennamen in Rom* (Helsinki).

Solin, H. *et al.* (eds) 1995. *Acta Colloquii epigraphici Latini Helsingiae 3.–6. sept. 1991 habiti* (Helsinki).

Solin, H. 2001. "Latin Cognomina in the Greek East", in *The Greek East in the Roman Context. Proceedings of a Colloquium, Finnish Institute at Athens, 1999*. O. Salomies (ed.) (Helsinki).

Solin, H. 2005. "Analecta epigraphica", *Arctos* 39, 176–77.

Strasser, J.-Y. 2002. "Deux autels de Messine rendus à Aigéai de Cilicie", *Epigraphica Anatolica* 34, 149–59.

Taeldeman, J. 2005. "The influence of urban centres on the spatial diffusion of dialect phenomena", in Auer *et al.* (eds) 2005, 263–83.

Varvaro, A. 1981. *Lingua e storia in Sicilia* (Palermo).

Vera, D. 1996. "Augusto, Plinio il Vecchio e la Sicilia in età imperiale. A proposito di recenti scoperte epigrafiche e archeologiche ad Agrigento", *Kókalos* 42, 31–58.

Wilson, R. J. A. 1988a. "Towns of Sicily during the Roman Empire", *ANRW* II 11.1, 90–206.

Wilson, R. J. A. 1988b. "A Wandering Inscription from Roma", *Zeitschrift für Papyrologie und Epigraphik* 71, 161–6.

Wilson, R. J. A. 1990. *Sicily under the Roman Empire. The Archaeology of a Roman Province, 36 B.C.–A.D. 535* (Warminster).

Wilson, R. J. A. 1995. "La topografia della Catania romana", in Gentili, B. (ed.) 1996, 149–73.

Wilson, R. J. A. 1996. "Sicily, Sardinia and Corsica", in *The Cambridge Ancient History*² X (Cambridge), 434–48.

Woolf, G. 1994. "Becoming Roman, Staying Greek: Culture, Identity and the Civilizing Process in the Roman East", *Proceedings of the Cambridge Philological Society* 40, 116–43.

Notes

1. See especially (in chronological order) Varvaro, A. 1981. *Lingua e storia in Sicilia* (Palermo), 33–59; Wilson, R. J. A. 1990. *Sicily under the Roman Empire. The Archaeology of a Roman Province, 36 B.C.–A.D. 535* (Warminster), 313–20; Lomas, K. 2000. "Between Greece and Italy", in *Sicily from Aeneas to Augustus. New Approaches in Archaeology and History*. Smith, C. and J. Serrati (eds) (Edinburgh), 161–73; Prag, J. R. W. 2002. "Epigraphy by Numbers. Latin and the Epigraphic Culture in Sicily", in *Becoming Roman, Writing Latin? Literacy and Epigraphy in the Roman West*. Cooley, A. E. (ed) (Portsmouth, RI), 15–31; Salmeri, G. 2004. "I caratteri della grecità di Sicilia e la colonizzazione romana", in *Colonie romane nel mondo greco*. Salmeri, G. et al. (eds) (Rome), 255–307; and, last but not least, numerous articles by G. Manganaro; see in particular 1993 "Greco nei *pagi* e latino nelle città della Sicilia 'romana' tra I e VI sec. D.C.", in *L'epigrafia del villaggio*. Calbi, A. *et al.* (eds) (Faenza), 543–94 and 1988. "La Sicilia da Sesto Pompeo a Diocleziano", in *ANRW* II 11.1, 3–89, here 41–64.

2. Wilson (Supra n. 1), 60, 76, 80–87; cf. for the Greek east, Woolf, G.1994. "Becoming Roman, Staying Greek: Culture, Identity and the Civilizing Process in the Roman East", *Proceedings of the Cambridge Philological Society* 40, 116–43, here 126–7.

3. Lomas (Supra n. 1), 170–1. A well-known case is Naples: see Leiwo, M. 1995. *Neapolitana* (Helsinki); Lomas, K. 2004. "Funerary Epigraphy and the Impact of Rome in Italy", in *Roman Rule and Civic Life: Local and Regional Perspectives. Impact of Empire (Roman Empire) 4*. de Ligt, L. *et al.* (eds) (Amsterdam), 179–97. The same phenomenon is visible in Rhegium (Reggio), on the other side of the Strait of Messina from Sicily: see the evidence in D'Amore, L. 2007. *Iscrizioni greche d'Italia: Reggio Calabria* (Rome).

4. See Rizakis, A. D. 1995. "Le grec face au latin. Le paysage linguistique dans la peninsule balkanique sous l'Empire", in *Acta Colloquii epigraphici Latini Helsingiae 3.–6. sept. 1991 habiti*. Solin, H. *et al.* (eds) (Helsinki), 373–91; Levick, B. 1995 "The Latin inscriptions of Asia Minor", op. cit., 393–402; Brélaz, C. 2008. "Le recours au Latin dans les documents officiels émis par les cités d'Asie Mineure", in *Bilinguisme gréco-latin et épigraphie. Actes du colloque organisé à l'Université Lumière-Lyon 2, mai 2004*. Biville, F. *et al.* (eds) (Lyons), 169–94, here 189, 191.

5. Cf. Salmeri (Supra n. 1), 283 n. 145. Diglossia is the extreme form of a situation in which two linguistic variants have a hierarchical relation in society, one being the more prestigious (High), the other the less prestigious (Low) variant; for definitions, see Adams, J. N. 2003. *Bilingualism and the Latin Language* (Cambridge), 537–41, 754–5.

6. See Varvaro (Supra n. 1), 45–6, who however sees a trend of progressive Latinization in the language choices of Sicilian literary authors.

7. Cf. Varvaro (Supra n. 1), 46; Salmeri (Supra n. 1), 282–6.

8. See Pinzone, A. 1999. "L'immigrazione e i suoi riflessi nella storia economica e sociale della Sicilia del II sec. a. C.", in *Magna Grecia e Sicilia. Stato degli studi e prospettive di ricerca*. Barra Bagnasco, M. *et al.* (eds) (Messina), 381–402. A masterly discussion of the epigraphic culture of late Hellenistic / republican Sicily in its historical context is provided by Prag, J. R. W. 2007. "Ciceronian Sicily: The Epigraphic Dimension", in *La Sicile de Cicéron: lectures des Verrines. Actes du colloque de Paris, 19–20 mai 2006*. Dubouloz, J. and S. Pittia (eds) (Besançon), 245–71.; cf. id. 2003. "Nouveau regard sur les élites locales de la Sicile républicaine", *Histoire et sociétés rurales* 19, 121–31.

9. A thorough survey on Oscan in Sicily would be needed; for an effort in this direction, see Sironen, T. 1995. "Position of Minority Languages in Sicily: Oscan and Elymian", in *Ancient Sicily* (Copenhagen), 185–94. On Messina in particular, see Pinzone, A. 1981. "Per la storia di Messana mamertina", *Archivio storico messinese* 32, 5–54 [repr. in id. 1999. *Provincia Sicilia* (Catania), 121–72].

10. See, in general, Wilson, R. J. A. 1996. "Sicily, Sardinia and Corsica", in *The Cambridge Ancient History*² X (Cambridge), 434–48, here 434–9.

11. Cass. Dio 48.48.6; cf. Manganaro, G. 1999. "Annotazioni sulla epigrafia di Lipara", in *Sicilia epigraphica. Atti del convegno di studi, Erice, 15–18 ottobre 1998*. Gulletta, M. I. (ed) (Pisa), 425–37, here 428.

12. Wilson (Supra n. 10), 437. If a colony was founded at

Panhormus by Augustus has been the subject of an intense debate; see especially Giardina, A. 1987. "Palermo in età imperiale romana", *Kókalos* 33, 225–55, here 226–31; Wilson (Supra n. 1), 39; Vera, D. 1996. "Augusto, Plinio il Vecchio e la Sicilia in età imperiale. A proposito di recenti scoperte epigrafiche e archeologiche ad Agrigento", *Kókalos* 42, 31–58, here 35 and 41. In this paper, I will use the modern names of the towns discussed.

13. Cf. Vera (Supra n. 12), 33–36.

14. Diod. Sic. 16.7.1: Καῖσαρος ἀναστήσαντος τοὺς Ταυρομενίτας ἐκ τῆς πατρίδος τῶν Ῥωμαίων ἀποικίαν ἐδέξατο. R. J. A. Wilson (1988. "Towns of Sicily during the Roman Empire", *ANRW* II 11.1, 90–206, here 95) suggests that the expulsion only concerned the elite; cf. Salmeri (Supra n. 1), 275.

15. Cf. Keppie, L. 1983. *Colonisation and Veteran Settlement in Italy 47–14 BC* (Rome), 102–4; Vera (Supra n. 12), 36.

16. *Res gestae* 28.1: *Colonias in Africa, Sicilia, [M]acedonia ... militum deduxi* (Greek translation: Ἀποικίας ἐν Λιβύῃ, Σικελίᾳ, Μακεδονίᾳ ... στρατιωτῶν κατήγαγον). Wilson (Supra n. 1, 38–9) points out the rarity of explicit epigraphic evidence on these veterans. However, this is not remarkable, as military service was not necessarily indicated in the kinds of inscriptions that survive; see Keppie (Supra n. 15), 104–5.

17. Keppie (Supra n. 15), 97–8; Wilson (Supra n. 1), 39, 45.

18. Wilson (Supra n. 1), 171. According to Strabo (6.2.4), Syracuse had notably diminished in size in comparison to the Hellenistic period, and that Augustus restored (ἀνέλαβε) it almost to its previous size; but the archaeological evidence does not support such a decrease: see Wilson (Supra n. 14), 113. Strabo also claims (6.2.3) that Catania had more inhabitants than Taormina.

19. See the list in *IMC Catania*, p. 79.

20. Bivona, in *IL TermIm* pp. 67–110.

21. For the concept of channelized migration, see Hall, J. M. 1997. *Ethnic Identity in Greek Antiquity* (Cambridge), 27–8.

22. Eck, W. 1996. "Senatorische Familien der Kaiserzeit in der Provinz Sizilien", *ZPE* 113, 109–28, here 109 [an earlier version "Senatoren und senatorischer Grundbesitz auf Sizilien", in *Catania antica. Atti del convegno della S.I.S.A.C., Catania 23–24 maggio 1992*. Gentili, B. (ed) (Pisa and Rome) 1996, 231–56, here 231].

23. The predominance of public inscriptions in the surviving record from the late Hellenistic / republican period is pointed out by Prag (Supra n. 8), 257. There is a strong contrast in the amount of epigraphic evidence of *gymnasia* in Sicily between the republican and imperial periods, see Prag, J. R. W. 2007. "*Auxilia* and *Gymnasia*: A Sicilian Model of Roman Imperialism", *Journal of Roman Studies* 97 (2007) 68–100, here 87–96.

24. See Bivona, L. 2001. "Brevi considerazioni sulla epigrafia latina di Sicilia", in *Varia epigraphica. Atti del Colloquio Bertinoro 8–10 giugno 2000* (Faenza), 49–61, here 49–54.

25. I shall return to the subject briefly below.

26. With "linguistic landscape" I refer to objects that mark the public space. "Public space" is used here in the meaning "every space in the community that is not private propriety". See Ben-Rafael, E. 2009. "A Sociological Approach to the Study of Linguistic Landscapes", in *Linguistic Landscape*. Shohamy, E. and D. Gorter (eds) (New York – London), 40–54.

27. On the role of such materials in administrative communication, see Eck, W. 2004. "Lateinisch, Griechisch, Germanisch ....? Wie sprach Rom mit seinen Untertanen?", in de Ligt *et al.* (eds) (Supra n. 3), 3–19, here 8–10.

28. Syracuse is the leading Sicilian town in the number of inscriptions known to us from that period: Prag (Supra n. 8), 258.

29. Thus Butler, S. 2002. *The Hand of Cicero* (London – New York), 37 (quoted in Prag [Supra n. 8], 251).

30. The inscriptions are Aneziri, S. 2002. *Die Vereine der dionysischen Techniten im Kontext der hellenistischen Gesellschaft* (Stuttgart), 400–2 nos. F1–F4 (*IG* XIV 12–13; Orsi, P. 1900. "Frammenti epigrafici sicelioti", *Rivista di storia antica* 5, 39–66, here 62 no. 41 = *IG Mus. Palermo* 106 = Manganaro, G. 1977 [1985]. "Per la storia dei culti nella Sicilia greca", *Cronache di archeologia e di storia dell'arte* 16, 148–64, here 157; Gentili, G.V. 1961. "Nuovi elementi di epigrafia siracusana", *Archivio storico siracusano* 7, 5–25, here 11–16 nos. 1–2). For discussion, see also Manganaro, G. 1963. "Nuove ricerche di epigrafia siceliota", *Siculorum Gymnasium* 16, 51–64, here 57–63; Moretti, L. 1963. "I technitai di Siracusa", *Rivista di filologia e di istruzione classica* 91, 38–45 [Repr. in *id.* 1990. *Tra epigrafia e storia* (Rome), 189–96]; for further references, see *SEG* L 1025.

31. I will comment the linguistic form of these inscriptions below, on p. 20.

32. *NSA* 1956, 96 = *SEG* XVI 535; an improved reading and a photograph in Manganaro, G. 2000. "Fenici, Cartaginesi, Numidi tra i Greci (IV–I sec. a.C.)", *Numismatica e antichità classiche* 29, 255–68, here 264–6 (*SEG* LII 933).

33. The transmitted text of the inscription, lost since the 17th century, is as follows: GN· OCTAVIO· A· F· MI· NICONOR· BOLONAR / VELIC· VENER· TARIC· PAVIMENTVM etc. See Gaggiotti, M. 2002. "Nuova luce sull'economia della Sicilia romana da una rilettura dell'iscrizione siracusana *ILLRP* 279", *L'Africa romana* 13, 1053–62 (*AE* 2002, 612), who deciphers the text as *Gn. Octavio A. f. mini(ster) cohor(tis) bolonar(um) / velic(us)* (= *vilicus*) *Vener(is) Taric(hinae) pavimentum* etc. *Minister* is somewhat anomalous in such a context, but no better explanations are at hand.

34. Line 1 seems to contain the ending of the dedicator's name, which was either the rare Πιτίων or a previously unattested Greek name. Πιτίων is attested only once (*LGPN* II 368: *IG* II² 12459); the rare Latin cognomen *Capitio* seems very unlikely. There is no way of connecting PITION to the Sicilian locality Καπίτιον / *Capitium* (Cic. *Verr.* II 3.103) or to the Latin word *propitius*.

35. On this administrative change, see the Appendix.

36. Manganaro, G. 1994. "Iscrizioni, epitaffi ed epigrammi in greco della Sicilia centro-orientale di epoca romana", *Mélanges de l'École française de Rome. Antiquité* 106, 79–118, here 79–82 (*SEG* XLIV 786).

37. The dating, proposed by Manganaro, is based on the word [τέτα]ρτον, plausibly part of Octavian's titulature, and on palaeography: the letters can hardly be later than Augustan.

38. Manganaro, G. 1989. "Iscrizioni latine nuove e vecchie della Sicilia", *Epigraphica* 51, 161–96, here 181 no. 57 (= *AE* 1989, 342b; ed. pr. Orsi [Supra n. 48], 65 no. 51):] IMP·DIV[/]ATVA·DIC [. The onomastic formula is uncommon: Manganaro supplied *[C. Iulio Caesari] / Imp(eratori) Div[i f(ilio) IIIviro r(ei) p(ublicae) c(onstituendae)] / [st]atua dic(ata) [---]*, but it is also

39. Much of the evidence can be found in Manganaro (Supra n. 38). I refer to the following documents: *Archivio storico siracusano* 7 (1961) 126a; *CIL* X 7120, 7126, 7128, 7131 (?), 7132 (?), 7134, 7137, 7138 and 7163 (?); *EE* VIII 679 (*CIL* X 7146 = Manganaro 181–2 no. 161); *EE* VIII 686; Gentili (Supra n. 30), 22–3 no. 1 (= Manganaro 181 no. 58 = *AE* 1989, 342c); Manganaro 181 no. 59 (= *AE* 342d, Trajan), 182 no. 62 (= 342e) 183 no. 65 (= 342h) and 183 nos. 66–67; *NSA* 1907, 753 (i); 1912, 293 (ii); 1951, 164–5 no. 1 (*AE* 1952, 158 = Eck (Supra n. 22), 109, from the year 227); 1951, 276; 1971, 634–5; Orsi (Supra n. 30), 64 no. 47 (statue base) and 65 no. 50; *Palladio* 23 (1973) 68–69 = Manganaro (Supra n. 1, 1988), 55; possibly also *NSA* 1905, 399 nos. 10 and 11. Inscribed *instrumentum* that refers to imperial or city property: *CIL* X 7140 (Claudius) and *NSA* 1915, 202 (*R(es) p(ublica) Syracusanorum*, 1st–2nd c.). Note that Manganaro 183 no. 64, Fig. 69 (= *AE* 1989, 342g) is the erroneous reading of a late fragment, published previously as *CIL* X 7133. To the fragments from late antiquity seems to belong Manganaro (Supra n. 1, 1993), 583 n. 102 = 561 Fig. 20 (= *SEG* XLIII 634), of which only a drawing has been published; it refers to a decision of the city council.

40. Manganaro 183 no. 65 (=*AE* 1989, 342h). The inscription Gentili (Supra n. 30), 22–3 no. 1 (= Manganaro 181 no. 58 = *AE* 1989, 342c) is datable to the first half of the first century CE: see Eck (Supra n. 22), 113, 123–5. *EE* VIII 679 might also be Augustan (= Manganaro 181–2 no. 161). – Note that *CIL* X 7135, mentioned by Prag (Supra n. 23, 96), is not from Syracuse, but a fragment of *CIL* VI 5688 found in 1788 in Rome: see Wilson, R. J. A. 1988. "A Wandering Inscription from Roma", *ZPE* 71, 161–6; Manganaro (Supra n. 38), 195–6 no. 91.

41. *NSA* 1891, 392, the reading of which was notably improved by Manganaro, G. 1999. *Sikelika: Studi di antichità e di epigrafia della Sicilia greca* (Pisa and Rome), 69 no. 65 (*SEG* XLIX 1330). Cf. Lazzarini, M. L. 2004. "Sopravvivenze istituzionali e culturali greche nell'Italia romana", in *L'Hellénisme d'époque romaine: nouveaux documents, nouvelles approches. Actes du Colloque international à la mémoire de Louis Robert, Paris 2000.* Follet, S. (ed) (Paris), 173–82, here 179.

42. See Manganaro (Supra n. 41), 69; Lazzarini (Supra n. 41), 178.

43. Gentili (Supra n. 40), 20–1 n. 2 (cf. Manganaro [Supra n. 30, 1963], 62; Moretti [Supra n. 30], 41 n. 1; Manganaro [Supra n. 1, 1988], 59): Κ. Καικίλ[ιος - -]των ... βιολόγος, ὀκ[λαδο?]παίκτης, φιλόξ[ενος]; Manganaro (Supra n. 41), 69 no. 66 (*SEG* XLIX 1333): [ὁ δεῖνα ...] καὶ σαλπίσας / [δ]ρόμοις κιρκησίοις [- - -].

44. No other attestations of the adjective κιρκήσιος (from Latin *circensis*) are known to me, but the plural noun κιρκήσια appears in literature (Arrian, *Epict.* 4.10.21) and in epigraphical sources (*IGL Syrie* 3.1 965).

45. The dedications *IG* XIV 4 (Nymphs) and Orsi (Supra n. 48), 63 no. 43 (Serapis) are very difficult to date.

46. L. Bernabò Brea, *NSA* 1947, 202, with a drawing. According to the publisher, the measurements of the monument are: height 49 cm, width 40 cm, height of the letters 5 cm.

47. The use of onomastic formulae in the epitaphs from Syracuse will be discussed below.

48. *Corpus inscriptionum Graecarum* 8886A; not in *IG*, but rescued from oblivion by Ferrua, A. 1940. "Nuovi studi nelle catacombe di Siracusa", *Rivista di archeologia cristiana* 17, 43–81, here 74–81: Ἀνάθη[μα - - -]Ι ΙΙΙ [- - -]ς Μα/ξίμου, Θεόδωρος [- - -]Μ / τὸν κρατῆρα [- - -]PON. [- - -]ς Μαξίμου could be a slave, but filiation is more likely here.

49. The Latin cognomen *Maximus* enjoyed some popularity in Greek-speaking areas especially after the 1st century CE: Solin, H. 2001. "Latin Cognomina in the Greek East", in *The Greek East in the Roman Context. Proceedings of a Colloquium, Finnish Institute at Athens, 1999.* Salomies, O. (ed) (Helsinki), 189–202, here 196.

50. "Tabella marmorea Syracusis reperta graeco idiomate, quam latine versam hic propono" (Gaetani, O. 1707 [posthumous]. *Isagoge ad historiam sacram Siculam* (Palermo), 19–20, quoted by Sgarlata, M. 1993 [1996]. *La raccolta epigrafica e l'epistolario archeologico di Cesare Gaetani Conte della Torre* [Palermo], 166–7). On this cult in Syracuse, see most recently Sfameni Gasparro, G. 2006. "I culti orientali nella Sicilia ellenistico-romana", in *Ethne e religioni nella Sicilia antica.* Anello, P. *et al.* (eds) (Rome), 251–342, here 324–5.

51. *P. Plotius P. f. [- - -?], M. Pomponius Di-?, L. Lucinius* (or *Licinius*, proposed by Kaibel in *IG*), *L. Octavius L. [- - -], T. Faecius [- - -]* (transmitted as *Phaecius*), *Attale (-us?) [- - -], Eutych[- - -].*

52. The praenomen *Tiberius*, even though attested, is not common in the republican period; see Salomies, O. 1987. *Die römischen Vornamen* (Helsinki), 56; cf. Solin (Supra n. 49), 194. Given the uncertainty of the text, it is not certain if all the officials had a cognomen.

53. See, most recently, L. Revell's illuminating discussion on the intricate dynamics of certain sites of worship in the provinces (2009. *Roman Imperialism and Local Identities* [Cambridge], 118–49).

54. For examples of conservative language choices (instead of Latin) in religious dedications, see Adams (Supra n. 5), 188–90 (Gaulish), 210–11 (Punic), 249–52 (Palmyrene), 271–3 (Hebrew).

55. Adams (Supra n. 5), 577–89.

56. See Manganaro (Supra n. 30, 1977 [1985]), 154 and 159, where he publishes a comparable inscription from Avola.

57. *NSA* 1947, 187 = Manganaro (Supra n. 38), 182 no. 62. Coarelli has proposed that the dedicator is to be identified with L. Papinius *locuples honestusque eques Romanus* (Cic. *Verr.* II 4.46; Coarelli, F. and M. Torelli 1984. *Sicilia* (Guide archeologiche Laterza, Bari), 243, but in my view the letter forms and the other characteristics of the inscription, although somewhat difficult to date, do not support this. See also Sfameni Gasparro (Supra n. 50), 268–9.

58. Manganaro (Supra n. 41), 70 no. 67 (*SEG* XLIX 1329).

59. Salmeri (Supra n. 1), 290–4.

60. See, in particular, Wilson (Supra n. 32), 101–53; *id.* (Supra n. 19), 46–57.

61. See Wilson (Supra n. 14), 113–15 and (Supra n. 1), 51–2; cf. Belvedere, O. 1988 "Opere pubbliche ed edifici per lo spettacolo nella Sicilia di età imperiale", *ANRW* II 11.1, 346–413, here 349–58. For an excellent map, see Wilson (Supra n. 1), 160.

62. Cf. Cic. *Verr.* II 4. 118.

63. Except those referring to Sextus Pompeius, if any. The dedication by king Masteabar discussed above (p. 9) was

evidently removed and, not long afterwards, the incision of a sculptured relief destroyed a part of the text. Manganaro (Supra n. 32, 265) connects the removal to the conquest of the city by the troops of Sextus Pompeius.

64. The *agora / forum* was located in the area now called Foro Siracusano (formerly known as Piazza d'Armi). Greek inscriptions: *IG* XIV 58a (cf. *NSA* 1889, 371, Hellenistic); Gentili (Supra n. 30), 11–16 nos 1–2 (1st c. BCE, see above, 3.1); Latin inscriptions: *CIL* I² 3429 and possibly 2224 (late republican); Gentili (Supra n. 30), 22–3 no. 1 = Manganaro (Supra n. 38), 181 no. 58 (*AE* 1989, 342c); *NSA* 1889, 371; 1907, 753 (three inscriptions); Orsi (Supra n. 30), 64 no. 47. *EE* VIII 684, from late antiquity was also found in the area.

65. For an up-to-date survey of evidence, see Prag, J. R. W. 2008. "Sicilia and Britannia: Epigraphic Evidence for Civic Administration", in *Le quotidien municipal dans l'Occident romain*. Berrendonner, C. *et al.* (eds) (Clermont-Ferrand), 67–81.

66. *IMC Catania* nos. 13–46 and the items listed on p. 134 (note that a few are from late antiquity, and that my category "Iscrizioni riguardanti i ceti più alti della società e la vita pubblica" also includes some epitaphs). The provenance of a dedication to Claudius in the Catania museum, *CIL* VI 31283 = *IMC Catania* 343, is very difficult to determine, and it might come from Catania (one of my arguments in *IMC Catania* against the local origin was flawed: in such a dedication, no individual name is needed).

67. The fragment has recently been discussed by Kajava, M. 2005–2006. "Laodicea al Mare e Catania", *Rendiconti della Pontificia Accademia Romana di Archeologia* 78, 527–41 (*SEG* LIV 897).

68. On language choice in the dedications of the towns of the Greek east in Italy, see now Brélaz (Supra n. 4), 186–9.

69. Naples: see Miranda, E. 1990. *Iscrizioni greche d'Italia 1: Napoli* (Roma), nos. 51–55. Furthermore, in an inscription from Mazara, the abbreviation Δ Δ B probably stands for δόγματι δεκουριώνων βουλῆς (of Lilybaeum / Marsala?), see *BE* 1936, 394; 1971, 767; Prag (Supra n. 65), 76.

70. In Sicily, concessions of burial places by the colonial senate are well attested in Termini: see the index in *IL TermIm* p. 310. Cf. Prag (Supra n. 65), 76.

71. Wilson (Supra n. 14), 125 and (Supra n. 1), 51; *id.*, "La topografia della Catania romana", in Gentili (ed) (Supra n. 22), 149–73, here 154–5. On the aqueduct, cf. *IMC Catania* p. 171.

72. *NSA* 1922, 494 = *AE* 1923, 75 = Manganaro (Supra n. 30, 1977 [1985]), 162–3 = Wilson (Supra n. 1), 314 = Manganaro (Supra n. 36), 110–11, all with photographs or drawings. Manganaro and Wilson suggest a dating to the 2nd or 3rd century; I prefer an earlier dating on palaeographical grounds and because of the filiation, *Rubri Sami fil.*

73. *BE* 1962, 388 = Manganaro (Supra n. 1, 1988), 49, 68 n. 346: Ἀρτεμίδωρος Κλήμεντος δ(οῦλος) κατ' ὄναρ; *IG* XIV 450 = Manganaro, *ibid.*, lost since the 17th century and difficult to date: Περσεφόνη Βασιλὶς κατ' <ὄ>να<ρ> (transmitted as ΚΑΤΑΝΑΛ). In *IMC Catania* (p. 70), I categorized the text under pre-Roman material.

74. The calendar: *Inscriptiones Italiae* XIII 2, p. 547, cf. Salomies, O. "Zu den Fasti consulares von Tauromenium", *ZPE* 86 (1991) 187–92; Ruck, B. 1996. "Die Fasten von Taormina, *ZPE* 111, 271–80; for the other texts, see Manganaro, G. 1964. "Iscrizioni latine e greche dal nuovo

edificio termale di Taormina", *Cronache di archeologia e di storia dell'arte* 3, 38–68.

75. *CIL* X 7472–7480, 8420; Manganaro (Supra n. 38), 162–3 nos. 2–11 (*AE* 1989, 338a–338g).

76. See Giardina (Supra n. 12), 231–7; Bivona (Supra n. 24), 55–7.

77. See Kajava, M. forthcoming. "Honorific and Other Dedications to Emperors in the Greek East", in: *Royal Cult and Emperor Worship in Classical and Late Antiquity. Proceedings of the Conference organized by the Belgian School at Athens (1–2 November, 2007)*. Iossif, P. and A. Chankowski (eds) (Studia Hellenistica, Leuven).

78. *CIL* X 7296 = *IG* XIV 297, text in two columns: Στῆλαι / ἐνθάδε / τυποῦνται καὶ / χαράσσονται / ναοῖς ἱεροῖς / σὺν ἐνεργείαις / δημοσίαις. // *Tituli / heic / ordinantur et / sculpuntur / aidibus sacreis / qum operum / publicorum.* See Alföldy, G. 1989. "Epigraphische Notizen aus Italien III", *ZPE* 77, 155–80, here 175, with references; Kruschwitz, P. 2000. "Die sprachlichen Anomalien der Werbeinschrift *CIL* X 7296", *ZPE* 130, 239–40; Adams (Supra n. 5) 429–31.

79. The stone belonged to the Museo Salnitriano, which contains material from several locations in Sicily and no certain items from Rome, and was published for the first time by Torremuzza in 1762 (references in *CIL*).

80. Alföldy (Supra n. 78), 175–6. Along similar lines Kruschwitz (Supra n. 78).

81. *IG* XIV 315 = *ILS* 8769 = *SIG*³ 677 = Brugnone, A. 1974. "Iscrizioni greche del Museo Civico di Termini Imerese", *Kòkalos* 20, 218–64, here 223 nos. 3–4. The contents of the two inscriptions are considered to be authentic. The lettering is not compatible with a second-century BCE date; Brugnone dated them to the 2nd or 3rd century CE (cf. Prag [Supra n. 8], 251 n. 23). On palaeographical grounds, there might be a connection between the copies and the local poet Ἀριστόδαμος Νεμηνίδα Πέρσιος of the early imperial period (*IG* XIV 316 = Brugnone, no. 5).

82. For evidence of local administrations, see Cordano, F. 1999. "Le istituzioni delle città greche nelle fonti epigrafiche", in Gulletta (ed) (Supra n. 11), 149–58; Lazzarini (Supra n. 41), 174–5.

83. See Wilson (Supra n. 1), 40–1, 43. Lipari had *duoviri* in the late republic, attested on coins as δύο ἄ(νδρες), see Manganaro (Supra n. 1, 1988), 12.

84. *IGL Lipari* 795: Ἄρχουσιν / [Σ]κρειβωνίοις Νωμεντανῷ καὶ Μοδέστῳ. Three more lines of the inscription survive (cf. the photograph and J.-P. Houël's drawing, *ibid.* p. 474, Fig. 10), but no reading is given in *IGL Lipari*. Of the list of names, only the traces of the first one can be seen in the drawing ("ΛΛ4ΙΟΣ ΛΥΙ ..."; one of Houel's signs does look like the modern number 4). In my opinion, it is unlikely that the inscription could be a "pierre errante" (suggested by R. A. Tybout, *SEG* LIII 1010).

85. The editio princeps is by Manganaro, G. 1992. "Tra epigrafia e numismatica", *Chiron* 22, 385–410, here 389–90, who dates the text to ca. 50 BCE. It is interesting that no filiation is given for the magistrates; Manganaro suggested that they were libertine, which would be remarkable.

86. Robert, L. 1963. "De Cilicie à Messine et à Plymouth", *Journal des Savants* 1963, 161–211; Strasser, J.-Y. 2002. "Deux autels de Messine rendus à Aigéai de Cilicie", *Epigraphica Anatolica* 34, 149–59. In favour of local provenance: G. Manganaro, "Asklepios e Hygieia 'divinità salvatrici e protettrici della città' a Messina", *ZPE* 113

(1996) 82–4; Bitto, in *IGL Messina* pp. 104–9; *ead.* 2002. "Testimonianze epigrafiche di Messina romana: iscrizione in onore di Asklepio e di Hygeia", in *Messina e Reggio nell'antichità*. Gentili, B. and A. Pinzone (eds) (Messina), 127–39. Bitto has brought forward previously unconsidered evidence of the cult (such as *IG* XIV 412), but the evidence of the cult of Asclepius in Messina does not solve the issue of the altars' provenance.

87. The earliest testimony of *IG* XIV 402 is G. Walther's (= Gualtherius) epigraphic corpus from 1624, when the stone was already in Messina.

88. In the late middle ages there was an active community of merchants in Messina who were well connected with e.g. Cyprus (Abulafia, D. 1986. "The Merchants of Messina: Levant Trade and Domestic Economy", *Papers of the British School in Rome* 54, 196–212), but it is not easy to grasp why the altars, which have no connection to Christianity, should have been brought to Messina in this period. The altar that found its way to Plymouth in England was transported much later.

89. Cf. Lomas (Supra n. 1), 171.

90. Adams (Supra n. 5), 8. For the background in socio-linguistics, see Romaine, S. 1995. *Bilingualism²* (Oxford), 7–22.

91. The situation in the city of Rome is concisely described by Adams (Supra n. 5), 761–2.

92. In some multilingual societies, no language has the complete range of communicative possibilities (cf. Croft, W. 2000. *Explaining Language Change* [Harlow], 90–4), but this was probably not the case in Sicily on the level of spoken communication.

93. Here I am not referring to the language some boys (and fewer girls) learned when they began the study of *litterae*, which is yet another matter (see Quintilian's famous passage, *Inst.* 1.1.12–14).

94. This can be seen *e.g.* in the "Monumentum Liviae" in Rome, on which see Joshel, S. R. 1992. *Work, Identity, and Legal Status at Rome. A Study of the Occupational Inscriptions* (Norman, OK), 100–1.

95. Cf. Hall's discussion (Supra n. 21, 123–31).

96. See most recently Adams (Supra n. 5), 84–90.

97. In the military context, using Latin in one's epitaph seems to have been an expression of Romanness or at least a marker of professional identity (see Levick [Supra n. 4], 397–8; Adams [Supra n. 5], 262, 616–17, 752). The fact that the evidence of the army is minimal in Sicily could be due to the fact that as in the republican period (on which see Prag [Supra n. 23], 96–9), the security of the province may have prevalently been maintained by local troops.

98. See Solin (Supra n. 49).

99. Solin, H. 1971. *Beiträge zur Kenntnis der griechischen Personennamen in Rom* (Helsinki), 135–8.

100. The indications of libertine status are nowhere common, for reasons that are easy to grasp. For the Greek east, see Rizakis, A. D. 1996. "Anthroponymie et société. Les noms romains dans les provinces hellénophones de l'Empire", in *id.* (ed.) *Roman Onomastics in the Greek East. Social and Political Aspects* (Athens), 11–29, here 25–6. At Lipari, Lazzarini (Supra n. 41, 180) has suggested that persons with an inverted onomastic formula, *i.e.*, of the cognomen preceding the gentilicium, could be interpreted as freed(wo)men, but I would be more cautious.

101. I refer to published material, scattered in numerous local and international publications and corpora. It is somewhat difficult to distinguish between pre-imperial and imperial pagan epitaphs, but the number of epitaphs datable before the Roman colonization seems to be small. The largest group of epitaphs excluded here comes from the cemetery published by Paolo Orsi in *NSA* 1892, 354–65 (8 epitaphs, 9 persons), which Orsi plausibly dated to the late 3rd – early 2nd century BCE. – In the distinction between "pagan" and "Christian" epitaphs, I rely on Antonio Ferrua (1941. "Epigrafia sicula pagana e cristiana", *Rivista di archeologia cristiana* 18, 151–243; 1989. *Note e giunte alle iscrizioni cristiane antiche della Sicilia* [Città del Vaticano]); cf. the lucid remarks by Felle, A. F. 2005. "Epigrafia pagana e cristiana in Sicilia: consonanze e peculiarità", *Vetera Christianorum* 42, 233–50.

102. On these attributes and social standing in Syracuse, see Korhonen, K. 2002. "Three Cases of Greek / Latin Imbalance in Roman Syracuse", in *Greek Romans and Roman Greeks. Studies in Cultural Interaction*. Ostenfeld, E. N. (ed) (Aarhus), 70–80, here 72–3.

103. Exceptional in this sense is the epitaph of a certain Εὐτύχης published by G. Manganaro, *Helikon* 2 (1962) 499, found in the vicinity of Priolo (*NSA* 1891, 359). It is a funerary altar with building and measuring tools in relief; apparently the deceased was a civil engineer. (Photographs in Rizzo, F. P. 1989 [1993]. *La menzione del lavoro nelle epigrafi della Sicilia antica* [Palermo], 108.)

104. Of the recent corpus, *IGL Lipari* (2003), I have obviously excluded the *cippi parallelepipedi* and the other *antiquiores* (nos. 5–331), but also a group of inscriptions that the editors of *IGL Lipari* have preferred to attribute neither to the *antiquiores* nor to the *recentiores* (nos. 554–649). These contain exclusively Greek names, which seems to have served as a criterion for classification. If all of them were from the early Empire, the proportion of Latin names would be reduced to ca. 10%, and the proportion of Greek names increased accordingly. But on the other hand, some of the inscriptions with Latin gentilicia could be from the republican period.

105. The material includes the epitaphs published in *IMC Catania*, as well as those listed on p. 134 of that work; for the photographs, see http://www.helsinki.fi/hum/kla/catania. One of the epitaphs with cognomina is bilingual (*IMC Catania* 109 = *CIL* X 7078 = *IG* XIV 491), which is why the totals in columns 2 and 3 are 239, but in columns 4–5 and 6 240. – The bilingual name is Πριμιγένης (*IMC Catania* 90), probably a fusion of Πρωτογένης and *Primigenius*.

106. Most of the epigraphic material from Messina has been put together by I. Bitto in *IGL Messina* (2001), but the volume does not contain the Greek inscriptions that are not in the Regional Museum; they are to appear in the second volume.

107. *IG* XIV 406 (Crete), 411 (Paphus) and 413 (Rome); *IGL Messina* 12 (Corinth), 15 (Apamea), 29 (Lycia; evidently four brothers), 33 (a Sebaste) and 34 (Antioch). For a list, see Malfitana, D. 2004. "Anfore e ceramiche fini da mensa orientali nella Sicilia tardo-ellenistica e romana", in *Transport Amphorae and Trade in the Eastern Mediterranean. Acts of the International Colloquium Athens 2002*. Eiring, J. and J. Lund (eds) (Athens), 239–50, here 249. (However, the list contains curious mistakes: *e.g.*, no. B6 is not from Messina; B7 belongs to Syracuse, not Messina; D2 to Syracuse, not Catania; E19 to Messina, not Syracuse).

108. Obviously, immigration was not always indicated in an

epitaph, and Αισαρις Σατταρας in *IGL Messina* 41, or at least her/his family, probably came from the Balkans or from North Africa (see Bitto, *IGL Messina* p. 113; note that for Αισαρις, the linguistic context should be the same as for Σατταρα(ς), and here it probably has little to do with Etruscan).

109. Principal corpora: *IL TermIm* (all the Latin texts from Termini; nos. B1 and B2 are also local, see Korhonen, K. 2001. "Osservazioni sul collezionismo epigrafico siciliano", *Arctos* 35, 85–102, here 98–102); Brugnone (Supra n. 81; Greek inscriptions in the City Museum). In my view, the inscriptions Brugnone nos. 5–21 are probably from early imperial times, although some of them could be earlier (*e.g.*, no. 17 = *IG* XIV 320; Brugnone's dating is misleading). I would not date any of them beyond the 2nd century CE.

110. Some inscriptions were imported from Rome, others from elsewhere in Sicily. My category of local pagan epitaphs includes the following: *IG* XIV 298 (= *IG Mus. Palermo* 138), 299 (= 145), 300 (= 33), 303 (= 152), 305, 306, 307, 310 (= 150); *CIL* X 7285 (= *IL Mus. Palermo* 27), 7288, 7289, 7290, 7291, 7292 (= 29), 7293, 7297, 7298, 7299, 7301, 7302, 7303, 7305 (= 32), 7306, 7307, 7308, 7309 (= 33), 7310, 7311 (= 34), 7312, 7313, 7314 (= 87), 7315, 7317, 7318 (cf. *EE* VIII 697), 7319, 7320, 7321, 7322, 7325, 7327 (= 83), 7328 (= 84); *IG Mus. Palermo* 137, 140, 142, 144, 147; *IL Mus. Palermo* 80, 86 and 90. I have the impression that some of the "iscrizioni urbane" in the Palermo museum are rather from Sicily than from Rome, but must return to this subject on another occasion. Only one of the Greek inscriptions listed above is certainly from Palermo (*IG* XIV 300).

111. The group "Other" in the inscriptions of Catania refers to bilingual texts.

112. *IMC Catania* 57, 65, 86, 90, 100, 114, 122, 128, 137, 140 and 142; *IG* XIV 478 and 497; *CIL* X 7055, 7060, 7075, 7076, 7088, 7090, 7092 and 7099; *Archivio storico per la Sicilia Orientale* 8 (1931) 49 no. 4 = *AE* 1984, 441 = *AE* 1987, 466; *NSA* 1915, 216 (ii).

113. In *IMC Catania*, I interpreted *Lecata* as a graphic variant of *Legata*, but the solution is unsatisfactory.

114. The transmitted text runs as follows: Κούιντος Σόσσις / καὶ Πετρονία / ΣΟΣΣΙΑ Χείᾳ / τῇ θυγατρὶ ζηάσῃ / ἔτη ι̅, ἡμέρα(ς) κβ̅. Kaibel interpreted the word ΣΟΣΣΙΑ as part of the mother's onomastic formula, but it could also belong, in the dative, to the name of the deceased (cf. *IMC Catania*, p. 88).

115. On the evidence of the senatorial members of this family in Sicily, see Eck (Supra n. 22).

116. The daughter's name has often been read as Ῥωμαντίλλα, not attested elsewhere, which requires interpreting the short horizontal line in the letter *iota* as a nexus of *tau* and *iota*. However, I agree with Solin, H. 2005. "Analecta epigraphica", *Arctos* 39, 176–7, 180, who takes the horizontal line as a stonecutter's error and argues that the well attested *Romanilla* must have been meant. The cognomina derived from *Roma* are listed in Kajanto, I. 1965. *The Latin Cognomina* (Helsinki), 182. For no evident reason, the previous editors have integrated the abbreviated gentilicium in these Latin inscriptions as *Claudius*, but in the Greek inscriptions as Κλώδιος; my interpretation is based on the cognomen *Claudianus*.

117. I shall discuss below why two epitaphs are in Greek and two in Latin.

118. T. Flavius Ionius, a benefactor in Catania: see *IMC Catania* p. 174.

119. Antia M. f. Cleopatra *sacerdos* from Termini, *IL TermIm* 18.

120. In a family in Messina (*IGL Messina* 18), the sons' cognomina are *Pudens* and *Pudentinus*; the parents have Greek cognomina.

121. *NSA* 1912, 298 (an early imperial Latin epitaph of a L. Arrius Dionusius) and *IG* XIV 23 (see Korhonen, K. 2007. "Erudite Forgeries or Families Seeking Distinction? Cesare Gaetani's Inscriptions from Syracuse", *ZPE* 161, 291–8, here 295).

122. The counts are my own.

123. Σικέλα and Σίκολος in Lipari: *IGL Lipari* 275 (certainly pre-Roman) and 693.

124. The development is discussed by Meyer, E.A. 1990. "Explaining the Epigraphic Habit in the Roman Empire. The Evidence of Epitaphs", *Journal of Roman Studies* 80, 74–96, here 75–83.

125. *IG* XIV 320 (= Brugnone, Supra n. 81, 246 no. 17), 322 (= *IG Mus. Palermo* 121), 324 (= Brugnone 247 no. 18), 325, 327 and 329 (= Brugnone 242 no. 14).

126. For Termini, see Bivona, *IL TermIm* pp. 39–40; add her no. B1 (p. 265; see above, n. 128), with *Epaφruitus*.

127. This development was also presented in Korhonen (Supra n. 102), 71–3.

128. The only instances in Greek epitaphs are *IG* XIV 34, in which the dedicator has a non-Greek name Ποδδα- (cf. Korhonen, Supra n. 140, 295), and Ferrua (Supra n. 119), 178. Latin epitaphs with dedicators shown: *CIL* X 7127, 7144, 7147, 7150, 7158; *EE* VIII 688, 690, 692; *NSA* 1889, 386; 1913, 268 (two); 1947, 205; 1951, p. 165 no. 2 and p. 297.

129. On the structures used in Catania, see my discussion in *IMC Catania*, pp. 83–9, 93–100.

130. Korhonen (Supra n. 102), 72.

131. A comparable case is *IL TermIm* 150.

132. I shall return to this document elsewhere.

133. Discussed in Korhonen (Supra n. 102), 73. The monument has been lost, but a fragment of the text survives as *IG* XIV 59a.

134. For the sake of simplicity, I have excluded the half a dozen fragmentary Greek epitaphs that could be either G2 or G2 + age, or either G2 + age or G3. The counts for Catania are from *IMC Catania*, in which such cases were included.

135. On Athens, see Meyer (Supra n. 124), 93–4.

136. See *IMC Catania* pp. 118–20; Korhonen, K. 2004. "La cultura epigrafica della colonia di *Catina* nell'Alto Impero", in Salmeri *et al.* (eds) (Supra n. 1), 233–53, here 243–9.

137. See also Korhonen (Supra n. 136), 249.

138. See Adams (Supra n. 5), 21–23.

139. One could suggest that the initial *D.M.S.* was already in place when the stone was ordered, but this seems less likely to me. For similar instances in modern written texts, but with English in the place of Latin, see

140. E.g., *IMC Catania* 66, 97, 102, 117, 134, 145 (Latin); 99, 108, 111 (Greek) (see the photographs at http://www.helsinki.fi/hum/kla/catania).

141 The recent interpretation of the situation at the colony of Cnossus as a diglossia by Baldwin Bowsky, M. 2004. "Of Two Tongues: Acculturation at Roman Knossos", in Salmeri *et al.* (eds) (Supra n. 1), 95–150, simplifies in my view the matters too much.

142. This was pointed out by P. Griffo in *NSA* 1942, 89.

143. According to Bitto (*IGL Messina*, p. 80), the marbles are different. I think that both inscriptions were made by the same stonecutter, but the lettering is slightly more uncertain in no. 22 than in no. 23, which could indicate a distance of some years, maybe a decade.

144. There may be some connection between the modest epitaphs in Greek *IGL Messina* 4 and 5 and the family of Theseus, although they were certainly not carved by the same stonecutters as the epitaphs dedicated by Claudius Theseus. The deceased women, Κλωδία Ῥωμανά and Κλωδία Σεβῆρα, have Latin cognomina, in the first case derived from *Roma*; no dedicators are shown.

145. See especially Hall (Supra n. 21) and the contributions in *Greek Identity in the Western Mediterranean. Papers in Honour of Brian Shefton*. Lomas, K. (ed.) (Leiden and Boston 2004).

146. Consani, C. 1995. "I dialetti greci in età ellenistica e romana: la documentazione epigrafica della Magna Grecia e di Sicilia", in *Studi di linguistica greca. Atti del I Incontro di linguistica greca, Pavia 1993* (Milan), 73–89.

147. See, as regards the "Aeolian" dialects of Asia Minor, Hodot, R. 2004. "Langue, identité et représentations dans le domaine éolien d'Asie", in Follet (ed.) (Supra n. 41), 247–54.

148. For the process, see Kerswill, P. and P. Trudgill 2005. "The birth of new dialects", in *Dialect Change: Convergence and Divergence in European Languages*. Auer, P. *et al.* (eds) (Cambridge), 196–220, here 196–202; for the consequences in the case of Latin, Adams, J. N. 2007. *The Regional Diversification of Latin 200 BC–AD 600* (Cambridge), 21–7.

149. Cf. Labov, W. 2001. *Principles of Linguistic Change* 2: *Social Factors* (Malden, MA and Oxford), 42; Taeldeman, J. "The influence of urban centres on the spatial diffusion of dialect phenomena", in Auer *et al.* (eds) (Supra n. 148), 263–83, especially 283 (overview of the factors); Adams (Supra n. 148), 18–20.

150. See Melazzo, L. 1984. "Latino e greco in Sicilia", in *Tre millenni di storia linguistica della Sicilia. Atti del Convegno della Società Italiana di Glottologia, Palermo 1983*. Quattordio Moreschini, A. (ed.) (Pisa), 37–54, here 42–50. – I plan to discuss the vowel systems of Sicilian Greek and Latin on another occasion.

151. *AE* 1964, 184 = *AE* 2004, 662.

152. Cf. the epitaphs of Aisaris in Messina (Supra p. 30 n. 108) and of T. Flavius Ganamio in Syracuse (p. 18).

153. The ambiguous phrase *Siculi trilingues* in Apuleius, *Met.* 11.5, is probably a reference to Greek, Latin and Punic – cf. most recently Salmeri (Supra n. 1), 289–90 – but it is not clear if it describes the situation at the time when Apuleius was writing. On the difficulties of the ethnic term "Punic", see Prag, J. R. W. 2006. "*Poenus plane est* – But Who Were the 'Punickes'?", *Papers of the British School in Rome* 74, 1–37.

154. See Millar, F. 1968. "Local Cultures in the Roman Empire: Libyan, Punic and Latin in Roman Africa", *Journal of Roman Studies* 58, 125–51 [repr. in Millar F. *et al.* 2004. *Rome, the Greek world, and the East 2: Government, Society and Culture in the Roman Empire* (Chapel Hill), 249–64], and Adams (Supra n. 5, 200–45).

155. Lomas, K. 2000. "The Polis in Italy", in *Alternatives to Athens. Varieties of Political Organization and Community in Ancient Greece*. Brock, R. and S. Hodkinson (eds) (Oxford), 167–85, here 184.

156. Lomas (Supra n. 1), 172–3.

157. Brélaz (Supra n. 4), 192–3.

158. P. Orsi, *NSA* 1895, 494 no. 192.

159. Wessel, C. *Inscriptiones Graecae Christianae veteres Occidentis* (ms. ca. 1940; published by A. Ferrua – C. Carletti, Bari 1989), no. 124.

160. G. Kaibel, the editor of *IG* XIV, did not see the inscription, but it arrived later in the Syracuse Museum, where Paolo Orsi confirmed the reading: see *NSA* 1907, 494. Orsi describes it as a limestone slab measuring 25 × 19 cm. – On the status of Centuripe, see especially Vera (Supra n. 12), 37–8.

161. ΙΣ ΑΓΟΡΑ could be Θεοῖς Ἀγοραίοις, but in that case, another word should have preceded the phrase, and the name of the dedicator would have followed between Ἀγοραίοις and δεκυρευ-. ΑΓΟΡΑ could also be the beginning of a name, and ΚΥΡΕΥ could, in theory, also be the ethnic Ἀντικυρεύς. The presence of the verb δεκυρεύω was noticed by Wessel (Supra n. 160).

162. A Greek onomastic formula would end in a filiation, and thus not in -ις; in inscriptions, Latin gentilicia in -*ius* could be written with the ending -ις, but even in that case, a filiation would be necessary. A combination of praenomen, gentilicium and cognomen is also thinkable, but quite unlikely in this period.

163. On ἀγορανόμοι in Roman times, see Bekker-Nielsen, T. 2007. "The One That Got Away: A Reassessment of the Agoranomos Inscription from Chersonesos", in *The Black Sea in Antiquity. Regional and Interregional Economic Exchanges*. Gabrielsen, V. and J. Lund (eds) (Aarhus), 123–31, in part. 125–7.

164. Apart from Polybius and before late antiquity, there appears to be only one attestation in literature: Dion. Hal. *Ant. Rom.* 2.7.4. For some epigraphic attestations, see *LSJ Suppl.* 1996, p. 84; there are others in the PHI database (http://epigraphy.packhum.org/inscriptions/), all from the imperial period.

165. The principal source for is Cic. *Att.* 14.12.1, written in April 44. Evidently Caesar conceded Latin rights to Sicilian towns not long before his death; Cicero also mentions Mark Antony's decision to extend Roman citizenship to free-born Sicilians. This did not necessarily take effect, but the Latin rights remained during the war between Octavian and Sextus Pompeius. See especially Vera (Supra n. 12), 33–5, and on the status of Centuripe in particular, 37–8; cf. Wilson (Supra n. 10), 434–5.

166. The object of the dedication may still have been a building.

3. "A Tale of Two Colonies": Augusta Emerita (Mérida) and Metellinum (Medellín) in Roman Lusitania

Jonathan Edmondson

Introduction

In 25 BCE Augustus' armies won what appeared at the time to be a decisive victory in the campaigns they had been conducting since the year 29 against the Cantabrians and Asturians in the far north of Spain. Augustus arrived in the Iberian Peninsula from Gaul in 26 to lead the troops himself. Although illness forced him to withdraw from the front-line to Tarraco, where he spent much of the year 25 recuperating, his legates C. Antistius Vetus and P. Carisius brought the armed resistance to an end through a series of important military successes, not least when Carisius captured the Asturian stronghold of Lancia.[1] According to Cassius Dio (53.26.1), once the war had come to a close, temporarily as it transpired, Augustus authorized the foundation of a settlement for the "older soldiers" of two of the legions involved in the campaigns: the V Alaudae and X Gemina. This new settlement was situated nowhere near the war-zone, but some 400 km to the south at modern Mérida on the river Anas (modern Guadiana) in Spanish Extremadura.

The town was granted a symbolically charged name, "Emerita", which emphasized its *raison d'être* as a settlement for veteran soldiers (*emeriti*), literally those who had deservedly earned their retirement after long years of military service.[2] In addition to these ex-soldiers, some indigenous inhabitants of the region were integrated into its initial population either as *incolae* or even as citizens. Strabo (3.2.15) includes Emerita among those Hispanic cities he terms *synoekismenai*, *i.e.*, with a mixed population of implanted colonists and indigenous settlers;[3] and confirmation of this is provided by the mixed nomenclature of certain inhabitants attested epigraphically: for instance, the Roman citizen C. Allius Tangini f(ilius) Pap(iria tribu) [?......], attested on the NW limit of the colony's

territory at Rincón de Gila, 20 km N of Badajoz,[4] or C. Iulius Mandi (f.) Sangenus, commemorated in a suburban burial area of Emerita in the very last years of the 1st c. BCE or right at the start of the 1st c. CE.[5] The colony's full name was *Colonia Iulia Augusta Emerita*, its titles "Iulia" and "Augusta" very much advertising its close ideological connection to the Roman imperial family.[6]

Soon after its foundation P. Carisius, who was almost certainly the colony's *deductor* and whose memory is still preserved in the toponym of Carija in a zone of granite quarries 4 km NW of the modern town of Mérida, issued a series of silver *denarii* and *quinarii* at Emerita. These coins commemorated the military campaigns in Cantabria and Asturia, by showing, on their reverse, images of captured enemy weapons; they celebrated the Roman victory in their depiction of military trophies; and they publicized the foundation of Emerita, by featuring the main gate of the new city on one of the *denarius* types, with the city's name proudly emblazoned across its upper section between its two flanking towers.[7] As W. Trillmich has argued, precisely the same underlying ideological programme may be discerned here in Carisius' provincial coin issue with its thematic sequence of war, victory and peace as had been developed a few years earlier for Octavian's so-called "Actium" *denarius*-series. On these coins images of Mars and various items of weaponry symbolized war, Diana and the military trophy shown within her shrine proclaimed the Augustan victory, while Actian Apollo and the pair of oxen ploughing the *sulcus primigenius* of a newly-founded city advertised the peace and stability that Octavian's victory would allegedly make possible.[8] Emerita, where ex-soldiers were to settle down to a life of peaceful agriculture on the land they were allotted, was to be a city of peace, and this message was clearly central to the political ideology that Augustus and his legates developed as they embarked on the far-reaching reorganization of the Hispanic provinces that began in the mid-20s BCE.

This paper aims to explore – in a necessarily selective manner for reasons of space – some of the ways in which the colony of Augusta Emerita developed during the first 100 years or so of its history from 25 BCE to *c*. CE 100 and to assess the impact that the foundation of a veteran colony such as Emerita had on its surrounding region. The fact that Emerita was soon chosen to be the administrative centre of the new Roman province of Lusitania, arguably from *c*. 16 BCE onwards, gave it a special connection to the centre of power, Rome, and meant that it developed a distinctly Roman physical appearance and a particularly Roman identity.[9] By the time of its foundation two other Roman colonies had already been established in this general region: Norba Caesarina (modern Cáceres), 70 km to the N of Emerita, and Metellinum (Medellín), 30 km due E. The second part of this paper will focus on how Emerita's foundation affected the development of the neighbouring colony of Metellinum. It will consider in particular whether it led to modifications in Metellinum's territory and how the urban centre of Metellinum evolved in light of urban developments at Emerita. It will also explore what the evidence of material culture and epigraphy reveals about the cultural and social relationship between the two colonies in the first 100 years of the principate.

The impact of the foundation of Augusta Emerita: Roman monuments and Roman identity

The foundation of Emerita in 25 BCE made an immediate and striking impact in the central SW of the Iberian Peninsula (see the map, Fig. 3.1). The size of the colony's urban centre and the extent of its territory were both exceptional. Emerita's wall-circuit enclosed an intramural area of *c*. 80 hectares. It was laid out immediately after the city's foundation. The internal grid-plan of *decumani* and *kardines* with their underlying sewers was oriented in such a way that the *decumanus maximus* followed the same alignment as the unusually long bridge, 800 m in span, over the river Anas, which carried the main Roman road that led south eventually to Italica and Hispalis (Sevilla) (Fig. 3.2).[10] Other Roman colonies in Lusitania were much smaller: Metellinum (Medellín), for instance, covered 25 hectares and Pax Iulia (Beja) just 24. (It is difficult to assess the urban

Figure 3.1. Map of SW Lusitania and N Baetica, showing the centuriated territory of Emerita due S of the colony (marked with a cross) and the territory of Metellinum (after Ariño Gil et al. 2004, 141, fig. 43)

areas of the other two colonies, Scallabis (Santarém) and Norba (Cáceres), because of subsequent urban growth at both these towns.)[11]

As for Emerita's territory, the *agrimensor* Agennius Urbicus was at pains to underline its magnitude in his work *De Controversiis Agrorum*; furthermore, even after a second and third assignation, he comments, there was still land left unassigned:[12]

I know that in Lusitania in the territory of the Emeritenses the not insubstantial river Anas flows through the very middle of the colony's *pertica*, around which plots of land have been assigned wherever the soil seemed at that time to be useful. Because of the magnitude of its territory he [sc. Augustus] distributed the veterans around the almost outermost edge as it were like boundary-markers; very few were settled around the colony and around the river Anas; the remainder had been left vacant so as to be filled up later. In the same way a second and third assignation took place subsequently. Even so such a process of division did not exhaust the limit of the land available, but there was still surplus land left unassigned.

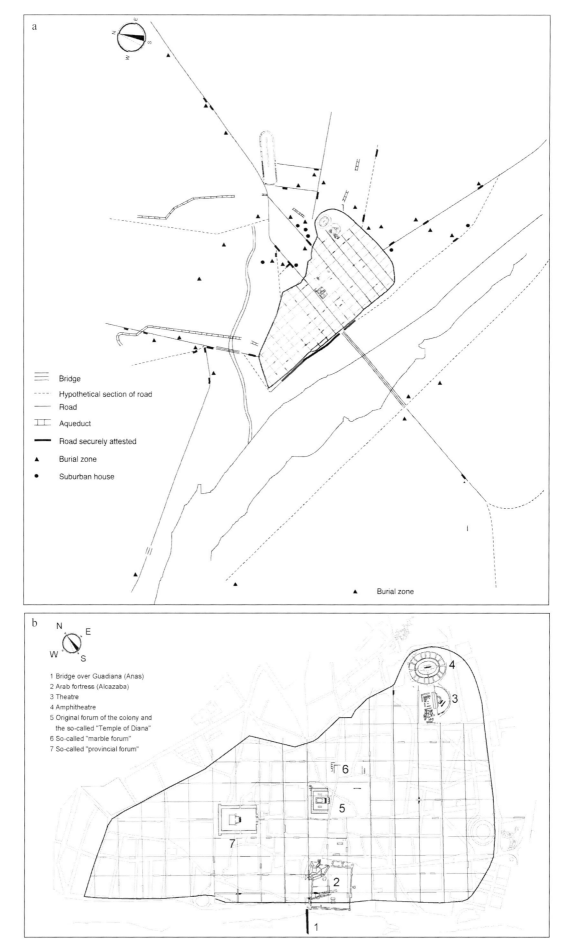

a

Bridge
Hypothetical section of road
Road
Aqueduct
Road securely attested
▲ Burial zone
● Suburban house

▲ Burial zone

b

1 Bridge over Guadiana (Anas)
2 Arab fortress (Alcazaba)
3 Theatre
4 Amphitheatre
5 Original forum of the colony and
  the so-called "Temple of Diana"
6 So-called "marble forum"
7 So-called "provincial forum"

Figure 3.2. (a) Schematic plan of Augusta Emerita and environs, showing major monuments, bridges, aqueducts, burial areas and suburban houses. (b) Urban centre of Emerita, showing street-plan, forums, theatre, amphitheatre (Plans courtesy of P. Mateos Cruz and Consorcio de la Ciudad Monumental de Mérida)

From the passage immediately following, it becomes clear that colonists had simply occupied such vacant land (known as *subseciva*) until Vespasian forced them to purchase it, a decision these colonists petitioned the provincial governor of Lusitania to have modified on the grounds that not all this land was of equally fertile quality:[13]

> In this territory when the *subseciva* were being reclaimed, those who had taken possession of them petitioned the governor of that province that in his adjudication he should designate a certain width to the river Anas. Since anyone who had occupied *subseciva* was being forced to purchase them, it was felt to be unfair if anyone should end up purchasing a public stream or unfertile soils that the river had deposited. As a result, a fixed limit was determined for the river.

The amplitude of Emerita's territory allowed the centuriation of the colony's *pertica* to be based on double the normal sized modules: *centuriae* of 400 rather than 200 *iugera*.[14] In addition, at least three *praefecturae* were added to Emerita's territory beyond the limits of the regular *pertica*: the Mullicensis, one in the *regio Turgaliensis* (*i.e.*, in the vicinity of Turgalium, modern Trujillo) and a third, whose name is not specified in the *agrimensores*;[15] as we shall see later, the colony also owned various enclaves of land within the territory of other communities in the region, some of which may have been these *praefecturae*.

The decision to make Emerita the administrative centre of the new province of Lusitania when Hispania Ulterior was split into two new provinces of Baetica and Lusitania, arguably in 16 BCE, further enhanced the colony's importance and prestige.[16] Work had already started on the colony's main forum with a monumental granite temple (known since the 17th c., without any secure basis, as the "Temple of Diana") as its focal point. Space had been reserved for it in the original city-plan at the intersection of the *decumanus maximus* and *kardo maximus* (Fig. 3.2).[17] This was demonstrably not the case with the so-called "provincial forum" in the NW sector of the town nor perhaps with the so-called "marble forum" (or *forum adiectum*) adjacent to the original colonial forum. When construction on the new "provincial forum" began during the reign of Tiberius, four *insulae* that had been laid out in the initial urban grid and which comprised, it has been calculated, 24 houses had to be removed.[18] The addition of the so-called "marble forum" alongside the colony's original forum may also have required one of the *kardines* to be eliminated, although it is possible that this *kardo* ran between the colonial forum and the new marble forum, providing access to both – an issue that can only be settled by future excavation.[19] The use of granite decorated with stucco for the temple in the original forum points to an early construction date in the reign of Augustus before the opening of the quarries 75 km W of Emerita in the vicinity of Estremoz, Borba and Vila Viçosa in modern Portugal provided ample supplies of marble for the colony's building works.[20]

From the moment it was selected to be the capital of the new province of Lusitania, Augustus and his son-in-law M. Agrippa took steps to ensure that Augusta Emerita would look like a distinctly "Augustan" city. The water-supply was a matter of immediate concern and at least one of the city's three aqueduct systems, the one that brought water from the reservoir at Cornalvo, 10 km NE of Emerita, dates back to the Augustan period.[21] This may be the AQVA AVGVSTA known from a monumental inscription composed of bronze letters 9.4 cm tall.[22] Its name may hint that Augustus provided the funding and technological expertise for the construction of this essential amenity.

M. Agrippa was patently implicated in the construction of one of the colony's most important public buildings: the theatre. No fewer that five monumental inscriptions survive from this building that name Agrippa.[23] The fact that in all of them he is named in the Nominative case suggests that he was a major benefactor of the initial building. His titles (consul for the third time, in the third year of tribunician power) date the inauguration, if not completion, of the building to 16/15 BCE. Furthermore, at least two of the inscribed blocks bearing his name appear to have been moved during subsequent remodelling from their original location, perhaps on the *scaenae frons*, it has been suggested, into new positions beneath the tribunals that were located over each of the facing lateral entrances to the orchestra.[24] This might suggest that they were seen as precious relics, as it were, preserving the memory of the colony's early benefactor and likely patron, that had to be maintained at all costs, even if their original function in the theatre's fabric had become obsolete.

Augustus took on the role of major benefactor for the construction of the amphitheatre constructed alongside the theatre. From here segments of at least three monumental inscriptions have been discovered, two of which were designed to run along the front of the tribunals on the W and E sides, while the third may have been set up across the N entrance to the arena.[25] All name Augustus in the Nominative. His titles include reference to his 16th year of tribunician power, which would date the inauguration of the original building project to the period between 26 June 8 and 25 June 7 BCE.

Figure 3.3. So-called "marble forum", Emerita (photo: J. Edmondson)

Over the next 75 years the colony came to be equipped with the full panoply of public buildings appropriate to a Roman colony (Fig. 3.2). A circus was laid out in the NE sector of the colony's *suburbium* initially under Tiberius, but its seating was not constructed in stone until the reign of Domitian and the central *spina* was monumentalized and equipped with water-fountains under Trajan or later.[26] It was also under Tiberius that a whole new forum was constructed in the NW half of the colony's urban plan, which had as its focal point a temple modeled on the Temple of Concord from the Roman Forum. This second forum was clearly not projected in the original city plan, since it was necessary to eliminate four housing blocks either side of the *kardo maximus* to clear space for its construction.[27] A number of inscribed pedestals (or fragments thereof) have long since been known to have come to light in the vicinity of this forum: for example, those dedicated to Tiberius, to Concordia Augusti, to Domitian, to a late-3rd or early-4th c. *praeses* of the province of Lusitania of equestrian rank.[28] And fragments of further inscriptions have emerged from the recent excavations that attest (a) the dedication of an object of 50 lbs (16.373 kg) of silver, in which a *legatus Augusti propraetore* of Lusitania was mentioned;[29] and (b) a plaque that formed part of a monument dedicated to Domitian or Trajan.[30] All this would suggest that the new forum was designed to be, or soon came to be, a major centre for the provincial imperial cult activities.[31]

Another porticoed square, of which details of just the NW corner have to date been published, was added adjacent to the original forum of the colony, most likely under Claudius and Nero.[32] The decorative scheme of its surrounding portico included *clipei* with heads of Jupiter Ammon and Medusa separated by semi-engaged pilasters with Karyatids (Fig. 3.3).[33] A series of rectangular niches were cut into the back wall of the portico for the display of sculptures, which included togate figures (possibly *summi viri*), mythological figures from early Roman history and a statue-group showing Aeneas leading his son Ascanius and carrying his father Anchises on his shoulder as they fled the flames of Troy (Fig. 3.4a). Trillmich's identification of the sculptural group was dramatically confirmed by the discovery in excavations in 1986 of parts of an inscribed *elogium* of Aeneas, clearly copied from the prototype that stood in the Forum Augustum in Rome and of which parts of a copy erected in the forum at Pompeii are known (Fig. 3.4b).[34] Recently another sculptural fragment excavated here in 1980 has been identified as part of an over-life-size statue of Romulus carrying the *spolia opima*.[35] These various elements confirm that it was an architectural complex, possibly an "Augusteum", closely modeled on the Forum Augustum in Rome. However, work on it did not commence in the late-Augustan period, as Trillmich originally suggested in 1990. As he himself has come to acknowledge, it was only begun under Claudius and completed under Nero.[36]

In addition, some of the public buildings set up in the Augustan period underwent significant

a

b

Figure 3.4. (a) Statue-group of Aeneas, Ascanius and Anchises. "Marble forum", Emerita (courtesy of Museo Nacional de Arte Romano, Mérida, based on a drawing by W. Trillmich, U. Städtler and T. Nogales Basarrate). (b) Fragments of elogium of Aeneas, "Marble forum", Emerita (photo: J. Edmondson)

modification within the first 100 years of the colony's existence. Recent studies have suggested that the amphitheatre, for example, was considerably remodeled and monumentalized in the Flavian period.[37] The theatre also experienced a series of reforms, most especially in the area of its *scaenae frons* which was increasingly monumentalized with shifts in its sculptural display and with major refurbishment in the Trajanic period.[38] The seating-area (*cavea*) was not immune to change either, as, for example, under Trajan, when a small *sacrarium* for the cult of the *Lares et imagines* was built into the *ima cavea*, in which a series of pedestals for statues in honour of the emperor was set up.[39] Similarly, as we have seen, it was also during the reign of Trajan that the central monumental *spina* of the circus was constructed.[40]

Perhaps the most important recent finding is that both theatre and amphitheatre were originally located outside the initial wall-circuit. This is not to say that scholars have returned to the early 20th century view, long since discounted, that Emerita was originally founded as a much smaller urban nucleus with the so-called Arch of Trajan one of its entrance gates. Far from it; the "Arch of Trajan" has now decisively been shown to form the monumental entrance-way to the so-called "provincial forum" constructed under Tiberius.[41] The full wall-circuit was laid out as part of the colony's foundation rituals and more or less followed its later outline, except in this NE zone near the two spectacle buildings. Remains of incineration

burials have been found both underneath the *cavea* of the amphitheatre and beneath the east wall of the portico behind the theatre's *scaena* that date to the early and mid-1st c. CE respectively.[42] Excavations have now confirmed on stratigraphic grounds that the wall-circuit where it abuts the amphitheatre dates to the Flavian period, which would appear to be when the theatre and amphitheatre were encompassed within the urban enceinte.[43] This helps to explain the evident irregularity of the city-plan in its north-east corner.

So not only was Emerita a strikingly large city in terms of its layout, but its many monuments, some of which were funded by benefactions of the emperor and imperial family, made it stand out as a centre of *Romanitas* in what had been, prior to 25 BCE, a thinly populated region of Hispania Ulterior and one in which there had not been much urban development in the pre-Augustan period.[44] Emerita very quickly became a centre for the diffusion of the image of Roman power. Its identity was fixed from the start as very much that of a Roman community, with strong links to the metropolis. These links were fostered by the residence here of much of the personnel tied to the administration of the Roman province of Lusitania and by the ongoing interest of the Roman authorities, in dialogue with the local colonial elite, in developing the monumental architecture of a town that was in many ways designed to resemble a miniature Rome. In the past, the Augustan period has been arguably over-privileged in much of the scholarly discussion, but it is clear that the Roman identity of the colony

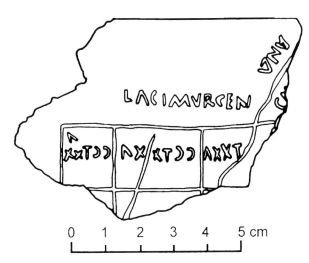

Figure 3.5. Fragment of a bronze forma showing a centuriated territory and the river Ana(s) (after Ariño Gil et al. 2004, 35, Fig. 5)

was enhanced over a much longer period through the building projects that took place under Tiberius (the construction of a circus and the so-called "provincial forum"), Claudius and Nero (the marble embellishment of the forum focused on the "Temple of Diana" and the adjacent "marble forum"), the Flavians (the amphitheatre and modifications to the wall circuit) and Trajan (important modifications to the theatre and embellishments to the circus). Although the close identification with Rome was initiated from the start of the colony's history, it took Emerita at least 100 years to develop its full panoply of Roman monuments.

The impact of the foundation of Emerita on the colony of Metellinum

When it was founded in 25 BCE, Emerita was not the only Roman colony in the region (Fig. 3.1). 70 km to the N the colony of Norba Caesarina (modern Cáceres) had been founded by C. Norbanus Flaccus (*cos.* 38 BCE) during his proconsulship in Hispania Ulterior from 36 to 34 BCE, probably completing a project initially planned by Julius Caesar (hence the "Caesarina" element in its official titulature),[45] while 30 km east of Emerita along the Guadiana Metellinum (modern Medellín), initially a Roman military base established by Q. Caecilius Metellus Pius (*cos.* 80 BCE) on the site of a prominent late-Iron-Age community during his campaigns against Sertorius, had been promoted to colonial status in all likelihood in the 40s BCE.[46] At 25 hectares, Metellinum was physically dwarfed by its new neighbour to the west.[47] What precise political,

economic and cultural impact did the foundation of Emerita have on pre-existing colonies such as these? Given its close geographical proximity to Emerita, the rest of this paper will explore the impact of the foundation of Emerita on the colony of Metellinum: the *colonia Metellinensis*.

i) the territory of Metellinum

First, what effect, if any, did the carving out of Emerita's enormous territory have on the territory of the neighbouring colony of Metellinum? Since the latter had been promoted to the rank of colony 15 to 20 years before Emerita was founded, it is to be expected that Metellinum's *pertica* had already been laid out and assigned to colonists by the time of Emerita's foundation in 25 BCE.[48] Although the presence of Roman citizens of Metellinum enrolled in the Galeria voting tribe might hint at a second Augustan phase of settlement,[49] it seems unlikely that Augustus would have wished to disrupt the landholding patterns already fixed for the neighbouring colony of Metellinum when his surveyors began to lay out the colonial *pertica* of Emerita. Two pieces of evidence, however, give us pause. First, a fragment of a bronze territorial map (*forma*), found at an uncertain location in the SE of the province of Lusitania near its boundary with both Baetica and Hispania Tarraconensis, shows (a) the river Anas (modern Guadiana), (b) part of a centuriated territory and (c) the abbreviated name of the Lusitanian community Lacimurga (Fig. 3.5).[50] This is a document that resists easy interpretation; if more of it had survived, it might be possible to construe it more reliably. Lacimurga was located at modern Cerro de Cogolludo, Navalvillar de Pela (prov. Badajoz), 40 km E of Metellinum and 10 km N of the river Guadiana.[51] The centuriated grid shown on the bronze *forma* clearly straddles the river, and this would be consistent with the most logical situation for the *pertica* of Metellinum. Since the urban centre of the colony was situated on the south bank of the Guadiana, we would expect its territory also to have extended south of the river, and indeed the most promising territory from an agricultural point of view and that most suitable for centuriation lies to the south and east of Medellín.[52] But the *pertica* of Emerita also extended to the south of the Guadiana, and indeed it is in this area that analysis of aerial photographs has revealed part of its centuriated grid.[53] So the centuriated grid on the bronze *forma* might relate to the territory of Emerita. However, the *centuriae* are marked as having an area of 275 *iugera* (CCLXXV in retrograde script). If these numerals do indeed indicate the area of each *centuria*, this would discount any notion that the centuriated land might be that of Emerita, since, as we have seen, the *agrimensores* insist that Emerita's territory was surveyed in modules of 400 *iugera*.[54] So the best interpretation of the *forma* is that it may show the centuriated territory of Metellinum at the point where it bordered the uncenturiated territory of the peregrine community of Lacimurga, that is, before the latter's promotion to municipal status under the Flavians.[55] Secondly, a boundary marker (*terminus Augustalis*) (Fig. 3.6) dated to the reign of Domitian (CE 81–96), found at Mojón Gordo, 13 km N of Valdecaballeros and 120 km to the E of Mérida, reveals that to the east of the territory of Metellinum and even about 30 km NE of Lacimurga in the area today known as the "Siberia" of Extremadura (the "Siberia Extremeña") lay territory owned by the colony of Augusta Emerita, within which was located land (probably a *praefectura*) owned by the colony of Ucubi, located at Espejo in the *conventus Astigitanus*, 20 km SE of Corduba.[56] This might lead to the view that Emerita came to take over some of the territory of the smaller colony of Metellinum, since its territory surrounded it on all sides. This can hardly be correct, and others have been quick to emphasize that the territory of Emerita attested on the boundary marker must have been one of the colony's *praefecturae* mentioned by the *agrimensores*.[57] Furthermore, these boundary-markers provide no indication of how the territory was organized in the Augustan period. They date to the Flavian period, when the promotion of Lacimurga to municipal status under Vespasian (perhaps in CE 73–4) must have provided the impetus to redefine territorial limits in this remote region.[58] This presumably required Lacimurga's territory to be surveyed, which in turn required its limits with the *praefectura* of Ucubi to be confirmed, as well as in due course those of this Ucubitan land with those of the *praefectura* of Emerita in this same area.

So although there was a *praefectura* of Emerita located well to the east of the territory of Metellinum, this does not appear to have affected the colonial assignations at Metellinum. On the other hand, the location of this *praefectura* does raise the question of how P. Carisius, Augustus' legate in Ulterior and very likely the *deductor* of Emerita, initially came to acquire the land in this area to assign to the new colonists of Emerita. It may have been relatively vacant – as it has been for much of its subsequent history; not for nothing is it known as the "Siberia" of Extremadura – or land may have been confiscated from the community of Lacimurga, which, though it does not appear in Pliny's list of

*Figure 3.6. Boundary-marker (*terminus Augustalis*) between the territory of Emerita and a* praefectura *of Ucubi. Reign of Domitian (81–96 CE). Mojón Gordo, Valdecaballeros, prov. Badajoz (CIL II 656 = II²/7, 871; photo Centro CIL II, Alcalá de Henares)*

Lusitanian communities, was at the time of Emerita's foundation a peregrine *civitas stipendiaria*.[59] This would be in line with Agennius Urbicus' remarks that *praefecturae* often comprised "land assigned in a territory was previously belonged to another community" (*coloniae quoque loca quaedam habent adsignata in alienis finibus, quae loca solemus praefecturas appellare*) and that "ownership of these *praefecturae* clearly belongs to the colonists, not to those whose territory has been reduced" (*harum praefecturarum proprietas manifeste ad colonos pertinet, non ad eos quorum fines sunt deminuti*).[60] So despite all the perturbations in land ownership and community's territories in the general region it would appear that the insertion of the new colony of Emerita into the physical landscape did not affect the much smaller territory of the already existing colony of Metellinum, but it might well have disturbed the landholdings of non-Roman communities in the vicinity such as Lacimurga.

Figure 3.7. View of the site of Metellinum (Medellín) with the 17th-c. bridge and remains of pontoons of the Roman bridge over the river Anas (Guadiana) in the foreground (photo: J. Edmondson)

ii) The urban centre of Metellinum

The relative lack of archaeological excavation of Roman, as opposed to pre-Roman, levels at Medellín (until very recently) makes it difficult to build up a coherent picture of the urban landscape of the *colonia Metellinensis* and its evolution over the first 100 years of its existence. The Roman colony was situated on an impressive and easily defensible hill (the "Cerro de Medellín") and an important community had been located here from at least the 7th/6th c. BCE controlling the main crossing-point of the Guadiana on the major land-route leading NW from Corduba and the Guadalquivir valley (Fig. 3.7).[61] Until the excavations that began in 2008 in and around the Roman theatre, archaeological work had focused more on the 7th- to 5th-century levels than on the Roman era, with discoveries of imported Phoenician and Greek pottery (included signed 6th-c. Attic black-figure vases), orientalizing silver jewelry and ivory-work in the large necropolis excavated on the left bank of the Guadiana and in the fortified settlement that extended *c.* 13.5 hectares on the hill that is still dominated by the walls of its 14th-c. castle.[62]

Some monuments are known from the Roman period. Remains of the foundations of seven pylons of the Roman bridge survive on the right bank of the river Guadiana alongside the modern bridge that was completed in 1630 to replace the Roman bridge that had been destroyed by storms in December 1603 (Fig. 3.7).[63] The main centre of the Roman colony developed on the same hillside on the left bank of the river that had been the nucleus of the earlier settlement at Medellín. Possible locations for

the colony's forum and various temples have been proposed (Fig. 3.8),[64] but much more work is needed to clarify their chronology and architectural plan. It would be particularly useful to isolate constructions from the late-Republican phase of the city's history, *i.e.*, when it was used as a military base by the troops of Q. Caecilius Metellus in the 70s BCE, but at the moment this is not possible.

Some standing remains of the Roman theatre, built into the hillside and supported on an artificial terrace, have long been visible on the site (Fig. 3.9). Excavations in 1969–70 allowed its basic ground-plan to be established, which shows that it was a rather small building – just 30 m wide compared to the theatre at Emerita, which is close to 80 m in width. This *scaenae frons* was constructed of local granite and decorated with painted stucco.[65] The precise date of the theatre's construction is not yet certain, and it is to be hoped that the current excavations will clarify this issue. The director of the excavations in the late 1960s, M. del Amo y de la Hera, argued that it was probably built in the last quarter of the 1st c. BCE, but others have proposed a Flavian date, based on the construction technique used for the *crypta*, which is very similar to the one excavated at the securely dated Flavian theatre at Regina (modern Casas de Reina, prov. Badajoz), 80 km to the S.[66] It will be instructive to compare the technique and artistic quality of the sculpture recently discovered from the *scaenae frons* of the theatre at Metellinum with the substantial body of sculptural material known from Emerita, to determine to what extent the workshops of the provincial capital influenced the craftsmen working on the decoration

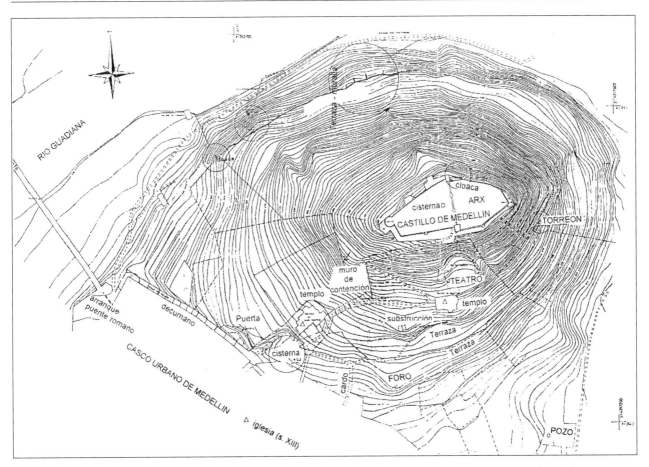

Figure 3.8. General topography of Metellinum (after Haba Quirós 1998, 402, fig. 13)

Figure 3.9. Roman theatre, Metellinum, from above, June 2008 (photo: J. Edmondson)

Figure 3.10. Equestrian statue-base for L. Caecilius L.f. Sca(ptia tribu) Rufus, provincial governor of Lusitania, from Mengabril, near Medellín. Late Augustan or early Tiberian (photos: courtesy of Centro CIL II, Alcalá de Henares)

of the theatre of this neighbouring colony; but that is work for the future.

Inscriptions, though not numerous, nevertheless, are sufficient to suggest that Metellinum enjoyed the standard civic life of a Roman colony, with magistrates of the colony engaged in public acts of homage towards the imperial house and Roman provincial authorities, at least during the 1st c. CE. No public inscriptions have survived from the 2nd or later centuries. Whether this is a sign of the colony's decline, as has sometimes been argued, is difficult to prove, since it is essentially an argument from silence in a situation where the data are not very numerous at all. It may simply be the result of the patchy survival of our epigraphic evidence.[67] From the 1st c. CE the harvest is, relatively speaking, quite impressive:

• a monument set up to honour Gaius Caesar as

princeps iuventutis (*CIL* II 607 = Haba Quirós 1998, 124–5, no. 39, now lost);
• a pedestal for an equestrian statue (22.5 cm tall; 51 cm wide; 175 cm deep), found at Mengabril (5 km S of Medellín), set up to honour (an otherwise unattested) provincial governor of Lusitania: L. Caecilius L.f. Rufus (Fig. 3.10; *HEp* 4, 159 = Haba Quirós 1998, 127–9, no. 43; not recorded in *AE*). His governorship has been dated to the late-Augustan or Tiberian period; *i.e.*, before the 10-year governorship of L. Fulcinius Trio that ran from *ca.* CE 21 to 31;[68]
• a statue-base honouring Drusus son of Germanicus as patron of the colony (*CIL* II 609 = Haba Quirós 1998, 122–3, no. 37, now lost);
• a monument honouring Claudius set up by [M. Porcius M.]f. Cato, provincial governor of Lusitania, *ca.* CE 45/46 (*CIL* II 608 = Haba Quirós 1998, 125–6, no. 41, now lost);[69]
• a statue set up to honour Domitia Augusta, wife of Domitian, to be dated after her assumption of the title "Augusta" in September 81, by the *II viri* of the colony, G. Licinius Saturninus and L. Mummius Pomponianus (*CIL* II 610 = Haba Quirós 1998, 123–4, no. 38, now lost).

The fact that two governors of the province of Lusitania are attested at or near Metellinum – one being honoured, the other honouring the reigning emperor – is notable since in Lusitania at least attestations of provincial governors outside Emerita, the provincial capital, are relatively rare.[70] It may be that the proximity of Emerita, the chief residence of the governor and his staff, as well as of the equestrian provincial procurator and his staff, was a factor here. This seems plausible, especially since there is a good deal of evidence for social and cultural links between the two colonies, as will become clear in the final section of this essay.

Cultural and social links between Emerita and Metellinum

The material culture of Metellinum in the late 1st c. BCE and 1st c. CE suggests that there were strong cultural links between this colony and Augusta Emerita. The earliest funerary monuments found at Metellinum – round-topped granite funerary stelae – are markedly similar in type to those found in the same period at Emerita (Fig. 3.11a–b).[71] The similarities go beyond the mere form of the monuments and extend to the precise textual formulae used: most particularly, in the frequent outlining of the dimensions of the burial plot along whose

Figure 3.11. Granite funerary stelae from (a) Emerita and (b) the Roman villa at "Las Galapagueras", near Medellín (photos: (a) J. Edmondson; (b) after Salas Martín and Haba Quirós 1987, Fig. 7)

Figure 3.12. Marble funerary altars from (a) the Roman villa at "Las Galapagueras", near Medellín and (b) Emerita (photos: (a) after Salas Martín and Haba Quirós 1987, Fig. 6; (b) J. Edmondson)

boundaries these stelae were often set up, conveyed most often in the formula *in fronte pedes XII, in agro pedes VIII*.[72] Is this a case of the material culture of the provincial capital Emerita influencing that of its neighbouring colony to the east? Perhaps, but it is also possible that both colonies were independently adopting the standard form of funerary monument and funerary formulae in use at Rome and in central Italy in the late Republic and Augustan period.[73]

However, the influence of Emerita can also be seen in marble funerary altars set up at Metellinum in the 2nd c. CE: for instance, the altar set up by Marcia Secundilla for her husband P. Nonius Mar(inus??) and herself[74] and another set up by Rufina for her homonymous daughter bear an uncanny resemblance to marble funerary altars set up in Emerita (Fig. 3.12a–b).[75] The influence of the workshops of Emerita on those of Metellinum seems clear. Similarly, private portraiture of a very high quality, at least equal in terms of craftsmanship to that found at Emerita, was on occasion commissioned by the local elite at Metellinum; for instance, the togate

a

b

Figure 3.13. Male portraits from (a) the villa at La Majona near Metellinum and (b) from Emerita (photos: J. Edmondson)

bust (Fig. 3.13a) of the Severan period found at the Roman villa site at La Majona, near Don Benito, some 8 km due E of Medellín, clearly owes much to the portraits produced at the provincial capital. The bust is particularly reminiscent of the portrait of L. Antestius Persicus, a *duumvir* and local *pontifex* at Emerita in the early 3rd c., that was incorporated into his funerary monument (Fig. 3.13b).[76]

The cultural interaction between Metellinum and the provincial capital is hardly surprising, given their proximity, but it was also facilitated by the fact that some citizens of either colony came to settle in the territory of the neighbouring community. So, for example, Satria Silvana, Emeritensis, was buried in the late-1st c. CE at the villa located on the modern *finca* El Tejar near Guareña, 20 km SW of Medellín.[77] Haba Quirós has argued that this was part of the territory of Metellinum, but it is just as possible that it was in the territory of Emerita.[78] But there can be less doubt that the soldier or, more likely, veteran

of the 10th legion, P. Talius Q.f. Pap(iria tribu), who was a citizen of Emerita and who was commemorated in the Augustan period at a villa site 14 km E of Medellín at Villanueva de la Serena, had settled in the territory of Metellinum.[79] This would hint at a fluidity of relations between the two neighbouring colonies, with citizens of one colony coming to acquire land in the territory of the other, perhaps as a result of intermarriage.

Similarly, two citizens of Metellinum are now attested in an area of Baetica just S of the frontier with Lusitania where there is such a remarkable concentration of citizens of Emerita documented that it seems to be a good candidate for one of the colony's *praefecturae* discussed by the *agrimensores* (see below, Appendix). In the area of La Serena centred around Castuera, some 45 km SE of Medellín, no fewer than nine Emeritenses are to date attested, including a freedwoman of the colony of Emerita and a man who had served in the 4th

Figure 3.14. Epitaph from Emerita of C. Sulpicius C.f. Gal. Superstes, duumvir three times at Metellinum (photo: J. C. Saquete Chamizo)

cohort of the Praetorian Guard (Appendix, nos. 7 and 9, respectively). Settled alongside them were at least two individuals from Metellinum: M. Helvius Sabinus, Metel(l)ine(nsis), whose burial at Castuera was looked after at the end of the 1st or start of the 2nd c. CE by an association known as the *sodales tabulae Salutaris*,[80] and Sentia Paulli liberta Sura, Metellinensis, commemorated in the mid-1st c. at Benquerencia de la Serena, 7 km SE of Castuera.[81]

The best evidence, however, for the close connections between the two colonies comes from the urban centre of Augusta Emerita. For here in the late-1st c. CE a local magistrate from Metellinum was granted a public burial by a joint decision of the decurions of both colonies, who provided a burial plot at public expense and covered all funerary expenses. As was recorded on his epitaph, C. Sulpicius C.f. Gal(eria tribu) Superstes had held the duumvirate no fewer than three times at Metellinum before his death aged 38 (Fig. 3.14).[82] One can see why the colony of Metellinum would have wished to honour such a devoted local public figure, but the reasons that lay behind his burial at Emerita and his being honoured by the town-council of that colony are more intriguing. One is, of course, reduced to speculation, but it may be that he had taken up residence in Emerita and had become a prominent figure in the life of the colony, even though he had continued to play an active political role in the colony of his birth, Metellinum. His reasons for taking up residence at the provincial capital are not difficult to suggest. It was a more vibrant and prominent community for a man of his status; like doubtless other members of the Lusitanian local elite

he was attracted to the amenities and social life of a centre of Roman power. The colony of Emerita had a variegated population. It included the Roman senatorial governor of Lusitania and his staff, the Roman equestrian provincial procurator and his staff, a number of imperial freedmen and slaves, as well as detachments of Roman soldiers who aided these Roman administrators. In addition, members of the provincial elite took up residence here, for instance, to serve as *flamines* of the province's imperial cult, while a significant group of immigrants came to settle at Emerita from elsewhere in Lusitania, the Iberian peninsula and sometimes even from other parts of the Roman world. This all made Emerita simply a livelier social community than any other Lusitanian city, with the possible exception of the port-city of Olisipo (modern Lisbon). Emerita was the place where connections to the centre of power could be established and maintained. For this a statue-base discovered near Tusculum in the vicinity of Rome provides very telling evidence (Fig. 3.15). It reveals that two ambassadors were officially dispatched by the colony of Emerita to Italy in the 30s CE to set up a statue of Sulpicia wife of L. Fulcinius Trio, the Roman senator who had governed Lusitania for about ten years from *c.* 21 to 31 before returning to Rome to become suffect consul in 31. This statue of Sulpicia offered by the colony to the former governor's wife through the agency of its ambassadors was to grace this family's villa near Tusculum.[83]

By comparison Metellinum, with its much smaller urban centre, much smaller territory and much smaller population, must have seemed a relative backwater. While some of its territory lay in the fertile alluvial

Figure 3.15. Statue-base set up to honour Sulpicia wife of (L. Fulcinius) Trio by the colony of Augusta Emerita, 30s CE, Tusculum (Italy) (photo: DAI-Rome inst. neg. 99–1234).

plain of the Guadiana, opportunities for social advancement were limited. By contrast, Emerita, as the centre of Roman administration and as one of the three Roman *conventus* centres of the province, where the Roman governor held assizes from early in its history, became a pole of attraction for a range of immigrants to come and settle here permanently: most of all from other parts of Lusitania and the rest of the Iberian peninsula, but occasionally from north Africa, Italy and the eastern Mediterranean.[84] As Dio Chrysostom observed in his 35th oration (35.15–16) about Apamea, a Roman juridical centre in Phrygia, the presence of the Roman governor and his holding of assizes had a profound impact upon the economic and social life of such a city:

> The courts are in session every year among you and they bring together a numerous crowd of people: litigants, jurors, advocates, elites, attendants, slaves, pimps, muleteers, traders, prostitutes and artisans. Consequently not only can those who have goods to sell obtain the highest prices, but also nobody in the city is out of work, neither the teams nor the houses nor the women. And this contributes not a little to prosperity; for wherever the greatest crowd of people come together, there necessarily we find money in greatest abundance, and it stands to reason that the place should thrive.

Similar factors were doubtless in play in southern Lusitania and may help to explain the relatively low profile of Metellinum and the fact that some at least of its *domi nobiles* felt drawn to the nearby provincial capital, where they could enhance their social connections, while still maintaining links to their original community. A similar process may be discerned in the case of the other Roman colony in the general vicinity, Norba Caesarina, located 70 km to the N of Emerita. In the second half of the 1st c. CE one of its Augustales, [L.] Postumius L.lib. Gal. Apollonius, Norbensis, had moved to Emerita, where he was buried alongside his wife.[85] He, like the duumvir, C. Sulpicius Superstes from Metellinum, was attracted to leave his home colony to take up residence at the more thriving community of Emerita, Roman colony and provincial capital. Whether we should assume that smaller colonies like Norba and Metellinum experienced "one hundred (or more) years of solitude" after the promotion of Emerita to the status of provincial capital remains unclear. But there can be little doubt that they were put into the shade by their more prominent neighbour and by the political, juridical and administrative imperatives of Roman provincial rule.

Acknowledgments

I am very grateful to Prof. Dr. José María Álvarez Martínez, Director, and all the staff of the Museo Nacional de Arte Romano, Dr Pedro Mateos Cruz, Director of the Instituto de Arqueología de Mérida, Dr Miguel Alba, Director Científico del Consorcio de la Ciudad Monumental de Mérida, Dña. Guadalupe Méndez Grande, co-director of the current excavations of the theatre at Medellín, and Dra. Helena Gimeno Pascual, Director of the Centro CIL II, Universidad de Alcalá de Henares, for their assistance in the preparation of this article. I would also like to thank the participants in the conference in St Andrews and the audiences at Brown University, McGill University, Trent University and at the York University/University of Toronto Work in Progress in Ancient History Seminar for their comments on various versions of this paper.

Appendix

Emeritenses (nos 1–10) and *Metellinenses* (nos 11–12) attested in the possible *praefectura* of Emerita located in the region of La Serena.

	Name(s)	Type of Monument	Date (all CE)	Reference
1–2	(1) Tongilia T. f. Maxuma Scaevini (uxor) Emeritensis (2) L. Granius L.f. Pap. Scaevinus	marble plaque (45 × 184 × 10)	end 1st/start 2nd c.	CIL II²/7, 922 (Iulipa, territory)
3	T. Flavius T.[f.] Pap. Procul[us]	granite stele (127 × (39) × 28)	end 1st/start 2nd c.	CIL II²/7, 906 (Iulipa)
4	P. Pomponius P.f. Pap. Sulpicianus (son of Sulpicia W.lib. Calirhoe)	unknown (lost)	1st c.	CIL II 2359 = II²/7, 907 (Iulipa)
5	C. Cavius C.f. Papiria Scaev[ae]us	granite stele (157 × 38 x 35/27)	early 1st c.	CIL II²/7, 939 (Esparragosa de la Serena, territory of Iulipa)
6	C. Sulpicius Taurus Emerite(n)si(s)	granite stele (163 × 53 x 15/25)	end 1st/start 2nd c.	CIL II²/7, 954 (Monterrubio de la Serena)
7	Publicia colon(iae) I(uliae) A(ugustae) E(meritae) l(iberta) Graecul[a]	granite stele (122 × 54 × ??)	end 1st/start 2nd c.	AE 1998, 747 = HEp 7, 150 (Monterrubio de la Serena)
8	S. Iu+[ius – f.] Ianuari[us] Papiria	granite stele (145 × 46 × 18)	end 1st/start 2nd c.	CIL II²/7, 952 (Monterrubio de la Serena)
9	L. Pontius L.f. Pap. Aquila, praetor(ianus) C(o)hort(is) IIII	granite stele (242 × 47/45 x 24/22)	mid-1st c.	FE 286 = HEp 10, 66 = AE 2000, 736 (Monterrubio de la Serena)
10	Cantia Celtibera Emeritensis (husband = L. V (- - -) I (- - -))	unknown (lost)	2nd c.	CIL II²/ 7, 966 (Magacela)
11	M. Helvius Sabinus Metel(l)ine(nsis)	granite stele (127 × 44 × 31/24)	end 1st / start 2nd c.	AE 1998, 746 = HEp 8, 9 (Castuera)
12	Sentia Paulli liber(ta) Sura Metellinensis	granite stele ((188) × 47 × 25)	mid-1st c.	FE 289 = HEp 10, 53 = AE 2000, 737 (Benquerencia de la Serena)

Bibliography

Aguilar Sáenz, A. and P. Guichard 1995. *La ciudad antigua de Lacimurga y su entorno rural* (Zafra).

Alarcão, J. de 1990. "A urbanização de Portugal nas épocas de César e de Augusto," in Trillmich and Zanker 1990, 43–57.

Alarcão, J. de and A. Tavares 1989. "A Roman marble quarry in Portugal," in *Studia Pompeiana & Classica in Honor of W. Jashemski. II. Classica* (New York) 1–12.

Alföldy, G. 1969. *Fasti hispanienses. Senatorische Reichsbeamte und Offiziere in den spanischen Provinzen des römischen Reiches von Augustus bis Diokletian* (Wiesbaden).

Almagro Gorbea, M. 1971. "La necrópolis de Medellín," *NAH Arq.* 16, 161–202.

Almagro Gorbea, M. 1977. *El bronce final y el periodo orientalizante en Extremadura* (Bibliotheca Praehistorica Hispana 14, Madrid).

Almagro Gorbea, M. (ed.) 1999a. *Las guerras cántabras* (Historia y documentos 14, Santander).

Almagro Gorbea, M. 1999b. "El territorio de Medellín en época protohistórica," in Gorges and Rodríguez Martín 1999, 17–38.

Almagro Gorbea, M. (ed.) 2006. *La necrópolis de Medellín.* I. *La excavación y sus hallazgos* (Bibliotheca Archaeologica Hispana 26.1, Madrid).

Almagro Gorbea, M. (ed.) 2008a. *La necrópolis de Medellín.* II. *Estudio de los hallazgos* (Bibliotheca Archaeologica Hispana 26.2, Madrid).

Almagro Gorbea, M. (ed.) 2008b. *La necrópolis de Medellín, III: Estudios analíticos. IV: Interpretación de la necrópolis; V: El marco histórico de Medellín-Conisturgis* (Bibliotheca Archaeologica Hispania 26.3, Madrid).

Almagro Gorbea, M. and J. M. Álvarez Martínez (eds) 1999. *Hispania: el legado de Roma* (Catálogo de la Exposición, Museo Nacional de Arte Romano, febrero–abril de 1999) (Zaragoza).

Almagro Gorbea, M. and A. M. Martín Bravo 1994. "Medellín 1991. La ladera norte del Cerro del Castillo," in M. Almagro-Gorbea and A. M. Martín Bravo (eds) *Castros y oppida en Extremadura* (*Complutum* Extra 4, Madrid) 77–127.

Álvarez Martínez, J. M. 1973. "Dos inscripciones funerarias emeritenses con la fórmula 'aeternae quieti'," *RABM* 76, 521–6.

Álvarez Martínez, J. M. 1988. "Algunas observaciones sobre el territorium emeritense," in *Homenaje a Samuel de los Santos (Albacete, 1984)* (Murcia) 185–92.

Álvarez Martínez, J. M. 2004. "Aspectos del urbanismo de *Augusta Emerita*," in Nogales Basarrate 2004, 129–69.

Álvarez Martínez, J. M. and E. E. Enríquez Navascués (eds) 1995. *El anfiteatro en la Hispania romana: Actas del Coloquio internacional, Mérida, 26–28 de noviembre de 1992* (Mérida).

Álvarez Martínez, J. M. and T. Nogales Basarrate 1990. "Schéma urbain d'Augusta Emerita: le portique du forum," in *Akten des XIII. Internationalen Kongresses für Klassische Archäologie Berlin 1988* (Berlin) 336–8.

Álvarez Martínez, J. M. and T. Nogales Basarrate 2003. *Forum Coloniae Augustae Emeritae: "Templo de Diana"* (Mérida).

Álvarez Martínez, J. M., F. G. Rodríguez Martín and J. C. Saquete Chamizo 2004. "La ciudad romana de *Regina*. Nuevas perspectivas sobre su configuración urbana," *Anas* 17, 11–45.

Álvarez y Sáenz de Buruaga, J. 1976. "La fundación de Mérida," in *Augusta Emerita: Actas del bimilenario* (Madrid) 19–32.

Ariño Gil, E. and J. M. Gurt Esparraguera 1994. "Catastros romanos en el entorno de Augusta Emerita. Fuentes literarias y documentación arqueológica," in Gorges and Salinas de Frías 1994, 45–66.

Ariño Gil, E., J. M. Gurt Esparraguera and J. M. Palet Martínez 2004. *El pasado presente. Arqueología de los paisajes en la Hispania romana* (Salamanca).

Arruda, A. M. and A. Guerra (eds) 2002. *De Scallabis a Santarém* (Lisbon).

Arruda, A. M. and C. Viegas 1999. "The Roman temple of Scallabis (Santarém, Portugal)," *Journal of Iberian Archaeology* 1, 185–224.

Auliard, C. and L. Bodiou (eds) 2004. *Au jardin des Hespérides: Histoire, société et épigraphie des mondes anciens. Mélanges offerts à Alain Tranoy* (Rennes).

Ayerbe Vélez, R. 2000. "Intervención arqueológica en la urbanización Jardines de Mérida de la Avenida Vía de la Plata. Excavación de un tramo de la conducción hidráulica 'Proserpina – Los Milagros'," in *Mérida. Excavaciones arqueológicas 1998* (Memoria 4) 39–58.

Beltrán Lloris, F. (ed.) 2007. *Zaragoza: Colonia Caesar Augusta* (Ciudades romanas de *Hispania* 4, Rome).

Bendala Galán, M. and R. Durán Cabello 1995. "El anfiteatro de Augusta Emerita: rasgos arquitectónicos y problemática urbanística y cronológica," in Álvarez Martínez and Enríquez Navascués 1995, 247–64.

Callejo Serrano, C. 1968. "La arqueología de Norba Caesarina," *AEspA* 41, 121–49.

Campbell, J. B. 2000. *The Writings of the Roman Land Surveyors: Introduction, Text, Translation and Commentary* (*JRS* Monograph 9, London).

Canto, A. M. 1982. "Sobre la cronología augustea del Acueducto de Los Milagros de Mérida," in *Homenaje a Sáenz de Buruaga* (Badajoz) 157–76.

Canto, A. M. 1989. "Colonia Iulia Augusta Emerita: consideraciones acerca de su fundación y territorio," *Gerión* 7, 149–205.

Canto, A. M. 2001. "Sinoicismo y *stolati* en Emerita, Caesaraugusta y Pax: una relectura de Estrabón III, 2, 15," *Gerión* 19, 425–76.

Castillo, C. 1988. "La tribu Galeria en Hispania: ciudades y ciudadanos," in J. González and J. Arce (eds) *Estudios sobre la Tabula Siarensis* (*AEspA* Anejo 9, Madrid) 233–43.

Cerrillo Martín de Cáceres, E., P. Le Roux and J. L. Ramírez Sádaba 2004. "Un pretoriano hallado en Cáceres (España)," in Auliard and Bodiou 2004, 157–66.

CIIAE = J. L. Ramírez Sádaba, *Catálogo de las inscripciones imperiales de Augusta Emerita* (Cuadernos Emeritenses 21, Mérida 2003).

Clavel-Lévêque, M. 1993. "Un plan cadastral à l'échelle. La forma de bronze de Lacimurga," *Estudios de la Antigüedad* 6–7, 175–82.

De la Barrera Antón, J. L. 2000. *La decoración arquitectónica de los foros de Augusta Emerita* (Bibliotheca Archaeologica 25, Rome).

De la Barrera Antón, J. L. and W. Trillmich 1996. "Eine Wiederholung der Aeneas-Gruppe vom Forum Augustum samt ihrer Inschrift in Mérida (Spanien)," *RM* 103, 119–38.

Del Amo y de la Hera, M. 1982. "El teatro romano de Medellín (Badajoz)," in *El teatro en la Hispania romana: Mérida, 13–15 de noviembre de 1980* (Badajoz) 317–24.

Dupré Raventós, X. (ed.) 2004. *Mérida. Colonia Augusta Emerita* (Las capitales provinciales de *Hispania* 2, Rome).

Durán Cabello, R. M. 2004. *El teatro y el anfiteatro de Augusta Emérita. Contribución al conocimiento histórico de la capital de Lusitania* (BAR Int. Series 1207, Oxford).

Edmondson, J. C. 1990. "Romanization and urban development in Lusitania," in T. F. C. Blagg and M. Millett (eds) *The Early Roman Empire in the West* (Oxford) 151–78.

Edmondson, J. C. 2005. "Inmigración y sociedad local en *Augusta Emerita*, 25 a.C.–250 d.C.," in Gorges *et al.* 2005, 321–68.

Edmondson, J. C. 2006. *Granite Funerary Stelae from Augusta Emerita* (Monografías Emeritenses 9, Mérida).

Edmondson, J. C. 2007. "The cult of Mars Augustus and Roman imperial power at Augusta Emerita in the third century A.D.: a new votive dedication," in Nogales Basarrate and González 2007, 541–75.

Edmondson, J. C., T. Nogales Basarrate and W. Trillmich 2001. *Imagen y memoria: monumentos funerarios con retratos en la colonia Augusta Emerita* (Bibliotheca Archaeologica Hispana 10; Monografías Emeritenses 6, Madrid).

Étienne, R. 1992. " L'horloge de la Civitas Igaeditanorum et la création de la province de Lusitanie," *REA* 94, 355–62.

Étienne, R. 1995. "À propos du territoire d'Augusta Emerita (Mérida)," in M. Clavel-Lévêque and R. Plana-Mallart (eds) *Cité et territoire (Béziers, 1994)* (Paris) 27–32.

Fishwick, D. 2000. "A new forum at Corduba," *Latomus* 59, 96–104.

Fishwick, D. 2007. *The Imperial Cult in the Latin West. III. Provincial Cult. 3. The Provincial Centre; Provincial Cult* (Leiden and Boston).

Galve, M. P., M. A. Magallón and M. Navarro Caballero 2005. "Las ciudades del valle medio del Ebro en época julio-claudia," in *L'Aquitaine et l'Hispanie septentrionale à l'époque julio-claudienne: Organisation et exploitation des espaces provinciaux* (*Aquitania* Suppl. 13, Bordeaux) 169–214.

Gamer, G. 1989. *Formen römischer Altäre auf der Hispanischen Halbinsel* (Madrider Beiträge 12, Mainz).

García y Bellido, A. 1953. "El puente romano de Medellín (antigua *Metellinum*)," *AEspA* 26, 407–18.

Gil Farrés, O. 1946. "¿Cuál fue la extensión urbana de la Mérida romana?," *AEspA* 19, 361–3.

Golvin, J.-C. 1988. *L'amphithéâtre romain: essai sur la théorisation de sa forme et de ses fonctions* (Paris).

González Cordero, A., J. Suárez de Venegas Sanz and M. de Alvarado Gonzalo 1990. "Nuevas aportaciones a la epigrafía de Extremadura," *Alcántara* 21, 113–50.

González, J. 1989. "Urso: ¿tribu Sergia o Galeria?," in J. González (ed.) *Estudios sobre Urso Colonia Iulia Genetiva* (Seville) 133–53.

González, J. 2004. "Límites entre provincias, ciudades y territorios," in M. G. Angeli Bertinelli and A. Donati (eds) *Epigrafia di confine, confine dell'epigrafia: Atti del colloquio AIEGL – Borghesi 2003* (Faenza) 49–64.

Gorges, J.-G. 1979. *Les villas hispano-romaines. Inventaire et problématique archéologiques* (Paris).

Gorges, J.-G. 1982. "Centuriation et organisation du territoire: notes préliminaires sur l'exemple de Mérida," in P.-A. Fevrier and P. Leveau (eds) *Villes et campagnes dans l'Empire romain* (Aix-en-Provence) 101–10.

Gorges, J.-G. 1986. "Prospections archéologiques autour d'Augusta Emerita. Soixante-dix sites ruraux en quête de signification," *REA* 88 [= *Hommage à Robert Étienne*], 215–36.

Gorges, J.-G. 1993. "Nouvelle lecture du fragment de *forma* d'un territoire voisin de Lacimurga," *MCV* 29, 7–23.

Gorges, J.-G., E. Cerrillo and T. Nogales Basarrate (eds) 2005. *V Mesa Redonda Internacional sobre Lusitania romana: Las comunicaciones* (Madrid).

Gorges, J.-G. and F. G. Rodríguez Martín (eds) 1999. *Économie et territoire en Lusitanie romaine* (Collection de la Casa de Velázquez 65, Madrid).

Gorges, J.-G. and F. G. Rodríguez Martín 2004. "Los territorios antiguos de Mérida. Un estudio del *territorium emeritense* y de sus áreas de influencia," in Nogales Basarrate 2004, 93–128.

Gorges, J.-G. and M. Salinas de Frías (eds) 1994. *Les campagnes de la Lusitanie romaine: occupation du sol et habitats* (Madrid and Salamanca)

Granino Cecere, M. G. 1996–7. "I *Sulpicii* e il Tuscolano," *Rend. della Pont. Accad. Rom. d'Arch.* 69, 233–51.

Haba Quirós, S. 1998. *Medellín romano. La Colonia Metellinensis y su territorio* (Badajoz).

Hiernard, J. and J. M. Álvarez Martínez 1982. "Aqua Augusta. Una inscripción con letras de bronce de Mérida," *Sautuola* 3, 221–9.

Humphrey, J. 1986. *Roman Circuses: Arenas for Chariot Racing* (London).

IMAPB = J. Salas Martín, J. Esteban Ortega, J. A. Redondo Rodríguez, J. L. Sánchez Abal (eds) *Inscripciones romanas y cristianas del Museo Arqueológico Provincial de Badajoz* (Badajoz 1997).

Jiménez Ávila, J. 2004. "El territorio emeritense en época protohistórica: antecedentes prerromanos de *Emerita Augusta*," in Nogales Basarrate 2004, 41–66.

Kraft, K. 1968. *Zur Münzprägung des Augustus* (Sitzungsberichte der Wissenschaftlichen Gesellschaft an der J. W. Goethe-Universität Frankfurt 7.5).

Le Roux, P. 1982. *L'armée romaine et l'organisation des provinces ibériques d'Auguste à l'invasion de 409* (Paris).

Le Roux, P. 1999. "Le territoire de la colonie auguste de Mérida: réflexions pour un bilan," in Gorges and Rodríguez Martín 1999, 263–76.

Le Roux, P. 2004. "La question des conventus dans la péninsule Ibérique d'époque romaine," in Auliard and Bodiou 2004, 337–56.

Le Roux, P. 2005. "Mérida capitale de la province romaine de Lusitanie," in Gorges *et al.* 2005, 17–31.

Lopes, M. Conceição 2003. *A cidade romana de Beja: percursos e debates acerca da "civitas" de Pax Iulia* (Coimbra).

Marcos Pous, A. 1961. "Dos tumbas emeritenses de incineración," *AEspA* 34, 90–103.

Marín Díaz, M. A. 1988. *Emigración, colonización y municipalización en la Hispania republicana* (Granada).

Márquez Moreno, C., R. García, J. García, and S. Vargas 2004. "Estudio de materiales de la excavación arqueológica en calle Morería, Córdoba," *Anuario Arqueológico de Andalucía 2001. 2. Actividades sistemáticas y puntuales* (Córdoba) 123–34.

Mateos Cruz, P. 1994–5 [1998]. "Reflexiones sobre la trama urbana de Augusta Emerita," *Anas* 7–8, 233–47.

Mateos Cruz, P. 2001. "*Augusta Emerita*. La investigación arqueológica en una ciudad de época romana," *AEspA* 74, 183–208.

Mateos Cruz, P. (ed.) 2006. *El "Foro Provincial" de Augusta Emerita: un conjunto monumental de culto imperial* (*AEspA* Anejo 42, Madrid).

Mateos Cruz, P. 2007. "El conjunto provincial de culto imperial de *Augusta Emerita*," in Nogales and González 2007, 369–93.

Mateos Cruz, P., R. Ayerbe Vélez, T. Barrientos Vera, and S. Feijoo Martínez 2002. "La gestión del agua en *Augusta Emerita*," *Empúries* 53, 67–88.

Mateos Cruz, P. and J. Márquez Pérez 1999. "Nuevas estructuras urbanas relacionadas con el Teatro Romano de Mérida: el pórtico de acceso," *Mérida: Excavaciones arqueológicas 1997* (Memoria 3) 301–20.

Mateos Cruz, P. and A. Pizzo 2008. "La costruzione del "foro provinciale" di *Augusta Emerita*," in S. Camporeale, H. Dessales and A. Pizzo (eds) *Arqueología de la construcción. I. Los procesos constructivos en el mundo romano: Italia y provincias occidentales* (*AEspA* Anejo 50, Mérida), 243–57.

Mateos Cruz, P. and A. Pizzo 2009. "El conjunto provincial de culto imperial de *Augusta Emerita*," in P. Mateos Cruz, S. Celestino, A. Pizzo and T. Tortosa (eds), *Santuarios, oppida y ciudades: arquitectura sacra en el origen y desarrollo urbano del Mediterraneo occidental* (*AEspA* Anejo 45, Mérida), 371–82.

Menéndez Pidal y Álvarez, J. 1957. "Restitución del texto y dimensiones de las inscripciones históricas del anfiteatro de Mérida," *AEspA* 30, 205–17.

Montalvo Frías, A. M., E. Gijón Gabriel and F. J. Sánchez-Palencia 1997. "Circo romano de Mérida: campaña de 1995,"

Mérida. Excavaciones Arqueológicas 1994–1995 (Memoria 1) 245–58.

Nogales Basarrate, T. 1997. *El retrato privado en Augusta Emerita* (Badajoz).

Nogales Basarrate, T. (ed.) 2004. *Augusta Emerita: Territorios, espacios, imágenes y gentes en Lusitania romana* (Monografías Emeritenses 8, Mérida).

Nogales Basarrate, T. 2007. "Culto imperial en *Augusta Emerita*: imágenes y programas urbanos," in Nogales Basarrate and González 2007, 447–539.

Nogales Basarrate, T. and J. M. Álvarez Martínez 2006. "*Fora Augustae Emeritae*: la *interpretatio* provincial de las patrones metropolitanos," in D. Vaquerizo and F. Murillo (eds) *El concepto de lo provincial en el mundo antiguo: Homenaje a Pilar León Alonso* (Córdoba) I, 413–44.

Nogales Basarrate, T. and M. L. Creus Luque 1999. "Escultura de *villae* en el territorio emeritense: nuevas aportaciones," in Gorges and Rodríguez Martín 1999, 499–523.

Nogales Basarrate, T. and J. González (eds) 2007. *Culto imperial: política y poder* (Hispania Antigua, Serie Arqueológica 1, Rome).

Pfanner, M. 1990. "Modelle römischer Stadtentwicklung am Beispiel Hispaniens und der westlichen Provinzen," in Trillmich and Zanker 1990, 59–116.

Pizzo, A. 2008. *El Arco de Trajano de Augusta Emerita* (Ataecina 4, Mérida).

Ramírez Sádaba, J. L. 1994a. "Nuevos datos para la historia de Metellinum: las inscripciones conservadas en el M.A.P. de Badajoz," *Homenaje al Profesor Presedo* (Seville) 637–53.

Ramírez Sádaba, J. L. 1994b. "La demografía del *territorium emeritense* (excepto el casco urbano) según la documentación epigráfica," in J.-G. Gorges and M. Salinas de Frías (eds), *Les campagnes de Lusitanie romaine* (Madrid), 131–47.

Ramírez Sádaba, J. L. 1995. "Epigrafía del anfiteatro romano de Mérida," in Álvarez Martínez and Enríquez Navascués 1995, 285–99.

Richardson, J. S. 1996. *The Romans in Spain* (Oxford).

Richmond, I. A. 1930. "The first years of Emerita Augusta," *Archaeological Journal* 87, 98–116.

Rizakis, A. D. 2004. "La littérature gromatique et la colonisation romaine en Orient," in G. Salmeri, A. Raggi and A. Baroni (eds) *Colonie romane nel mondo greco* (*Minima epigraphica et papyrologica*, Suppl. 3, Rome) 69–94.

Roddaz, J.-M. 1984. *Marcus Agrippa* (BEFAR 253, Rome).

Rodríguez Martín, F. G. 2004. "El paisaje urbano de *Augusta Emerita*: reflexiones en torno al Guadiana y las puertas de acceso a la ciudad," *Revista Portuguesa de Arqueología* 7.2, 365–405.

Sáez Fernández, P. 1990. "Estudios sobre una inscripción catastral colindante con Lacimurga," *Habis* 21, 205–27 (with addendum, including a better photo, at *Habis* 22, 1991, 437).

Sáez Fernández, P. 1994. "Nuevas perspectivas en relación a la ordenación territorial del sur de la Lusitania española," in Gorges and Salinas de Frías 1994, 99–108.

Salas Martín, J. 1982. "Consideraciones acerca de la fundación y evolución de la colonia *Norba Caesarina*," *Norba* 2, 145–55.

Salas Martín, J. 2001. "Fuentes antiguas para el estudio de la *Colonia Metellinensis*," *Norba: Revista de Historia* 15, 101–16.

Salas Martín, J. and J. Esteban Ortega 1994. *La Colonia Norba Caesarina y la gens Norbana en Hispania* (Cáceres).

Salas Martín, J. and S. Haba Quirós 1987. "Nuevas aportaciones a la epigrafía romana de Extremadura. 2. Inscripciones inéditas de la colonia Metellinensis," *Veleia* 4, 134–8.

Sánchez-Palencia, F. J., A. Montalvo Frías and E. Gijón Gabriel 2001. "El circo romano de *Augusta Emerita*," in T. Nogales Basarrate and F. J. Sánchez-Palencia (edd.) *El circo en Hispania romana. Actas del congreso internacional, MNAR, Mérida, 22, 23 y 24 de marzo de 2001* (Mérida) 75–95.

Saquete Chamizo, J. C. 1997. *Las elites sociales de Augusta Emerita* (Cuadernos emeritenses 13, Mérida).

Saquete Chamizo, J. C. 2004. "Territorios y gentes en el contexto histórico de la fundación de la colonia *Augusta Emerita*," in Nogales Basarrate 2004, 373–97.

Saquete Chamizo, J. C. 2005a. "*L. Fulcinius Trio*, Tiberio y el gran templo de culto imperial de *Augusta Emerita*," *Epigraphica* 67, 279–308.

Saquete Chamizo, J. C. 2005b. "Materiales epigráficos procedentes del área del gran templo de culto imperial de *Augusta Emerita*: una revisión necesaria," *Habis* 36, 277–97.

Sillières, P. 1982. "Centuriation et voie romaine au sud de Mérida: contribution à la délimitation de la Bétique et de la Lusitanie," *MCV* 18, 437–48.

Sillières, P. 1990. *Les voies de communication de l'Hispanie méridionale* (Paris).

Sillières, P. 2003. "Voies romaines et contrôle de l'Hispanie à l'époque republicaine: l'exemple de l'Espagne ultérieure," in A. Morillo, F. Cadiou and D. Hourcade (eds) *Defensa y territorio en Hispania de los Escipiones a Augusto* (León and Madrid) 25–40.

Stylow, A. U. 1986. "Apuntes sobre epigrafía de época flavia en Hispania," *Gerión* 4, 285–311.

Stylow, A. U. 1991. "El *Municipium Flavium V(...)* de Azuaga (Badajoz) y la municipalización de la *Baeturia Turdulorum*," *Studia Historica: Historia Antigua* 9, 11–27.

Stylow, A. U. 1995. "Apuntes sobre las tribus romanas en Hispania," *Veleia* 12, 105–23.

Stylow, A. U. 2006. "Nuevos epígrafes del conjunto provincial de culto imperial de Augusta Emerita," in Mateos Cruz 2006, 297–314.

Stylow, A. U. 2008. "Ein neuer Statthalter der Baetica und frühe Reiterstatuenpostamente in Hispanien" in M. L. Caldelli, G. L. Gregori and S. Orlandi (eds) *Epigrafia 2006. Atti della XVIe rencontre sur l'épigraphie in onore di Silvio Panciera con altri contributi di colleghi, allievi e collaboratori* (Rome) 1051–62.

Syme, R. 1970. "The conquest of north-west Spain," in *Legio VII Gemina* (León) 79–107.

Trillmich, W. 1989–90. "Un *sacrarium* del culto imperial en el teatro de Mérida," *Anas* 2–3, 87–102.

Trillmich, W. 1990. "Colonia Augusta Emerita, die Hauptstadt von Lusitanien," in Trillmich and Zanker 1990, 299–318. Revised English version in J. Edmondson (ed.), *Augustus* (Edinburgh Readings on the Ancient World, Edinburgh 2009) 427–67 (ch. 14).

Trillmich, W. 1995. "Gestalt und Ausstattung des 'Marmorforums' in Mérida. Kenntnisstand und Perspektiven," *MM* 36, 269–91.

Trillmich, W. 2004. "Monumentalización del espacio público emeritense como reflejo de la evolución histórica colonial: el ejemplo del teatro emeritense y sus fases," in Nogales Basarrate 2004, 275–84.

Trillmich, W. 2007. "Espacios públicos de culto imperial en *Augusta Emerita*: entre hipótesis y dudas," in Nogales

Basarrate and González 2007, 415–45.

Trillmich, W. and P. Zanker (eds) 1990. *Stadtbild und Ideologie: Die Monumentalisierung hispanischer Städte zwischen Republik und Kaiserzeit* (ABAW, Phil-hist. Kl., n. F. 103, Munich).

Ventura Villanueva, A. 2007. "Reflexiones sobre la arquitectura y advocación del templo de la calle Morería en el *forum adiectum* de *Colonia Patricia Corduba*," in Nogales Basarrate and González 2007, 215–37.

Wiegels, R. 1976. "Zum Territorium der augusteischen Kolonie Emerita," *MM* 17, 258–84.

Notes

1. On the wars, Syme 1970; Almagro Gorbea 1999a.

2. Cf. Isid. *Etym.* 15.1.69: *Emeritam Caesar Augustus ... dans ei nomen ab eo quod ibi milites veteranos constituisset: nam emeriti dicuntur veterani solutique milites.* For the foundation of Emerita, see Álvarez y Sáenz de Buruaga 1976; Le Roux 1982, 69–72; Saquete Chamizo 1997, 24–39 and 2004.

3. Le Roux 1982, 70, n. 284; cf. Canto 2001.

4. *AE* 1993, 892 = *HEp* 5, 53 (since this granite stele is broken, it is unclear whether a *cognomen* needs to be restored after the mention of his votive tribe).

5. *HEp* 9, 95 = *AE* 2006, 597 = Edmondson 2006, 145–6, no. 15 and pl. Xa.

6. See Saquete Chamizo 2004, esp. 386–8, summarizing the evidence for the abbreviation C.I.A.E. on inscriptions (*e.g. AE* 1998, 747 = *HEp* 8, 150) and on stamps on tiles (*e.g. AE* 1984, 491 = *AE* 1976, 274), *terra sigillata* bowls (*AE* 1984, 490) and lead pipes (*AE* 2002, 684, dated to CE 180).

7. Trillmich 1990, 300–2 and plate 22.1–6; *BMCRE* I 51–4, nos. 277–97 and plate 5, 1–14. City gate: *BMCRE* I 53, nos. 288–92; Trillmich 1990, 301 and plate 22.6.

8. Trillmich 1990, 300–2 and plate 22.7–12 ("Actium" series). For this interpretation of the Actium series, see also Kraft 1968, 205–225.

9. For discussion of the date of the creation of the province of Lusitania, see below, n. 16.

10. In general see Trillmich 1990, 302–10; Mateos Cruz 1994–5; Álvarez Martínez 2004; Rodríguez Martín 2004.

11. See Le Roux 2005, 21 and n. 17. On Pax Iulia, see Lopes 2003; for Scallabis, Arruda and Viegas 1999; Arruda and Guerra 2002; on Pax Iulia and Scallabis, see Alarcão 1990, 44–9; for Norba, Callejo Serrano 1968; Salas Martín and Esteban Ortega 1994.

12. Agennius Urbicus *De Contr. Agr.* 44 Thulin = 40 Campbell: *scio in Lusitania, finibus Emeritensium, non exiguum per mediam coloniae perticam ire flumen Anam, circa quod agri sunt adsignati qua usque tunc solum utile visum est. propter magnitudinem enim agrorum veteranos circa extremum fere finem velut terminos disposuit, paucissimos circa coloniam et circa flumen A<nam>: reliquum ita remanserat, ut postea repleretur. nihilo minus et secunda et tertia postea facta est adsignatio. nec tamen agrorum modus divisione vinci potuit, sed superfuit inadsignatus.* In general on Emerita's territory, see Wiegels 1976; Gorges 1986; Álvarez Martínez 1988; Étienne 1995; Le Roux 1999 and 2005; Gorges and Rodríguez Martín 2004; Ariño Gil *et al.* 2004, 44–6, 68–72, 98, 138–44.

13. Ibid.: *in his agris cum subseciva requirerentur, impetraverunt possessores a praeside provinciae eius, ut aliquam latitudinem An<ae> flumini daret. quoniam subseciva qua quis occupaverat redimere cogebatur, iniquum iudicatum est, ut quisquam amnem publicum emeret aut sterilia quae alluebat: modus itaque flumi<ni> est constitutus.* For Vespasian's involvement, see the comments of Campbell 2000, 344–6 *ad loc.*

14. Hyginus, *Constitutio limitum* 136 Thulin = 136 Campbell = 171 Lachmann: i.e., each *centuria* was 40 *actus* in length and 20 in breadth rather than the usual 20 x 20 *actus*.

15. Ibid.: *in Emeritensium finibus aliquae sunt praefecturae, quarum decimani aeque in orientem diriguntur, kardines in meridianum; sed in praefecturis Mullicensis et Turgaliensis regionis decimani habent actus XX, kardines actus XL. nam et in alia praefectura aliter converse sunt limites.*

16. For the division of Ulterior, Strabo 3.2.15; for its date, Étienne 1992; Le Roux 1982, 54–6, 74–5; Richardson 1996, 135–6.

17. For this forum and temple, see now Álvarez Martínez and Nogales Basarrate 2003. The results of more recent excavations, allowing the full extent of this forum to be ascertained and bringing to light a second temple in an adjoining forum, will be published in 2009 by the Instituto de Arqueología de Mérida as an *AEspA* supplement edited by R. Ayerbe, T. Barrientos and F. Palma.

18. Mateos Cruz 2006, 68–118, esp. 110–14 and Fig. 109; Mateos Cruz and Pizzo 2008 and 2009.

19. In the meantime, see the discussion in Mateos Cruz 2001, 194; *id.* 2006, 343–4; cf. Álvarez Martínez 2004, 141–2.

20. See Trillmich 1990, 305–9; Álvarez Martínez and Nogales Basarrate 2003, 77–118, 133–9. On the opening of the marble quarries near Estremoz, Borba and Vila Viçosa, see Alarcão and Tavares 1989.

21. For Emerita's water supply in general, see recently Mateos Cruz *et al.* 2002. Earlier scholars had dated at least one of the other aqueduct systems to the Augustan period (*e.g.* Canto 1982; Pfanner 1990, 90, 99, fig. 31), but the so-called "Los Milagros" aqueduct has recently been firmly dated to the mid-1st c. CE, which is probably also the date of the third aqueduct know as the "San Lázaro aqueduct": see Ayerbe Vélez 2000.

22. Hiernard and Álvarez Martínez 1982 = *AE* 1984, 493 = *CIIAE* 1 (31 cm tall × 121.5 cm long × 8 cm wide), dating to the Augustan period. An "Aqua Augusta" does not necessarily have to belong to the Augustan period; note the Flavian or Trajanic Aqua Augusta constructed at Capera (Cáparra, prov. Cáceres) in Lusitania *[pro sa]lute municipi Flavi Ca[perens(is)]*: *AE* 1941, 307, rev. Stylow 1986, 303–7, no. 3 = *AE* 1986, 307. For other examples from Hispania and elsewhere, see Stylow 1986, 288–9 and n. 8.

23. Two lintel blocks: *CIL* II 474 = *ILS* 130 = *CIIAE* 2–3: *M(arcus) • Agrippa • L(uci) • f(ilius) • co(n)s(ul) • III trib(unicia) pot(estate) • III.* Three separate granite friezes with holes for bronze letters (a) in situ over the E. entrance to the theatre: Richmond 1930, 115–16, fig. 4 and pl. 6b = *CIIAE* 4 = Trillmich 1990, 304, n. 46 and pl. 23e: *M(arcus) • Agrippa • L(uci) • f(ilius) • co(n)[s(ul) • tert(ium) / trib(unicia) • potest(ate) t[ert(ium)]]*; (b) and (c) original location unclear, but perhaps on the *scaenae frons*: *CIIAE* 5: *M(arcus) Agrippa [•] L(uci) • f(ilius) • co(n)s(ul) • III • [tri]b(unicia) • pot(estate) • III]*; *CIIAE* 6: *M. Agr[- - -*

- - -]. See briefly Roddaz 1984, 416–18.

24. Trillmich 1990, 310, pointing out the parallel with the reuse of the Augustan inscription of M. Agrippa in the reign of Hadrian on the facade of the redesigned Pantheon in Rome: *CIL* VI 896 = *ILS* 129.

25. See Menéndez Pidal y Álvarez 1957; Ramírez Sádaba 1995. (More work, however, is needed on the physical situation of these inscriptions within the amphitheatre.)

26. Humphrey 1986, 362–76; Montalvo Frías *et al.* 1997; Sánchez-Palencia *et al.* 2001.

27. For the definitive publication, see Mateos Cruz 2006. For a new larger forum built under Tiberius in Caesaraugusta, see Galve *et al.* 2005, 177–8; J. A. Hernández Vera and J. Núñez in Beltrán Lloris 2007, 50–6. For the late-Augustan/Tiberian "forum adiectum" in Corduba, see Fishwick 2000 and 2007, 79–83; Márquez *et al.* 2004; Ventura Villanueva 2007.

28. For recent discussion of these, see Saquete Chamizo 2005a and 2005b; Stylow 2006, 299–304, nos. A–F and figs 285–8.

29. Stylow 2006, 308–11, no. 3 and fig. 292 (photo) = *AE* 2006, 585: - - - - - - / [- - -] +one • leg / [- - - ex? arge]nti p(ondo) L. This inscription may be restored to attest L. Fulcinius Trio, governor from *c.* CE 21 to 31, M. Porcius Cato, whose governorship Alföldy places under Claudius, or M. Salvius Otho, governor from 58 to 68: see Stylow, loc.cit. For these senators as governors of Lusitania, see Alföldy 1969, 135–6 (Trio), 138–9 (Cato), 139 (Otho).

30. Stylow 2006, 311–12, no. 4 and fig. 293 (photo) = *AE* 2006, 586: [- - -] ARI • DIVI / [- - -] AVG • GER / - - - - - -, which may be expanded either as *[Imp(eratori) Caes]ari Divi / [Nervae f(ilio) Nervae Traiano] Aug(usto) Ger(manico) / - - - - -* or as *[Imp(eratori) Caes]ari Divi / [Vespasiani f(ilio) Domitiano / Aug(usto) Ger(manico) / - - - - - -*.

31. See also Mateos Cruz 2007; Fishwick 2007.

32. Álvarez Martínez and Nogales Basarrate 1990; Trillmich 1990, 310–15 (dating it to late-Augustan period); cf. *id.* 1995 and 2007, 434–41 (preferring a Claudian-Neronian date); Nogales Basarrate and Álvarez Martínez 2006. More recent excavations of other parts of this complex will be published in 2009 in an *AEspA* supplement, ed. R. Ayerbe, T. Barrientos and F. Palma.

33. De la Barrera Antón 2000.

34. De la Barrera Antón and Trillmich 1996 = *AE* 1996, 864a-b = *HEp* 7, 109a–b = *CIIAE* 76a–b. Copy from Pompeii: *CIL* X 808 = *Inscr. It.* XIII.3, no. 85.

35. Nogales Basarrate 2007, 493–5 and fig. 11d (photo).

36. See above, n. 32. For its identification as an Augusteum, see Nogales Basarrate 2007, 490–7 (with previous literature), but it might also have incorporated a temple in the same manner, for example, as the Forum Augustum in Rome.

37. For this, see Durán Cabello 2004, esp. 131–221 (esp. 212–16), 242–7, with a summary by the same author in Dupré Raventós 2004, 58–61, updating the work of Golvin 1988, esp. 109–10, no. 77.

38. Trillmich 2004; Durán Cabello 2004, esp. 31–129 (esp. 118–27), 239–42, with a summary in Dupré Raventós 2004, 55–8.

39. Trillmich 1989–90, with an inscription dating the reform to the 130th year of the colony, *i.e.*, CE 105: *AE* 1990, 515 = *HEp* 4, 167 = *CIIAE* 26: *[anno] coloniae CXXX / [- - - C]aes. Aug. Ger. Dacic.[- - - / - - - provi]nciae Lusit[aniae - - - sacr]ari ? Larum et imaginum / [- - -]D*

dat[- - - / - - -]A D[- - -]. A full epigraphic study is still needed to discuss various possible restorations of this important inscription. For the six surviving pedestals with the inscription AVG. SACR. see *CIL* II 471 = *CIIAE* 27; *CIIAE* 28–32 = *AE* 2003, 868–872.

40. Montalvo Frías *et al.* 1997, 248–51; Sánchez-Palencia *et al.* 2001, 91.

41. On this arch see Mateos Cruz 2006, 146–56 (P. Mateos, A. Pizzo, T. Cordero) and esp. 207–49 (A. Pizzo); Pizzo 2008. For the older view of the *urbs quadrata* of Emerita, see the discussion in Richmond 1930; Gil Farrés 1946; Álvarez y Sáenz de Buruaga 1976.

42. For the burial beneath the *media cavea* of the amphitheatre, see Marcos Pous 1961, esp. 91–6 (but erroneously dating it to the Augustan period prior to 8 BCE); Bendala Galán and Durán Cabello 1995, 255–8; Durán Cabello 2004, 213–15 (dating it to the Claudian or early Neronian period). For the burial to the east of the portico *post scaenam*, Mateos Cruz and Márquez Pérez 1999.

43. Mateos Cruz 2001, 187–8.

44. On urban development in Lusitania prior to Augustus, see Edmondson 1990; in the area around Mérida, Jiménez Ávila 2004.

45. See Callejo Serrano 1968; Salas Martín 1982; Salas Martín and Esteban Ortega 1994.

46. Haba Quirós 1998; Salas Martín 2001. Initially Metellinum was a *civitas stipendiaria* until its promotion to colonial status under Caesar: so Marín Díaz 1988, 198–9.

47. It is now clear that the citizens of each of these colonies were enrolled in one of two Roman voting tribes: the Sergia and the Galeria. For Norba, note Q. Pomponius Potentinus Ser(gia tribu), father (or perhaps brother) of G. Pomponius Potentinus, who served in the 4th cohort of the praetorian guard (Cerrillo *et al.* 2004 = *AE* 2004, 724 = *HEp* 13, 216) and [L. P]ostumius L.lib. Gal(eria tribu) Apollonius Norbensis, who died aged 80 at Emerita (*AE* 1997, 781 [with transcription errors] = *HEp* 7, 125). For Metellinum, note Q. Blaesienus Q.f. Ser(gia tribu) Potitus (*AE* 1987, 487 = *HEp* 2, 33) and C. Sulpicius C.f. Gal(eria tribu) Superstes, IIvir III Metellinensium (*AE* 1993, 909 = *HEp* 5, 94, Emerita). (For another possible attestation of a person registered in the Sergia, from a villa at Mengagil Grande, 3.5 km W of Medellín, see Gorges 1979, 192, cat. no. BA 13 = Haba Quirós 1998, 101–2, no. 11, although SER could also be expanded as *ser(vus)*.) This would indicate that there were two separate phases of settlement at each of these colonies: an initial one, perhaps under Caesar, when citizens were enrolled in the Sergia tribe, and a second phase under Augustus when they were enrolled in the Galeria. For the phenomenon, see Castillo 1988; González 1989; Stylow 1995.

48. For the foundation of Metellinum by Q. Caecilius Metellus Pius, probably in 80/79 BCE during his campaigns against Q. Sertorius and then its promotion to the status of a Roman colony under Julius Caesar, see Haba Quirós 1998, 406–11. For its status as a colony, note Plin. *NH* 4.35.117.

49. See above, n. 47.

50. First published by Sáez Fernández 1990 = *AE* 1990, 529 = 1991, 1016= *HEp* 4, 983.

51. On Lacimurga, see Aguilar Sáenz and Guichard 1995.

52. See Haba Quirós 1998, 295–356, esp. 284.

53. Gorges 1982, 1986; Sillières 1982; Ariño Gil and Gurt Esparraguera 1994; Ariño Gil *et al.* 2004, 44–46, with fig.

9 (map), 70–2, with fig. 18 (aerial photograph), 98–99 with fig. 29.

54. See above, p. 35 and n. 14. For doubts that the figure represents the area of each *centuria*, see Ariño Gil and Gurt Esparraguera 1994, 62–4 and Ariño Gil *et al.* 2004, 34–5, preferring to argue, implausibly in my view, that it represents the area of *subseciva* (unassigned land) in each *centuria*.

55. For this tentative suggestion, see also Sáez Fernández 1994, 105; Haba Quirós 1998, 293–4, 424. Other scholars have argued that it may show the centuriated territory of a *praefectura* of the colony of Ucubi: see Clavel-Lévêque 1993; Gorges 1993; Gorges and Rodríguez Martín 2004, 112–13; González 2004, 55–6; but for a rejection of this view, see A. M. Canto's comments at *HEp* 6, 1006a.

56. *CIL* II 656 = II²/7, 871 (found at Mojón Gordo, 13 km N of Valdecaballeros): *Imp(eratori) Domiti/ano Caes(ari) Aug(usto) / Divi Aug(usti) Vesp(asiani) f(ilio) / Augustalis te/rminus c(olonorum) c(oloniae) C(laritatis) Iul(iae) / Ucubitanor(um) / inter Aug(ustanos) Emeri(tenses).* (Note the correction of the final word from the text published as *CIL* II²/7, 871.) Another boundary stone set up under Vespasian between March and July 73 settled limits between this same land owned by Ucubi and the territory of Lacimurga: *CIL* II²/7, 870 (also found at Mojón Gordo): *Imp(erator) Caes(ar) Aug(ustus) / Vespasianus po/ntif(ex) [max(imus)] trib(unicia) p/ot(estate) [IIII i]mp(erator) X p(ater) / p(atriae) co(n)s(ul) IIII design(atus) / V ter(minavit?) inter Laci/nimurg(enses) et Ucu/bitanos c(olonos) c(oloniae) Claritatis Iulia.*

57. Álvarez Martínez 1988, 186–7; Canto 1989, 150, fig. 1 and 198; Gorges and Rodríguez Martín 2004, 111–13.

58. For arguments that Lacimurga was probably promoted to municipal status under the Flavians, see Stylow 1991, 24, arguing against the view of, *e.g.*, Sáez Fernández 1994, 100–5, that it was promoted under Augustus. The latter view is based on an erroneous conflation of Lusitanian Lacimurga with the Baetican Constantia Iulia Lacimurga, an Augustan *municipium* according to Plin. *NH* 3.3.14.

59. Plin. *NH* 4.118, where he explicitly states that he is only going to list those stipendiary communities "worthy of mention": *stipendiariorum quos nominare non pigeat.*

60. *De Contr. Agr.* p. 40 Thulin = p. 80 Lachmann = p. 36 Campbell. For *praefecturae* in the works of the *agrimensores* more generally, see Rizakis 2004, 77–81.

61. Sillières 1990, 454–66 and 2003, 32–3.

62. Almagro Gorbea 1971, 1977, 1999b, 2006, 2008a, 2008b; Almagro Gorbea and Martín Bravo 1994; Haba Quirós 1998, 31–68.

63. On the Roman bridge, see García y Bellido 1953, esp. 410–15 (for its destruction in 1603 and replacement with a new bridge by 1630); Haba Quirós 1998, 382–97.

64. Haba Quirós 1998, 264–70, 402 (site plan).

65. For the theatre, see Del Amo y de la Hera 1982; Haba Quirós 1998, 257–64. During the completion of this article major excavations of the theatre recommenced in March 2008 by an archaeological team of the Junta de Extremadura, resulting in a series of spectacular discoveries of much of the sculptural display from its *scaenae frons*: a large stolate female figure, a smaller female figure, the base and feet of a statue representing a heroic figure (perhaps a divinized Roman emperor), two Sileni, as well as over-life-size fragments of a right arm and

a fine marble head of the Cnidian Aprodite type. A large bronze letter M from a monumental inscription and several other fragments of inscriptions have also been reported. For provisional reports (in advance of full publication), see, for the discoveries prior to March 2008, www.terraeantiquae.blogia.com/2008/031501–excavacion-del-teatro-romano-de-medellin-php; www.hoy.es/multimedia/fotos/11636.html; for the finds made from July to November 2008: www.webislam.com/?idn=13423; http://mundohistoria.portalmundos.com/los-ultimos-hallazgos-encontrados-en-las-excavaciones-del-teatro-romano-de-medellin-son-de-una-calidad-cientifica-suprema; and www.hoy.es/multimedia/fotos/23480.html (all last consulted, 18.xi.08).

66. See Haba Quirós 1998, 262. For the theatre at Regina, see, most recently, Álvarez Martínez *et al.* 2004, esp. 24–33 (with references).

67. The epigraphic catalogue compiled by Haba Quirós (1998, 87–114) comprises 53 inscriptions, plus 1 early Christian inscription, from Metellinum and its territory. For the assertion of the supposed decline of Metellinum in the 2nd c., see, *e.g.*, García y Bellido 1953, 408–9.

68. González Cordero *et al.* 1990, 147–8, no. 24, with line-drawing = *HEp* 4, 159 = Haba Quirós 1998, 127–9, no. 43 and pl. X,3 (erroneously describing it as a stele): *L. Caecilio L.f. / Sca(ptia tribu) Rufo / leg(ato) pro(praetore) pr(ovinciae) / - - - - - -.* For his date, see the comments of A. U. Stylow at *HEp* 4, 159 and at Stylow 2008, 1054–6.

69. For the date of Cato's governorship, see Alföldy 1969, 138–9.

70. Cf. *AE* 1969/70, 233 = *IRCP* 479 (*hospitium* pact with L. Fulcinius Trio, Juromenha, 21 January, CE 31); *CIL* II 172 = *ILS* 190 (oath of allegiance to Caligula taken by the people of Aritium Vetus in the presence of C. Ummidius Durmius Quadratus, 11 May, CE 37); *CIL* II 189, with Alföldy 1969, 142–3 ([A. Avellius Urina]tius Quadratus, Olisipo, CE 154); *CIL* II 258 and 259, rev. Alföldy 1969, 143 and 147 (dedications to Sol and Luna by Sex. Tigidius Perennis and D. Iulius Coelianus, Colares, territory of Olisipo, *c*. CE 185 and *c*. CE 200–9 respectively). For governors attested at Emerita, *CIL* II 5264 = *ILS* 261 (C. Arruntius Catellius Celer, *c*. CE 75–77); *AE* 1915, 35 = 1990, 514 = *HEp* 4, 172 (Q. Acutius Faienanus, Domitianic/Trajanic; cf. Alföldy 1969, 133–4: Augustan); *AE* 1952, 116 (Sex. Furnius Iulianus, *c*. CE 210–213); *AE* 1993, 264 (P. Clodius Laetus Macrinus, CE 261); Edmondson 2007 (Iul. Maximinus, mid-3rd c.); *AE* 1992, 957 (Aemilius Aemilianus, Diocletianic).

71. For such stelae at Emerita, see Edmondson 2006 (*passim*); for parallels from Metellinum, Ramírez Sádaba 1994a; Edmondson 2006, 29 and figs 1.6–7. The stelae illustrated in Fig. 3.11 are *HEp* 9, 97 = *AE* 2006, 594 = Edmondson 2006, 134–6, no. 6 and pl. IVa–b ((70) × 56 × 38/35 cm, Emerita) and *AE* 1987, 487 = *HEp* 2, 33 = Salas Martín and Haba Quirós 1987, 135–8, no. 2 and fig. 7 = Haba Quirós 1998, 103–4, no. 14 and pl. VII,4 ((67) × 43 × 20 cm; villa at "Las Galapagueras", 3 km from Metellinum).

72. Among many others, from Emerita see: *EE* VIII 17; *HEp* 6, 120; *ERAE* 386 = Edmondson 2006, cat. nos. 4, 7, 9; see further Edmondson 2006, 65–73; from Metellinum: *AE* 1997, 793–5 = *IMAPB* nos 38–40 and pls XXXIX–XLI, revising *AE* 1994, 872–4; cf. *CIL* II 611, rev. *AE* 1994, 870 = *IMAPB* no. 37 and pl. XXXVIII (*l(ocus) p(edum) XII*).

73. See Edmondson 2006, 28, 49–51 (with references).

74. *HEp* 6, 80 = *HEp* 8, 19 = *AE* 1994, 871 = Haba Quirós 1998, 98–100, no. 9: *D(is) M(anibus) s(acrum) // P(ublius) Nonius Mar(inus?) / an(norum) LXX si[bi(?)] / [et] Marcia / [Secu]ndilla / [ma]rito p(i)en/[tiss]imo fe/[cit et] sibi // Marcia Se/cundilla / ann(orum) [- - -] / sibi et ma/rito pien/tissimo / fecit h(ic) s(ita) e(st) s(it) t(erra) l(evis)*.

75. Fig. 3.12 shows *AE* 1987, 486 = Salas Martín and Haba Quirós 1987, 134–5, no. 1 and fig. 6 = Haba Quirós 1998, 102–3, no. 12 and plate VII.3: *D(is) M(anibus) s(acrum) / Rufina / mater / fili(a)e Ru/fin(a)e an(n)o(rum) / XVIII fili(a)e / pientissi/m(a)e fecit / s(it) t(ibi) t(erra) l(evis)* and Álvarez Martínez 1973, 521–4, with photo: *aeternae quieti / sacr(um) / Publiliae Fla/vianae ann(orum) XXVI (et uncia) Ti(berius) Cl(audius) / Eutychus fil(iae) / piissimae / s(it) t(ibi) t(erra) l(evis)*. For a survey of funerary altars from Emerita, see Gamer 1989, 190–9, cat. nos BA 1–69 (with photos).

76. For the bust from La Majona, see Almagro Gorbea and Álvarez Martínez 1999, 651, no. 253 (with photo); Nogales Basarrate and Creus Luque 1999, 511–16 and figs 4–5; for private portraiture at Emerita, Nogales Basarrate 1997; for the funerary monument of L. Antestius Persicus, see *AE* 1952, 117 = Edmondson, Nogales Basarrate and Trillmich 2001, 120–3, no. 2 and plate 1C–D and figs 1.34–5 (with further references).

77. *HEp* 4, 147 = Haba Quirós 1998, 109, no. 19 (marble plaque, 41 x 60 x 13 cm): *Satria Silvana / Imiritensiu(m) / h(ic) s(ita) e(st) s(it) t(ibi) t(erra) l(evis)*.

78. As a result, it is included in the list of inscriptions from the territory of Emerita prepared by Ramírez Sádaba 1994b, 143–4.

79. *HEp* 4, 186 (ex ms, 1779) = Haba Quirós 1998, 117, no. 29: *P. Talius Q.f. Pap. leg. X / hic situs est*.

80. *AE* 1998, 746 = *HEp* 8, 9 (Castuera): *M. Helv/[i]us Sab/inus M/etel(l)ine(nsis) an(norum) LX h(ic) s(itus) e(st) s(it) t(ibi) t(erra) l(evis) sod(ales) tab(ulae) saluta(ris) f(aciendum) c(uraverunt)*.

81. *FE* 289 = *HEp* 10, 53 = *AE* 2000, 737 (Benquerencia de la Serena): *Sentia / Paulli / liber(ta) Su/ra Metel/linensis a/nn(orum) XXXVI / h(ic) s(ita) e(st) t(ibi) t(erra) l(evis)*.

82. *AE* 1993, 909 = *HEp* 5, 94: *Valeria / Allage ann(orum) LX h(ic) s(ita) e(st) s(it) / t(ibi) t(erra) l(evis) / C(aius) Sulpicius C(ai) f(ilius) Gal(eria tribu) Superstes / ann(orum) XXXVIII II vir III Metellinensium / huic col(onia) Emeritensis et col(onia) Metelli(nensis) / d(ecreto) d(ecurionum) locum sepulturae et funeris inpen(sam) / decreverunt h(ic) s(itus) e(st) s(it) t(ibi) t(erra) l(evis)*.

83. Granino Cecere 1996–7, 239–51 with fig. 5 (photo) = *AE* 1999, 417: *Sulpiciae Gali f(iliae) Ser. n(epti) Ser. pro[n(epti)] Trionis (uxori) ex provinc(ia) Lusitania colonia Augusta Emerita agentib(us) leg(atis) T. Furio Ocriculano et L. Flavio Urso*. The statue-base measures 24.6 cm high by 60 cm wide by 39 cm deep.

84. For the *conventus* in the Hispanic provinces, see recently Le Roux 2004; for immigration to Emerita, Edmondson 2005.

85. *AE* 1997, 781 (with errors in transcription) = *HEp* 7, 125: *[L(ucius) P]ostumius L. lib. Gal(eria) / Apollonius Norbensis / Aug(ustalis) ann(orum) LXXX / Volosinia Secundina uxor / ann(orum) XXX hic s(ita) e(st) s(it) t(ibi) t(erra) l(evis)*.

4. *Corduba*/*Colonia Patricia*: the colony that was founded twice

Alicia Jiménez and José R. Carrillo

Introduction

Corduba is an exceptionally interesting example for understanding the different processes associated with the complex phenomenon of Roman colonisation and territorial expansion in the provinces. The first Roman settlement in the area took place during the earliest stage of the conquest, at the beginning of the 2nd c. BCE, in a phase contemporary with the development of the very concept of colony on the Italian Peninsula. The archaeological evidence from *Corduba* is also especially valuable for exploring the material culture of a town inhabited from the outset by Romans and local peoples and for analysing, from a critical perspective, the relationship between the legal status and its material representation. In this respect, our accounts of the monumental character of colonies can, at least in part, be linked to ancient discourses on the reproduction of the model of the city of Rome, or the creation of 'little Romes' in colonies abroad. *Corduba* can be seen as an example of an old Republican colony that was refounded (enlarged, remodeled and embellished) and given a new name, *Colonia Patricia*, in the context of the extensive colonial programmes of Caesar and Augustus.

In the first section of this paper, the evidence provided by the ancient sources on the establishment of a Roman settlement next to an important native *oppidum* is contrasted with the archaeological remains discovered in the town in recent years. The traceable changes that occurred in the image of the town during the first one hundred years of the colony are then analysed. Next, we tackle the question of the coexistence of several discourses on the meaning of 'being Roman' in *Colonia Patricia* through a comparison of the representation of collective identities in public spaces and of individual or family identities in houses and tombs and their

relevance in the transformation of the Republican colony of *Corduba* into the *Colonia Patricia* of the early Empire.

The problem of the origins

According to Strabo (III.2.1.), *Corduba* was founded by Marcellus and, together with Gades, it was one of the towns that had grown most in fame and power in the Turdetania: "...because of the excellence of its soil and the extent of its territory, though the Baetis River has also contributed in great measure to its growth; and it has been inhabited from the beginning by picked men of the Romans and of the native Iberians; what is more, the first colony which the Romans sent to these regions was that to *Corduba*."[1] Marcellus has been identified as the Republican consul *Claudius Marcellus*, praetor of *Hispania Ulterior* and *Hispania Citerior* in 169–168 BCE[2] and proconsular legate in *Hispania Citerior* in 152–151 BCE,[3] and therefore it is usually claimed that Roman *Corduba* was founded in the second quarter of the 2nd c. BCE.[4] However, this short passage has caused decades of controversy. The mere mention of *Corduba* as the first colony in southern Spain has been considered problematic, since we know of at least two Roman towns founded before 169 BCE: Carteia[5] and Italica.[6] Carteia should be dismissed, according to Canto and Stylow,[7] since it is located near Gadir on the Mediterranean coast and in this passage Strabo gives us information only about Turdetania. The colonial status of *Italica* in this early phase remains a thorny issue, although some scholars include it in the list of early Republican colonies.[8] Also, the very use of the Greek terms *Markéllou ktísma* and *apoikía* are difficult to interpret. Canto has suggested, taking into account Casevitz's work,[9] that Strabo, like other Greek authors of Roman times, used this word not to refer to the founder-hero of a Greek colony, as Greek writers did many centuries before, but to a 'new founder' or 'benefactor' of the town. If this was the case, the expression must be then understood in the context of a profound transformation of a town where the first Roman settlement may have taken place some years before.[10] In this respect, the role of Marcellus could be compared to that of Scipio's in *Tarraco*, which Pliny, describing the Republican origins of the town, refers to as *Scipionum opus*.[11] Strabo may have used the word *apoikía* not in the administrative sense of the colonial foundations of Caesar and Augustus, something inconceivable in the mid 2nd c. BCE, but to allude to a contingent of immigrants, an alternative meaning of the concept more in tune with the migratory currents from the Italian Peninsula in the late Republic[12] as Bispham has pointed out, what in the early 2nd c. BCE counted as a colony, such as a small garrison.[13] Recently, García (2002, 268; 2009, 385) has proposed a different reading of Strabo, that the reference to the *apoikía* must be related to the second phase of the town founded as a *colonia civium Romanorum* by Caesar and not with the Latin colony of Marcellus. According to this interpretation, *Corduba* was the first Roman colony founded by the Romans in southern Iberia and, therefore, no contradiction is to be found in considering *Cartago Iunonia* as the first Roman colony established outside Italy (123 BCE) and in asserting that the foundation of Latin colonies such as *Italica* and *Carteia* were earlier than that of *Corduba*.

Leaving aside the problematic translation of the word *apoikía* in modern texts, and the uncertain definition of the legal status of the first settlement (to be discussed briefly later), it is usually admitted that *Corduba* may have enjoyed the status of Latin colony from the very beginning and probably accommodated a *conventus civium Romanorum*.[14] In any case, Strabo describes the town as being inhabited from the start by individuals selected from the local and Roman communities.[15] This is a characteristic that many Roman towns of southern Iberia may have had in common, even in those colonies founded *ex nihilo* in the areas surrounding native settlements, although this fact is not commonly acknowledged by modern scholars.[16] In the case of *Corduba*, the local elite must have originated from the native settlement of Colina de los Quemados, which prompted a "change of domicile" and the creation of a new town by adding population from neighbouring settlements, almost in the fashion of the Greek synoecism.[17] It must also be borne in mind that, according to the use of the term *Romaioi* by Hellenistic authors,

the Roman population settled in *Corduba* must have been quite heterogeneous, including not only Roman citizens, but also mostly Italics and probably also the descendants of Roman soldiers and native women (*hybridae*).[18] In fact, as Rodríguez Neila has pointed out, in *Hispania Ulterior* Italic *nomina* are predominant over Roman names, which might be related to the settling of Italic *socii*, who served as *auxilia* in the Roman army, in important towns like *Tarraco*, *Emporiae*, *Carteia*, *Castulo* or *Corduba* itself.[19]

Although speculation on the subject was common from the sixteenth century on, the exact location of the pre-Roman settlement of *Corduba* remained unknown until the 1960s, when excavations took place for the first time on the Colina de los Quemados (present day Parque Cruz Conde)[20] (Fig. 4.1). The latest archaeological investigations by Murillo have been crucial for demonstrating that the site had been occupied from the Copper Age to the end of the 2nd c. BCE and probably even the beginning of the 1st c. BCE.[21] The data recovered showed for the first time that the 'Turdetanian' *oppidum* had not been abandoned immediately after the foundation of the Roman settlement, as had been earlier thought. By the eighth century BCE the native *oppidum* of *Corduba* had become one of the most important towns on the Guadalquivir River, covering *c*. 50 hectares, according to some possibly optimistic estimates.[22] There seem to be no evident breaks in the archaeological record, as is shown by the continuity of some structures and the typology of pottery sherds, up to the end of the settlement during the late Iron Age.[23] However, a certain lack of definition is characteristic of the site's 2nd century BCE layers, leaving open the question of the magnitude of the impact of the new Roman settlement founded at that time next to Colina de los Quemados.

The uncertainty about the first stages of Roman *Corduba* is also important. Even though we are still lacking materials that can be unequivocally linked to the Roman army in the first phase of the site, the idea that the Roman town may have had its origins in the *cannabae* of a Roman camp is not new. The involvement of the army in the origins of Roman *Corduba* has been claimed a number of times,[24] although not all the researchers agree with this idea.[25]

Some of the earliest Roman towns of *Hispania*, such as *Emporiae*[26] and *Tarraco*,[27] are believed to have originated from or have been the result of the growth of military camps set up next to pre-existing settlements;[28] others were founded, according to the ancient sources, to settle soldiers that had been

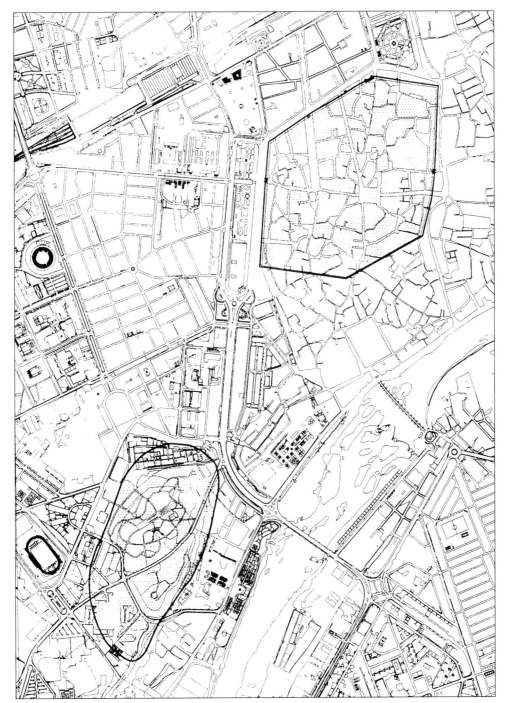

Figure 4.1. Map of Corduba in the late Republic. On the left, the native oppidum located in Colina de los Quemados (Parque Cruz Conde), on the right the Roman town founded by Marcellus. Late 3rd c. BCE–2nd c. BCE (Carrillo et al. 1999, fig. 1).

involved in the early years of the wars in the Iberian Peninsula, as is the case of *Italica*[29] or *Valentia*.[30] In support of the hypothesis of the existence of a *castellum* or *praesidium* opposite the native town, right after the beginning of the Roman conquest of the Iberian Peninsula, the following evidence is usually enumerated: the mention by several sources of *Corduba* as a place of sojourn for the troops in

the early stages of the war,[31] some of the geostrategic characteristics of the colony (control over the crossing of the Guadalquivir and the harbour to ship minerals from the neighbouring mountain ranges and its location at a key communications junction),[32] the disproportionate size of the Republican town (perhaps an indication of its use as a place to station the troops), and pottery finds that can be dated to between the end of the 3rd c. BCE and the first quarter of the 2nd c. BCE.[33]

The earliest archaeological contexts found so far in the north of the Roman town, which include house walls, local pottery and Campanian and Dressel 1 amphorae, can be dated to the second quarter of the 2nd c. BCE. At least in this part of the colony, the first inhabitants of Roman *Corduba* lived in houses built using the same construction techniques as those found in the pre-Roman *oppidum*.[34] Probably around the same date, or maybe a little earlier, the impressive town walls were built. They were two metres thick with a six-metre *agger*, a 15–metre deep fosse and several towers.[35]

The absence of levels from the first half of the 2nd c. BCE in the early Roman towns of Hispania can be regarded almost as a common pattern. In *Tarraco*, the town walls of the first phase of the upper enclosure of the Roman *castrum* have been dated to between the end of the 3rd c. BCE and the beginning of the 2nd c. BCE, although contemporary structures inside the enclosure are still missing. However, materials from this and earlier dates have been recorded in the native *oppidum*, located next to the Roman military base set up by Scipio in 218 BCE in the lower town.[36] Another good example from Republican times is *Valentia*. Having been founded in 138 BCE after the settlement of veterans from the wars of conquest in an uninhabited spot, in the first stage the town bore a close resemblance to a Roman camp, including tents and wooden structures. Probably only some months later, these dwellings were replaced by new houses built with masonry foundations and brick walls, although solid structures only began to appear in the course of the late 2nd c. BCE.[37]

The verification of the first founding of *Corduba* in the early 2nd c. BCE brings us back to the problem of studying the legal status of the town and its inhabitants and the early stages of the Roman colonisation using the written sources of the early Empire, such as Strabo or Pliny, as our main interpretative tools. This question goes far beyond the specific example of *Corduba* and applies to the first Roman settlements of the earlier provinces, at a stage when legal formulas of colonization implemented so far in the Italian Peninsula and the Cisalpin Gaul, such as the Latin colony, were probably tested for the first time after the Second Punic War in the new conquered land, as the ancient sources show for the case of *Carteia*.[38] The very meaning of the concept of 'colony' was the subject of antiquarian debate among different writers in the Gracchan period and in the 1st century BCE, after the modification of the former status of different settlements in the Italian Peninsula as a consequence of the *leges Iulia* and *Pompeia*.[39] The nature and purpose of *coloniae* seem to have been more blurred than the clear-cut legal categories used by modern scholars today. Bispham has showed how the juridical boundaries between colonies and other types of settlements, and between Roman and Latin colonies, usually established in the archaeological literature since Salmon,[40] may not adequately describe the colonial situation prior to the late 2nd c. BCE.[41] How, for example, did the 'citizens' of colonies established before the foundation of the first Roman colony outside Italy (Carthage, in 123 BCE), perceive themselves and how were they perceived by others? The conundrum, in the case of *Corduba*, as we have seen, has been solved by stating that the Roman town was founded first as Latin colony in the early 2nd c. BCE[42] and remained as such probably up to the time of Caesar or Augustus, when, after being razed to the ground for supporting Pompey's side in the civil wars,[43] the city named *Corduba*, according to the legends of the coins,[44] was reborn as a *colonia civium Romanorum* with a new name: *Colonia Patricia*. Perhaps the double *tribus* traced in the epigraphic record of the colony (*Sergia* and *Galeria*) is the testimony of two different *deductiones*, the first taking place during the time of Caesar and the second performed by Augustus with veterans from the Spanish wars.[45] A new series of coins showing the legionary eagle and two standards and, for the first time, a *completely* Roman name (*Colonia Patricia*), is usually claimed as evidence of the settlement of retired soldiers.[46] Thus, *Corduba* could be considered as a colony that was founded twice, first probably as a *colonia Latina* and later as a *colonia civium Romanorum*,[47] showing at the same time the extent to which it is important to make a distinction between the material reality of the ancient towns, the *actual* origins of a given Roman settlement, and its legal status.

The image of a town: the first one hundred years of the colony

In the following section we will approach the question of how the successive changes in the legal status of *Corduba* influenced its town planning and the settlement of a heterogeneous population group in the *colonia*. We will attempt to ascertain whether there is a direct relationship between the creation of a colony and the 'monumentalization' of civic spaces,[48] or if those phenomena could be better interpreted, in the case of *Colonia Patricia*, within the framework of wider a process that affected different regions during the transition between the Republic and the Empire.

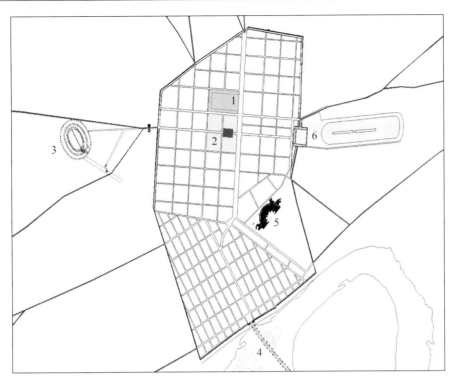

Figure 4.2. Map of Colonia Patricia in the early Empire. 1. Forum coloniae, 2. Forum adiectum, 3. Amphitheatre, 4. Bridge over the Gualquivir river, 5. Theatre, 6. Forum provinciae and circus (Courtesy of J. F. Murillo, Gerencia Municipal de Urbanismo of Córdoba).

Finally, we will take into account, in this context, the dialogue established between the expression of collective identity symbolized in civic spaces by public buildings or state symbols and the self-representation of individuals in houses and tombs.

Leaving aside the town walls, which can be considered the most impressive element of the Republican town's urban landscape, the construction of the first monumental buildings took place several generations after the foundation of the settlement and also some decades after the consolidation of *Corduba* as capital of the *provincia Ulterior* (197 BCE), probably during the transition from the 2nd to the 1st c. BCE. The existence of an early forum, which could have been in use during the first phase of the town, or at least from the middle of the 2nd c. BCE, judging from recent excavations,[49] is also attested by ancient sources at least from 112 BCE.[50] Around the transition between the 2nd and the 1st centuries BCE, a phase of intensive restructuring of the urban fabric of various Roman towns in southern *Hispania*,[51] new building techniques (walls built of ashlars covered with stucco, *tegulae* and *opus signinum*) are attested for the first time,[52] together with the construction of a new public building associated with an open space in the south end of *Corduba* (Section 1, Casa Carbonell),[53] probably a temple with Doric-Tuscan

capitals, similar to that found in the Republican *forum* of Ampurias.[54] The ancient writers also inform us of the existence of a *forum* with a basilica around the same period (80–70 BCE).[55]

The destruction of the town by Caesar's troops during the civil wars may have left its mark in the archaeological record, since thick deposits of ashes and debris dating from this time have been documented in some stratigraphic sequences,[56] although the basic layout of the street grid and the organisation of public and private spaces remained unaffected.

During the reign of Augustus, coinciding with a series of administrative measures that would transform *Colonia Patricia* into the capital of the *provincia Baetica* and the *conventus Cordubensis*, the town underwent a profound programme of remodelling (Fig. 4.2). The old *pomerium* was altered extending the city walls towards the south to meet the banks of the river;[57] the first stone bridge over the Guadalquivir and an aqueduct, *aqua Augusta*,[58] were built and the streets were paved with stone slabs and adorned with porticos and fountains[59]. Marble imported from Carrara-Luna was introduced at this time as a construction material in public buildings and decorative patterns in fashion in the *Urbs* were adopted in certain monuments.[60] Some of the larger civic projects date also from this time. The largest

theatre in *Hispania* (Fig. 4.3), based on the model of
the theatre of *Marcellus* in Rome, was probably built
before 5 BCE,[61] and the old Republican *forum* was
remodelled to meet width-length ratio recommended
by *Vitruvius*. This space was probably decorated with
the addition of a large temple and a new arch over the
entrance to the square. Soon after, a new *forum* was
annexed (*forum novum* or *adiectum*),[62] although it
was not completed until the Julio-Claudian dynasty.[63]
The design of this new space was inspired by the
forum Augusti in Rome[64] and included a temple *c.*
30 m high, similar to the one consecrated to *Mars
Ultor* in the capital of the Empire, with columns of
1.59 m in diameter, a group of sculptures with a
colossal representation of Aeneas or, according to
Spannagel,[65] Romulus (Fig. 4.4), as well as several
structures with marble facing, in stark contrast to the
stucco or terracotta decoration of the late-Republican
buildings.

Even more ambitious projects were undertaken
during the Julio-Claudian dynasty. The largest
amphitheatre in *Hispania* known to us so far, with
a capacity of 30,000 spectators, was built outside
the walls, on the western side of the town.[66] On the
eastern flank, an enormous structure of three terraces,
with a temple and an altar surrounded by a porticoed
square at the top and a circus at the bottom, created
a new monumental façade for those who approached
the colony from that end.[67] Some scholars believe
that this space, completed during the Flavian age,
should be identified as a provincial forum, where the
cult to the Imperial family for the whole of Baetica
province would have been located.[68] In addition to
these large-scale interventions in the town planning
of the colony, it must be remembered that the largest
number of sculptures erected to honour the acts of
evergetism of distinguished citizens also belong to
the Julio-Claudian period,[69] probably impacting an
urban landscape that only changed drastically two
hundred years after the establishment of the first
Roman colony in *Corduba*, setting the town within a
Mediterranean pattern of transformations undergone
by various towns in the Empire approximately at the
same time, although on different scales.[70]

The house and the tomb: representing family and individuals

The first inhabitants of 'Roman Cordoba' are as
difficult to trace in the archaeological record as the first
public monuments and town planning of the colony.
Despite all the archaeological research conducted in
the city in recent decades, it has been impossible to
find evidence of the pre-Roman necropoleis. However,

a few years ago Murillo published a summary of the
materials found in a cremation tomb that belonged to
a necropolis in use, in his opinion, between the 7th
and the 2nd c. BCE and located in the eastern part
of Parque Cruz Conde.[71] According to him, a number
of tombs from this cemetery were plundered in the
early 1990s and the artefacts were dispersed in several
private collections. He announced in this article that
he was conducting a study of the materials from the
site, of which the data on this tomb, consisting of a
painted funerary urn, a bowl and a *lagynos*,[72] were an
advance (Fig. 4.5). This humble burial is of enormous
relevance: firstly, because pre-Roman necropoleis
are few in the area identified by archaeologists as
Turdetania, known from the ancient texts and also
because the possible causes of this absence in the
archaeological record of Andalusia have become the
subject of a vehement debate among scholars;[73] and
secondly, because it is the oldest record of funerary
practices in Cordoba known to date and it documents
roughly the time of the first Roman foundation next to
the native settlement. Moreover, the finds published
to date show that at least some of the Republican
forefathers of the subsequent Roman colony made use
of a characteristic painted local urn as a receptacle
for their ashes and covered them with a drinking
bowl, following a standard funerary ritual in the
Mediterranean areas of pre-Roman Iberia. *Corduba*
was, in this respect no exception, since this type of
burial and funerary receptacle were still in use in
Colonia Patricia and other Roman towns in southern
Iberia well into the years of the early Empire.[74]

The Republican phase houses are also barely
known, although it is possible to confirm that
thirty or forty years after the founding of the first
settlement, by the mid 2nd c. BCE, most of them
were still made of rubble bases and mud walls, a
construction technique also used, incidentally, in
the ancient and contemporary native settlement.[75]
The first tombs we know of in the Roman town are
even later and have been dated to almost a century
after the first Roman settlement, between the end of
the 2nd c. BCE and the beginning of the 1st c. BCE.
Precisely at that time a change in private architecture
was introduced and for the first time houses with an
atrium and perhaps a peristyle were built with ashlar
masonry and *tegulae* roofs. These houses also had
stucco walls and *signinum* floors (Fig. 4.6).[76] These
changes coincide with the progressive abandonment
of the native town of Colina de los Quemados, where
the most recent evidence belongs to the beginning
of the 1st c. BCE.

It is almost two hundred years after the establishment
of the first Roman *apoikía* in *Corduba* that some

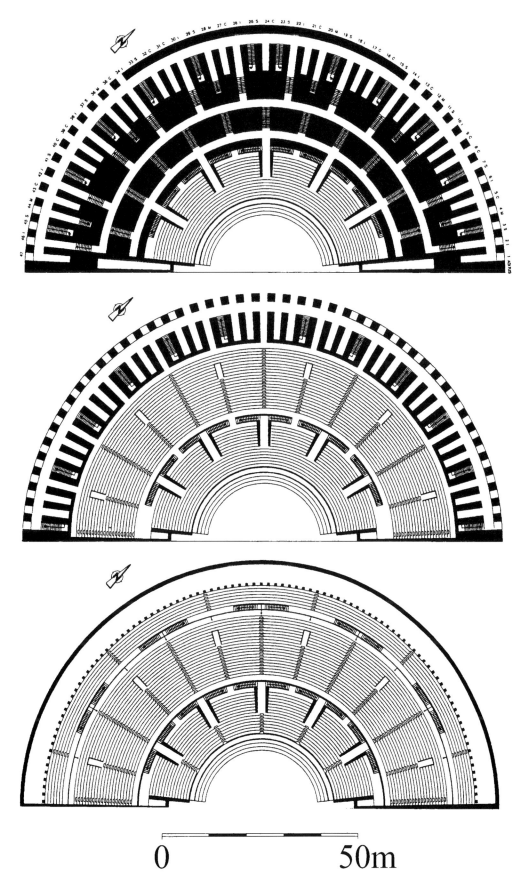

Figure 4.3. Plan of the different levels of the Roman theatre of Colonia Patricia (After Ventura 2002, figs 5, 6 and 7).

important changes can be seen in the funerary contexts of the town. With the location of monuments at this time along the roads leading out of the town from different gates in the walls, the cemeteries of *Colonia Patricia* resembled the funerary areas of other Roman towns on the Italian and the Iberian peninsulas. The very concept of displaying the tombs in this way implies a new notion of the funerary space and what was then thought of as an appropriate place for ancestors. Before the Roman conquest, necropoleis were usually located at some distance from the town, typically in a near hill or area that could be seen from the settlement. On the other hand, during the early years of the Empire in *Colonia Patricia* a gallery of ancestors (represented by gladiatorial gravestones, funerary enclosures with altars and statues, chamber tombs, funerary aediculae and monuments decorated with reliefs) greeted passers-by as they entered or left the town.[77] Tombs were then also placed, following the Roman custom, outside the religious limits of the *pomerium*, sometimes in funerary plots measured in Roman units (*in agro pedes*, *in fronte pedes*), as can

Figure 4.4 (left). Thoracata, interpreted as a representation of Romulus or Aeneas. (Baena 2007).

Figure 4.5 (below). Pre-Roman oppidum of Corduba. Objects from a tomb found in Parque Cruz Conde (Colina de los Quemados) (after Murillo and Jiménez Salvador 2002, 186).

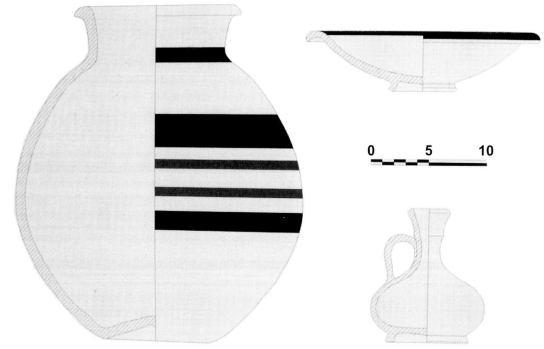

be read in inscriptions found in Cordoba.[78] We also see at the time a novel need to record the name of the deceased on epigraphs carved in stone, and in doing so, leaving behind evidence of their place within a nexus of social relationships,[79] something previously unknown in the local cemeteries of southern Iberia. In fact, one of the highest concentrations of gladiatorial epitaphs outside Rome has been unearthed in *Colonia Patricia* along a Roman road that leads to the recently discovered amphitheatre.[80] The inscriptions must have been placed not only in *stelae*, but also in the walls of funerary enclosures and other types of structures, including funerary altars and *aediculae*, similar to those that were being erected on the Italian Peninsula or in the *Urbs*.[81] At the western gate of the town were even built, in the late first c. BCE, a pair of monuments resembling the tomb of Augustus itself (Fig. 4.7).[82] These new cemeteries, reminiscent of their Roman counterparts, can only be fully understood when analysed in conjunction with the coexistence of alternative ways of honouring the dead in *Colonia Patricia*.[83] Fancy memorials and gladiators' epitaphs were intermingled in some funerary spaces with tombs in which the ashes of the dead were kept in painted funerary pots very similar to those used for the same purpose in the region for four hundred years before Augustus[84] (Fig. 4.8). At the beginning of the 1st century CE a drinking bowl was used to seal the top of such containers, as was also customary in pre-Roman necropoleis. However, it is very important to bear in mind that this sort of pottery, which has only been found in small quantities in the contemporary town, was not an exact copy of the Iberian types, but Roman ware freely inspired in the linear painted decorations and the shape of ancient local urns to confer on these receptacles a 'traditional' appearance. The comparison of different burial areas in the same town is relevant in this respect. Local pottery predominates in some funerary areas of Roman *Corduba*, such as Camino Viejo de Almodóvar, while imports such as *sigillata* seem to have been virtually absent in the early years of the Empire.[85] In other necropoleis in the town, such as La Constancia, the lower percentage of local pottery found during excavations masks the fact that, although traditional ware is not abundant, its presence and function are significant, as the painted local ware usually corresponds, precisely, to the funerary urn.[86]

With regard to funerary spaces, the founding of a Roman colony in *Colonia Patricia* meant not only the reframing of the Italic material culture in the provinces, but also the development of ways particular to the region of expressing a link with local pasts. In the new cemeteries of the colony, which were divided into Roman funerary plots

Figure 4.6. Roman Corduba. Domus found under the ancient palace Castejón (Photo A. Cánovas).

and located along the roadsides during the 1st c. CE, sometimes no memorials of the Roman type were to be found, only the traditional painted urns accompanied by some grave goods, as well as simple inhumations or even funerary chambers similar to the Punic *hypogea* from North Africa (Fig. 4.9). In fact, some architectural and ritual aspects of these underground funerary chambers are reminiscent of the Punic necropoleis of southern Iberia, including that of Villaricos (Almería), where this type of tomb was in use between the 6th/5th c. BCE and the early Empire,[87] or that of Carmona (Seville). The Carmona funerary chambers (dated to the 1st and 2nd c. CE), as well as three monumental tombs found in Cordoba and some monuments from Punic necropoleis,[88] had in common the presence of an entrance ritually blocked with ashlars that were only removed to bury a new body. This feature would have made it difficult to enter the tomb during the mandatory visit to the dead that was part of Roman festivities such as *lemuria* or *parentalia*. Instead, libations were probably poured through the ritual cavities found in some of the Carmona and *Corduba* chambers.

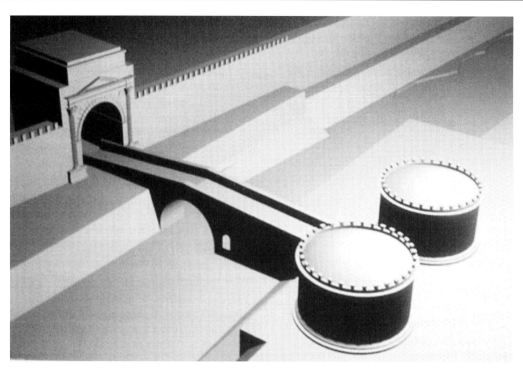

Figure 4.7. Colonia Patricia, western necropolis next to one of the monumental gates of the city. Virtual model of the mausolea found on Paseo de la Victoria (Murillo et al. 2002, fig. 20).

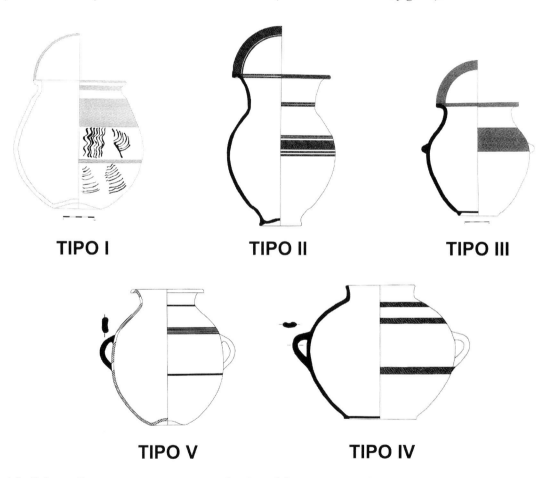

Figure 4.8. Colonia Patricia, western necropolis. Local funerary urns found in Camino Viejo de Almodovar, according to the typology of García Matamala (Modified from García Matamala 2002, figs 2, 4, 6, 7 and 9. No scale in the original figures).

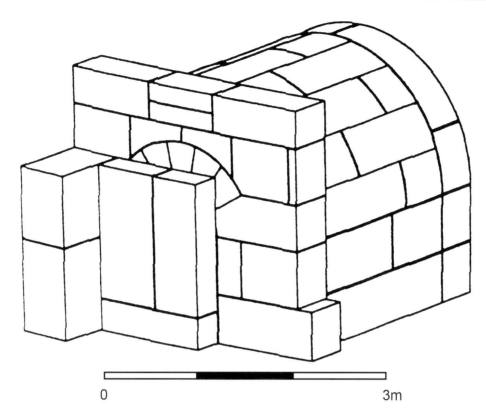

0   3m

Figure 4.9. Colonia Patricia. Northern necropolis. Chamber tomb found in Bodega St. (after Vaquerizo, 2002b, fig. 17).

Thus, the most important changes in funerary commemorations took place during the time of Augustus, approximately at the same time as the second foundation of the town. However, it is very important to state that this transformation happened simultaneously in other settlements in the province, where we find funerary monuments that 'resemble' their Roman counterparts, regardless of their legal status. It was precisely at this time that Rome itself underwent a transformation in the ways of remembering the dead through monumental architecture.[89] In the context of the new monuments that were erected in the forum and along the roadsides, the existence of a dialogue between different ways of commemorating family ancestors in the tombs and the images of 'collective' Rome forefathers depicted in public spaces is especially meaningful.[90]

From *Corduba* to *Colonia Patricia*

According to a frequently quoted passage by Aulus Gellius (*NA* 16, 13, 9.), the Roman colonies in the Empire were "*quasi efigies parvae simulacraque*", a reflection, almost a 'double' (a small copy), of the *Urbs* itself. *Corduba* could thus be seen as a provincial mirror, something that 'resembles', but

cannot be compared with the greatness of the city of Rome. As archaeologists and historians interested in the so-called 'Romanization' process, we have searched carefully for signs of this desire to create small, although imperfect, 'Romes' in the provincial colonies and other towns. However, the statement should be placed in the administrative, legal[91] and certainly propagandistic context of Hadrianic times, where it belongs.[92] According to Zanker, the slow pace of urban development in Rome and its particular layout meant that the *Urbs* was a difficult model to imitate in specific ways. The imitation of the outward appearance of Rome was limited to specific urban political structures and buildings, such as the *forum* (including a *comitium* and a *curia*), the basilica or the baths. However, Zanker argues that "'Romanization' can also be understood as something abstract and idealized, that is, the notion of how a Roman imagined the ideal city (or certain elements of this ideal city) ought to look... ."[93] This could explain why colonies abroad did not look like Rome, but did look like each other, because of the presence of a *cardo* and a *decumanus* that intersected in a central public square and certain public buildings.[94] To what extent these provincial towns tell us more about an evolving provincial idea of the Roman town than about a static and unitary Roman idea of a city is open to further exploration.

It is certainly interesting to note that the best examples of the aforementioned emulation phenomenon took place in political spaces that were particularly useful for Imperial propaganda, such as theatres or fora. Caryatids and *clipei* decorated with the head of Zeus-Ammon and Medusa, similar to those placed in the forum of Augustus in Rome, have been unearthed in the three provincial capitals of *Hispania*: *Corduba*,[95] *Tarraco*[96] and *Emerita Augusta*.[97] Perhaps even more important for building of a collective identity through the setting of images in the forum was the placement of sculptures closely linked to the 'ancestors' of the Imperial family and the Roman people, including the kings of Alba Longa or Aeneas with Ascanius.[98] This attempt to mimic the metropolis, which can be seen particularly in certain urban spaces or in buildings often related to the Imperial cult, such as theatres, can be equated to the discourse spread by the literary sources during the reign of Augustus.[99] Both can be considered as parallel elite discourses taking place during a significant phase of intensive change that would turn the conquered land into provinces and Rome into the capital of an Empire. It is quite probable that some kind of nexus existed at this time between the ability to read Latin texts and the capacity to 'read' or interpret the symbols displayed in the forum and the building of a Roman identity in the colonies.

The old *Corduba*, the defeated town that had supported Pompey during the civil war and had been razed to the ground by Cesar, was reborn as *Colonia Patricia*. The adjective '*Patricia*' added to the new name given to the city after its refoundation has been interpreted in different ways. Traditionally a connection with a single famous ancestor, Caesar, of patrician origins, as founder or *deductor*, has been made by modern scholars.[100] However, it is certainly interesting to verify the presence in some colonies of southern Iberia of names that could be loosely linked to alleged Roman/Italic forefathers or founders.[101] Apart from *Colonia Patricia*, the examples of *Iulia Romula Hispalis* (a reference to Romulus), *Iulia Genetiva Urbanorum* (a name that links the town to the Urbs) or *Italica* (founded according to the ancient sources by retired allied Italic troops after the Punic wars) could be cases in point.

Colonia Patricia became a *colonia civium Romanorum* not by chance during the implementation of the ambitious colonization programme carried out by Caesar and Augustus, at a time when most of the colonies were promoted or founded in Baetica and built over or next to pre-existing local towns (Fig.

4.10).[102] Pliny mentions nine:[103] *Colonia Patricia/ Corduba, Colonia Romula Hispal, Hasta Regia, Asido Caesarina, Augusta Fima Astigi, Augusta Gemella Tucci, Ituci Virtus Iulia, Ucubi Clairtas Iulia* and *Iulia Genitiva Urbanorum Urso*. According to some scholars, another four towns in southern Iberia may be added to the list: *Colonia Iulia Gemella Acci*,[104] *Colonia Salariense, Italica*[105] and *Colonia Iliturgitana*,[106] although the legal status of the last two is particularly problematic. Some of these towns acquired their new status during Caesar's reign only as titular colonies, meaning that even though they may already have accommodated a *conventus civium Romanorum*, there was no real *deductio* of citizens, which has obvious implications for our analysis of the composition of the town's population; it was more common in Augustan foundations to settle new citizens, frequently veterans from the army. The first foundation of *Corduba* in the early 2nd c. BCE must, in any case, be placed within a context in which the very process of creating fixed colonial categories in the provinces was taking place. While the 'second' foundation, in the second half of the 1st c. BCE, coincides with an extensive political programme of colonization in southern Hispania and the creation of a monumental setting in many towns, regardless of the date they were founded or their legal status. It might be possible to find here a common pattern with the other provincial capitals in Hispania, such as Tarraco, which was also founded during the Republic (although its legal status in this early phase remains hard to define as well) and was probably granted later the title of Roman colony during the time of Caesar (49 BCE).[107] *Emerita Augusta*, appointed as the capital of the *provincia Lusitania* and as a Roman colony by Augustus, received also in 25 BCE a *deductio* of veterans from the Cantabrian wars under this Emperor.[108]

In *Corduba*, the old name of the town disappears in the official records that have come down to us, almost after the fashion of a *damnatio memoriae*.[109] However, the brand-new *Colonia Patricia*, refounded in the time of Caesar and Augustus, transforms itself into a monumental scenario, essential for Imperial propaganda in southern Hispania. *Colonia Patricia* became then the capital of the conventus and the capital of *Baetica* province, as the result of the administrative reforms of the first emperor. *Colonia Patricia*, the seat of the governor, received a *deductio* probably of veterans from the Cantabrian wars. To pay these soldiers, Augustus minted in *Colonia Patricia* a series of coins with a particular connection to the Imperial propaganda and the honours granted by the senate to Octavius. Around this time, *Colonia Patricia* became a particularly

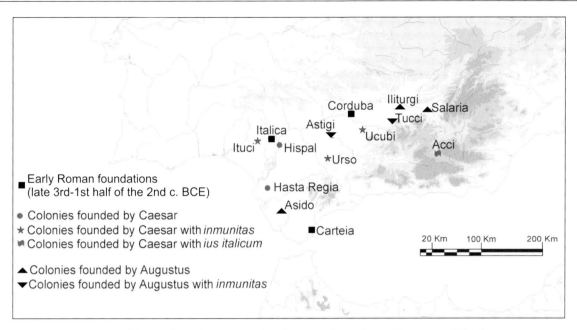

Figure 4.10. Roman Republican foundations and colonies of southern Hispania (Blank map courtesy of F. Quesada and J. de Hoz. Research projects PB97/0057 and Hesperia*).*

attractive place for the elites of the region, who were eager to establish connections with members of the Imperial administration or to be promoted to one of the privileged *ordines*.[110] Leaving aside *Tarraco*, *Corduba* stands out in our records as having produced the highest number of *equites* from Hispania. From *Italica* and *Corduba* come too the largest number of Baetican senators known to us. The fact that *Corduba* at the time offered a wide range of opportunities may also explain the presence of other population groups. According to a recent survey, *Corduba* was, at least qualitatively, the Baetican town that received the largest number of *alieni* and immigrants from Hispania during the early Empire.[111] It is interesting to turn now to the metaphor of Rome as a cosmopolis advanced by Edwards and Woolf. During the early Empire, the trope of the *Urbs* as a cosmopolis or the epitome of the civilized world appears in the texts of some authors in parallel to the presence in Rome of works of art or spoils from different conquered regions. The city absorbed the world by placing in a new context objects and images dragged from distant lands now under the Roman control but, at the same time and to a certain extent, was itself taken in by the world, as citizens of different origins created small colonies in the capital of the Empire.[112] Meanwhile, in the provinces, different representations of the ideal Roman town were implemented, especially in monumental settings, but also new interpretations of local identities in contrast to, or in dialogue with, an image of Rome that was perceived diversely.

The metaphor of provincial colonies as a multiple mirror of the magnificence of Rome can be qualified through the study of private spaces such as cemeteries. The Roman town was a mixture, as Zanker[113] has reminded us, of both state planning and a long term process carried out by its inhabitants, which is especially true in Baetica, where most Roman towns were 'founded' above of or next to pre-Roman settlements. The reflection of the image of Rome is thus much more complex and interesting. In this new scenario it is possible to see provincial capitals such as *Colonia Patricia,* the recipients of a ready-made set of symbols of the Imperial power, as cosmopolitan centres. In these towns alternative or parallel versions of the meaning of being a citizen of *Corduba* were as 'real' as those offered by the official Roman history on the expansion of its own culture all over the Mediterranean.

Acknowledgements

Some of the ideas presented in this paper have been explored in greater depth in Jiménez (2008a). We are grateful to the editors of the volume, to an anonymous referee, to Estela García (Universidad Complutense de Madrid) and Juan José R. Villarías (CSIC) for their comments on an earlier version of the text and also to all the participants in the conference "100 years of Solitude" held at St. Andrews University (12th–14th September 2007) for their feed-back. We would also like to thank Sebastián Vargas (CSIC) and

Antonio Jesús Pinto (CSIC) for their generous help during the writing of the text. Research funded by the European Social Fund (I3P-CSIC). Project HUM 2007 – 64045/HIST).

Bibliography

Almagro Gorbea, M. J. 1984. *La necrópolis de Baria*, Excavaciones Arqueológicas de España 129 (Madrid).

Amela, L. 2004. "La ceca de Córdoba en época republicana" *XII Congreso Nacional de Numismática* (Madrid), 177–93.

Arce, J. 2004. "Introducción histórica" in X. Dupré Raventós (ed.), *Las capitales provinciales de Hispania. II. Mérida. Colonia Augusta Emerita* (Roma) 7–13.

Astruc, M. 1951. *La Necrópolis de Villaricos*, Informes y Memorias 25 (Madrid).

Baena, M. D. (ed.) 2007. *Thoracata. La imagen del poder* (Córdoba).

Bandelli, G. 2002. "La colonizzazione romana della Penisola Iberica da Scipione Africano a Bruto Callaico", in G. Urso (ed.) *Hispania terris omnibus felicior. Premesse et esiti di un proceso di integrazione* (Pisa) 105–142.

Barrera J. L. de la and W. Trillmich 1996. "Eine Wiederholung der Aeneas-Gruppe vom Forum Augustum samt ihrer Inschrift in Mérida (Spanien)", *Mitteilungen des deutschen archäologischen Instituts (Abt. Röm.)* 103, 119–38.

Bendala, M. 1976. *La necrópolis romana de Carmona (Sevilla)* (Sevilla).

Bendala, M. 1981. "La etapa final de la cultura ibero-turdetana y el impacto romanizador", in *La baja época de la cultura ibérica* (Madrid) 33–48.

Bendala, M. 1990. "El plan urbanístico de Augusto en Hispania: precedentes y pautas macroterritoriales", in W. Trillmich and P. Zanker (eds), *Stadtbild und Ideologie: die Monumentalisierung hispanischer Städte zwischen Republik und Kaiserzeit*, (Madrid, 19–23 octubre de 1987) (Madrid) 25–40.

Bendala, M. 1992. "Tartessos: ¿concierto o desconcierto?", *Arqrítica* 3, 20–22.

Bendala, M. 2002. "Perduraciones y romanización en *Hispania* a la luz de la arqueología funeraria: notas para una discusión", *Archivo Español de Arqueología* 75, 137–58.

Bendala, M. 2003. "*De Iberia in Hispaniam*: el fenómeno urbano", in L. Abad (ed.), *'De Iberia in Hispaniam'. La adaptación de las sociedades ibéricas a los modelos romanos* (Alicante) 17–35.

Bendala M. and L. Roldán 1999. "El cambio tecnológico en la arquitectura hispanorromana: perduración, novedades y peculiaridades", in R. de Balbín and P. Bueno (eds), *II Congreso de Arqueología Peninsular. Tomo IV – Arqueología Romana y Medieval* (Zamora, 1996) (Alcalá de Henares) 103–15.

Bernier, J. and J. Fortea 1963. "Niveles arqueológicos del Valle del Guadalquivir", *Boletín de la Real Academia de Córdoba* 85, 199–206.

Bispham, E. 2006. "*Coloniam deducere*: how Roman was Roman colonization during the middle Republic?", in G. Bradley and J. P. Wilson (eds), *Greek and Roman colonization. Origins, ideologies and interactions* (Wales) 73–160.

Blanco, A. 1970. "Vestigios de Córdoba romana", *Habis* 1, 109–23.

Caballos, A. 1994. *Italica y los italicenses. Aproximación a su historia* (Sevilla).

Caballos, A. 2006. *El nuevo bronce de Osuna y la política colonizadora romana*, (Sevilla).

Cadiou, F. 2008. *Hibera in terra miles. Les armées romaines et la conquête de l'Hispanie sous la République (218–45 av. J.-C.)* (Madrid).

Canto, A. 1991. "*Colonia Patricia Corduba*: nuevas hipótesis sobre su fundación y nombre", *Latomus* L, 4, 846–57.

Canto, A. 1997. "Algo más sobre Marcelo, Corduba y las Colonias Romanas del año 45 a. C.", *Gerión* 15, 223–81.

Canto, A. 1999. "La *Vetus Urbs* de Itálica, quince años después. La planta hipodámica de D. Demetrio de los Ríos, con otras novedades", *Cuadernos de Prehistoria y Arqueología de la Universidad Autónoma de Madrid* 25.2, 145–191.

Carrasco, I. 2001. "Intervención arqueológica de urgencia en un solar sito en calle Góngora número 13 esquina a calle Teniente Braulio Laportilla (Córdoba)", *Anuario Arqueológico de Andalucía 1997*, III, (Sevilla) 199–208.

Carrillo, J. R. 1999. "Evolución de la arquitectura doméstica en la *Colonia Patricia Corduba*" in F. R. García Verdugo and F. Acosta (eds), *Córdoba en la Historia: La Construcción de la Urbe*, Actas del Congreso, (Córdoba, 20–23 de Mayo 1997) (Córdoba), 75–86.

Carrillo, J. R., R. Hidalgo, J. F. Murillo and A. Ventura 1999. "Córdoba. De los orígenes a la Antigüedad Tardía", in F. R. García Verdugo and F. Acosta (eds), *Córdoba en la Historia: La Construcción de la Urbe*, Actas del Congreso, (Córdoba, 20–23 de Mayo 1997) (Córdoba) 37–74.

Casevitz, M. 1985. *Le vocabulaire de la colonisation en grec ancien. Étude lexicologique: les familles de κτίζω et de οἰκέω-οἰκίζω* (Paris).

Castillo, C. 1974. "Hispanos y romanos en Córdoba", *Hispania Antiqua* IV, 191–7.

Chaves Tristán, F. 1977. *La Córdoba hispano-romana y sus monedas* (Sevilla).

Conde, M. J. 1998. "Estado actual de la investigación sobre la cerámica ibérica pintada de época plena y tardía", *Revista de Estudios Ibéricos* 3, 299–335.

Edwards, C. and G. Woolf 2003. "Cosmopolis: Rome as a world city", in C. Edwards and G. Woolf (eds), *Rome the Cosmopolis* (Cambridge) 1–20.

Escacena, J. L. 1987. "El poblamiento ibérico en el Bajo Guadalquivir", in A. Ruiz and M. Molinos (eds), *Iberos. Actas de las primeras Jornadas sobre el Mundo Ibérico* (Jaén, 1985) (Jaén) 273–98.

Escacena, J. L. 1989. "Los Turdetanos o la recuperación de la identidad perdida", *Tartessos. Arqueología Protohistórica del Bajo Guadalquivir* (Barcelona) 433–76.

Escacena, J. L. 1992. "Indicadores étnicos en la Andalucía prerromana", *Spal* 1, 321–43.

Escacena, J. L. and M. Belén 1994. "Sobre las necrópolis turdetanas", Homenaje al Profesor Presedo, P. Sáez and S. Ordóñez (eds) (Sevilla) 237–65.

Fishwick, D. 2000. "A new forum at Corduba", *Latomus* 59.1, 96–104.

Fishwick, D. 2004. *The Imperial Cult in the Latin West. Studies in the Ruler Cult of the Western Provinces of the Roman Empire. Volume III: Provincial Cult. Parte 3: The Provincial Centre; Provincial Cult* (Leiden-Boston).

Galsterer, H. 1997. "Die Stadt Italica: Status und Verwaltung" in A. Caballos and P. León (eds), *Italica MMCC. Actas de las Jornadas del 2.200 Aniversario de la Fundación de Italica (Sevilla, 8–11 noviembre 1994)* (Sevilla) 49–64.

García, E. 2002. "Observaciones jurídicas sobre la fundación de *Corduba* y la *tribus Sergia*", in S. Crespo and Á. Alonso (eds), *Scripta Antiqua in honorem Ángel Montenegro Duque et José María Blázquez Martínez* (Valladolid) 265–72.

García, E. 2009. "Reflexiones sobre la latinización de *Hispania* en época republicana", in I. Rodá, J. Andreu and J. Cabrero (eds), *Hispaniae: las provincias hispanas en el mundo romano* (Tarragona) 377–90.

García y Bellido, A. 1952. "Nuevos datos sobre la cronología final de la cerámica ibérica y sobre su expansión extrapeninsular", *Archivo Español de Arqueología* XXV, 39–45.

García-Bellido, M. P. 2006. "*Corduba* y *Colonia Patricia*: Historia de dos ciudades", in D. Vaquerizo and J. F. Murillo (eds), *El concepto de lo provincial en el mundo antiguo. Homenaje a la Prof. Pilar León*, Vol. I (Córdoba) 251–66.

García Matamala, B. 2002. "Enterramientos con urnas de tradición indígena en Corduba", in D.Vaquerizo (ed.), *Espacio y usos funerarios en el Occidente Romano* (Córdoba) 275–295.

García Matamala, B. 2002–2003. "Enterramientos de tradición indígena en Corduba", *Anales de Arqueología Cordobesa* 13–14, 251–277.

García Prósper, E. and P. Guérin 2002. "Nuevas aportaciones en torno a la necrópolis romana de la Calle Quart de Valencia (s. II a.C.–IV d.C.)", in D. Vaquerizo (ed.), *Espacio y usos funerarios en el Occidente Romano* (Córdoba) 203–215.

Garriguet, J. A. 2002. *El culto imperial en la Córdoba romana: Una aproximación arqueológica* (Córdoba).

González Román, C. 1991. "Las colonias romanas de la *Hispania* meridional en sus aspectos socio-jurídicos", in C. González Román (ed.), *La Bética en su problemática histórica* (Granada) 87–100.

González Román, C. 1998. "Ciudad y privilegio en la Bética", in M. J. Hidalgo, D. Pérez and M. J. R. Gervás (eds), *"Romanización" y "reconquista" en la Península Ibérica: nuevas perspectivas* (Salamanca) 129–40.

González Román, C. 2002. *Ciudad y privilegio en Andalucía en época romana* (Granada).

Gros, P. 2001. *L'architecture romaine: du début du IIIe siècle av. J.-C. à la fin du Haut-Empire. Vol. 2: Maisons, palais, villas et tombeaux* (Paris).

Haselberger, L. 2007. *Urbem adornare: die Stadt Rom und ihre Gestaltumwandlung unter Augustus*, Journal of Roman Archaeology, Suplementary Series 64 (Portsmouth, RI).

Hesberg, H. von. 1992. *Römische Grabbauten* (Darmstadt).

Hesberg, H. von 1996. "La decorazione architettonica di Cordova. Sulla funzione dell'ornamentazione architettonica in una città romana" in León, P. (ed.) *Colonia Patricia Corduba una reflexión arqueológica* (Sevilla) 155–74.

Hita, J. M., P. Marfil and N. Marín 1993. "Aproximación a la Corduba prerromana a través de la cerámica de barniz negro", in *I Coloquio de Historia Antigua de Andalucía* (Córdoba) 403–20.

Hidalgo, R. 1993. "Nuevos datos sobre el urbanismo de Colonia Patricia Corduba excavación arqueológica en la c/ Ramírez de las Casas-Deza 13", *Anales de Arqueología Cordobesa* 4, 91–134.

Jiménez, A. 2006. "Contextos funerarios en la transición del mundo prerromano al romano en el sur peninsular», *Anales de Arqueología Cordobesa* 17, vol. I, 67–97.

Jiménez, A. 2008a. *Imagines Hibridae. Una aproximación postcolonialista al estudio de las necrópolis de la Bética*, Anejos del Archivo Español de Arqueología 43 (Madrid).

Jiménez, A. 2008b. "A critical approach to the concept of resistance: new 'traditional' rituals and objects in funerary contexts of Roman Baetica" in Fenwick, M. Wiggins and D. Wythe (eds), *TRAC 2007: Proceedings of the Seventeenth Theoretical Roman Archaeology Conference* (London 2007) (Oxford) 15–30.

Jiménez Salvador, J. L. 2002. "Últimas novedades en relación al mundo funerario romano en el Este y Sureste de Hispania (siglos II. a.C.–IV d.C.)", in D. Vaquerizo (ed.), *Espacios y usos funerarios en el Occidente romano*, vol. 1 (Córdoba), 181–202.

Keay, S. 1997. "Early Roman Italica and the Romanisation of western Baetica", in A. Caballos and P. León (eds), *Italica MMCC. Actas de las Jornadas del 2.200 Aniversario de la Fundación de Italica (Sevilla, 8–11 noviembre 1994)* (Sevilla) 21–47.

Keay, S. 1998. "The development of towns in Early Roman Baetica", in S. Keay (ed.), *The Archaeology of Early Roman Baetica* (Portsmouth, Rhode Island) 54–83.

Knapp, R. C. 1977. *Aspects of the Roman Experience in Iberia, 206–100 B.C.* (Valladolid).

Knapp, R. C. 1983. *Roman Córdoba* (Berkeley).

Laffi, U. 2002. "La colonización romana desde el final de la guerra de Aníbal a los Gracos", in J. L. Jiménez Salvador and A. Ribera i Lacomba (eds), *Valencia y las primeras ciudades romanas de Hispania* (Valencia) 19–26.

León, P. 1999. "Itinerario de monumentalización y cambio de imagen en *Colonia Patricia* (Córdoba)", *Archivo Español de Arqueología* 72, 39–56.

León Pastor, E. 2007. *La secuencia cultural de la "Corduba" prerromana a través de sus complejos cerámicos* (Córdoba).

López, I. M. 1998. *Estatuas masculinas togadas y estatuas femeninas vestidas de colecciones cordobesas* (Córdoba).

Luzón, J. M. and D. Ruiz Mata 1973. *Las raíces de Córdoba. Estratigrafía de la Colina de los Quemados* (Córdoba).

Mar, R. (ed.) 1993. *Els monuments provincials de Tàrraco. Noves aportacions al seu coneixement*, Documents d'Arqueologia Clàssica, n. 1 (Tarragona).

Marín, M. A. 2002. "Observaciones sobre las colonias latinas en la Hispania meridional", in C. González Román and A. Padilla (eds), *Estudios sobre las ciudades de la Bética* (Granada) 277–87.

Marín, C. and A. Ribera i Lacomba 2002. "La realidad arqueológica de la fundación de Valencia: magia, basureros y cabañas", in L. Jiménez Salvador, A. Ribera and Lacomba (eds), *Valencia y las primeras ciudades romanas de Hispania* (Valencia) 287–98.

Márquez, C. 1998a. *La decoración arquitectónica de Colonia Patricia*, Córdoba.

Márquez, C. 1998b. "Acerca de la función e inserción urbanística de las plazas en *Colonia Patricia*", *Empúries* 51, 63–78.

Márquez, C. 1998c. "Modelos romanos en la arquitectura monumental de Colonia Patricia Corduba", *Archivo Español de Arqueología* 71, 113–37.

Márquez, C. 1999. "Colonia Patricia Corduba paradigma urbano de la Bética" in J. González (ed.) *Ciudades privilegiadas en el Occidente romano* (Sevilla) 351–363.

Márquez, C. 2002. "La ornamentación arquitectónica en ámbito funerario de *Colonia Patricia*", in D. Vaquerizo (ed.), *Espacios y usos funerarios en el Occidente Romano* (Córdoba) 223–46.

Márquez, C. 2004a. "Baeticae Templa", in *Simulacra Romae. Roma y las capitales provinciales del occidente europeo* (Tarragona), 109–25.

Márquez, C. 2004b. "La decoración arquitectónica en *Colonia Patricia* en el período julio-claudio", in S. Ramallo (ed.), *La decoración arquitectónica en las ciudades romanas de Occidente* (Murcia), 337–53.

Márquez, C. 2004c. "Arquitectura oficial", in X. Dupré Raventós (ed.), *Las capitales provinciales de Hispania. I. Córdoba. Colonia Patricia Corduba* (Roma) 55–62.

Márquez, C. 2005. "Córdoba romana: dos décadas de investigación arqueológica", *Mainake* 27, 33–60.

Mattingly, D. J. 2004. "Being Roman: expressing identity in a provincial setting", *Journal of Roman Archaeology* 17, 5–26.

Mattingly, D. J. 2006. *An Imperial Possession. Britain in the Roman Empire* (London).

Melchor, E. 2006. "*Corduba, caput provinciae* y foco de atracción para las élites locales de la *Hispania Ulterior Baetica*", *Gerión* 24.1, 251–79.

Morillo, A. and J. Aurrecoechea (eds) 2006. *The Roman Army in Hispania. An Archaeological Guide* (León).

Murillo, J. F. 1995. "Nuevos trabajos arqueológicos en Colina de los Quemados: el sector del Teatro de la Axerquía. (Parque Cruz Conde, Córdoba)", *Anuario Arqueológico de Andalucía 1992*, III, 188–99.

Murillo, J. F. 2004. "Topografía y evolución urbana", in X. Dupré Raventós (ed.), *Las capitales provinciales de Hispania. I. Córdoba. Colonia Patricia Corduba* (Roma) 39–54.

Murillo, J. F. and D. Vaquerizo 1996. "La Corduba prerromana", in P. León (ed.), *Colonia Patricia Corduba. Una reflexión arqueológica* (Córdoba) 37–47.

Murillo, J. F., A. Ventura, S. Carmona, J. R. Carrillo, R. Hidalgo, J. L. Jiménez, M. Moreno and D. Ruiz 2001. "El circo oriental de *Colonia Patricia*" in T. Nogales and F. J. Sánchez Palencia (eds), *El Circo en Hispania Romana (Mérida 2001)* (Madrid) 57–74.

Murillo, J. F. and J. L. Jiménez Salvador 2002. "Nuevas evidencias sobre la fundación de Corduba y su primera imagen urbana", J. L. Jiménez Salvador and A. Ribera i Lacomba (eds), *Valencia y las primeras ciudades romanas de Hispania* (Valencia) 183–93.

Murillo, J. F., J. R. Carrillo, M. Moreno, D. Ruiz and S. Vargas 2002. "Los monumentos funerarios de Puerta de Gallegos. Colonia Patricia Corduba", in D. Vaquerizo (ed.) *Espacios y usos funerarios en el Occidente Romano* (Córdoba) 247–74.

Murillo, J. F., M. Moreno, J. L. Jiménez and D. Ruiz 2003. "El templo de la c/ Claudio Marcelo (Córdoba). Aproximación al foro provincial de la Bética", *Romula* 2, 53–88.

Nogales, T. 2008. "Rómulo en el Augusteum del foro colonial emeritense". In E. La Rocca, P. León and C. Parisi Presicce (eds), *Le due patrie acquisite: studi di archeologia dedicati a Walter Trillmich*, (Roma), 301–312.

Nogales, T. and J. M. Álvarez 2006. "*Fora Augustae Emeritae*: la 'interpretatio' provincial de los patrones metropolitanos" in D. Vaquerizo and J. F. Murillo Redondo, *El concepto de lo provincial en el mundo antiguo: homenaje a la profesora Pilar León Alonso*, Vol. 1, (Córdoba) 419–50.

Olmos, R. 1994. "Algunos problemas historiográficos de cerámica e iconografía ibéricas: de los pioneros a 1950", *Revista de Estudios Ibéricos* 1, 311–34.

Olmos, R. and P. Rouillard 2004. *La vajilla ibérica en época helenística (siglos IV–III al cambio de era)* (Madrid).

Padilla, A. 2006. "La integración de las oligarquías indígenas en las elites coloniales del sur de Hispania", in A. Caballos and S. Demougin (eds), *Migrare. La formation des élites dans L'Hispanie romaine* (Bordeaux) 205–40.

Panzram, S. 2003. "Los *Flamines Provinciae* de la *Baetica*: Autorrepresentación y culto imperial" *Archivo Español de Arqueología* 76, 121–30.

Peña, A. 2007. "Reflejos del *Forum Augustum* en *Italica*". In T. Nogales and J. González (eds), *Culto Imperial: política y poder* (Roma), 323–45.

Ramallo, S. F. 1989. *Cartagena, la documentación arqueológica*, Murcia.

Remolà, J. A. 2004. "Arquitectura funeraria", X. Dupré (ed.), *Las capitales provinciales de Hispania. III. Tarragona. Colonia Iulia Vrbs Triumphalis Tarraco* (Roma) 83–95.

Ribera i Lacomba, A. 2006. "The Roman foundation of Valencia and the town in the 2nd–1st c. B.C.", in L. Abad, S. Keay and S. Ramallo (eds), *Early Roman Towns in Hispania Tarraconensis, Journal of Roman archaeology*. Supplementary series 62 (Portsmouth, Rhode Island), 75–89.

Ripollès, P. P. 1998. "Las acuñaciones cívicas romanas de la Península Ibérica", in C. Alfaro, A. Arévalo, M. Campo, F. Chaves, A. Domínguez and P. P. Ripollés, *Historia monetaria de la Hispania Antigua* (Madrid), 335–95.

Rodríguez Neila, J. F. 1976. "Consideraciones sobre el concepto de *vicus* en la *Hispania* romana. Los *vici* de Corduba", *Corduba* n. 2, vol. I, fasc. 2, 99 -118.

Rodríguez Neila, J. F. 1981. "Introducción a la 'Corduba' romana en época republicana", *Córdoba. Apuntes para su historia* (Córdoba) 107–34.

Rodríguez Neila, J. F. 1992. "Corduba", *Conquista y modos de intervención en la organización urbana y territorial, Dialoghi di Archeologia* 1–2, 177–94.

Ruiz de Arbulo, J. 2002. "La fundación de la colonia Tárraco y los estandartes de César", in J. L. Jiménez Salvador and A. Ribera i Lacomba (eds), *Valencia y las primeras ciudades romanas de Hispania* (Valencia) 137–56.

Ruiz de Arbulo, J. 2006. "*Scipionum opus* and something more: an Iberian reading of the provincial capital (2nd–1st c. B.C.)", in L. Abad, S. Keay and S. Ramallo (eds), *Early Roman Towns in Hispania Tarraconensis, Journal of Roman archaeology*. Supplementary series 62 (Portsmouth, Rhode Island), 33–43.

Ruiz Osuna, A. 2007. *El proceso de monumentalización en las áreas funerarias de Colonia Patricia Corduba (ss. I a.C.–II d.C.)* (Córdoba).

Ruiz, A. and M. Molinos 1993. *Los iberos. Análisis arqueológico de un proceso histórico* (Barcelona).

Sillières, P. 2003. "Voies romaines et contrôle de l'Hispanie à l'époque républicaine: l'exemple de l'Espagne ultérieure", in A. Morillo, F. Cadiou and D. Hourcade (eds), *Defensa y territorio en Hispania de los Escipiones a Augusto* (Salamanca) 25–40.

Spannagel, M. 1999. *Exemplaria principis: Untersuchungen zu Entstehung und Ausstattung des Augustusforums* (Heidelberg).

Stylow, A. U. 1990. "Apuntes sobre el urbanismo de la *Corduba* romana", in W. Trillmich and P. Zanker (eds), *Stadtbild und Ideologie. Die Monumentalisierung hispanischer Städte zwischen Republik und Kaiserzeit (Kolloquium in Madrid vom 19 bis 23 Oktober 1987)* (München) 259–82.

Stylow, A. U. 1996. "De Corduba a Colonia Patricia. La fundación de la Córdoba romana", in P. León (ed.), *Colonia Patricia Corduba, una reflexión arqueológica*, (Sevilla) 77–85.

Stylow, A. U., C. González Román and G. Alföldy (eds) 1995. *Corpus Inscriptionum Latinarum. Vol. 2. Inscriptiones Hispaniae Antiquae. Editio altera. Pars. 7. Conventus Cordubensis* (Berolini).

Taller Escola d'Arqueologia 1989. "El Foro Provincial de Tárraco. Un complejo arquitectónico de época flavia", *Archivo Español de Arqueología* 62, 141–91.

Torelli, M. 1988. "Aspetti ideologici della colonizzazione romana più antica", *Dialoghi di Archeologia* 3, 6.2, 65–72.

Trillmich, W. 1996. "Los tres foros de *Augusta Emerita* y el caso de *Corduba*", in P. León (ed.) *Colonia Patricia Corduba: una reflexión arqueológica* (Córdoba), 175–95.

Trillmich, W. 1998. "Las ciudades hispanorromanas: reflejos de la metrópoli" in *Hispania: el legado de Roma, en el año de Trajano* (Zaragoza) 163–74.

Van Dommelen, P. 2001a. "Cultural imaginings. Punic tradition and local identity in Roman Republican Sardinia", in S. Keay and N. Terrenato (eds), *Italy and the West. Comparative Issues in Romanization* (Oxford) 68–84.

Van Dommelen, P. 2001b. "Ambiguous Matters: Colonialism and Local Identities in Punic Sardinia", in C. L. Lyons and J. K. Papadopoulos (eds), *The Archaeology of Colonialism* (Los Angeles) 121–47.

Van Dommelen, P. 2007. "Beyond resistance: Roman power and local traditions in Punic Sardinia", in P. van Dommelen and N. Terrenato (eds) *Articulating local cultures. Power and identity under the expanding Roman Republic*, Journal of Roman Archaeology, Supplementary Series. (Portsmouth, Rhode Island) 55–70.

Vaquerizo, D. (ed.) 1996. *Córdoba en tiempos de Séneca* (Córdoba).

Vaquerizo, D. 2001. "Formas arquitectónicas funerarias de carácter monumental en *Colonia Patricia Corduba*", *Archivo Español de Arqueología* 74, 131–60.

Vaquerizo, D. (ed.) 2002a *Espacios y usos funerarios en el Occidente romano* (Córdoba).

Vaquerizo, D. 2002b. "Espacios y usos funerarios en *Corduba*", in D. Vaquerizo (ed.), *Espacios y usos funerarios en el Occidente Romano* (Córdoba) 143–200.

Vaquerizo, D. 2002c. "Recintos y acotados funerarios en Colonia Patricia Corduba", *Madrider Mitteilungen* 43, 168–206.

Vaquerizo, D. (ed.) 2003. *Guía arqueológica de Córdoba* (Córdoba).

Vaquerizo, D. 2004. "Arquitectura doméstica y funeraria", X. Dupré Raventós (ed.), *Las capitales provinciales de Hispania. I. Córdoba. Colonia Patricia Corduba*, Roma, 81–94.

Vaquerizo, D. 2005. "Arqueología de la *Corduba* republicana", in E. Melchor, J. Mellado and J. F. Rodríguez Neila (eds), *Julio César y* Corduba*: tiempo y espacio en la campaña de Munda (49–45 a.C.)* (Córdoba) 165–205.

Vaquerizo, D. 2006. "Corduba: una ciudad puente" in *Civilización: un viaje a las ciudades de la España antigua: catálogo de la exposición* (Alcalá de Henares) 123–41.

Vaquerizo, D. 2008. "Topografía y usos funerarios en la capital de *Baetica*" *Archeologia Classica* LIX, 63–111.

Vaquerizo, D. and S. Sánchez 2008. "Entre lo público y lo privado. *Indicatio pedaturae* en la epigrafía funeraria hispana", *Archivo Español de Arqueología* 81, 101–31.

Vargas, S. 2002. "El conjunto funerario de La Constancia (Córdoba). Ajuares y cronología", in D. Vaquerizo (ed.), *Espacio y usos funerarios en el Occidente Romano* (Córdoba) 297–310.

Ventura Martínez, J. J. 1992. "Cerámica campaniense de la Corduba romana", *Anales de Arqueología Cordobesa* 3, 137–70.

Ventura Martínez, J. J. 1996. "El origen de la Córdoba romana a través del estudio de las cerámicas de barniz negro", in P. León (ed), *Colonia Patricia Corduba, una reflexión arqueológica* (Sevilla) 49–62.

Ventura Villanueva, A. 1993. *El abastecimiento de agua a la Córdoba romana I: El acueducto de Valdepuentes* (Córdoba).

Ventura Villanueva, A. 1996. *El abastecimiento de agua a la Córdoba romana II: Acueductos, ciclo de distribución y urbanismo* (Córdoba).

Ventura Villanueva, A. 1999. "El teatro en el contexto urbano de Colonia Patricia (Córdoba). Ambiente epigráfico, evergetas

y culto imperial", *Archivo Español de Arqueología* 72, 57–72.

Ventura Villanueva, A. 2002. "El teatro romano de Córdoba: caracterización arquitectónica", in A. Ventura, C. Márquez, A. Monterroso and M. A. Carmona (eds), *El teatro romano de Córdoba* (Córdoba), 107–116.

Ventura Villanueva, A. 2003. "Los edificios administrativos de la Córdoba romana: problemas de localización e identificación", *Romula* 2, 183–96.

Ventura Villanueva, A. 2007a. "Bauliche und literarische Inszenierung: die Eliten der Colonia Patricia und das Jahr 5 v. Chr." in S. Panzram (Hg.), *Städte im Wandel. Bauliche Inszenierung und literarische Stilisierung lokaler Eliten auf der Iberischen Halbinsel* (Münster) 87–126.

Ventura Villanueva, A. 2007b. "Reflexiones sobre la arquitectura y advocación del templo de la calle Morería en el *Forum Adiectum* de *Colonia Patricia Corduba*" in T. Nogales and J. González (eds), *Culto imperial: política y poder. Actas del Congreso Internacional* (Roma) 215–238.

Ventura Villanueva, A. 2008. "Una lastra 'campana' en Córdoba: *Asinius Pollio*, el *auguraculum* y la *deductio* de *Colonia Patricia*", M. P. García-Bellido, A. Mostalac and A. Jiménez (eds), *Del imperium de Pompeyo a la auctoritas de Augusto*, Anejos del Archivo Español de Arqueología XLVII (Madrid) 85–105.

Ventura Villanueva, A., P. León and C. Márquez 1998. "Roman Cordoba in the light of recent archaeological research", in S. Keay (ed.), *The Archaeology of Early Roman Baetica*, JRA Supp. Series 29 (Portsmouth, Rhode Island) 87–107.

Ventura Villanueva, A., C. Márquez, A. Monterroso and M. A. Carmona (eds) 2002. *El teatro romano de Córdoba* (Catálogo de la exposición) (Córdoba).

Ventura Villanueva, A. and C. Márquez 2005. "Corduba tras las Guerras Civiles" in J. F. Rodríguez, E. Melchor and J. Mellado (eds) *Julio César y Corduba: tiempo y espacio en la campaña de Munda (49–45 A.C.)* (Córdoba) 431–68.

Wallace-Hadrill, A. 2008. *Rome's Cultural Revolution* (Cambridge).

Woolf, G. 1996. "Monumental writing and the expansion of Roman society in the early Empire", *Journal of Roman Studies* LXXXVI, 22–39.

Woolf, G. 1998. *Becoming Roman: the origins of provincial civilization in Gaul* (Cambridge).

Zanker, P. 1987. *Augusto y el poder de las imágenes* (Madrid).

Zanker, P. 2000. "The city as a symbol: Rome and the creation of an urban image", in E. Fentress (ed.), *Romanization and the city. Creation, transformations and failures*, JRA, Supp. Series 38 (Portsmouth, Rhode Island) 25–41.

Notes

1. English translation by Horace Leonard Jones, The Loeb Classical Library (Cambridge, Mass) 1960: πλεῖστον δ', ἥ τε Κόρδυβα ηὔξηται, Μαρκέλλου κτίσμα, καὶ δόξῃ καὶ δυνάμει, καὶ ἡ τῶν Γαδιτανῶν πόλις, ἡ μὲν διὰ τὰς ναυτιλίας καὶ διὰ τὸ προσθέσθαι Ῥωμαίοις κατὰ συμμαχίας, ἡ δὲ χώρας ἀρετῇ καὶ μεγέθει, προσλαμβάνοντος καὶ τοῦ ποταμοῦ Βαίτιος μέγα μέρος· ᾤκησάν τε ἐξ ἀρχῆς Ῥωμαῖόν τε καὶ τῶν ἐπιχωρίων ἄνδρες ἐπίλεκτοι· καὶ δὴ καὶ πρώτην ἀποικίαν ταύτην εἰς τούσδε τοὺς τόπους ἔστειλαν Ῥωμαῖοι.

2. Liv. XLV.4.

3. App., *Iber*. 48–49.

4. Some authors have shown their preference for the first of these dates (Knapp, 1983, 10; Stylow, 1990, 262; Stylow, 1996, 77–78). Rodríguez Neila (1992, 177) however considers 152 /151 BCE as a more likely date for the foundation of *Corduba*. See Stylow 1996: note 1 and Knapp, 1983, note 61 for previous references. Canto has proposed a completely different interpretation, assimilating the Marcellus of the Strabonian text with the ill-fated nephew of Augustus (Canto 1991; *eadem* 1997). The main criticism of this hypothesis is found in Stylow, 1996 and Ventura Villanueva 2008, 89–91.

5. Founded as a *colonia Latina* in 171 BCE, according to Livy 43.2.3.

6. According to Appian (*Ib.* 38. 153), Publius Cornelius Scipio chose to settle the soldiers wounded in the battle of Ilipa (Alcalá del Río, Seville) in 206–205 BCE in a town he named *Italica* after Italy.

7. Canto 1991, 847–8; Stylow *et al.* (eds) 1995, 61; Stylow 1996, 80.

8. See *infra* for a brief discussion on the legal status of early Republican colonies in southern Iberia. See note 105 on the colonial status of Italica. Some scholars have adopted a restrictive view of the colonial phenomenon in this area and include only Carteia in the group of early Republican colonies, while others consider that towns such as *Corduba*, *Italica* or *Castulo* can be also regarded as Latin colonies. See González Román 1998, 131, note 6; Marín 2002, 281 and Bandelli 2002, 121–2 with previous bibliography.

9. Casevitz 1985.

10. Canto 1991, 847. Canto made this point in connection with the identification of Marcellus with the nephew of Augustus, but the correct interpretation of the term is relevant in a general sense.

11. Plin. *NH* 3.21. Castillo 1974, 191; Rodríguez Neila 1981, 112.

12. Rodríguez Neila 1992, 181.

13. Bispham 2006, 83, 122.

14. Stylow 1996, 80; Knapp 1983, 11; Ventura 2008, 100; García 2009. According to the latter (2009, 379), all the colonies founded *ex novo* in *Hispania* during the 2nd c. BCE, like *Italica*, *Carteia* or *Corduba* must be considered Latin colonies of Italian type, which followed the colonial model implemented in Italy probably until the foundation of *Aquileia* in 181 BCE. They had a military nature and were located in strategic positions to stabilize recently conquered regions.

15. Trying to isolate the native population through prosographic studies has proven to be difficult (Knapp, 1983: note 76). Other evidence to take into account when analysing the hybrid nature of the Roman town are the high percentages of Roman imported ware attested in the Republican colony compared to the native *oppidum*, native building techniques, references to ancient Etruscan cults (Bendala 1981, 45), the survival of a non-Latin pre-Roman town name (*Corduba*) (Rodríguez Neila 1981, 108) or the use of some archaic Latin words in the 1st c. BCE (Blanco, 1970: 109).

16. González Román, 2002, 61.

17. Bendala 1990, 32; *idem* 2003, 28.

18. Knapp 1977, 138; Stylow 1996, 78.

19. Rodríguez Neila 1992, 180.

20. Bernier and Fortea 1963; Luzón and Ruiz Mata 1973.

21. Murillo 1995, 196, with previous bibliography. The study of the pottery sequence has been updated by León Pastor 2007.

22. It is necessary to remember that the size of *Corduba* in the late Republic – probably one of the largest Roman towns of the time in the Iberian Peninsula – has been calculated in 47 hectares (Vaquerizo 1996, ed., 26; Carrillo *et al.* 1999, 42).

23. Murillo, 1995; Murillo and Vaquerizo 1996, 39–40; Carrillo *et al.* 1999, 38–9.

24. Bendala 1990, 33; Rodríguez Neila, 1992, 178, 186; Murillo and Vaquerizo 1996, 42; Ventura Martínez 1996, 56; Carrillo *et al.* 1999, 41; Murillo and Jiménez Salvador 2002, 184–7; Murillo 2004, 39–40; Vaquerizo 2005, 171–2.

25. Against this hypothesis Knapp 1983, 9: "...permanent legionary bases were not normal at this period; arrangements varied from year to year according to the theatres and fortunes of war. Troops were billeted in various towns, not in a single camp, for the winter months. At best, the prefoundation Roman presence at Córdoba was limited to some resident Roman businessmen and, perhaps, a garrison such as that attested at Ilipa, a little downstream from the town." See also Stylow 1996, 78–9 and most recently Cadiou 2008, 351–2, 359–60.

26. The archaeological evidence of the first Roman fortification is still scarce in *Emporiae*. See Morillo and Aurrecoechea eds, 2006, 242–5, for a recent summary on the literary and archaeological evidence.

27. The literary and archaeological evidence has also been recently summarized in Morillo and Aurrecoechea eds, 2006, 281–287.

28. See, however, the criticisms to the evidence traditionally related to the presence of permanent *praesidia* in these cities in Cadiou 2008, 328–50.

29. Apian *Iber.* 38. A section of ditch excavated in El Olivar to the west of Santiponce was identified as part of a rectangular Roman camp. However, it is difficult to ascertain, on the one hand, if the ditch enclosed the whole settlement and on the other, rectangular military camps are not characteristic of this early date (Keay 1997, 28; Galsterer, 1997, 52).

30. Liv., *Per.* 55. Recent excavations seem to confirm the possibility of the existence of an early military camp in *Valentia*. The archaeological evidence consist mainly of foundation of huts, alignments of stones from the barracks, postholes from tents, remains of bonfires, sallow ditches, rubbish deposits and a large midden (Ribera i Lacomba 2006, 79–80).

31. Polib. XXXV, 22; Sal., *Hist.*, II, 20, 28; App., *Ib.*, 65–66; Cic., *Pro Arch.*, 26; *Bell. Hisp.*, IV, VI, XII. Although this does not imply that the troops were always stationed *intra-muros* (Stylow 1996; Cadiou 2008, 369).

32. *Corduba* was located in the intersection of the so-called *via Heraclea* (that linked *Tarraco*, *Valentia* and *Corduba*) and the road that reached *Castra Caecilia*, crossing in its way *Carteia*, *Munda* and *Corduba*. For that reason, *Corduba* became a strategic centre, both for controlling the territories south of the Guadalquivir and as military base for the troops involved in the conquest of the Meseta in the north. That explains the frequent reference to Cordoba during the 1st c. BCE as a place to station the troops during the winter, especially in the 1st c. BCE (Sillières, 2003).

33. Rodríguez Neila 1976, 113; *idem* 1981, 115; Bendala, 2003, 20; Murillo and Jiménez Salvador, 2002, 189; Hita *et al.* 1993; Carrillo *et al.* 1999, 42, note 8; Sillières 2003, 33. Unfortunately these materials come from two tips, where the debris from a couple of construction plots had been dumped. The location of one of them is unknown, but the

other was for sure situated outside the Roman walls. The five sherds dated before the 2nd c. BCE can be identified as Morel 2234a 1, 2764a 1, 1324c 1, P321b 2, 7712 (Hita *et al.* 1993). Other ceramics found in the centre of the Republican city or in one of its roads can only be loosely dated to the first half of the 2nd c. BCE (Ventura Martínez, 1992; Ventura Martínez, 1996). Recent rescue excavations in different points of the city, the *forum* of the colony and the *decumanus maximus* seem to confirm the early date of some of the ceramics found in *Corduba*. Carrillo *et al.* 1999, 42, note 8; Murillo and Jiménez Salvador, 2002, 184.

34. Murillo and Vaquerizo 1996, 45; Carrillo, 1999: 75; Murillo and Jiménez Salvador 2002, 184, 189–92.
35. Murillo and Jiménez Salvador 2002, 187.
36. Murillo and Vaquerizo 1996, 46; Ventura Villanueva, León and Márquez, 1998, 91; Ruiz de Arbulo 2002, *idem* 2006; 146; Morillo and Aurrecoechea eds 2006, 287.
37. Marín and Ribera i Lacomba 2002: 289, 297. Ribera i Lacomba 2006, 80.
38. Liv., 43, 3, 1–4. Rome had founded Latin colonies in Gallia Cisalpina during the 3rd century, but this process ends in the Italian Peninsula quite likely with the establishment of Aquileia in 181 BCE (Laffi 2002; García 2009, 383).
39. Bispham 2006, 83–5. The earliest contemporary reference to any kind of *colonia* is recorded in an inscription from early-second-century Aquileia (CIL I² 621, Bispham 2006, 81). The town was founded in 181 BCE, therefore, after *Italica* (206–205 BCE) and just some years earlier than Carteia (171 BCE) and *Corduba* (169–168/152–151 BCE).
40. E. T. Salmon, *Roman Colonization under the Republic*, London, 1969.
41. Bispham 2006, 84.
42. See note 14.
43. Caes. *Bell. Hisp.* 34.
44. The first series are dated to the beginning of the 1st c. BCE. Chaves 1977; Amela 2004; García-Bellido, 2006.
45. Ventura Villanueva (2008) has suggested in a recent article that the *deductor* of the Roman colony under Caesar might have been *C. Asinius Pollio* during his stay as governor in Cordoba between 44–43 BCE. It is known now (thanks to the information contained in the new bronze found in Osuna – *Lex Coloniae Genetivae Iuliae*, cap. XV) that he probably acted as *deductor* in other colonies of the *provincia Ulterior* such as *Urso* (Caballos 2006, 340–1).
46. However, we must bear in mind that this type of images are not unusual in the coinage of Roman colonies, regardless of the origin of the first citizens. Ripollès 1998, 346.
47. Stylow 1990, 263; *idem* 1996, 80–81; Knapp 1983, 28; García 2002; Marín 2002, 287.
48. The bibliography on the monuments and public spaces of *Corduba/Colonia Patricia* is too numerous to be quoted here. For an overview on this vast topic see: Carrillo *et al.* 1999; von Hesberg 1996; León 1999; Márquez 1998a, 1999, 2005; Murillo 2004; Stylow 1990; Vaquerizo 2003, 2005, 2006; Ventura Villanueva 2003; Ventura and Márquez, 2005; Ventura *et al.* 1998, with previous references.
49. Carrasco 2001, 205; Márquez 2004c, 56.
50. Cic. Verr. 2, 4, 56.
51. Bendala and Roldán 1999.
52. Murillo 2004, 44
53. León 1999, 40.
54. Márquez 1998c, 122, Fig. 17.

55. Bel. Alex. 52, 2. Márquez 1998b. See also Ventura Villanueva, 2007a for the date, location and denomination of this building.
56. Some Republican buildings were also demolished around the same phase, and structures with a different orientation were built over them in Imperial times. Hidalgo 1993, 105.
57. Carrillo *et al.* 1999, 46.
58. Ventura Villanueva 1993, *idem* 1996.
59. Murillo 2004, 46.
60. Von Hesberg 1996; Ventura Villanueva *et al.* 1998, 95.
61. Ventura Villanueva 1999; Ventura Villanueva *et al.* (eds) 2002.
62. Márquez 1998a, 176 ff., *idem* 2004a, 109–17.
63. Ventura Villanueva, 2007b; See also Fishwick 2000 and 2004, 79–83.
64. Márquez 1998a, 178.
65. Spannagel 1999, 132. For possible representations of *summi viri*, see López 1998. Trillmich (1996, 1998) was the first to establish a connection between the iconographic programme of the forum of Augustus in Rome and similar representations found in the capitals of the Hispanic provinces. The same phenomenon has been described in towns such as Arlés, Pompei, Vienne or Nyon. See infra and note 97.
66. The first references to these findings have been published in Vaquerizo (ed.) 2003.
67. Murillo *et al.* 2001.
68. Murillo *et al.* 2003, 65 ff. In recent years there has been a lively debate about the identification of the public spaces of the city in relation to the Imperial cult and its "provincial" or "colonial" character. See, for example, Fishwick 2004, Garriguet 2002, Panzram 2003 and most recently the new proposal by Ventura Villanueva 2007b, 234–236.
69. Stylow *et al.* (eds) 1995.
70. For the concept of the 'Roman cultural revolution' and the important changes in Augustan times see Wallace-Hadrill 2008 and Woolf 1998, 238 with further references.
71. Murillo and Jiménez Salvador 2002, 186.
72. M5422/Lamb. 59, 210–190 BCE.
73. Escacena 1987, *idem* 1989, *idem* 1992, 332–334; Escacena and Belén 1994; Bendala 1992; Jiménez 2006; *eadem* 2008a, 73–4, 140–5.
74. The survival of the traditional painted ware in Imperial times was a fact already noticed by García y Bellido in the early 1950s (García y Bellido 1952, 42). The 'survival' of local pottery used as funerary urns has been noticed in other early Roman towns of *Hispania*, such as *Tarraco* (Remolà 2004), *Valentia* (García-Prosper and Guerin 2002), *Carthago Nova* (Ramallo 1989, 122) or *Lucentum* (Jiménez Salvador 2002, 195). On the problem of establishing an accurate chronology for the pre-Roman pottery of southern Spain see Ruiz and Molinos (1993, 23–52). For the "characteristically Iberian" painted ware of Oliva-Llíria and Elche-Archena, displaying complex iconographies depicting hunters, warriors and women wearing local dresses, produced precisely during the first two centuries of the Roman occupation in some areas of the Mediterranean coast, see various contributions in Olmos and Rouillard (2004) and also the synthesis in Olmos 1994 and Conde 1998 with previous bibliographical references.
75. Murillo and Vaquerizo 1996, 45; Murillo and Jiménez Salvador 2002, 184, 189–92.
76. Carrillo 1999; Vaquerizo 2004.

77. Vaquerizo 2001; *idem* 2008, 80–93; Ruiz Osuna 2007.
78. Vaquerizo 2002c; Vaquerizo and Sánchez 2008.
79. Woolf 1996, 29.
80. Stylow *et al.* 1995; Jiménez 2008a, 291–2, 327–8, with previous references.
81. Vaquerizo 2008, 93–7.
82. Vaquerizo 2001; *idem* 2002a; *idem* 2002b; Márquez 2002; Murillo *et al.* 2002.
83. See Mattingly 2004, 22; *idem* 2006, *passim*, for the concept of 'discrepant experiences'.
84. Van Dommelen, 2001a: 81; *idem*, 2001b: 141 on the notion of 'local culture' in the regions conquered by Rome and the importance of this concept to go beyond binary oppositions such as Roman:native in our analysis of provincial cultures.
85. On the contrary imported Campanian ware was present in the earlier layers of this cemetery. García Matamala 2002, *idem* 2002–2003. Jiménez 2008a, 343.
86. Vargas 2002, 298, fig. 8; Jiménez 2008a, 273–4.
87. Astruc 1951; Almagro Gorbea 1984.
88. Carmona and Punic necropolis, Bendala, 1976, 36, 82–83; *idem* 2002, 150–152. See for the *hypogea* on Calle de la Bodega, Palacio de la Merced and the so-called "Gran Tumba" of Camino Viejo de Almodóvar, Jiménez 2008a, 261–2, 266–7, 285, with previous references.
89. Gros 2001, 440–443; von Hesberg 1992, 26–37.
90. See van Dommelen 2007 and Jiménez 2008b for a critical approach to the relation between 'traditional-looking' material culture and different forms of resistance.
91. However, even from a legal point of view, many Roman colonies in southern Spain did not enjoy all the privileges attached to this status in Italy and therefore can not be compared to Rome in this sense. Only *Acci* was granted the *ius italicum*, according to the ancient sources; *Tucci, Ituci, Ucubi, Urso* and *Astigi* were endowed with *inmunitas* and the rest did not have special privileges (González Román 1991, 92–93).
92. Torelli 1988, 65–6; Bispham 2006, 78–9. For a different interpretation see Zanker (2000, 41): "In this famous passage, Gellius is apparently not interested in the concrete physical appearance of these cities, but rather their aesthetic effect and the quality of life that they offered their people."
93. Zanker 2000, 26.
94. Bispham, 2006, 75.
95. See Márquez (2004b, 342, fig. 8) for a *clipeus* that has been recently put in connection to the so-called *forum adiectum* of the *colonia*. A statue from the Tienda collection has been identified as a representation of Aeneas or Romulus (see Fig. 4.4 and note 65).
96. Taller Escola d'Arqueologia 1989; Mar (ed.) 1993.
97. In Mérida *clipei* and caryatids, as well as fragments of sculptures dressed in a *toga picta* have been found; these probably correspond to representations of *summi viri*, a figure that might have been a portrait of a mythical king of Alba Longa and a depiction of Aeneas, Ascanio and Anquises related to the flight from Troy. Attention has also been brought to an inscription interpreted as an *elogium* of Aeneas by de la Barrera and Trillmich. See Trillmich 1996; *idem* 1998; de la Barrera and Trillmich 1996; Nogales and Álvarez 2006 and Nogales 2008 with previous bibliography. Recently, A. Peña 2007 has suggested that the model of the forum of Augustus in Rome was also followed in Hispania by Roman towns other than the provincial capitals, such us *Italica*, where fragments of *clipei* and monumental statues have also been found.
98. Zanker 1987, 230–55 Spannagel 1999; Haselberger 2007, 156–160.
99. It is true that similar images can also be found in the decoration of private spaces or objects, however, the meaning usually changes within different contexts and, for example, the image of Aeneas carrying his father Ascanio on his shoulder can be read more as a symbol of individual loyalty and *pietas* than as a sign of political support for the Imperial family (Zanker 1987, 321–5).
100. For a summary of the main views on this issue, see Vaquerizo 2005, 169 ff.; Canto (1991, 855–6) suggests a possible relation with the homage paid to the Senate (the *patres*) by Augustus, an idea rejected by Stylow (1996, 81).
101. Rodríguez Neila has collected a series of examples in Rome and provincial towns, where it is possible to trace a connection between the supposed ethnic origin of the population and the name of a *vicus*, such as the *vicus Tuscus* in Rome. It was also not unusual to name provincial *vici* after the *vici* of the *Urbs*, as we can see from the *vicus Patricius* in the *Colonia Caesarea Antiochia*. For more examples of this phenomenon and the possible connection of the new name of *Corduba* with an early *vicus* see Rodríguez Neila (1976, 106, 116, note 72) and also Bispham 2006, 87 for an example of Republican date in Cales.
102. See Keay 1998, 63 and Apendix III for a list of Roman *coloniae* and other privileged towns in Baetica.
103. Nat. 3.3.7; 3.3.10–12. Caesar is considered to be responsible for the foundation of *Hasta Regia, Iulia Romula Hispal, Ituci Virtus Iulia, Claritas Iulia Ucubi, Genitiva Iulia Urbanourm Urso* and *Iulia Gemella Acci*. Augustus may have been the founder of *Augusta Gemella Tucci, Augusta Firma Astigi*, and *Caesarina Augusta Asido*. *Hispalis* and *Corduba* are thought to have been refounded in time of Augustus. *Italica* was granted the status of *colonia civium Romanorum* by Hadrian.
104. Plin. Nat. 3.3.25.
105. The legal status of the earliest Republican settlement remains unclear and it is somehow remarkable that the only mention to the Scipio's settlement in 206–205 BCE is recorded in a text dated in middle of the 2nd c. CE (Apian, Iber. 38) and not by earlier writers like Livy (Galsterer 1997, 51). For Canto (1999, 145–82) and García (2009, 379), the early settlement may have had the status of *colonia Latina*. See against this hypothesis Caballos 1994, 30; Keay 1997, 26; Galsterer 1997, 53. *Italica* was granted the status of *municipium civium Romanorum* some time in the second half of the 1st century BCE, probably between 16 and 13 BCE (Caballos 1994, 61–4) and became a *colonia Civium Romanorum* under Hadrian (Aul. Gelius, *Noct. Attic.* XVI, 13, 4) changing its name to *Colonia Aelia Augusta Italica*.
106. See González Román 1991, 89, with previous bibliography, for the problematic inscription used as evidence of the colonial status of Iliturgi under Hadrian.
107. Ruiz de Arbulo 2006, 41.
108. Arce 2004.
109. Canto 1997, 274, 280; García-Bellido 2006, 256.
110. Melchor 2006.
111. Melchor 2006, 252, for the integration of the local elites in the colonies of southern Hispania, see Padilla 2006.
112. Edwards and Woolf 2003, 2.
113. 2000, 25.

5. Imperial Cult and Imperial Reconciliation

Paul D. Scotton

Julius Caesar had to have realized the strategic significance of the Corinthia and the benefit of direct Roman control of it. The refounding of the city of Corinth as a Roman colony by Caesar in 44 BCE was, I would say,[1] the result of that realization.[2] Shortly after the founding, however, there was a turning point as Julius Caesar was assassinated. Just how strong a role as benefactor Caesar may have had in the development of the colony can only be guessed. But, his death and the subsequent turmoil appears to have had an effect on the development of the city. Although Corinth played, at best, a minor role in the events that unfolded between Caesar's partisans and those of Brutus and Cassius in Italy and in Greece, those events may well have had an impact on the newly founded colony. There is little evidence of Roman building activity to be found in Corinth in general, and in the forum in particular, for the first two decades. That Corinth sided with Antony in the civil war between him and Octavian could not have helped.[3] What transpired politically in Corinth for the next twenty years is unknown but it is clear that the forum was virtually empty until the tenth decade of the 1st century BCE. Why it took Corinth over thirty years to find the ways and means is left for speculation and beyond what I will address here.[4] Something happened, however, during the last decade that appears to have changed that. Several threads in the archaeological – and historical – record document rather sudden and significant changes in the fabric of Corinth, and suggest why it occurred. This activity seems to have been brought about through reciprocal favors between Augustus and the colony, favors facilitated by and manifested in Corinth embracing the imperial cult.

Although there is no question as to where the civic center of Roman Corinth came to be, the earliest construction within the city was elsewhere, *i.e.* around Peirene Fountain, adjacent to the Lechaion Road.[5] For this activity to cluster around an abundant and ready water supply (see below) is not surprising. That those structures are dated post Actium and by around ten to twenty years is. The most secure date we have for this activity is that of Peirene Fountain itself. Recent work by B. Robinson dates the first Roman remodeling of the fountain to the 20s or 10s BCE.[6] But, her understanding of the state of Peirene before the remodeling is that it was not only visible but serviceable.[7] Accordingly, it seems reasonable that this was the first center of building activity in Roman Corinth. Just north of Peirene there is evidence of early industrial manufacturing, apparently bronze. Sometime afterwards, and on the site of the later Peribolos of Apollo, shops around a courtyard and a macellum were built. To the north of the courtyard, and contemporary with it, was a *macellum piscarium*.[8] Across the Lechaion Road, the North Building, dated late 5th to early 4th century BCE, had been put into use after its destruction and before a post-Augustan basilica had been built on the site.[9] In spite of not knowing the precise composition of this group, its importance is clear. Regardless of whether or not the market courtyard and macella antedate the earliest construction in the forum, the activity at Peirene, the bronze works, and perhaps the North Building, do and we should consider that the area around Peirene and the adjacent Lechaion Road to have been an earlier center of activity in the colony.

What then of the area of the later forum? For the past thirty years or so the belief that the forum was the first center of Roman Corinth has slowly unraveled. The composite of studies by several scholars has shown that the forum was largely empty until late in the Augustan era.[10] That is not to say there were no structures and no activity, but the center of the city was elsewhere. Certainly present in some form was the South Stoa, although its state of repair and the earliest colonial use are uncertain.[11] Broneer thought that the first activity was at the west end and included replacing the gutter, step and stylobate.[12] Since Broneer, most have held that the earliest restorations in the building proper began at the east end of the stoa with the conversion of the first seven Greek shops into three rooms.[13] Although a fully synthetic study of the coins, architecture, and lotted pottery has not been done since Broneer, Roman chronologies are well documented in specific rooms and areas by Hayes, Williams, and Slane in individual studies.[14] Hayes found a Neronian date for the deposits he examined in the bouleterion and behind shops XXV–XXVII.[15] Williams found earlier fills in three areas, behind shops XX and XXI and in an area south of them.[16] This last area was one of those Hayes had studied. Although the fills are earlier than what Hayes found, they are no earlier than the Augustan period or slightly later. Slane's findings were consistent with those of Williams.[17] In sum, the earliest documented Roman activity in the South Stoa dates to the Augustan/Tiberian periods.

Adjacent to the east end of the South Stoa and oriented perpendicular to it, lies the Southeast Building (Fig. 5.1). Two phases of the Roman building have been recognized, the first of which has been identified as antedating the Julian Basilica.[18] This belief was based upon the understanding that the north wall of the Southeast Building was moved southward at some time to accommodate the construction of the basilica. If this is true, how far south is not clear as the northern terminus of the west wall is ambiguous. What appears to be a finished corner viewed from the west is far less certain when viewed from the east. Compounding the difficulty in interpretation is the fact that all of the ashlar blocks are reused and of varying dimensions.[19] Until, and if, the building phases and configurations of those phases are settled, the assertion that the relocation of the north wall was required by the construction of the Julian Basilica is questionable (Fig. 5.2).[20] It is more likely that if the north wall was relocated,[21] it should be associated with the rebuilding of the Southeast Building in the 5th century CE, a rebuilding that was undertaken after the collapse and abandonment of the Julian Basilica.[22] Regardless of the current uncertainties of its first Roman phase configuration, the Southeast Building stood contemporary with the Julian Basilica and may well have been built at the same time.

Off the northwest corner of the Southeast Building was the Circular Monument. This was originally a Greek monument, remodeled in Hellenistic times, and still visible when the colony was founded. Farther to the west was the Rostra, better known today as the Bema (Fig. 5.1). The assumption has been that in its earliest form it was one of the first structures built by the colony.[23] Three phases of construction have been identified,[24] but only the first two concern us here. This first phase is characterized by Walbank as a "carefully-cut poros block" facing over a rubble and mortar core. The second phase, the addition of scholae on the east and west ends, has been dated Augustan by the letter forms on an inscribed epistyle block.[25] Furthermore, the Attic influence of the decorative elements are held to be consistent with Augustan and early Julio-Claudian periods.[26] As cited above,[27] Kent's criteria for dating by letter form for the Augustan period in Corinth called to question and with the decorative elements possibly early Julio-Claudian, the date of the second phase is uncertain and may well be later than Augustan. Furthermore, carefully cut poros block is indeed characteristic of Augustan period masonry in Corinth[28] but it is also characteristic of the Julio-Claudian period and later.[29] With the evidence at hand, we cannot date the rostra with any more specificity than Augustan/Julio-Claudian.

The site of the *locus gromae* may have been to the north and east of the rostra.[30] To the north and west was an altar. This has been dated as Early Roman but there is evidence that speaks against that.[31] The foundation blocks, *c.* 0.37 to 0.42 m high, are laid on a bedding of cemented poros fragments and stones *c.* 0.22 m high. The east side of the altar foundations is built entirely of cemented poros stones mixed with some block fragments. The top of the foundation blocks is set to the level where the mortar was laid for the marble paving of the forum. This level is *c.* 0.60 m above that of the floor of the first Roman forum. None of the blocks has any indication of dowel holes for setting revetment or any traces of stucco. This means that if the altar had been built at the level of the floor of the first Roman forum, and were it contemporary with that level, its bedding and roughly finished faces would have been visible. What would appear to be more likely is that this altar was built either at the same time or after the forum level was raised and the marble paving installed, *i.e.* post CE 77.

Across the forum area, near and behind the Sacred Spring, stood a small monopteros of Roman construction. The consensus is that it was Early Roman in date.[32] Lastly, just outside of the southwest corner of the forum between two roads was the Early Roman Cellar Building (Fig. 5.1). The function of the building remains unknown but the pottery and

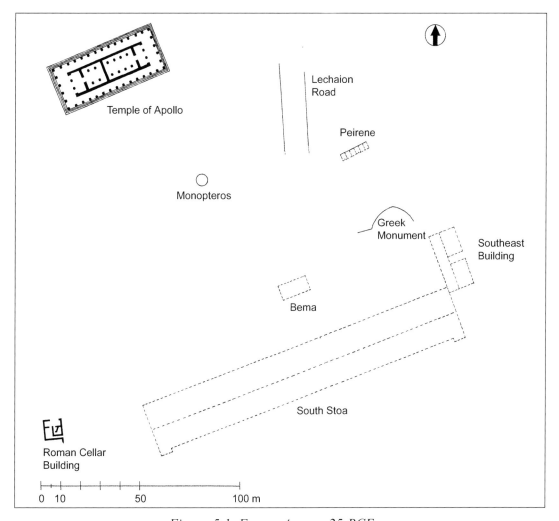

Figure 5.1. Forum Area c. 25 BCE

glassware found within are suggestive of a restaurant or tavern.[33] It was built in the last decade of the 1st century BCE, damaged in the early Tiberian period during the earthquake of CE 22/23, and rebuilt likely during Caligula's reign.[34]

In sum, there is very little evidence of a significant Roman presence in the forum area until *c.* post 10 BCE. Present in some form prior to 10 BCE were the Circular Monument and perhaps renovated rooms XVII–XXIII of the South Stoa, the Monopteros above the Sacred Spring, and maybe the Locus Gromae. The rest was empty but for whatever portions, if any, of the Hellenistic race course were visible.[35] The Hellenistic race course is important for this discussion for at some point during the second half of the 1st century BCE and the first half of the 1st century CE it may have been the site for the Isthmian games. It has been commonly held that at some time during the Augustan period and more specifically between 7 BCE and CE 3 control of the Isthmian games was returned to Corinth.[36] E.

Gephard has determined that the games themselves did not return to the Isthmus until *c.* CE 50–60.[37] The assumption has been that after the return of Corinthian control and before the games returned to the sanctuary at the Isthmus, the games were held somewhere in Corinth and perhaps on the old Hellenistic race course. Gephard dates the return of the control of the games to 40 BCE based upon the issue of a Corinthian coin with a hydria on the obverse and a victors wreath encircling the name of the city on the reverse. She interprets both as symbols of the Isthmian games and questions why Corinth would commemorate the Isthmian games if they were still under the control of Sikyon.[38] This is plausible but also would be the hydria as a symbol of "well watered Corinth" and the wreath an easily recognizable and long established symbol for Corinth just as were Poseidon and Bellerophon who appear on the first coin issues from Roman Corinth. The counter view to the date of the return of the games holds that it was "some time between 7 B.C. and

A.D. 3, probably the year 2 B.C. ...".[39] This view is based upon a victors' list found in the gymnasium at Corinth.

We may not have a consensus on when the games returned to Corinthian control but we do know when they had to have left the forum at Corinth, if they ever were there. On top of the west end of the dromos, late in the 1 century BCE, the Fountain of Poseidon was built.[40] On the east end, the porch of the Julian Basilica was laid on top of and extending beyond to the west of the Hellenistic starting line (Fig. 5.2). From the efforts of Williams and Scotton in the Julian Basilica, we can date with some precision when the basilica was built. That is, between 2/1 BCE and *c*. CE 4/5. The *postquem* date is provided by coins found in a well sealed during the construction of the basilica and construction fill in the foundation trenches. The approximate *antequem* date is provided by the deaths of Gaius and Lucius Caesar.[41] Thus, if the Isthmian games had been held in the forum, they had to have moved elsewhere by no later than *c*. CE 4/5. There is no certainty at all to the games having been held in the forum during Roman times but if they were, this may explain why the forum was so empty.

Less speculative is the increase in construction in the area of the forum beginning with Peirene. Sometime in the 20s or 10s BCE a Roman facade was added to Peirene Fountain.[42] Apparently associated with the two storey facade and perhaps contemporary with it the Northeast Stoa was added behind and above Peirene in the northeast corner of the forum.[43] Both structures share the same orientation and the same construction techniques, in particular the use of "large, squared poros blocks joined by swallow-tailed clamps."[44] If these two structures are indeed contemporaries, the Northeast Stoa was likely the first Roman built public building in the forum. The stoa was soon followed by the construction of the Julian Basilica, likely the Southeast Building, and then the Fountain of Poseidon. All four of these seem to have been built within roughly a ten to fifteen year period (Fig. 5.2). Although the benefactor of the Julian Basilica is unknown and that of the Northeast Stoa at best suspected,[45] Cn. Babbius Philinus is known as the benefactor of the Southeast Building[46] and the Fountain of Poseidon.[47] It is reasonable to assume that Babbius' buildings were a coordinated effort. Whether all four were is less certain but the effort was at least a coherent one. Although there is no hard evidence of a building program in the epigraphic record and what is presented below is a circumstantial case, it is a reasonable interpretation of several intersecting threads.

First, we will consider the Julian Basilica.[48] The basilica was an imposing structure on the east end of forum standing on a podium over 4 m high and rising in total *c*. 18 m above the forum floor. Inside along the south interior wall was a tribunal. The tribunal helps to identify one of the primary functions of the building. That is, the seat of the imperial court of law in the Corinthia and later in the province of Achaia.

Near the tribunal, in the southwest corner of the basilica, in a sealed deposit from its collapse was found one of the best known sculptures from Corinth, Augustus Caesar in the guise of pontifix maximus.[49] Although the date of the statue has swung from Augustan through Claudian, recent consensus places it in the Augustan period.[50] Contemporary sculptures of Gaius and Lucius Caesar were found in the east aisle: Gaius, nearly complete and undisturbed from where he was placed in the cryptoporticus sometime in the 2nd century CE;[51] Lucius, missing the lower half of his body and built into a medieval wall.[52] These three statues were the first in the Julian Basilica of an ever increasing group of imperial statues, ultimately second in number only to those found in the theatre. The recognition of the imperial family in Corinth has been known for some time but the association between the statues of Augustus, Gaius, and Lucius has been diminished by the original dating of the construction of the Julian Basilica. According to the original theory, the statues were first placed elsewhere and *c*. 30 years later moved into the basilica shortly after its construction in the Claudian period.[53] With the basilica date now known to be contemporary with the statues, *i.e. c.* 2/1 BCE to CE 4/5, it is safe to assume the statues were always housed in the basilica.

That Augustus, Gaius, and Lucius were venerated in Corinth is further attested by specific evidence in the archaeological record. Previously published is a dedication to Augustus found in the destruction debris in the basilica near the tribunal and not far from his statue.[54] In the numismatic record, and with examples of it found within the basilica, is a coin issued in 2/1 BCE with busts of Gaius and Lucius.[55] Recent work in the epigraphic record in the Julian Basilica has revealed that the statues of Augustus, Gaius and Lucius held special significance in that building.

Additional fragments have been found of two previously published inscriptions. The first was placed in the north aisle opposite the tribunal in the south aisle.[56] I have restored the dedication as to the CAESARES AVGVSTI and to the colony of Corinth, cited in the inscription as LAVS IVLIA

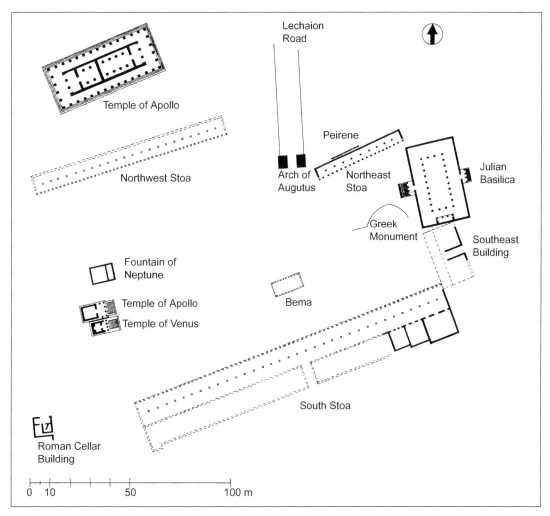

Figure 5.2. Forum Area c. *10 CE*

COLONIA CORINTHENSIS, although abbreviated. Which Caesares is not specified but I have posited an Augustan/Julio-Claudian date based upon the letter forms.[57] The safest interpretation for this then would be a dedication to the Caesars both living and deceased.

A second inscription, unpublished in its more complete form, is a dedication to the genius of Augustus.[58] All the fragments were found in the south aisle of the basilica east of the site of the tribunal. The presence of these statues and dedications to Augustus, his genius, and Caesares Augusti indicate the presence of the imperial cult within the Julian Basilica.

Imperial statuary and dedications within the context of a basilica is not unusual. I would suggest that the presence of another type of dedication found within the Julian Basilica is indicative of a particular aspect of the imperial cult. Within this basilica was found the greatest concentration of dedications to agonothetai in Corinth. These agonothetai are particularly significant for they were the ranking officials of the Isthmian games. What is more, post-Actium, every other Isthmian games included the celebration of the Casesaria, founded originally in honor of Julius Caesar, but soon evolved into general honors for the imperial family. The agonothetai were the highest ranking officials of the imperial cult in the Corinthia and these officers had a particular focus in Corinth, *i.e.* the Julian Basilica.[59]

The presence of the agonothetai inscriptions in the basilica would seem to support a revised interpretation of what guise the statues of Gaius and Lucius hold. Their nudity has been assumed to be indicative of their heroic stature and hence posthumous. There are, however, other explanations for their nudity. In a Greek context nudity would have been commonplace and in a Roman one not extraordinary.[60] It was also appropriate for *principes iuventutis* and more especially for athletes. In fact, Ridgway, Pollini, and de Grazia Vanderpool, among others, see the deliberate conjuring of specific athletes, the dioskouri.[61] I am not suggesting that Gaius and Lucius participated in the Isthmian games; rather, that the portrayal of them as athletes seems a fitting symbol for the tie between the Isthmian games and the Augustan family and for the recognition of the debt owed by Corinth for the return of the Isthmian games to their control.

On the west end of the forum, considerable building activity begins at approximately this same time, *i.e.* Augustan in general, and more likely late Augustan in particular. Of these, Temple F is "a candidate for the earliest temple in the Forum."[62] This determination is based upon architectural style and the identification of Temple F as that of Venus Genetrix.[63] This identification seems quite reasonable given that Julius Caesar founded the colony. Adjacent to it, and later in date, is Temple G.[64] Based upon the identification of the Temple of Venus and Pausanias' description of the forum in Corinth, Temple G is a Temple of Apollo, perhaps Apollo Clarios.[65]

North of the Venus and Apollo temples, and placed in nearly the middle of the west end, is the Fountain of Poseidon. Built early in the career of Cn. Babbius Philinus, this is dated to late 1st century BCE or early 1st century CE by Robinson.[66] Standing next to the fountain and also built by Babbius was his monopteros monument, but this is dated Tiberian.[67] Also to be excluded from the Augustan period building program is Temple D, which according to Williams is later than the Northwest Stoa.[68] Temple K is later still, and Temple E, "probably not much after the death of Augustus, or, possibly, as late as the reign of Caligula."[69]

One other building and an arch may belong to the Augustan phase: the Northwest Stoa and the Lechaion Road Arch. According to Williams, the Northwest Stoa "cannot be earlier than late Augustan, at the earliest."[70] This is significant because the date of the first phase of the Lechaion Road Basilica has to be later than the Northwest Stoa. The south end of the basilica was truncated because of the presence of the east end of the Northwest Stoa.[71] That is, the Northwest Stoa was already standing when the Lechaion Road Basilica was built. With the stoa built no earlier than late Augustan at the earliest, the basilica has to have been built sometime later. Immediately to the east of the south end of the basilica stood a monumental arch over the Lechaion Road. This arch has been dated late Augustan.[72]

It would seem then that the earliest Roman building activity in the area of the forum is in the South Stoa in the vicinity of where the so-called road to Kenchreai passes through the stoa and in the Roman Cellar Building. For the former, the well

deposits only indicate there was activity and not what that activity was. For the latter, the cellar building is, although close, outside of the forum and does not appear to be civic in nature, *i.e.* the pottery found within it is consistent with that of a restaurant or tavern. Of the earliest buildings in the forum built by the Romans we can say the following: none are earlier than middle Augustan, and late Augustan seems more likely. The earliest structure may be the Northeast Stoa, above Peirene, in the ninth or tenth decade of the 1st century BCE, if it were built during or shortly after the first Roman remodeling of Peirene. The rest seem to be clustered in a fifteen to twenty year period. Of these the most secure date begins at *c.* 2 BCE with the construction of the Julian Basilica and perhaps also the adjoining Southeast Building, although Temple F (Venus Genetrix) may be earlier. Also in this group are the Southeast Building, Temple G (Apollo), the Fountain of Poseidon, and perhaps the Babbius Monument, the Northwest Stoa, and the Lechaion Road Arch.[73] In other words what we know with reasonable surety are a large basilica housing multiple guises of the imperial cult and with an adjoining smaller building, a temple to the genetrix of the founding father of the colony, another which may have been dedicated to the patron god of the current emperor,[74] a fountain dedicated to one of the patron gods of the city since Greek times, and lastly, a large public fountain that may have been an imperial benefaction.[75] There is no explicit evidence that these structures were part of a building program but, it is difficult to imagine that two temples, a basilica with an adjacent (and perhaps attached) building, a stoa, a fountain dedicated to a god, and a monumental entrance in the form of an imperial arch into the what was then becoming the forum, all built within a fifteen to twenty year period, were random events.

The absence of significant Roman building in the forum at Corinth until late in the 1st century BCE is certain. Knowing that the Julian Basilica housed one of the major sites of the imperial cult in Corinth is suggestive. That is, prominent manifestations of the imperial cult in the largest and most imposing of the earliest Roman buildings in the forum suggests a link between the construction of those buildings and imperial favor courted, granted, and recognized through the imperial cult. Although we should not diminish Agrippa's efforts in Peirene Fountain, if true, the return of the Isthmian games to Corinthian control seems to have been the impetus for a major building program which included the Julian Basilica, the Southeast Building, the Fountain of Poseidon, and the Temples of Venus Genetrix and Apollo. Of these structures the archaeological record suggests particular importance for the Julian Basilica in this program. The presence of the tribunal, the statues of Augustus, Gaius, and Lucius, the dedications to Augustus, his genius, to the CAESARIBVS AVGVSTIS, and to the agonothetai suggest not just the presence of the imperial cult in the building but a deliberate and very visible attempt to recognize favors granted and to perhaps encourage favors to come.

Acknowledgments

I would like to thank Rebecca Sweetman for all her efforts to make the 100 Years of Solitude conference a success, the faculty and staff at St. Andrews for being such good hosts, the editors of Oxbow for providing a venue for our papers, and my anonymous reviewer for keen insight. Any errors or omissions are my fault alone.

Bibliography

Corinth I.iii = R. Scranton, *Monuments in the Lower Agora and North of the Archaic Temple,* Princeton, NJ, ASCSA 1951.

Corinth I.iv, = O. Broneer, *The South Stoa and its Roman Successors,* Princeton, NJ, ASCSA 1954.

Corinth I.v = S. Weinberg, *The Southeast Building, the Twin Basilicas, the Mosaic House,* Princeton, NJ, ASCSA, 1960

Corinth VIII.ii = A. B. West, *Latin Inscriptions, 1896–1926,* Cambridge, Mass., Harvard University Press, 1931.

Corinth VIII.iii = J. Kent, *The Inscriptions 1926–1950,* Princeton, NJ, ASCSA 1966.

Corinth XX = C. K. Williams II and N. Bookidis, *Results of Excavations: Corinth, the Centenary,* ASCSA, 2003.

Amandry, M. *Le monnayage des duovirs Corinthiens,* (BCH Suppl. 15) (Paris) 1988.

Edwards, C. 1994, "The Arch Over the Lechaion Road at Corinth and Its Sculpture," *Hesperia* 63 (1994) 263–308.

Gebhard, E. 1993, "The Isthmian Games and the Sanctuary of Poseidon in the early Empire," *The Corinthia in the Roman Period, JRA Suppl.8,* Ann Arbor, 1993, 78–94.

de Grazia Vanderpool, C. "Roman Portraiture, The Many Faces of Corinth", in C. K. Williams II and N. Bookidis, *Corinth XX Results of Excavations: Corinth, the Centenary,* ASCSA, 2003, 371–382.

Gros, P. 1967, "Trois temples de la Fortune des Ier et II siècles de notre ère, Remarques sur l'origine des sanctuaires romains à abside " *MEFRA* 79 (1967) 503–66.

Hallet, C. 2005, *The Roman Nude:Heroic Portrait Statuary 200 BC–AD 300* Oxford 2005

Hayes, J. 1973, "Roman Pottery from the South Stoa at Corinth," *Hesperia* 42 (1973) 416–470.

Hellenkemper-Salies, G. 1986 "Römische Mosaiken in Griechenland," *BJb* 186 (1986) 241–284.

Kajava, M. 2002. "When Did the Isthmian Games Return to the Isthmus? (Rereading 'Corinth 8.3.153)", *Classical Philology* 97 (2002) 168–178.

Millis, B."'Miserable Huts' in Post-146 B.C. Corinth," *Hesperia* 75 (2006) 397–404.

Pollini, J. 1987, *The Portraiture of Gaius and Lucius Caesar* Fordham University Press 1987.

Ridgway, B. 1981 "Sculpture from Corinth" *Hesperia* 50 (1981) 422–48.

Robinson, B. 2001 "Fountains and the Culture of Water in Roman Corinth", PhD diss. University of Pennsylvania 2001.

Robinson, B. 2005 "Fountains and Formation of Cultural Identity," *Urban Religion in Roman Corinth,* D. Schowalter and S. Friesen (eds) 2005 111–40.

Romano, I. 1994, "A Hellenistic Deposit from Corinth: Evidence for Interim Period Activity (146–44 B.C.)," *Hesperia* 63 (1994) 57–104.

Rose, C. B. 1997 *Dynastic Commemoration and Imperial Portraiture in the Julio-Claudian Period,* Cambridge, 1997.

Scotton, P. 1997. "The Julian Basilica at Corinth: An Architectural Investigation," PhD diss. University of Pennsylvania 1997.

Scotton, P. 2005 "A New Fragment of an Inscription from the Julian Basilica at Roman Corinth," *Hesperia* 74 (2005) 95–100.

Shoe, L. T. 1964"The Roman Ionic Base in Corinth", *Essays in Memory of Karl Lehman,* New York, Institute of Fine Arts, 300–303.

Slane, K. 1986, "Two Deposits from the Early Roman Cellar Building, Corinth," *Hesperia* 55 (1986) 271–318.

Slane, K. 2004, "Corinth: Italian sigillata and other Italian imports to the early colony," *Early Italian Sigillata, Proceedings of the First International ROCT-Congress,* Leuven 2004 31–42.

Slane Wright, K. 1980, "A Tiberian Pottery Deposit from Corinth," *Hesperia* 49 (1980) 135–75.

Spawforth, A. J. S. 1978, "Balbilla, the Euryclids, and Memorials for a Greek Magnate," *BSA* 73 (1978) 249–260.

Walbank, M. 1997. "The foundation and planning of early Roman Corinth", *JRA* 10 (1997) 95–130.

White, L. M. 2005, "Favorinus's 'Corinthian Oration': A Piqued Panorama of the Hadrianic Forum", *Urban Religion in Roman Corinth,* D. Schowalter and S. Friesen (eds) 2005 61–110.

Williams, C. K. 1989, "A Re-evaluation of Temple E and the West End of the Forum of Corinth," *The Greek and Roman Renaissance in the Roman Empire,* Papers from the Tenth British Museum Classical Colloquium, S. Walker and A. Cameron (eds) 1989 156–62.

Williams, C. K. 1993, "Roman Corinth as a commercial center," *The Corinthia in the Roman Period, JRA Suppl.8,* Ann Arbor, 31–46.

Williams, C. K. and P. Russell 1981 "Corinth: Excavations of 1980," *Hesperia* 50 (1981) 1–44.

Williams, C. K. 1980, "Corinth Excavations, 1979," Hesperia 49 (1980) 107–134.

Williams, C. K 1977, "Corinth 1976: Forum Southwest," *Hesperia* 46 (1977) 40–81.

Williams, C. K. and J. E. Fisher 1975, "Corinth 1974: Forum Southwest", *Hesperia* 44 (1975) 99–162.

Williams, C. K. 1970, "Corinth, 1969: Forum Area," *Hesperia* 39 (1970) 1–39.

Wiseman, J. 1979, "Corinth and Rome I," *ANRW* 7.1 438–548.

Notes

1. As Strabo did similarly: "πολὺν δὲ χρόνον ἐρήμη μείνασα ἡ Κόρινθος ἀνελήφθη πάλιν ὑπὸ Καίσαρος τοῦ θεοῦ διὰ τὴν εὐφυΐαν, ἐποίκους πέμψαντος τοῦ ἀπελευθερικοῦ γένους πλείστους." 8.6.23

2. Amandry considers the date of 44 BCE to be uncertain, Amandry, A. 1988 Le *monnayage des duovirs Corinthiens,* (BCH Suppl. 15) (Paris) 1988 13. Strabo, who as Amandry

cites (1988 8), visited Corinth in 29 BCE and attributed the foundation to Caesar but does not say when it occured. (See Fn. 2 above.) Regardless of this imprecision and his uncertainty, Amandry proposes a chronology of the duovires issues begining with Aeficius Certus and C. Iulius in 44 or 43 BCE and continuing uniterrupted through M. Antonius Theophilus and P. Aebutius 30 BCE afterwhich the Augustan period issues begin.

3. It is hard to judge the depth of Corinth's support of Antony. His early conscription of Corinth into his forces, however, would seem to have diverted the colony's resources toward his needs and not those of the the colony. (Robinson, B. 2001, "Fountains and the Culture of Water in Roman Corinth" PhD diss. University of Pennsylvania 2001 31, and Walbank, M. 1997, "The foundation and planning of early Roman Corinth", *JRA* 10 (1997) 95–130, esp. 123. Regardless of how partisan the Corinthians were, its strategic importance was great enough that Agrippa neutralized it before Actium *(Dio 50.13.5)*

4. According to Vitruvius I.3–7 the sequence of events in laying out a town are: 1) selecting a site, 2) laying the foundations for the city walls and towers, 3) laying out the streets, and 4) siting the temples, forum, and other public buildings. Although we should understand the initiation of these events to be sequential, with the exception of item 1, work toward the completion of the remaining three would have been ongoing simultaneously. A thirty year wait before undertaking major construction in the forum and civic center seems unusual.

5. N.B. In Corinth publications "Early Roman Corinth" has been used as a general descriptive for events prior to the earthquake of CE 77. Unless specified by a particular author, it does not necessarily mean events Augustan or prior. A good recent discussion of Early Roman Corinth is Walbank 1997.

6. Robinson, 2005. "Fountains and the Formation of Cultural Identity", in D. Schowalter and S. Friesen (eds), *Urban Religion in Roman Corinth (Harvard Theological Studies 53)*, 121.

7. Robinson 2001 29–31, wherein she cites Cicero's apparent first hand knowledge of the spring in *c*. 79–77 BCE during his travels in Greece, his letter to Atticus in 46 BCE, and B. H. Hill's understanding that the earliest colonists used the fountain pretty much as they found it.

8. Wallbank 1997 123, believes the industrial site was probably the shop of a bronze smithy. The presence of a macellum and a macellum piscarium is attested epigraphically, *Corinth VIII.ii* (=West) nos 124 and 125, and *Corinth VIII.iii* (=Kent) no. 321. West includes a discussion of the siting of these structures based upon the find spots of the fragments. Two of the additional three fragments Kent associates with W-124 were found east of Peirene in 1914 and are consistent with West's analysis. The third Kent fragment, found in the South Basilica, does not subvert the preponderance of evidence placing these inscriptions in the area to the north of Peirene. West dates the inscriptions "to the last years of Augustus or to the reign of Tiberius" based upon the historical record. Kent dates the three of them Augustan by letter form, citing the "characteristic tail of the letter Q". Spawforth, A. 1978, "Balbillia, the Euryclids, and Memorials for a Greek Magnate", *BSA* 73 249–260, esp. p. 258, has challenged Kent. Although Spawforth 1978 does not address K-321

specifically, the challenge is not over using letter forms for dating but over Kent's specific Augustan criteria and his use of the tail of the letter Q in particular. Exactly when these macella appeared remains a question but West's assessment remains sound.

9. Its particular use may have been quite utilitarian. For the problems with its use and dating see Millis, B. 2006, "'Miserable Huts' in post-146 BC Corinth," *Hesperia* 75 (2006) 397–404. See p. 80 below for a revised dating of the Lechaion Road Basilica.

10. Williams, C. K. and Slane, K. have produced the most extensive works, see bibliography; Walbank 1997 has offered an overview of the early colony based upon an interpretive synthesis of their work; Scotton, P. 1997, "The Julian Basilica at Corinth: An Architectural Investigation," PhD diss. University of Pennsylvania, based upon a reexamination of the architectural evidence and archaeological record, has presented a revised date for the construction of the Julian Basilica; Robinson 2001for the buildings on the west end of the forum and the Fountain of Poseidon in particular. Specific citations will be referenced by building.

11. All studies of the South Stoa at Corinth must begin with *Corinth I.iv* = O. Broneer *The South Stoa and its Roman Successors*, Princeton, NJ, ASCSA 1954. His discussion of the early Roman period is pp. 100–102. Perhaps the best evidence for dating comes in the form of the unpublished pottery lots, some of which have been studied by Slane. New evidence and anaylyses, based in part upon the pottery lots, has been provided by Williams, C. K. 1993, "Roman Corinth as a commercial center," *The Corinthia in the Roman Period, JRA Suppl.8*, Ann Arbor, 31–46 esp. 37–38, Wallbank 1997 118–120, and Robinson 2001 264–292. The architecture of the South Stoa is currently being restudied by David Scahill for his University of Bath dissertation.

12. Broneer 1954 100–101.

13. Walbank 1997 118–120.

14. Hayes, J. 1973, "Roman Pottery from the South Stoa at Corinth" *Hesperia* 42 (1973) 416–470, Williams, C. K. "Corinth Excavations, 1979" *Hesperia* 49 (1980) 107–134, and Slane, K. unpublished study of the pottery lots from shops XVII–XXIII.

15. Hayes 1973 417.

16. Williams 1980 117–125.

17. Private conversations with Kathleen Slane.

18. *Corinth I.v* 3–31 and for the first phase of the Roman Building 5–13. The date of the Julian Basilica will be presented below.

19. The phasing and various forms of the Southeast Building is one of the thorniest problems remaining in the forum. Complicating the matter is the presence of at least a Hellenistic period structure on the site, see Romano, I. 1994, "A Hellenistic Deposit from Corinth: Evidence for Interim Period Activity (146–44 BC)," *Hesperia* 63 (1994) 57–104. It is not at all clear what elements are to be associated with this structure. Two new drawings of the two Roman phases have recently been produced and published, White, L. M. 2005 "Favorinus's 'Corinthian Oration': A Piqued Panorama of the Hadrianic Forum", *Urban Religion in Roman Corinth*, D. Schowalter and S. Friesen eds, 2005, 85 and 87. Of these drawings, the earlier phase is speculative but it should be noted that it shows no need to reposition the north wall to facilitate

the construction of the Julian Basilica. The second phase, as depicted, incorporates the remains after the collapse of the basilica late in the 4th century CE.

20. As with the Julian Basilica, there are difficulties with the published interpretation of the architecture of the Southwast Building. My dissertation, Scotton 1997, addressed some of the problems with the Julian Basilica and my forthcoming monograph on the subject will address more. I have begun architectural studies of the Southeast Building in an attempt to resolve its issues.

21. Which may well be. The north wall does not begin to bond with the west until its fourth course and only abuts it in its first three courses.

22. These findings are based upon my completed study of the Julian Basilica and my ongoing investigation of the Southeast Building.

23. *Corinth I.*iii = Scranton, R. 1951, *Monuments in the Lower Agora and North of the Archaic Temple*, Princeton 1951 91–110 for a full discussion and 91–92 for the foundations and core; Walbank 1997, 120–122; Wiseman, J. 1979, "Corinth and Rome I," *ANRW* 7.1 515–516, offers an Augustan date tying it to the formation of the province of Achaia.

24. Walbank 1997 121.

25. Kent no. 157.

26. Walbank 1997 121 fn. 95

27. Spawforth fn. 9.

28. Well dated examples of Augustan era poros masonry can be found in the second Roman phase of Peirene Fountain, the first phase of the Julian Basilica, and in the Fountain of Poseidon.

29. The masonry in the South Basilica, for example, is now dated to sometime in the 70s CE. The most comprehensive analysis of the materials and methods employed in the South Basilica may be found in Herbst, J. 2001, "Quarrying and Construction Methods in the Twin Basilicas at Corinth", MS thesis, Berkeley 2001.

30. Walbank 1997 116.

31. Corinth I.iii 139–141and 148–154.

32. *Corinth* I.vi 151–153; Shoe, L. T. 1964 "The Roman Ionic Base in Corinth", *Essays in Memory of Karl Lehman*, New York, Institute of Fine Arts, 300–303; Williams C. K. 1970, "Corinth, 1969: Forum Area," *Hesperia* XXXIX (1970) 29 and Fig. 8; Williams, C. K. and J. E. Fisher 1975, "Corinth 1974: Forum Southwest", *Hesperia* XLIV (1975) 28; Walbank 1997 122–123; and Robinson 2001 236–238.

33. Slane Wright, K. 1980, "A Tiberian Pottery Deposit from Corinth," *Hesperia* 49 (1980) 135–176, esp. 174.

34. For the phases of its construction and dates see: Williams, C. K. 1977, "Corinth 1976: Forum Southwest," *Hesperia* 46 (1977) 58–62; Slane Wright 1980 174–5; Slane, K. 1986, "Two Deposits from the Early Roman Cellar Building, Corinth," *Hesperia* 55 (1986) 271–318, esp. 317 (for a revised date), and Walbank 1997 123.

35. The west porch of the Julian Basilica is set upon and across the starting line. Whether or not it was exposed before the construction of the basilica is uncertain. For a discussion of the remains in situ see Scotton 1997 103–107.

36. This view is perhaps best expressed in *Corinth VIII.iii* 28–29 and based upon Kent 152.

37. Gebhard, E. 1993, "The Isthmian Games and the Sanctuary of Poseion in the early Empire," *The Corinthia in the Roman Period, JRA Suppl. 8*, Ann Arbor, 1993, 82–89. Kajava, M. 2002, "When Did the Isthmian Games Return to the Isthmus? (Rereading 'Corinth 8.3.153)," *Classical Philology* 97 (2002) 168–178 aruging from epigraphic and historic sources dates the return to the Isthmus to CE 43.

38. Gebhard 1993 81–82. See also Kajava 2002 170–171.

39. Corinth VIII.iii 28 and 70, with the latter discussing the reasons why.

40. Robinson 2001 246–249 esp. 249 for the most recent discussion of dating the fountain.

41. More about this evidence below.

42. Robinson 2001 44–45 and 2005 121–123.

43. Williams, C. K. and Russell, P. 1981, "Corinth: Excavations of 1980," *Hesperia* L (1981) 27–29. Based upon Robinson's dating of the First Roman phase in Peirene this is contra to Walbank 1997 123 who agreed that Peirene and the Northeast Stoa are contemporaries but wrote before Robinson's revised dating.

44. Williams and Russell 1981 28.

45. If the Northeast Stoa was indeed contemporary with and designed to act as a screen for the upper reaches of the Pierene facade, it too may have been at the benefaction of Agrippa.

46. W-122 and K-323.

47. Robinson 2001 246–249.

48. See Corinth I.v and Scotton 1997 for discussions of the form and function of the building.

49. S-1116a–e. For a relatively recent short discussion of the statue and its date see Rose, C. B. 1997, *Dynastic Commemoration and Imperial Portraiture in the Julio-Claudian Period*, Cambridge, 1997 139.

50. de Grazia Vanderpool, C. "Roman Portraiture, The Many Faces of Corinth", *Corinth XX Results of Excavations: Corinth, the Centenary*, ASCSA, 2003, 369–384 esp. 372–373 and 375–379.

51. S-1065.

52. S-1080. For the dating of both the Gaius and Lucius statues see de GraziaVanderpool 2003 ibid.

53. *Corinth I.v* 54.

54. *Corinth VIII.iii* no. 69.

55. This is the same type of coin that was sealed in the well by the construction of the building.

56. Scotton, P. 2005, "A New Fragment of an Inscription from the Julian Basilica at Roman Corinth," *Hesperia* 74 (2005) 95–100.

57. *Ibid.* 99. A Julio/Claudian date was possited by Joyce Reynolds, *ibid.* 99 fn. 35.

58. An article producing the full evidence of the inscription is forthcoming.

59. Broneer tentatively identifed Room C of the South Stoa as the agonotheteion, *Corinth I.iv.* 107–111. The evidence for this is a mosaic depicting an athete before a seated female figure who may be Eutyche. Broneer considered this identification to be conjectural, *ibid.* 111. Weakening the relevance of the mosaic to the early colony is the fact that it is now considered to be late 1st or more likely 2nd century CE. See Hellenkemper-Salies, G. 1986, "Römische Mosaiken in Griechenland," *BJb* 186 (1986) 241–284. Even if Broneer's identification of Room C as the agonotheteion is correct and it was so used in the early colony, the presence of the agonothetai in the Julian Basilica is not diminished, especially in the context of the trappings of the imperial cult.

60. Hallet, C. 2005, *The Roman Nude:Heroic Portrait Statuary 200 BC–AD 300* Oxford 2005 172–176 argues this is reasonable in a Greek context and cites examples of clad parents and nude sons.

61. Ridgway, B. 1981, "Sculpture from Corinth" *Hesperia* L (1981) 422–448, esp. 432; Pollini, J. 1987, *The Portraiture of Gaius and Lucius Caesar* Fordham University Press 1987 19–20; de GraziaVanderpool 2003 376–377.

62. The discussion of the temples on the west end is derived largely from Williams, C. K. 1989, "A Re-evaluation of Temple E and the West End of the Forum of Corinth," *The Greek and Roman Renaissance in the Roman Empire*, Papers from the Tenth British Museum Classical Colloquium, Susan Walker and Averil Cameron eds, 1989 156–162 Buidling specific references are cited by footnote. The dates for these structures are determined largely by architectural analyses.

63. *Ibid.*; Gros, P. 1967, "Trois temples de la Fortune des Ier et II siècles de notre ère," *MEFRA* 79 (1967) esp. 503–24. Kent, *Corinth VIII.iii* no. 56, dates the fragmentary inscription on the marble tympanun, VE]NERI - - -, in the first half of the 1st century CE but Williams' early date seems more consistent with the architecture.

64. Williams 1989 156–157.

65. Williams 1975 27–28.

66. Robinson 2001 246–249 and 260.

67. *Ibid.* 249.

68. Williams 1989 158.

69. Williams 1989 159–160 esp. 160. Accepting Williams, the construction sequence in the northwest corner of the forum would then seem to be the Northwest Stoa, Temple D, and then Temple K. It is unclear where Temple E, standing west and above this group, fits in this chronological scheme but none of them is earlier than late Augustan.

70. Williams 1989 156.

71. Williams 1993, fig. 1

72. Edwards, C. Edwards, C. 1994, "The Arch Over the Lechaion Road at Corinth and Its Sculpture," Hesperia 63 (1994) 263–308, esp. 272–273.

73. How much later the Lechaion Road Basilica was built is uncertain. Quarrying was ongoing on the east face of Temple Hill until Claudian times. It is hard to imagine the basilica standing and quarrying underway five to ten or even twenty meters distant. Conversation with C. K. Williams II.

74. That this may have been a temple to Apollo Clarios is a possibility but Pausanias only cites it as a Temple of Apollo.

75. Robinson 2001 46 where she speculates, and on reasonable grounds, that Marcus Agrippa may well have been the benefactor behind the first Roman renovation of Peirene.

6. Between Atticus and Aeneas:
the making of a colonial elite at Roman Butrint

Inge Lyse Hansen

Three times during the latter half of the 1st c. BCE the city of Butrint (ancient Buthrotum in Epirus) was shaped directly and unequivocally by the intervention of Rome. On two separate occasions grants of Roman colonial status were conferred upon it, in 44 and 27 BCE, connecting its political foundation to the two most powerful individuals of the late Republic, Caesar and Augustus.[1] By the end of the century long-standing traditions of Epirote links to Troy had been formalised and promoted as a proper Trojan ancestral myth for Butrint in no less than the court-sponsored epic of the *Aeneid*.[2] In legal and in mythical origin Butrint was, in other words, directly linked to Rome and the Julio-Claudian family, and for the first century of its existence this would shape its very identity as a city.

Situated on the mainland of Epirus close to the narrowest point of the Straits of Corfu, Butrint benefited from its access to the Ionian Sea to the west and to the sheltered Lake Butrint to the east (Fig. 6.1).[3] Its location made it one of the nodal points in the routes connecting Italy and Sicily with the eastern Adriatic and mainland Greece. Above all, it offered safe anchorage and gave access to rich natural resources in grazing and fisheries of its hinterland (Figs 6.2–3). Despite its advantageous position, which alone could explain it becoming an object of interest for Roman colonisation in the area, the status and identity of Butrint, until the early Principate, remained overshadowed by its more powerful neighbours, Corcyra and Phoenice. Even historical references to the city remained short and tersely geographical in intent. Dionysius of Halicarnassus, for example, in his account of the travels of Aeneas provides little more information than Butrint is "a seaport of Epirus"; Caesar's is more laconic still describing Butrint as "a city over by Corcyra".[4]

With the publication of the *Aeneid*, a fulsome description of the city and its origins was provided by Virgil. Butrint is here portrayed as a mirror image of Troy – with gates, a brook and an acropolis, all a miniature version of the Phrygian city, and its foundation is directly attributed to two of the most exemplary and virtuous Trojans, Helenus and Andromache, who populated the city with their own kin. Crucially, Aeneas not only pays a lengthy visit, but it is at Butrint that he receives the good auspices for his journey towards Rome, an event formerly intimately connected to the great oracular sanctuary at Dodona in inland Epirus.[5] The tradition of links between Troy and Epirus was well established by the time of Virgil, though for Butrint never as unequivocally expressed as it now became.[6] Virgil provided the first description and characterization of Butrint as a city, formalized its foundation history linking it implicitly to that of Rome, and conferred on it a participatory role in the heroic narrative of Rome itself. In the *Aeneid* one other important stopover is made by Aeneas in the Ionian: at Actium, where the men celebrate Trojan games.[7] For a contemporary audience this could not but have invoked Octavian's recent victory and the foundation of the new city, Nicopolis, by the battle site.[8] Hence, Butrint was presented not simply as one of the stops along the route of Aeneas but could now appear as *the* urban counterpart to Augustus' own city of Nicopolis in the Ionian (Fig. 6.1).[9]

This extraordinary singling out of an otherwise seemingly undistinguished city provides the starting-point for my discussion of the colonising effort at Butrint. Could persons – or interests – at Butrint itself have made this mythmaking appropriate? I want to examine the composition of the magisterial elite of the new Roman city and of the Roman patrons with whom they are linked. My main objective is

Figure 6.1. The location of Butrint (Butrint Foundation)

to review the nature of early Roman Butrint and the interests invested in this city, and, drawing on onomastic and artistic evidence, this paper will discuss the social make-up and political loyalties of the new governing class between the Caesarian and Augustan colonial grants.

The discussion is intended as an articulation of the identity of the magisterial elite in Roman Butrint, and with it that of the colonial group as a whole. It will provide a prism for assessing the motivations behind the establishment of the colony (and with it Rome's approach to this region), as well as Butrint's own employment of its new identity – at a local and regional level as well as in its dealings with Rome. Integral to the discussion is the related issue of patronage. Most straightforwardly this comprises the personal relationships that conditioned the choice of the colonists and their access to local power. Conversely, these relationships also

indicate the ability of influential individuals and families to act as patrons in this area: practically and within the contemporary political climate of Rome. Certainly, the fortunes of the local magisterial elite appear to mirror the fortunes of their patrons, and the engagement of the latter in the wider circles of patronage and influence in Rome. In the same manner, Virgil's promotion of Butrint may be read both as furnishing local characteristics and as a discourse of metropolitan Roman interests, and so this paper will start by examining local identities and relationships and close with a discussion of the patrons of the new city.

The material evidence

The physical expansion of Butrint as a result of the grants of colonial status is clear in the archaeological record. In particular, the recent investigations on

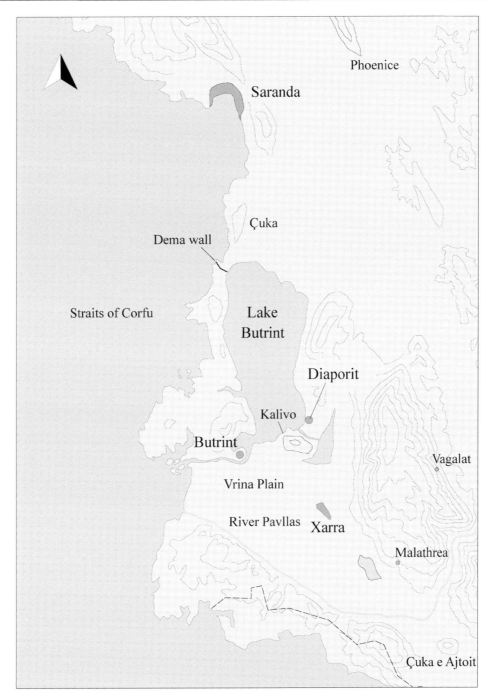

Figure 6.2. Butrint and immediate environs (Butrint Foundation)

the flat alluvial plain facing Butrint have provided evidence for the establishment of an urban extension, or suburb, to the city here (Fig. 6.4).[10] By the mid 1st c. CE an area along the waterfront and close to the main access point to Butrint had developed into a planned settlement consisting of a mixture of residential, commercial and public structures. Antedating this may conceivably have been the domestic structures associated with the early colonists; unfortunately the raised water level makes deeper excavation impossible.[11] Further south, in the fertile valley evidence of centuriation has been found in landscape features. Differences in the units used (respectively 20 × 20 actus and 12 × 16 actus) suggest the centuriation programme was established in two main phases; further research will establish if it conforms to the alignment of the layout of the settlement and are contemporary with this.[12]

What is of interest here is the composition of the colonists and, in particular, the composition of the new magisterial elite. The primary material for colonial magistrates at Butrint is the names

Figure 6.3. Aerial view of Butrint towards the Straits of Corfu (Butrint Foundation, photo by A. Islami)

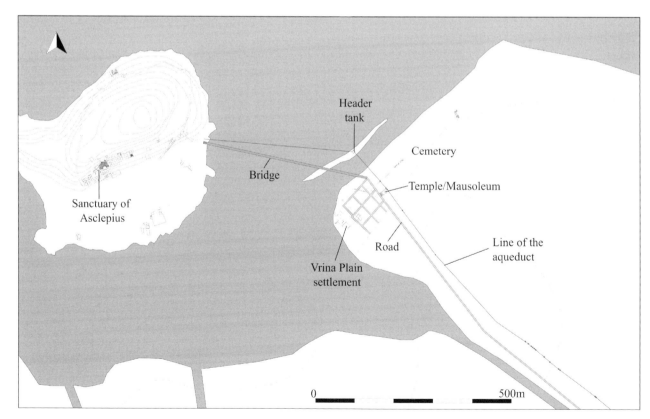

Figure 6.4. Reconstruction of the ancient shoreline with the Vrina Plain settlement and the alignment of the main road and aqueduct (Butrint Foundation)

Table 6.1 Magistrates at Butrint 44 BCE–CE 14

	Name	Magistracy
Triumviral period	Q. CAECILIUS [--]IBUS	Praefectus iure dicundo
	P. DASTIDIUS	IIvir quaestor aerarii, Praefectus
	L. CORNELIUS	IIvir quaestor aerarii
	SURA	IIvir iter
Augustan period	Q NAEVI SURA	IIvir
	A. HIRTUL. NIGER	IIvir
	T. POMPONIUS	IIvir quinq & iter
	C. IULIUS	IIvir quinq
	A. COCCEIUS	IIvir iter
	M. PULLIENUS	quinq / [quinq iter]
	L. ATEIUS FUSCUS	quinq
	P. POMPONIUS GRAECINUS	IIvir /quinq /quinq iter/quinq tert
	MILESIUS	IIvir
	SILVIUS	IIvir quin iter
	A. TEIDIUS	IIvir
	C. IULIUS STRABO	Praefectus

provided in the epigraphic and, in particular, the numismatic material. With colonial status came also the establishment of a mint. This remained active at Butrint during the period between the mid-1st century BCE and the mid-1st century CE, producing a wider range of issues than any other city in the immediate region.[13] The names of the issuing *duovirs* are included on the Triumviral and Augustan coinage with enough detail to establish a relative chronological order (Table 6.1).[14] Unfortunately the tradition is not maintained in the Claudian or Neronian coinage, and no longer-term evaluation of the magisterial elite can hence be undertaken.[15] However, though the material evidence provided covers a rather short period – only 57 years – 14 different people are named as holding the office of *duovir* or *duovir quinquennal* – five of whom held office over multiple terms. Added to this are three men listed as *praefecti* – one of whom also held the office of *duovir* (Table 6.1). That is, 24 terms of office, shared among 16 individuals, representing roughly 27% of the total number of terms of office in this period. Though far from comprehensive, the sample size is comparative to that of similar studies from Corinth.[16]

Corinth, Dyme and Patras in Achaea, with which Butrint shares a common history of colonisation, provide interesting comparative evidence.[17] Like Butrint, Corinth and Dyme were both Caesarian colonies; the colony at Dyme replaced the settlement of pirates installed by Pompey, before being absorbed absorbed into the territory of Patras in the Early Tiberian period.[18] The duoviral magistrates in both cities appear mainly to be of civilian background.

Corinth, with its large port and important regional status, presents the most varied social background of its civic elite: provincial Greek notables, veteran families, clients of powerful Romans and, overwhelmingly, clients of Roman *negotiatores*.[19] At Dyme the magistrates appear to be predominantly clients or freedmen of powerful Roman individuals rather than *negotiatores*.[20] Patras instead was an Augustan colony founded in the aftermath of Actium, with a second wave of colonist settled in 16/15 BCE coinciding with the travels of Agrippa in the East.[21] Here, the epigraphic record points to it being a predominantly veteran settlement. As the examination of the Butrint material will show, the colony at Butrint appears overwhelmingly to have been composed of urban freedmen and clients of powerful individuals in Rome. Even accounting for the inherent difficulties in prosopographical investigations, the Butrint sample in composition resembles that of Corinth and, in particular, Dyme. Hence, as at other Caesarian colonies, the colonists must have benefited from the *Lex Coloniae Genetivae Juliae*, which allowed freedmen access to the office of municipal *decurion* and hence the office of *duovir*.[22]

To date, only two inscriptions have been linked to a military presence at Butrint. A fragmentary, possibly funerary, inscription from Çuka e Ajtoit in the Pavllas Valley south of Butrint may be dedicated to a veteran of the IX Legion Hispana or Macedonica, which served with Augustus till Actium.[23] A better preserved inscription from Butrint itself, dated to the Claudian–Neronian period, is dedicated to a person celebrated as twice *duovir*, *quinquennal* and patron of the colony, previously serving with the V Legion Macedonia. Nothing, unfortunately, remains of the person's name.[24]

```
  Co po
[I]I vir II qui[nq]
[L]eg V Macedoni[c]
[au]guri patrono col
[praef ue]hiclor et
[praef] castr
  Orestarum
  suo
```

The legion had belonged to Octavian before Actium and was stationed in Macedonia between 30 BCE and CE 6, and our unknown patron's links with Butrint may have been established then unless he was, as suggested by Deniaux, originally from Butrint.[25] To obtain the property assets required to qualify for the local curia, the person to whom the dedication is made must have been an officer, undoubtedly with additional personal funds. Hence, his presence is not *per se* indicative of an organised settlement of veterans post Actium.

A large, but rather damaged, limestone inscription provides details for the very earliest period of the Triumviral colony. It lists the *magistri* and administrators serving the colony, and the mixture of citizen and freedman status of these names support the identification of the early settlement as consisting of civilians.[26]

```
Ge[nio coloniae]
c]oll[egium iuuenum]
    ...]oto[...
L. Turranio L. l. Attalo ma[g(istro)]
P. Dastidio P. f. Ouf(entina) Rufo pr[aef(ecto)]
Q. Caecilio L. n. [Sos]ibio praef(ecto)
i(ure) d(icundo)
L. Licinio L. l. Philotecno lapidario
M'. Otacilio M'. l. Eum[eni]o librar[io]
C. Plaetorio C. l. Phil[ipp]o scalpt[o]re
A. Granio [s]criba [colla]tione [pleb]is
```

The two most high-ranking persons mentioned, the prefects Publius Dastidius Rufus (son of Publius and of the Oufentina tribe) and Quintus Caecilius [Sos]ibius (grandson of Lucius), are both Roman citizens, as is the Aulus Granius acting as scribe. The remaining four are all freedmen. The scribe, Aulus Granius, may be the same person recorded as being *magister vicus* in two later inscriptions, suggesting that he was a member of the original colonial settlement who maintained local standing into his late middle age.[27] His Campanian name, common in Puteoli, is well attested among *negotiatores*

and appears among the magistrates of Corinth.[28] Another *magister*, the *libertus* Lucius Turranius Attalus, might, as suggested by Deniaux, instead be a freedman of a person with commercial interests based on landholdings in Epirus; that is, one of the *synepirotae* referred to by Varro.[29] The Manius Otacilius Eumenius listed as *libertus* and *librarius* may be linked to a later Manius Otacilius Mystes who appears as dedicator of a shrine to Minerva Augusta in an early 1st-c. CE inscription.[30] Various possibilities have been suggested for the presence of Otacilii at Butrint, based on links to Roman generals then active in the Adriatic or to commercial interests in Delos or Sicily.[31] The background of Licinius and Plaetorius are difficult to establish but may conceivably be linked to the Adriatic.[32]

With the exception of the two prefects, the office-holders listed here all appear as having links to patrons with commercial interests in the area. None of these families (again, with the exception of the prefects) appear among those named on the coinage as *duoviri* or in other capacities among the higher echelons of municipal power. Whereas the importance of the port of Corinth provided access to high office for clients of *negotiatores*, at Butrint, by contrast, this seems not to have been the case. Instead, the promotion to power seems to be linked to the patronage of persons of political significance in Rome.

The Triumviral colony

Thanks to the correspondence of Cicero the earliest history of the colonial *deductio* is known in some detail.[33] The first decree designating Butrint as a colony was issued by Caesar using a claim of unpaid taxes as justification. Responding to this threat of land confiscations the inhabitants appealed for help to Titus Pomponius Atticus who had owned major properties in the area since at least 68 BCE.[34] Atticus not only paid the outstanding amount on behalf of the city, but lobbied Caesar – through friends and associates in Rome – for a promise that a colony would not be established at Butrint. The promise seems to have been granted but the death of the dictator left its ratification by the senate in the hands of the consuls of 44 BCE, Marcus Antonius and Publius Cornelius Dolabella. Despite the best efforts of Cicero and Atticus, and the expressed support of the consuls, the colonists arrived late in the summer of 44 BCE led by the praetor designate C. Munatius Plancus.[35]

M. Antonius' failure to redirect the colonist elsewhere must have been influenced by the same strategic concerns that had originally motivated Caesar: to protect the routes between Italy and the East, and to safeguard access to the important island of Corcyra as well as to supplies for the troops in an area that had been a theatre of conflict in the Civil War.[36] For M. Antonius, Caius Plancus must have seemed a safe choice: chosen by Caesar to oversee the settlement in Epirus, he had already proved himself a staunch Caesarian supporter, fighting on his side at Dyrrhachium in 48 BCE.[37] Besides, Plancus' more illustrious brother Lucius, the consul of 42 BCE, could – at least until 32 BCE – be counted among the Antonian camp.[38]

Among the Triumviral magistrates at Butrint, Lucius Cornelius and Sura may equally be linked to political allies (Table 6.1). Cornelius offers various possibilities: the Cornelii were one of the oldest patrician families in Rome and is well represented among *negotiatores* in the east; the Buthrotan *duovir* could be linked to Sulla, possibly a descendant of one the 10,000 manumitted by him; or he could be associated with the family of Antonius' fellow consul Cornelius Dolabella.[39] The latter appears as a viable possibility given the particular role afforded to Cornelius: with Publius Dastidius he is the earliest recorded *duovir* at Butrint, both men unusually holding the office as *quaestor aerarii*, in recognition, presumably, of their role in organising the new colony.[40] That matters relating to the establishment of the colony fell within the sphere of interest of the consul is suggested also in an effusive letter from Cicero in June 44 BCE in which Dolabella is thanked for "having put the cause and community of Buthrotum on a secure footing" and requested to take the city "under your perpetual patronage".[41] For the latest of the Triumviral magistrates, a man known only as Sura, it is tempting to see a link with the Cateline conspirator and consul of 71 BCE, P. Cornelius Lentulus, nicknamed Sura. Lentulus had died already in 63 BCE, but leaving no heirs some of his clients would undoubtedly have been inherited by his wife Julia, the mother of Marcus Antonius and kinswoman of Julius Caesar. Twice *duovir*, the link to Antonius' family may account for the long-standing political influence of the Butrint Sura.[42] Indeed, one may only speculate if the family's link to the respected Julia was a factor in their political survival into the Augustan period.[43] The family is the only one of the Triumviral office holders to succeed as magistrates after Actium – undoubtedly by calling on their links with the family of Caesar.

Despite the limited number of names available, there is much to suggest that elite power in the new colony was afforded to individuals with patrons who could be counted as Caesarian supporters favourable to M. Antonius. In this respect, the greatest surprise is the complete absence of Antonii among the Butrint magistrates, unlike at Corinth and Dyme.[44] Butrint does not appear to have been a *primary* object of military interest for Antony and his control of the Ionian Sea. Rather, he focussed his interests on the islands of Corcyra and Zakynthus.[45] It seems likely that the all-important role of Butrint, which warranted the colonial settlement, must instead have been as a supply-base for the troops, as the area had been previously for Caesar.[46] The Caesarian support evident among the patrons of the colonist must have been considered sufficient to ensure loyalty to the triumvir, and to enable influence at Butrint to be managed obliquely with the city as an appendage to the more important Corcyra.

The most interesting of the magistrates is Quintus Caecilius [Sos]ibius. His name appears on the early Triumviral inscription noted above, together with that of P. Dastidius Rufus – undoubtedly the same person as the *duovir* sharing office with L. Cornelius, confirming the early date of the inscription.[47] Both magistrates are honoured as *praefectus* (*iure dicundo*). The reason for their appointment as *praefecti* rather than *duoviri* is unknown; the details included on the stone suggest a role as eponymous magistrates, possibly replacing the *duoviri* at a moment of exceptional circumstance.[48] Q. Caecilius carries the formal name of T. Pomponius Atticus after the latter's adoption in 58 BCE – as is the case also for Q. Caecilius Epirota, the teacher of Atticus' daughter Attica, manumitted by Atticus some time after 58 BCE – and there can be little doubt that he gained his position due to Atticus' patronage.[49] The Butrint Caecilius is not the least interesting by a rather extrovert display of his family's long-standing Roman citizenship. Rather than providing an affiliation to his father he refers to his grandfather, calling himself *Lucius nepos*. It is likely that Caecilius was of an indigenous provincial family, granted Roman citizenship prior to the settlement of the colony, and whose link with Atticus provided the access into the reconfigured elite circle of Butrint.[50]

Despite his opposition to the colonial settlement, Atticus clearly sought influence in its fashioning, and hence to safeguard his interests and affirm his status as a patron of Butrint.[51] What may surprise is that the patronage of Atticus is not more evident: two other members of the Caecilii are known from funerary inscriptions but the name does not appear again among the magistrates.[52] It is possible that this may be another aspect of Atticus' customary reluctance to get directly involved in politics; it is also possible that he simply did not need to. His property may not have been affected by any claim made on the *ager publicus* for the colonial settlement; essential instead would have been to protect his business interests and his links to powerful men in Rome. Nicholas Horsfall has suggested that army supply contracts may explain Roman land investments in Epirus, and access to these would need the support of the triumvirs not the local community.[53] However, Atticus would need to be able to count on the loyalty of his client base to provide weight in his dealings with the generals, as much as he needed good relations with influential men in Rome to fulfil his obligations as a patron towards the Buthrotians. The support offered to Brutus in Epirus indicates Atticus' continued access to funds and ability to grant support in the area Cicero jokingly refers to as "Atticus' province".[54] To support Brutus, in Epirus particularly, looks like an implicit counter-measure to the recent Antonian influence at Butrint; a political balancing act almost immediately countered by his support to Fulvia in the face of Antonian military losses at Mutina.[55] The measures paid off: Atticus neither lost his property in the proscriptions or his influence in Epirus, nor injured his relationships with the triumvirs. It is possible that the long-term influence of Atticus at Butrint depended on just this continuity of presence and the perceived ability to champion the city's cause; on his ability, in other words, to be like Q. Fabius Sanga for the Allobroges "their nation's principal patron".[56]

The Augustan colony

Only a single family, the Surae, is able to maintain high office after 31 BCE and it is on their issues that the change in Butrint's title from *Colonia Julia* to *Colonia Augusta* can be traced (Table 6.1).[57] It obviously served this family well to advertise its allegiance to the new princeps in an explicit manner; certainly, all other Augustan issues from Butrint simply use the ethic BUTHR. Some of the new magistrates may be mature members of the original colonists, or descendants of these. This may be the case for the two Caius Iulii – one holding the office of *quinquennal*, the other a prefect acting on behalf

of Germanicus honoured as *duovir quinquennal* in CE 12 – whose family must be clients or freedmen of Caesar.[58] Similarly the *duovir* Aulus Cocceius whose family may be linked to that of the Cocceius Nerva brothers, consul suffects respectively in 39 and 36 BCE, who – like the Plancii – shifted their support from Antonius to Octavian and similarly may have been able to maintain a client base at Butrint.[59] It may also be the case of the duovir known only as Milesius. His name is known from the coinage and from a substantial stone inscription from a public building, and it has been linked to that of M. Antonius Milesius, who was responsible for the restoration of the Asclepieion in the Roman colony of Corinth.[60] If this is the case, he may be a first- or second-generation colonist from Corinth – where Antonian clients are well attested – now settled in Butrint.[61]

As suggested by the change in its title, Butrint was formally refounded as a colony by Augustus in, or soon after, 27 BCE.[62] The grant provided the catalyst for investment in the urban fabric of Butrint, most notably in the construction of an aqueduct (the singularly most prominent structure featuring on the coinage of Butrint until the late 60s CE).[63] This transported water from springs 4 km away and not only allowed the city to participated in a lifestyle of conspicuous public use of water for bath-houses and fountains, but also provided the conditions for the expansion of the city on the plain facing Butrint to the south (Fig. 6.4).[64] The refoundation also provided opportunities for new patrons of the city, like the Domitii Ahenobarbi, even conceivably the introduction of new colonists.[65] A recent find of a new coin type attributed to the mint of Butrint suggests that a particular interim administration was put in place in the period immediately after Actium (Fig. 6.5). The coin in question was discovered at Phoenice, the old Chaeonian capital 19 km north of Butrint, and depicts on the obverse two antithetic fish and, on the reverse, a legend giving the names of two *praefecti*, Nepos and Siculus.[66] No ethic for the mint is given and the attribution to Butrint is based on an iconographic similarity to two Neronian issues from here, and on the deliberate use of Latin for the legend. The coin is dated to the late Republic or very early Principate. The date is particularly intriguing, not the least given the correspondence with the name of T. Marius Siculus from Urbino. Marius Siculus held a series of civic and religious offices in his hometown as well as being military tribune of the XII Legion and twice *praefectus* of the fleet in Sicily.[67] He is usually identified with the T. Marius described by Valerius Maximus as having intended

Figure 6.5. Late Republican coin found at Phoenice (after Gjongecaj 2005, with permission)

Figure 6.6. Portrait of Augustus from Butrint (Butrint Foundation, photo by J. Barclay-Brown)

Figure 6.7. Portrait of Agrippa from Butrint (Butrint Foundation, photo by J. Barclay-Brown)

Augustus as his heir in gratitude for the wealth and high office won due to him.[68] Siculus appears to have fought first on the side of Sex. Pompeius, then against him as part of the joint forces of Octavian and Antonius in 36 BCE.[69] In his epitaph he carefully avoids mentioning either of the defeated generals by name, but his position within the XII Legion is well advertised indicating that in this case he served with the Augustan forces; that is, with the *XII Fulminata*.[70] Veterans of this legion, together with those from the *X Equestris*, formed the main body of colonists at Patras, settled in two waves, first immediately after Actium then in 16/15 BCE coinciding with Agrippa's travels in the East.[71] Siculus' political loyalties and military abilities on both sea and land would make him an able choice to administer an area of strategic importance in the immediate aftermath of Actium, and it is possible that he may be the very person mentioned on the coin found at Phoenice. Parallels for the deployment of a general at sensitive strategic positions in the Ionian can be found in the installation of G. Sosius by Antonius to oversee the fleet-station on Zakynthus at various times during 39–36 BCE, and in the position of C. Proculeius on Kephallonia in 30–28 BCE, granted by Octavian.[72]

The position of Siculus and Nepos may hence have been to manage a local reorganisation required after 31 BCE, with which the re-foundation of Butrint can be associated. A consequence, as already noted, of this at a local level is clearly that the opportunities extended to individual families were by no means equal. The success of particular families after the Augustan re-foundation appears to follow the same general pattern as during the Triumviral period: those who could point to links with supporters of the princeps (or to the family of the princeps as for the C. Iulii) rose to high office. However, for Butrint the influence from the circle around the princeps increasingly became centred on a single person: Augustus' friend and general, Marcus Vipsanius Agrippa.

There can be no doubt that Agrippa was afforded a particular status at Butrint. No less than two portrait statues were erected in his honour, both of which mirror the idealised imperial style established by Augustus more closely than any found in Italy, as if stressing the allegiance and complementary status between the two (Figs 6.6–7).[73] In local politics, after 27 BCE the duoviral office became overwhelmingly dominated by persons and families associated with

Agrippa. For the magistrates Marcus Pullienus and Lucius Ateius Fuscus, it is the iconographic choice for one of their joint coin issues that betrays their link to the general. Though a bull, the symbol of Butrint, is normally their preferred image, one issue depicts a dolphin and trident. The motif is strikingly similar to an issue commemorating Agrippa at Nicopolis and must have been modelled on the latter type.[74] The dolphin motif is one of the symbols most closely associated with Agrippa and his achievements at Actium. The deliberate adoption of this rather than an Augustan type – combined with the relative rarity of the image on the Butrint coinage – must surely characterise the duovirs as clients of the famous general. Another example of the use of the dolphin motif by persons linked to Agrippa is furnished by the issues of the Segestan duovirs M. Vipsanius Athenaeus and C. Iulius Dionysius; the name of the former betrays his links to the Vipsanii but the continuity of the use of the image on several issues may indicate that both men were linked to the general.[75]

However, the most striking aspect of the period is the domination of the *quinquennial* office by the Pomponii. If Q. Caecilius in the Triumviral period had held a single extraordinary office, now both Titus Pomponius and Publius Pomponius Graecinus are multiple office holders: Titus holding the office of quinquennal twice, Graecinus holding it three times. In other words, between them they were actively engaged in politics for more than 25 years, and a deliberate repetition of imagery on their coin issues suggests that they are related.[76] The Pomponii, as suggested by their name, clearly owed their citizen status to Atticus under whose patronage the family prospered. However, it would have owed its present status to Agrippa as the son-in-law of Atticus, through his marriage to Caecilia Attica. In other words, the career of four of the eleven magistrates can be linked directly to the patronage of Agrippa and his family.

Agrippa was not the only powerful general with access to an established client base in this part of the Ionian after 31 BCE. In 16 BCE L. Domitius Ahenobarbus was honoured as the patron of Butrint and a statue was erected to commemorate this.[77] Lucius' father Gnaeus, the consul of 32 BCE, had been a commanding presence in the Ionian in 42–40 BCE, controlling access in this area in a manner similar to Sex. Pompeius in Sicily.[78] An ostentatious inscription set in the pavement of the main civic area of Butrint indicates the presence of a continued client base in the area. The refurbishment of the pavement, and possibly of nearby key civic buildings, was undertaken by the freedman Cn.

Domitius Eros, undoubtedly manumitted by Cn. Domitius Ahenobarbus the consul of 32 BCE and father of Lucius, the later patron of Butrint.[79] Eros' status may have prevented him holding office after the revocation of the *Lex Coloniae Genetivae Juliae* but his display of civic euergetism indicates that he must have amassed enough wealth to make it feasible for a descendent to hold office. However, none appear. Though silence cannot automatically be taken as evidence, the complete absence of Domitii Ahenobarbi from the list of Augustan period duovirs adds weight to the predominant role of Agrippa and the Pomponii at Butrint.

In this connection the absence of duoviral magistrates on the post-Augustan coinage is particularly unfortunate. The marriage of the younger Cn. Domitius Ahenobarbus (consul CE 32) to Agrippina the Younger, the granddaughter of Agrippa, in CE 28 might have aided the advancement of the Domitii at Butrint.[80] This possibility must have been accentuated in CE 66–67 when their son, the Emperor Nero, visited Achaea.[81] The imperial visit and the freedom granted to the province by him clearly provided a fresh impetus for development at Butrint, as evidenced by its re-invigorated mint and the emphatic presence of the image of the aqueduct on the issues in the period.[82] Being able to call upon direct links to several strands of the emperor's family may well have promoted the local standing of the family at Butrint; however, neither the coinage nor epigraphic sources attest to their presence.[83]

The legacy of Atticus

If Q. Caecilius, as suggested, originated from an indigenous provincial family of longstanding Roman citizen status, the Pomponii could call upon Roman status of even longer standing. As indicated by their name they could trace their links back to the very earliest period of Atticus' involvement in Epirus – that is *prior* to his adoption in 58 BCE. The use of the *praenomen* Titus for the Butrint *duovir* – and for a further three individuals known through epigraphic sources – reveal the continuity and deliberate promotion of the link to Atticus.[84] Hence, it is possible that this family too may have been of indigenous origins. In this light, the somewhat self-conscious indication of long-standing citizenship status used by the *praefectus* Q. Caecilius in the reference to his grandfather appears as a response not just to an influx of colonists of predominantly freedman status but also as a competitive statement aimed at the Butrint Pomponii. However, no other families are as well represented in the epigraphic record as the Pomponii and Caecilii. Accepting their provincial background, their presence at Butrint would have formed significant Roman element in the city, even prior to the colonial grant.[85]

At Butrint, the assistance extended to the city by Atticus was recognised in the erection of a statue in his honour.[86] The Civil War may have forced Atticus to spend most of the 40s in Rome, but repeated offers made to his friends to make use of his property in Epirus as a place of refuge through the 50s and 40s indicate that his engagement with the region continued as unabatedly as his economic interests here.[87] Atticus had passed away in 32 BCE, but by then Agrippa had been married to his daughter Caecilia Attica for at least five years, and together they had a young daughter, Vipsania Agrippina, already betrothed to Augustus' stepson, the future emperor Tiberius.[88] The clients of Atticus would hence, at the time of the regional reorganisation in the aftermath of Actium, have passed to Caecilia Attica and Agrippa, and to a system of family alliances distinctly pro-Octavian.[89]

According to Nepos, Atticus, when not able to regain health, decided to put an end to his suffering by starving himself to death, and called his son-in-law, and two intimate friends, to his deathbed to inform them of this decision.[90] The care and foresight displayed suggest that testamentary issues must have formed part of the discussion too. The scene is reminiscent of the moment of the formal testamentary adoption of Atticus himself by his uncle Q. Caecilius at which he was also made heir to three quarters of the estate.[91] The only securely recorded child of Atticus and Pilia is Caecilia Attica and as a girl the *Lex Voconia* of 169 BCE would have prevented her inheriting more than half her father's wealth. This was a problem faced also by Julius Caesar, and it is possible that the two adopted similar measures to circumvent the law. Caesar adopted his then son-in-law Pompey as his heir, presumably to safeguard his daughter Julia's inheritance by including stipulations that the estate was to be passed to her.[92] It would seem likely that Atticus' elaborate deathbed scene may have provided the setting to make a similar arrangement, with provisos for Agrippa either to benefit Caecilia Attica directly or to make their child the eventual beneficiary in his will. Certainly, Vipsania Agrippina would, within a few years of her father's death in 12 BCE, have been legally independent and hence able to manage the control of her grandfather's Epirote estates, should this have been part of his will. Not only does the *Lex Voconia* appear to have had little effect by the time of Augustus, but from her marriages to

Tiberius and C. Asinius Gallus she had more than the three children required by the terms of the *ius trium liberorum* (Augustus' law of three children) to exempt her from having a guardian.[93] After 28 BCE Agrippa was brought more tightly into the imperial family by marriage first to Augustus' niece Claudia Marcella, then to his daughter Julia.[94] The continuity of support of the Butrint Pomponii combined with the lack of a single recorded Agrippa or Vipsanius at Butrint suggest that direct patronage was carried out by, or in the name of, the descendants of Atticus with the person of Agrippa appearing rather as a focal point of loyalty for the city as a whole.[95]

The close links with powerful political figures and with families close to the imperial court would explain the remarkable appearance of Butrint in Virgil, and its participation as an agent in the new official mythology of Rome. For Butrint, post-31 BCE was not simply a strategic harbour in the Ionian, but in its political make-up presented a composite web of alliances and links with Rome. The decisive appearance of Butrint in the *Aeneid* also epitomises the changing relationships of patronage that occurred throughout the Roman world between the Republic and the Principate.[96]

In the complex relationships of patronage between individuals, and between individuals and Butrint, during the Triumviral period, public and private interests are virtually indistinguishable. The colonial settlement was one way to secure bases in the Adriatic and Mediterranean for Rome and her ruling generals, and individual relationships of patronage and *clientelae* provided an efficient medium through which the new community was made a participant in the workings of Empire. The city and its citizenry needed strong patrons to champion its cause and to give it an access to the political centre, as well as to provide a framework for its own local aspirations. In the competition for influence, the success of a patron depended as much on an ability to command the loyalty of his clients as on an ability to gain authority in Rome, and hence the 'management' of the Triumviral colony displays a complex network of interpersonal relationships, favours and advancements that explains the diverse links of patronage by powerful Roman families that the city could call upon.

The appearance of Butrint in the *Aeneid*, as a major element in the journey of Aeneas and as a complement to Nicopolis, is an evocative mirror for how the Augustan city was perceived. As a city its purported Trojan ancestry and antiquarian reproduction of Troy highlights the presence of local families already of long-standing citizen status and well integrated among the new colonial elite, which must have been such a striking element of its civic character. It also deftly – if implicitly – draws attention to its longstanding links to a former patron, a man of exemplary Republican tradition and arguably the progenitor of its loyalty to Rome. However, the inclusion of Butrint on a revised itinerary of Aeneas reserved in its essence the greater compliment for the princeps, for within its language of heroic ancestry the very singling out of the city subtly acknowledged the very real presence here of economic interests and a client base linked directly to members of his immediate circle.

The creation of the Principate did not do away with the system of patronage *per se* but it did trigger a profound transformation of its expression. At Butrint the notable change in the composition of its ruling elite after 31 BCE, as well as the evidence for praetors acting on behalf of Octavian in the period immediately following Actium, denote the continued use of individual patronage as a system of social and political control. However, the identification between the state and the princeps increasingly converged ties of loyalty and networks of patronage around the very person of the emperor. In this transformation Butrint found itself in the fortunate position of being able to conform to an altered world even before the changes had fully taken place, for it could invoke an alliance network belonging to the Octavian camp already by 32 BCE.[97] There can be little doubt that the city attempted to use this to its advantage in the period following the Actium victory, for with the combined events of the outcome of the battle and the death of its most famous patron the city was suddenly to all intents and purposes an area of authority of persons directly linked to the imperial family itself.

Acknowledgements

The excavations at Butrint are sponsored by the Butrint Foundation and the Packard Humanitites Institute. I would like to thank both for the opportunity to work on this material as well as John Cabot University for financial assistance for the preparation of this paper. I am grateful to Carina Chitta and Kathryn Welch for their generous assistance and advice on family loyalties and inheritance, and to Richard Hodges, Rebecca Sweetman and the anonymous readers who all suggested improvements to the text. My thanks also to Sandro De Maria and Shpresa Gjongecaj for the permission to illustrate the coin shown in Fig. 6.5, and to Andrew Crowson, Oliver Gilkes and Simon Greenslade who patiently made the maps Figs 6.1–2, 6.4.

Bibliography

Alcock S. E. 1994. "Nero at play? The emperor's Grecian odyssey" in J. Elsner and J. Masters (eds) *Reflections of Nero. Culture, History and Representation*: 98–111 (London).

Anamali, Sk., H. Ceka and É. Deniaux 2009. *Corpus des inscriptions latines d'Albanie. (Collection de l'École française de Rome 410)* (Rome).

Bergemann, J. 1998. *Die römische Kolonie von Butrint und die Romaniserung Griechenlands* (Munich).

Bescoby, D. J. 2007. "Geoarchaeological investigation at Butrint", in I. L. Hansen and R. Hodges (eds) *Roman Butrint: An Assessment* (Oxford) 95–188.

Bispham, E. 2005. "Inscriptions", in I. L. Hansen, O. J. Gilkes and A. Crowson (eds) *Kalivo and Çuka e Aitoit, Albania. Interim Report on Surveys and Excavations 1928–2004* (www.butrintfoundation.co.uk) chapter 9.

Braund, D. 1989. "Function and dysfunction: personal patronage in Roman imperialism", in A. Wallace-Hadrill (ed.) *Patronage in Ancient Society* (London/New York) 137–52.

Burnett, A., M. Amandry and P. P. Ripollès 1992 *Roman Provincial Coinage. Vol 1: From the Death of Caesar to the Death of Vitellius (44 BC–AD 69)* (London/Paris).

Cabanes, P. 1996 "Les noms latins dans les inscriptions grecques d'Épidamne-Dyrrhachion, d'Apollonia et de Bouthrotos", in A. D. Rizakis (ed.) *Roman Onomastics in the Greek East – Social and Political Aspects* (Athens) 89–104.

Crawford, M. H. (ed.) 1996. *Roman Statutes (Bulletin of the Institute of Classical Studies, Supplement 64)* (London).

Criniti, N. 1970. *L'epigrafe di Asculum di Cn. Pompeo Strabone* (Milan).

Crowson, A. and O. J. Gilkes 2007. "The archaeology of the Vrina Plain: an assessment", in I. L. Hansen and R. Hodges (eds) *Roman Butrint: An Assessment* (Oxford) 119–64.

de Franciscis, A. 1941. "Iscrizioni di Butrinto" *Rendiconti della Reale Accademia di Archeologia Lettere e Belle Arti* n.s. 21: 273–90.

Deniaux, É. 1987. "Atticus et l'Épire", in P. Cabanes (ed.) *L'Illyrie méridionale et l'Epire dans l'antiquité I (Actes du colloque international de Clermont-Ferrand, oct. 1984)* (Clermont-Ferrand) 245–54.

Deniaux, É. 1993. *Clientèles et pouvoir à l'époque de Cicéron (Collection de l'École Française de Rome 182)* (Rome).

Deniaux, É. 1999. "La traversée de l'Adriatique à l'époque des Guerres Civiles: liberté et contrôle: Cn. Domitius Ahenobarbus et le Canal d'Otrante (42–40 av. J.-C.)", in P. Cabanes (ed.) *L'Illyrie méridionale et l'Epire dans l'antiquité III* (Paris) 249–54.

Deniaux, É. 2004. "Recherches sur la societé de Buthrote, colonie romaine", in P. Cabanes and J.-L Lamboley, eds, *L'Illyrie méridionale et l'Epire dans l'antiquité IV* (Paris) 391–97.

Deniaux, É. 2005. "La colonie romaine de Buthrote. Charges civiques et fonctionnement de la vie municipale" *Mélange de l'École française de Rome. Antiquité* 117.2: 507–15.

Deniaux, É. 2006. "Epigraphie et émergence d'une colonie, l'exemple de Buthrote", in S. Demougin, X. Loriot, P. Cosme and S. Lefebvre (eds), *H.-G. Pflaum: un historien du XXe siècle* (Geneva) 343–67.

Deniaux, É. 2007a. "L'île de Corcyre et la maîtrise de la mer avant la bataille d'Actium (48–31 av. J.-C.)", in K. L. Zachos (ed.) *Nicopolis B* (Preveza) 77–85.

Deniaux, É. 2007b. "La structure politique de la colonie romaine de Buthrotum", in I. L. Hansen and R. Hodges (eds) *Roman Butrint. An Assessment* (Oxford) 33–39.

Freis, H. 1985. "Zwei latenische Inschriften aus Albanien" *Zeitschrift für Papyrologie und Epigraphik* 61: 224–8.

Giorgi, E. 2006. "Problemi metodologici per lo studio del paesaggio antico: considerazioni sul territorio di Phoinike in epoca romana", in L. Bejko and R. Hodges (eds) *New Directions in Albanian Archaeology* (Tirana) 207–22.

Gjongecaj, S. 2005. "Nuovi dati numismatici da Phoinike", in S. De Maria and S. Gjongecaj (eds) *Phoinike III. Rapporto preliminare sulle campagne di scavi e ricerche 2002–2003* (Bologna) 161–79.

Grant, M. 1946. *From Imperium to Auctoritas* (Cambridge).

Greenslade, S. forthcoming. "The Vrina Plain settlement between the 1st–3rd centuries AD", in I. L. Hansen, R. Hodges and S. Leppard (eds) *Butrint Reappraised* (Oxford).

Groag, E. 1915. "Beiträge zur Geschichte des zweiten Triumvirats" *Klio* 14: 43–68.

Hansen, I. L. 2007. "The Trojan connection: Butrint and Rome", in I. L. Hansen and R. Hodges (eds) *Roman Butrint: An Assessment* (Oxford) 44–61.

Hansen, I. L. 2009. *Hellenistic and Roman Butrint.* (London/ Tirana).

Hansen, I. L. and R. Hodges (eds) 2007. *Roman Butrint: An Assessment* (Oxford).

Hansen, I. L. and I. Pojani forthcoming. "Two new togate statues from Roman Butrint: the impact of Actium", in S. walker and K. Zachos (eds) *After Actium: New Archaeological Results from Roman Greece* (London).

Hatzfeld, J. 1919. *Les trafiquants italiens dans l'Orient hellénique* (*Bibliothéque des Écoles Française d'Athene et de Rome 115*) (Paris).

Horsfall, N. 1989. "Atticus brings home the bacon" *Liverpool Classical Monthly* 14.4: 60–62.

Horster, M. 2004 "Substitutes for emperors and members of the imperial families as local magistrates", in L. De Ligt, E. A. Hemelrijk and H. W. Singor (eds) *Roman Rule and Civic Life: Local and Regional Perspectives* (*Impact of Empire* 4) (Amsterdam) 331–55.

Jones, D. 2006 *The Bankers of Puteoli. Finance, Trade and Industry in the Roman World* (Stroud).

Keppie, L. 1984. *The Making of the Roman Army* (London).

Keppie, L. 2000. *Legions and Veterans. Roman Army Papers 1971–2000* (Stuttgart).

Lloyd, R. B. 1957. "Aeneid III and the Aeneas legend" *American Journal of Philology* 78.4: 382–400.

Melfi, M. 2007. "The sanctuary of Asclepius", in I. L. Hansen and R. Hodges (eds) *Roman Butrint: An Assessment* (Oxford) 17–32.

Millar, F. 1988. "Cornelius Nepos, "Atticus" and the Roman revolution" *Greece and Rome* 35: 40–55

Moorhead, S., S. Gjongecaj and R. Abdy 2007. "Coins from the excavations at Butrint, Diaporit and the Vrina Plain", in I. L. Hansen and R. Hodges (eds) *Roman Butrint. An Assessment* (Oxford) 78–94.

Patterson, J. R. 2007. "A dedication to Minerva Augusta from Butrint", in I. L. Hansen and R. Hodges (eds) *Roman Butrint. An Assessment* (Oxford) 40–43.

Pollo, C. 1990. "Die Germanicus-Inschrift aus Buthrotum" *Tyche* 5: 105–8.

Reinhold, M. 1972. "Marcus Agrippa's son-in-law P. Quinctilius Varus" *Classical Philology* 67.2: 119–21.

Rizakis, A. D. 1997. "Roman colonies in the province of Achaia: territories, land and population", in S. E. Alcock (ed.) *The Early Roman Empire in the East* (Oxford) 15–36.

Rizakis, A. D. 2001. "La constitution des élites municipales dans les colonies romaines de la province d'Achaïe", in

O. Salomies (ed.) *The Greek East in the Roman Context* (Helsinki) 37–49.

Salmon, E. T. 1969. *Roman colonization under the Republic* (London).

Salomies, O. 1996. "Contacts between Italy, Macedonia and Asia Minor during the principate", in A. D. Rizakis (ed.) *Roman Onomastics in the Greek East – Social and Political Aspects* (Athens) 111–27.

Spawforth, A. J. S. 1996. "Roman Corinth: the formation of a colonial elite", in A. D. Rizakis (ed.) *Roman Onomastics in the Greek East – Social and Political Aspects* (Athens) 167–82.

Stahl, H.-P. 1998. "Political Stop-overs on a Mythological Travel Route: from Battling Harpies to the Battle of Actium (Aen. 3.268–93)", in H.-P. Stahl (ed.) *Vergil's Aeneid: Augustan epic and political context* (London) 37–84.

Syme, R. 1986. *The Augustan Aristocracy* (Oxford).

Treggiari, S. 1969. *Roman Freedmen during the Late Republic* (Oxford).

Treggiari, S. 1991. *Roman Marriage. Iusti coniugi from the Time of Cicero to the Time of Ulpian* (Oxford).

Ugolini, L. M. 1942. *L'acropoli di Butrinto. (Albania antica III)* (Rome).

Wallace-Hadrill, A. 1989. "Patronage in Roman society: from republic to Empire", in A. Wallace-Hadrill, A. (ed.) *Patronage in Ancient Society* (London/New York) 63–87.

Welch, K. 1996. "T. Pomponius Atticus. A banker in politics?" *Historia* 45: 450–71.

Wilson, A. forthcoming. "The aqueduct at Butrint", in I. L. Hansen, R. Hodges and S. Leppard (eds), *Butrint Reappraised* (Oxford).

Wiseman, T. P. 1971. *New Men in the Roman Senate 139 BC–AD 14* (Oxford).

Notes

1. The details of the Caesarian settlement are summarized in Cic. *Ad Att.* 16.16a. The legends on the Butrint coinage use respectively *Colonia Julia Buthrotum* during the Triumviral period and *Colonia Augusta Buthrotum* in the Augustan period; the latter provides the primary evidence for the Augustan refoundation of the colony. Burnett, Amandry and Ripollès 1992, 275; Deniaux 1987; Deniaux 1993, 362–6.

2. Verg. *Aen.* 3.349–51 is entirely devoted to a description of Aeneas' visit to Butrint, including a description of the city and its history. For a discussion of the use of Trojan ancestry for Butrint in the Julio-Claudian period, see Hansen 2007.

3. Provincial reorganisation meant that Butrint in various periods could count itself as belonging respectively to Macedonia (pre 27 BCE), Achaea (post 27 BCE) and Epirus (early 2nd c. CE). For a discussion of Roman Butrint, see Hansen and Hodges 2007, and, more generally, Hansen 2009.

4. Caes. *B Civ.* 3.16; Dion. Hal. 1.51.1. For the latter the temporary presence of the Trojan camp in the area is further indicated by a hill being called Troy. For the importance of Corcyra prior to 31 BCE, see Deniaux 2007a.

5. Verg. *Aen.* 3.349–51. Ovid provides a similar, if greatly more succinct, description of the city, its origins and its impact on Aeneas, *Met.* 13.715–17.

6. On links between Butrint and Troy, see Dion. Hal. *Ant.*

Rom. 1.51.1–2; Serv. *Ad Aeneidem* 3.293, 3.349; Steph. Byz. *Ethnica* s.v. "Troia" and "Buthrotos". On Epirote links to Troy, see Dion. Hal. *Ant. Rom.* 1.51.2; Eur. *Andr.* 1244–53; Paus. *Description of Greece* 1.11.1–2 and 2.23.6; Procop. 8.22.31; Serv. *Ad Aeneidem* 3.297, 3.349; Varro *Rust.* 2.2.1

7. Verg. *Aen.* 3.278–90.
8. Cf. Stahl 1998 58–61. See also Lloyd 1957 for a discussion of Aeneas' route through the Ionian.
9. See also Stahl 1998, 44–46.
10. Crowson and Gilkes 2007; Greenslade forthcoming.
11. Greenslade forthcoming.
12. Bescoby 2007, 112–3. See also Giorgi 2006 for evidence of centuriation around nearby Phoenice.
13. Burnett, Amandry and Ripollès 1992, 274–9 nos 1378–1417. The issues appear to have been interrupted during the period between Tiberius and Gaius (Caligula). No new coinage is minted after the death of Nero; instead the Neronian issues are countermarked and probably staid in official circulation for some time – possibly as late as the reign of Trajan.
14. Cf. Burnett, Amandry and Ripollès 1992, 275 whose chronological order is followed here. In Table 6.1, the duvoir Aulus Teidius, known only from epigraphic sources, may have held his magistracy in the early Augustan period, but his name has been added at the end of the list given the uncertainty of the date of the inscription.
15. Neither does the body of published epigraphic material from Butrint add any salient information.
16. Rizakis 2001; Spawforth 1996, 168. At Corinth the sample constitutes 21% of the total number of terms; here the names of duoviral magistrates are included on the coinage until CE 68/69, though numerically weighted in favour of the Triumviral and Augustan period.
17. See, in particular, Rizakis 1997, 15–19; Rizakis 2001, 39–41, 46–49; cf. Strabo 8.7.5. Dyme, like Butrint, does not record duoviral names beyond the Augustan period; at Patras no magistrates are named on its coinages and all evidence is epigraphic in nature.
18. Paus. 7.17.5; Plut. *Pomp* 28.4. Rizakis 2001, 46–47.
19. Rizakis 2001, 41–6, 49; Spawforth 1996, 169, 171–3, 174–5.
20. Rizakis 2001, 46–49.
21. Rizakis 1997, 19–21; Rizakis 2001, 48.
22. Salmon 1969, 135; Treggiari 1969, 63–64; cf. the *Lex Ursoniensis*, Crawford 1996, 409/428 no. CV. The law was revoked by Augustus already in 24 BCE; however, by then the main part of his own programme of colonisation had been completed.
23. MAX / VIIII / COELIV[S] ('Max(imus?) / 9 / Coelius'). Bispham 2005 suggests a date in the Julio-Claudian period, perhaps in the reign of Augustus. See Anamali, Ceka and Deniaux 2009, 201 no. 280 for a reading as:] pont(ifex) / max(imus) / trib(unicia) potestate VIII / Coeliu[s].
24. *AE* 1950.0170; de Franciscis 1941, 284–7 (see also 285 for the mention of another inscription restored as l]EG V M[aced; no further details are provided for the latter), and, most recently, Anamali, Ceka and Deniaux 2009, 174–6 no. 236.
25. Anamali, Ceka and Deniaux 2009, 174–6 no. 236; Deniaux 2006. On the V Legion see Keppie 1984, 207; Keppie 2000, 87, 91.
26. *AE* 2004.1341 = *AE* 2005.1405; Anamali, Ceka and Deniaux 2009, 209–10 no. 236; Deniaux 2004; Deniaux 2005; Deniaux 2006; Deniaux 2007b, 35–36.

27. The other two inscriptions with his name are both dated to before 7 BC (A GRANIUS / MAG VICI / LAR VIC SACR and [A GR]ANIUS MAG VICI / STATAE MATRI SAC); *AE* 1987.0904; Deniaux 2007b, 34.
28. Caes. *B Civ.* 3.71; Cic. *Att.* 2.8; Deniaux 2004, 396; Hatzfeld 1919, 392–3; Jones 2006, 35–36; Spawforth 1996, 172, 177.
29. Deniaux 2004, 395. Varro *Rust.* 2.5.1
30. [M]INERVAE / AUGUST(AE) SACR(UM) / M(ANIUS) OTACILIUS MYSTES / ET AEDEM D(E) S(UA) P(ECUNIA) F(ACIENDAM) C(URAVIT) / L(OCUS) D(ATUS) D(ECRETO) D(ECURIONUM), Patterson 2007.
31. Cic. *Fam.* 13.33; Deniaux 1993, 535–6; Deniaux 2004, 396; Patterson 2007, 42. An association with the Sicilian interests of Otacilius Naso is not the least appealing since the evocatively Macedonian name of his freedman Antigonus, indicates links to the Adriatic mainland.
32. See Deniaux 2004, 396 who notes the widespread occurrence of the name Licinius, including in Dalmatia, and the possible Illyrian origin of Plaetorius.
33. The course of events is summarised by Cicero himself in *Att.* 16.16a. See also Deniaux 1987; Deniaux 1993, 362–6.
34. The date is based on a reference by Cicero (*Att.* 1.5.7) in late 68 BCE to Atticus being pleased with his purchase in Epirus, but business interests may antedate this; cf. Horsfall 1989, 60. His estate is likely to have comprised landholdings on Corcyra, around the river Thyamis on the mainland, as well as at Butrint. No convincing archaeological evidence for the location of the Butrint property has yet been found, but the fertile and airy Pavllas Valley to the south present an attractive possibility.
35. Cicero *Att.* 15. 29.3, 16.1.2, 16.4.3, 16.16a–d; Deniaux 1993, 362–66.
36. Deniaux 1999; Deniaux 2007a; Rizakis 1997, 15.
37. Support to Caesar: Caes. *B Civ.* 3.19.7; authority invested by Caesar: Cic. *Att.* 16.16a.3. Plancus became L. Plautius Plancus by adoption, cf. Wiseman 1971, 252 (no 328).
38. Lucius Munatius Plancus fought with Caesar in Spain and Africa during the Civil War, held the consulship 42 BCE and was honoured with a statue on the Esquiline hill in Rome, *CIL* 6. 9673; Wiseman 1971, 242 (no 262). Changing to the Octavian side he famously made Marcus Antonius' will available to the future princeps in 32 BCE, and was the person formally to propose to the senate Octavian's adoption of the name Augustus in 27 BCE, cf. Plut. *Ant.* 58.2–3; Suet. *Aug.* 7.2, 17; *RE* 16.1, 546–54 (no 30). No magistrates related to this family hold high office at Butrint, but the family may well have had a client-base in the Ionian; cf. a 1st-c. CE inscription from Butrint (CI / A / MUNATI[O] / VIRO) and a tile-stamp from Corcyra with the name Munatius; *AE* 1950.0172; Anamali, Ceka and Deniaux 2009, 177–8 no. 238; de Franciscis 1941, 287–8. The name is also found at Corinth and at Delos linked to negotiatores, though in the particular circumstances of Butrint a link to the senatorial family may be more convincing; Hatzfeld 1919, 397; Spawforth 1996, 172.
39. Hatzfeld 1919, 389; Treggiari 1969, 171.
40. For the attribution of their title of 'duovir q.a.' as *duovir quaestor aerarii*, see Burnett, Amandry and Ripollès 1992, 275 and Grant 1946, 270 with discussion of office as coincidental with the duovirate. Deniaux 2004, 393 reads their title as *duovir quinquennal*. See also Moorhead,

Gjongecaj and Abdy 2007, 83 for a new coin type by the two magistrates.

41. Cic. *Att.* 15.14.3 (Loeb Classical Library 1999, translated by D.R. Shackleton Bailey).

42. Alternatively, a Sura is mentioned by Cicero (*Fam.* 5.11.2) as a friend or freedman of P. Vatinius, the consul of 64 and 47 BCE and triumphator of 42 BCE In 48/7 BCE Vatinius had defended Brundisium on behalf of Caesar and in 45–43 BCE he was proconsul in Illyricum, cf. *RE* 8 A.1, 495–519 (no 3); see also Cic. *Att.* 11.5.4; *Fam.* 5.9, 5.10a-c. A link to Adriatic command may equally be reflected in the name of the Augustan duovir Q. Naevius Sura, since Q. Naevius Crista in 214 BCE was the general to take Apollonia and force Phillip V out of Illyria, Livy 24.40.8–17; *RE* 16.2, 1563 (no 14).

43. Julia is by Plut. (*Ant.* 2.1; Loeb 1959, transl. B. Perrin) described as among the 'noblest and most discreet women of her time'; she died in 39 BCE

44. Rizakis 2001, 42–43; Spawforth 1996, 170.

45. For Corcyra, see Deniaux 2007a, 81, 83. Zacynthus in the southern Ionian was long associated with C. Sosius who issues coins there between 39 and 32 BCE, cf. Burnett, Amandry and Ripollès 1992, 263, nos 1290–3.

46. Cf. Caes. *B Civ.* 3.16.1 where Caesar is at Butrint to expedite the food supply; 3.42.3 where two assistants are sent to Epirus to get provisions and set up granaries; and 3.47.3 where meat from Epirus is described as being in large supply and held in high favour by the troops.

47. *AE* 2004.1341 = *AE* 2005.1405; Deniaux 2004; Deniaux 2006; Deniaux 2007b, 35.

48. Deniaux 2004, 393; Horster 2004, 335–7.

49. For Q. Caecilius Epirota see Suet. *Gram.* 16; Treggiari 1969, 123, 248. A Q. Caecilius Niger, duovir at Corinth 34–31 BCE, has been linked to the Sicilian quaestor of 72 BCE whose family was enfranchised by the Caecilii Metelli, Spawforth 1996, 176; Wiseman 1971, 22.

50. Deniaux 2007b, 36. The name Lucius is common among the Caecilii Metelli, the maternal family of Atticus.

51. Atticus' concern to protect his status as benefactor of Butrint is a recurring theme in the appeals made by Cicero to Plancus, cf. *Att.* 16.16a, 16.16e.

52. Q. Caecilius Epagatus (child died at age 7), 1st c. CE: *AE* 1978.0770; Anamali, Ceka and Deniaux 2009, 174 no. 235; de Franciscis 1941, 284. Caeciliu[s] Nicostratu[s]: AE 1978.0776; Anamali, Ceka and Deniaux 2009, 186–7 no. 257; Ugolini 1942, 221, fig. 235. At Butrint the name is recorded in no other contexts.

53. Horsfall 1989. Could a deal of this nature have formed the basis of the enigmatic meeting between M. Antonius and Atticus in July 44 BCE, referred to by Cicero (*Att.* 16.3.1) with the words, 'our money will stand by us longer than our liberties'?

54. Cic. *Att.* 6.3.2.

55. For support to Brutus: Nep. *Att.* 8.6; for support to Fulvia: Nep. *Att.* 9.4–5, 10.4. See also Millar 1988, 45 and Welch 1996, 454, 470–1.

56. Cf. Sal. *Cat.* 41 (Loeb 1960, transl. by J.C. Rolfe).

57. Burnett, Amandry and Ripollès 1992, 275–7 nos 1379–80.

58. For C. Iulius Strabo acting on behalf of Germanicus see, *AE* 1989.642 and 1990.872; Anamali, Ceka and Deniaux 2009, 196 no. 274; Deniaux 2007b, 35; Horster 2004, 353 (no 86); Pollo 1990. At Corinth two of the earliest duovirs are Iulii; cf. Burnett, Amandry and Ripollès 1992, 250 nos

1116–17; Spawforth 1996, 169.

59. *RE* 4, 130–1 (nos 12–13). Other mature or second-generation colonists may the duovirs Silvius, A. Teidius and A. Hirtuleius Niger. The name of the latter carries the reminder of the Hirtuleii brothers respectively recorded as fighting for Sertorius in Spain and participating in the *consilium* of Pompeius Strabo, cf. Criniti 1970, 140–1; Wiseman 1971, 235 no. 208. A relative, A. Hirtuleius Asiaticus, is known from a dedication to Asclepius found inside the shine/treasury building next to the theatre at Butrint (A. HIRTULEIUS / ASIATICUS / AESCULAPIUS), cf. AE 1949.0264; Anamali, Ceka and Deniaux 2009, 179–80 no. 241; Ugolini 1942, 124. Aulus Teidius, known only from a recently published inscription carries a name known from incriptions in central Italy; he may be linked to the senatorial family whose most famous member was the Sex. Teidius who brought Clodius' body back to Rome; cf. RE 5-A1; Anamali, Ceka and Deniaux 2009, 193–4 no. 270. The name appears among Roman freedmen and is represented on the list of participants at the concilium of 89 BC by an M. Teiedius; all of whom may be linked to the senatorial family; CIL 6.37810, 6.36408; Criniti 1970, 119–20.

60. Melfi 2007, 27. For the inscription see *AE* 1950.0169; Anamali, Ceka and Deniaux 2009, 173 no. 234; Bergemann 1998, 57; de Franciscis 1941, 282–4; cf. note 77.

61. Spawforth 1996, 176.

62. Burnett, Amandry and Ripollès 1992, 275.

63. Wilson forthcoming. For the coin imagery see Burnett, Amandry and Ripollès 1992, nos. 1381, 1388, 1400, 1402, 1404–5, 1407, 1409.

64. Greenslade forthcoming; Hansen 2009, 41–49; Hansen and Hodges 2007, passim.

65. For the Domitii Ahenobarbi see below and note 78.

66. Gjongecaj 2005, 161–2, 175 no. 321 (fig. 10.3–321) interprets the obverse as two dolphins. The iconographically similar Neronian issues from Butrint are by Burnett, Amandry and Ripollès 1992 (279, nos 1416–17) described as two fishes. Neronian Butrint issues are largely characterised by types recalling Augustan and Claudian ones and hence it is not unlikely that the type with fishes may have its roots in an earlier period too.

67. *CIL* 11.6058; Groag 1915, 51–57; *PIR*² M 319; *RE* 14.2, 1822 no 30

68. Valerius Maximus 7.8.6.

69. Groag 1915, 51–57.

70. For the *XII Fulminata* see, Keppie 1984, 158, 209; Keppie 2000, 85–86. Keppie identifies it as a continuation of the former *XII Antiqua* of Antonius, which was kept in the East, rather than the Octavian *XII Victrix*. The *XII Fulminata* may have been stationed in Egypt immediately after Actium before joining the garrison at Syria.

71. Keppie 2000, 83–86; Rizakis 2001, 48.

72. Burnett, Amandry and Ripollès 1992, 263 nos 1290–3 (Sosius) and 271–2 nos 1359–62 (Proculeius).

73. Hansen 2007, 48; Hansen and Pojani forthcoming – both with further bibliography.

74. Burnett, Amandry and Ripollès 1992, 277 no 1386 (Pullienus and Fuscus) and 273 no 1367. See also Hansen 2007, 50. Pulienus holds the office of *quinquennal* both with Ateius Fuscus and Pomponius Graecinus and hence is listed as 'quinq iter' in Table 6.1. A Lucius Pulienus also is mentioned among the *consilium* of Pompeius Strabo and the Butrint duovir may have a military background and

have served with Agrippa, cf. Criniti 1970, 176, 178.

75. Burnett, Amandry and Ripollès 1992, 174 nos 648–50; the date of the issues is suggested as the Triumviral period, though the possibility of a later (post 21 BC) date is left open. The dolphin symbol can also be found on an Augustan issue by Pomponius Graecinus at Butrint (who may be linked to the family of Agrippa, see below), on anonymous Triumviral issues from Corinth, and on a single issue of Sosios from Zakythus, Burnett, Amandry and Ripollès 1992, 277 no. 1392, 257 nos 1223, 1229–31 and 263 no. 1293. The control of the sea implied in all of these became intimately linked to the Actian victory.

76. For the similarity in coinage note especially Burnett, Amandry and Ripollès 1992, 277 nos 1381, 1388. Though no indication of status as *quinquennal* is given for Graecinus in the coinage issued with Milesius, in a fragmentary dedication from a public building (Butrint Archaeological Museum inv 495) the two appear already to be holding that office (F GRAECINUS / MILESIUS / [IIVIRI Q]UINQUENNAL), cf. *AE* 1950.0169; Anamali, Ceka and Deniaux 2009, 173 no. 234; Bergemann 1998, 57; de Franciscis 1941, 282–4; Hansen 2009, 58.

77. [L DO]MITIO CN F AHENOB / PONTIF COS / D D PATRON COLONEI; part of the base carrying this honorific inscription is currently on display in the Butrint Archaeological Museum (inv 496). *AE* 1985.0771 no 5 = *AE* 1999.1451; Anamali, Ceka and Deniaux 2009, 196–7 no. 275; Deniaux 2007b, 34; Freis 1985, 224–6; Hansen 2009, 39.

78. Appian 4.15.115; Deniaux 1999.

79. CN. DOMITIUS CN. L. EROS. Anamali, Ceka and Deniaux 2009, 198 no. 276; Deniaux 2007b, 35; Melfi 2007, 27, fig. 2.13.

80. Tac. *Ann.* 4.75; Suet. *Nero* 5.

81. Alcock 1994.

82. Burnett, Amandry and Ripollès 1992, nos 1400, 1402, 1404–5, 1407, 1409. See also Hansen 2007, 52–56 for a discussion of Butrint in this period. Stahl (1998, 45–46) attributes the presence of Butrint in the *Aeneid* to the patronage of the Domitii Ahenobarbi; though, on the present evidence that of Agrippa and his family appears more likely.

83. At Corinth the presence of the Antonii, after disappearing from the magisterial records in the Augustan period, reappear during the reign of Nero, cf. Rizakis 2001, 43. It would seem likely that they called upon their ties to the emperor through the Domitii Ahenobarbi (Marcus Antonius' daughter Antonia the Elder was the mother of Cn. Domitius Ahenobarbus (*cos* CE 32) and grandmother of Nero).

84. Three funerary inscriptions can be linked to client families of Atticus: T. Pomponius Alkaios; T. Pomponius Lupercus and T. Pomponius Dalmaticus, cf. *CIL* 3.581; Anamali, Ceka and Deniaux 2009, 172 no. 232, 187–8 no. 260; Cabanes 1996, 97, 104; Deniaux 1987, 253, fig. 1; Ugolini 1942, 210, fig. 215, 233.

85. An example of a provincial family reaching high office at Corinth may be found in P. Caninius Agrippa duovir in CE 21/22 or 16/17 whose father Alexiades may have assisted Octavian. Spawforth 1996, 173–4, 176–7.

86. [P]OMPONIANI / Q F ATTICO / [ME]RIT; only part of the inscribed statue base survives; *AE* 1950.0168; Anamali, Ceka and Deniaux 2009, 172–3 no. 233; Bergemann 1998, fig. 37; de Franciscis 1941, 281 no. 5; Hansen 2009, 31.

87. For offers of the use of his villa extended to Cicero and (possibly) Brutus, see Deniaux 1987, 249–50. See Nep. *Att.* 14.3 for the claim that all Atticus' income came from possessions in Epirus and Rome.

88. Nep. *Att.* 12.1–2, 19.4. The marriage of Agrippa and Caecilia Attica is normally thought to have taken place in 37 BCE; however, see Reinhold 1972, 121 for the suggestion that it took place in 43/42 BCE. For possible other children of Agrippa and Caecilia Attica, see Reinhold 1972; Syme 1986, 145–7.

89. Though see Millar 1988, 42, 52 for the 'coolness' displayed in Nepos for Octavian.

90. Nep. *Att.* 21.4–6.

91. Nep. *Att.* 21.4–6 and 5.2. Cf. Val. Max. 7.8.5, 8 for other examples of the deathbed as venue for inheritance issues.

92. Treggiari 1991, 365–6. I am grateful to Kathryn Welch for drawing my attention to the legal implications of inheritance for women.

93. Treggiari 1991, 366, 67–69.

94. Syme 1986, 36–37, 143–4.

95. Several Vipsanii and Agrippae are recorded at Corinth were Agrippa was honoured as patron, though none achieve duoviral status until Tiberius or later; the absence at Butrint could conceivably be due to the lack of magisterial names recorded later than Augustus, cf. Burnett, Amandry and Ripollès 1992, 252–6; Spawforth 1996, 168, 181–2.

96. Braund 1989; Millar 1988; Wallace-Hadrill 1989; Welch 1996.

97. Presuming that Caecilia Attica was Atticus' only child, after Atticus' death in 32 BCE her inheritance – of clients as well as property – would effectively have been linked to her husband Agrippa, who now – and particularly after Actium – provided a potent link between the family of Atticus and the princeps.

7. "Alien settlers consisting of Romans": identity and built environment in the Julio-Claudian foundations of Epirus in the century after Actium

William Bowden

Introduction

The relationship between "the Romans" and their conquered subjects has provided one of the most fertile areas of scholarly discourse in the last two decades, with traditional models of Romanisation increasingly being abandoned as discredited imperialist constructs. These models, which saw a monolithic "Roman" system encompassing material culture and social structures exported in a one-way traffic to Rome's provinces, have been replaced by a giddying range of theoretical constructs encompassing post-colonial theory, globalisation, "discrepant identity", creolisation and structuration. This has led to an increasing awareness of the role of the usually voiceless indigenous inhabitants of the regions that came under Roman political control, aided by increasing post-colonial consciousness on the part of a new generation of western scholars.

The increasing importance of post-colonial theory in Roman studies has led to a re-evaluation of the complex ways in which identities such as "Roman" and "native" were flexible rather than being fixed and immutable categories. This recent trend has perhaps focused more on indigenous experience rather than that of the incoming Romans, as part of a natural tendency to move away from the "Romanocentric" scholarship that dominated most of the 20th century. However, it is worth noting that the ordinary "Roman" (whatever part of the Empire he or she originated from) is often as voiceless as the native in many parts of the Empire, unless their lives are illuminated by chance survivals such as the Vindolanda tablets. Equally, an incoming colonist or soldier whether Italian, British, Baetican, Batavian, or Punic in origin will have become "Roman" to an indigenous population by the simple fact of his or her arrival. The extent to which their own view of their identity was changed through the process of moving from one part of the Empire to another is a different matter. Was a "Roman" identity strengthened through being perceived as the Other by their new neighbours?

The reality of the colonial experience was doubtless disconcerting to the colonists, if not to the same extent that it was disconcerting to those who were forcibly dispossessed of their land. Those who moved to Epirus, for example, were suddenly within an environment in which their neighbours spoke Greek, a language that may have been unfamiliar to many, and were probably as hostile as might be expected given the loss of land involved in colonisation. As with any powerful minority in a similar situation, their (in this case) Italian identity is likely to have become more important and have been increasingly emphasised. However, people from the Italian peninsula had long been present in the area, evidenced for example by the names on some of the manumission inscriptions from the theatre at Butrint.[1] Most famously, we have the members of the Roman aristocracy, such as Titus Pomponius Atticus, who already had major land-holdings and villas in Epirus. Cicero's correspondence with Atticus on the arrival of the colonists shows that the arrival of other "Romans" was deeply unwelcome. What effect did the arrival of the colonists, described by Strabo as "alien settlers consisting of Romans",[2] have on the Roman identity of Atticus and his contemporaries? Atticus, as his adoption of that name suggests, subscribed to the idealised Hellenism that was common among the Roman upper class, adding a further level of complexity to the situation.

In an area that had already been under Roman control for more than a century, we must question to what extent the Roman identity of the colonists and the Roman identity of those already living in the area were subsumed in other more dominant identities relating to social class and regional origins. In particular we must consider the role of the identities forged in the civil war that culminated in the decisive battle at Actium and which shaped the provincial landscape of Epirus. The factions that sided with Octavian (which had to be rewarded), and the factions that opposed him (which had to be either punished or appeased) were all ostensibly Roman in one sense, but this *romanitas* was only one element of a myriad of competing social and political identities.

It appears, therefore, that it would be wholly inaccurate to refer to "the Romans" in Epirus as a homogeneous body with shared cultural values and aspirations. Roman identity was only one of a range of co-existing and conflicting identities that constantly changed and shifted through time and circumstance. The new foundations of the Julio-Claudian period took place in a context that was neither simply Greek nor Roman but one that was specific to the social and political circumstances that had shaped the area during the 2nd and 1st centuries BCE.

Is it possible to trace any aspect of this within the archaeological record? Can we see any elements of this complexity in the material culture and traces of the built environment that are left to us? It is surely legitimate to try to do so, and to devise archaeological methodologies that are appropriate to these questions. At the very least, we must seek to question some of the assumptions on which our definitions and interpretations are based. Rather than viewing Epirus in the period of the Julio-Claudian foundations in terms of that which was Roman and that which was not, we must seek to understand the archaeological record as a reflection of the ideological complexity described above. This paper is an attempt to move in that direction. I will discuss the evidence that we have and how we might interpret it, while highlighting some gaps in our evidential record and suggesting how these gaps might be filled. While I will be discussing the region of Epirus, with which I have some familiarity, much of what I say will also be of relevance in other contexts.

A brief historical outline of Rome's foundations in Epirus

Roman intervention in Epirus occurred initially in the context of Rome's successive conflicts with Macedonia. This culminated in Aemilius Paullus's activities in Epirus in 167 BCE in the aftermath of the 3rd Macedonian war, which reportedly involved

the sacking of 70 *oppida* and the taking of 150,000 people as slaves.[3] Epirus was eventually formally incorporated into Rome's domains as part of the province of Macedonia in 146 BCE. According to Strabo, in his day Epirus, which had previously been "well populated, though mountainous", had become "a wilderness, with here and there a decaying village".[4] While rural decline and depopulation are constantly recurring *topoi* for Roman writers, this situation may have been one of the factors in the process which saw the senatorial aristocracy of Rome establish major land holdings and estates within Epirus, the first area outside the Italian peninsula where this occurred to a significant level. These were the "Epirote men" noted by Cicero and Varro, of which the most famous was Titus Pomponius Atticus, Cicero's correspondent, who owned an estate in the territory of Butrint.[5]

It was under the Julio-Claudians that the first colonies were founded in Epirus (Fig. 7.1). At Butrint, a colony was established by Caesar around 44 BCE, possibly as a reflection of the strategic and political importance of Kerkyra which is separated from the mainland by a narrow strait some 3 miles wide.[6] The imposition of the colony was ostensibly a punishment for an outstanding tax debt on the part of the town. Although Atticus discharged the debt in return for a promise that the colony would not be established, Caesar's death meant that the redirection of the colony was never ratified. Subsequently in the summer of 44 BCE, a small detachment of colonists arrived at Butrint. They were almost certainly civilians rather than veterans, a mixture of freedmen and clients of powerful individuals in Rome, a situation analogous to that of the Caesarean colony at Corinth.[7]

Soon after his victory at Actium in 31 BCE, Augustus renewed Butrint's colonial status, a change noted in the title *Colonia Augusta* which appears on the town's coinage at this time. This ushered in an extraordinary period in the town's history, when its purported Trojan ancestry gave it an important role in the creation of the new iconography of the Augustan period, including its use as a setting for a key part of the *Aeneid*. This new role was reflected in the patronage of the Julio-Claudian dynasty, evidenced in the epigraphic record of the colony and in a rich assemblage of sculpture from the period.[8]

The major Augustan foundation in Epirus, however, was Nikopolis, the victory city on the plain beneath the site of the camp occupied by Octavian before the battle of Actium. The camp itself was marked by the extraordinary *tropaeum* that overlooked the sanctuary of Apollo with its theatre and the stadium

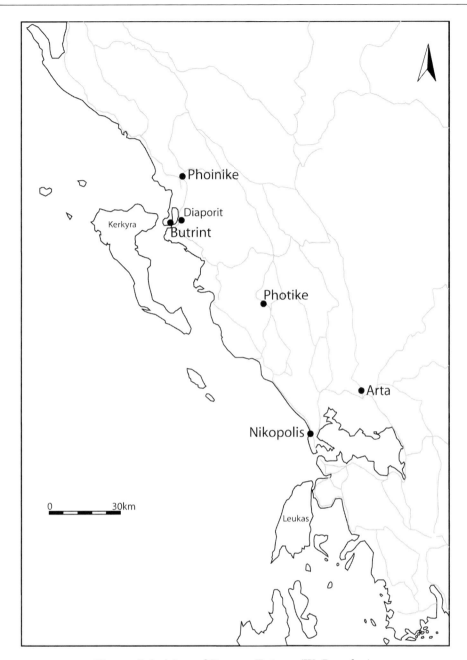

Figure 7.1. Map of Roman Epirus (W. Bowden).

used for the quinquennial Actian games (moved by Augustus from their original home on the southern side of the strait of Actium).

The city was founded sometime after 31 BCE. Its creation involved a process of synoecism in which the inhabitants, deities and sculptural decoration from numerous nearby settlements were more or less forcibly co-opted into the new settlement. Most commentators have argued that it is, to all intents and purposes, a Greek city, founded by a victorious ruler in the manner of a Hellenistic king and populated through an act of synoecism. Strabo describes the foundation and synoecism thus:

In later times, however, the Macedonians and Romans, by their continuous wars, so completely reduced both Cassope and the other Epeirote cities because of their disobedience that finally Augustus, seeing that the cities had utterly failed, settled what inhabitants were left in one city together – the city on this gulf which was called by him Nicopolis; and he so named it after the victory which he won in the naval battle before the mouth of the gulf over Antonius and Cleopatra the queen of the Egyptians, who was also present at the fight. (7.7.6)

However, Pliny refers to its status as a colony, describing it as "the colony founded by Augustus, Actium, with the famous temple of Apollo, and the free city of Nicopolis" (...*et in ore ipso colonia Augusti Actium cum templo Apollinis nobili ac civitate libera Nicopolitana*). Tacitus also mentions *Nicopolim Romanam coloniam*, but he also calls the city *urbem Achaiae Nicopolim*.[9]

This has led some, such as Purcell, to suggest that the settlement may have included colonists, probably civilians displaced by veteran settlements in Italy. He argued that, like the neighbouring city of Patrae, it had dual status as both *colonia* and *civitas libera*.[10] Lange argues, however, that the evidence for a colony at Nicopolis is very limited, noting that neither Strabo nor Suetonius refer to Nikopolis as a colony in otherwise lengthy descriptions of the town and its foundation. Furthermore he argues that unlike Patrae, which minted Latin coins that explicitly referred to its colonial status, all the coins minted at Nikopolis are in Greek and make no mention of the city as a colony. Butrint's colonial coins are also Latin (as indeed are all colonial coins) and explicitly mention its status as a colony under both Caesar and Augustus. Similarly, there is remarkably little Latin epigraphy from Nikopolis (comprising less than 5% of the total epigraphic corpus).[11] However, the extensive centuriation traced on the Margarona peninsula and further afield would perhaps argue in favour of the presence of a colony, a point to which I shall return below.

Lange insists that Nikopolis is therefore a Greek city, and suggests that the only way to reconcile the evidence with the testimony of Pliny and Tacitus is to hypothesize a separate colonial foundation at Actium itself on the south side of the Strait. However, as Lange himself admits, this is fairly unlikely given that there is no archaeological, numismatic or epigraphic evidence for such a foundation. A further possible explanation is that Nikopolis was given colonial status subsequent to its foundation, which could explain why the colony was not mentioned by Strabo although it does not explain why it was not mentioned by Suetonius and Dio. The simplest explanation (if a slightly unsatisfactory one) is that Pliny and Tacitus were inaccurate in describing Nikopolis as a colony.

If we accept Lange's argument that there is little evidence for a colony at Nikopolis, then we might say that further discussion of it has little place in this volume. However, colony or not, the evidence from Nikopolis will serve as a valuable point of reference in the discussion that follows. Equally it allows us to question the extent to which labels such as "Roman", "Greek", or even "colony" advances or hinders the study of these settlements.

A second (or third) colony in Epirus is that of Photike in Thesprotia, though by Rizakis to be a Caesarean foundation.[12] We have very little understanding of Photike, which remains unexcavated with knowledge of the town and its inhabitants restricted to epigraphic sources. At least 37 inscriptions relating to the town are known, mainly Latin funerary monuments.[13] The predominance of Latin inscriptions from Photike also provides an interesting comparison to Nikopolis where, as noted above, Latin texts form a very small part of the epigraphic corpus.

Apart from a few chance finds, almost nothing is known of the topography of Photike, although most scholars agree on its approximate location in the area of Liboni slightly north-west of Paramythia.[14] This area is also associated with the *ad Dianam* mentioned on the Peutinger Table on the basis of the discovery of an inscription dedicated to Diana together with a small statue of the goddess, perhaps suggesting the presence of a sanctuary.[15]

Archaeological evidence for Augustan Butrint and Nikopolis.

An immediate problem when trying to ascertain the impact of these colonies on the lives of the region's inhabitants and on the lives of the colonists themselves lies in the nature of the evidence that we have, much of which is ill-suited to discussion of the sorts of issues outlined in the introduction.

The reason for this in part relates to the history of study of the region, which understandably reflects the research questions of 20th century classical archaeology with its emphasis on political history on the one hand and art history on the other. This meant primarily a focus on public areas which produced the most impressive discoveries, helped by an archaeological strategy that involved simply digging around visible pieces of standing masonry. Much of what is visible at Butrint was excavated in this fashion, first by the Italians under Luigi Ugolini and then in the 1970s and 1980s by successive Albanian excavators.[16] More recent work at the site has focused first on the late antique and medieval phases and subsequently on the topography of the Roman town.[17]

At Nikopolis, early Greek excavation focused almost exclusively on the city's Early Christian monuments,[18] although Italian interest in the site during the fascist period focused on the Roman monuments.[19] The latter resulted in the site being surveyed by the Italian army, creating what were until

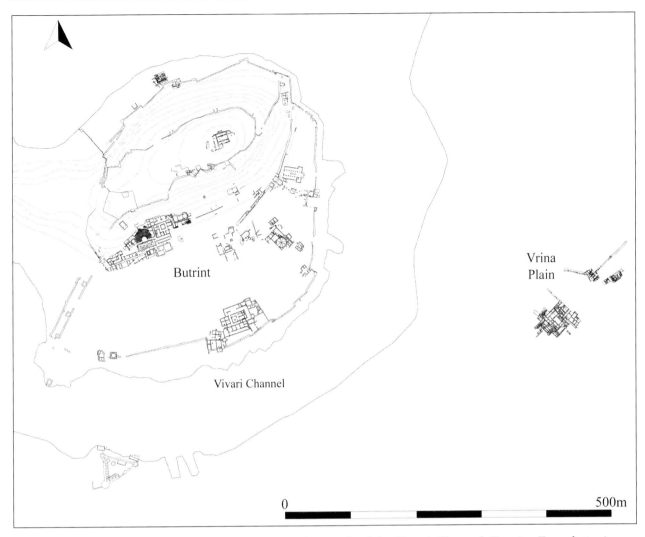

Figure 7.2. Butrint, including the suburb to the south of the Vivari Channel (Butrint Foundation).

relatively recently the most detailed plans of the city and its monuments.[20] More recent work has targeted the monuments of the Roman city, in particular the Actium *tropaeum*, the walls, the cemeteries and the villa of Manius Antoninous, although much of the more recent work has been focused on developing Nikopolis as a heritage site.[21]

I do not intend to provide a detailed description of Augustan Butrint and Nikopolis here, primarily because I have recently attempted to do that elsewhere.[22] Instead I will focus on particular aspects of these towns that may give some indication of the ways in which the inhabitants viewed themselves and presented themselves to the neighbours and the wider world.

Public areas and elite display

At Butrint, the site that we know to have been a colony, despite very extensive excavations, the evidence for physical change within the town that can be definitely associated with the early years of the colony is relatively limited. This is in part due to the difficulties encountered in excavating to the depth of the town's earliest levels, caused by high groundwater. The evidence, summarised elsewhere, relates almost exclusively to the public areas of the town, primarily to the construction of the aqueduct and bridge across the channel (seeming depicted on Augustan coins of the colony), and the area of the sanctuary of Asclepius (Figs 7.2 and 7.3).[23] Here, a large east-west oriented forum was laid out, together with a tripartite building which can be reasonably dated to the late 1st century BCE, or possibly the early years of the 1st century CE.[24] The tripartite building contained an inscription erected by Manius Otacilius Mystes dedicating a shrine to Minerva Augusta. Otacilius Mystes was probably a freedman, possibly one of the colonists sent by Caesar, or a freedman of one of the colonists or of

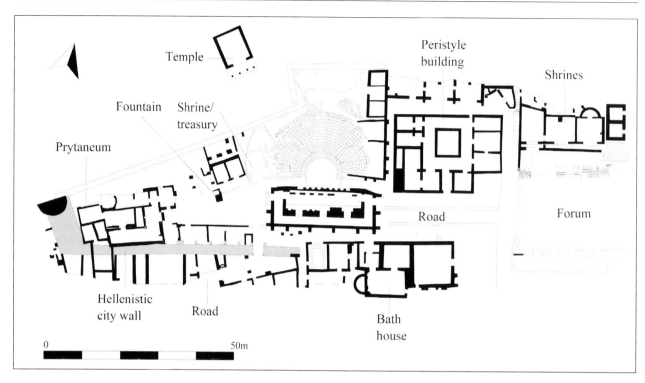

Figure 7.3. The forum and Sanctuary of Asclepius at Butrint (Butrint Foundation).

one of the colonists' descendants, and it is likely that this building is the *capitoleum* of the colony.[25] The theatre may also have been altered at this time with the addition of the *scaenae frons* and further seating banks, although the dates of these additions are a matter of speculation.[26]

The political institutions of the colony were seemingly devised to mirror those of Rome itself, with the city divided into *vici* controlled by *magistri.* One of these *magistri*, Aulus Granius, is recorded on two inscriptions, one dedicated to the *Lares* of the *vicus*, while the second is dedicated to Stata Mater, a cult associated with protection from fire and the protection of the pavement of the forum in Rome.[27] Thus we have divisions of civic space and the presence of civic cults that are directly modelled on those of the capital.

The relatively rich epigraphic record from Butrint shows a clear change in the language of epigraphic display from Greek to Latin, a change which as noted above did not occur at Nicopolis where the language of epigraphy was predominantly Greek from the outset. The longevity of Latin as a public language at Butrint is an interesting question. Certainly, by the time Junia Rufina paid for the aggrandisement of the well on the north east side of the city (probably during the 2nd century), it was more appropriate for the inscription to appear in Greek, although a probable 2nd-century funerary inscription from the

Vrina Plain is in Latin, recording an individual with a Greek name (Olympus).[28] Certainly by around CE 400, when the owner of the large *domus* known as the Triconch Palace had his name and rank (*lamprotatos*) commemorated in the mosaic pavement of his house's entrance vestibule, he chose to do it in Greek. Subsequent to this date all epigraphic evidence from Butrint (including texts on items of jewellery) is in Greek. However, it seems most likely that the use of Latin began to decline much earlier, probably during the 2nd century. In this context it should also be noted that minting of the colony's coins ceased after the reign of Nero.[29] It is unknown whether Latin was ever spoken by a significant section of the town's population, but it is clear that it was the language of public display during the first century of the colony's history, and that the audience that mattered to those erecting the inscriptions was a Latin literate one.

In this context it is also interesting to note a bilingual inscription from Photike, probably dating to the 2nd or 3rd century. The first part (in Latin) reads "To the spirits of the dead. The relatives put up (the grave) for the steward (?) slave Tychicus and for themselves". The following section (in Greek) reads "If somebody else puts someone into this grave, he shall give 2,500 denarii to the treasury".[30] A similar message (and an identical fine) is recorded on another funerary inscription from Photike (this time entirely in Greek).[31] The bilingual inscription clearly implies that the dedicators wished to emphasise their membership of a Latin literate elite (who were the principal intended audience) but to prevent future violation of the grave they were required to stipulate the penalty in a language that all could understand.

At Butrint, despite Atticus's well documented opposition to the colony, the Pomponii occupied a position of prominence within the town in the decades that followed, with a second Titus Pomponius and Publius Pomponius Graecinus holding a series of offices within the town. This was the result of a complex system of patronage in which the Pomponii were linked to Agrippa though his marriage to Atticus's daughter, Caecilia Attica, while the town's purported Trojan ancestry, as noted above, also stimulated the patronage of the Julio-Claudian dynasty.[32]

It is clear then that the inhabitants of Butrint found themselves in a rapidly changing urban environment in which the imperial family and members of a colonial elite were prominently represented through both sculpture and epigraphy. The administrative organisation of the town was also changed fundamentally and the public areas of the town saw alteration through the insertion of the forum. As Rizakis shows in the case of Patrae, we must presume that the new colonial elite was a dominant force in the region that was able to mould the political framework in which they operated to suit their own interests.[33]

At Nikopolis we know little of the public areas within the walled town (Fig. 7.4). The location of the forum is unknown, although it presumably lies in the area of the intersection of the *cardo maximus* and *decumanus maximus*. It is clear, however, that in the manner of a Classical or Hellenistic *polis*, the principal sanctuary lay outside the city.[34] This "thoroughly equipped sacred precinct" as Strabo described it lay beneath the "hill that is sacred to Apollo" on which the Actium monument stood and comprised a theatre, a stadium and a gymnasium.[35] A recently discovered inscription records that a certain Mnasïlaidas, son of Archonida, and his wife Polikrita, daughter of Euchitheou built a gymnasium in honour of the memory of Archonida for the gods and for the town.[36]

Although this inscription was found near the Odeion, almost 1km from the sanctuary area, Faklari contends on the basis of the letter forms that it is of Augustan date and is associated with the gymnasium described by Strabo, although there seems no overpowering reason why the latter should be the case. However, whether or not the inscription records the gymnasium associated with the sanctuary, it is interesting to note, as Faklari does, that all the names recorded are Greek and that similar names are

recorded in other local contexts (as well as elsewhere in Greece) in earlier times.[37] Similar gymnasium dedications are known from Messene and other Greek sites. If the inscription is of Augustan date, it represents a significant difference from Butrint in terms of the identity of the early elite of the city, who are clearly local. Equally, whatever the enforced nature of the synoecism, it seems that the new inhabitants of Nikopolis were willing to participate in the civic life of the city at an early stage.

Dominating the sanctuary area was the Actium monument, an extraordinary construction commemorating Augustus's victory and decorated with 36 bronze rams from captured enemy ships. The monument and the discoveries from Zachos's recent excavations have been discussed in considerable detail elsewhere.[38] Here I will only briefly mention two aspects of relevance to this paper. The first is the use of *opus reticulatum* in the monument, more specifically for the facing of the large retaining wall that supported the terrace immediately below the monument. Malcrino suggests that this is the first example of the use of *opus reticulatum* outside Italy, and together with other techniques used in the monument would have required the presence of a team of workers from Italy.[39] The same technique was also used, albeit sparingly, in the *cavea* of the theatre, while other examples appear in a wall within the *domus* of Manius Antoninus, and within a tract of wall beneath Basilica A. Many of the other buildings of the city also utilise building techniques that originate in Italy notably *opus caementicum* used in the odeion together with a decorative *cortina* that Malcrino suggests is an attempt to imitate the pattern of *opus reticulatum*.[40] He argues that the use of this building technique in Greece represents a deliberate choice on the part of local elites to utilise an architectural symbol of *romanitas*.

A single example of *opus reticulatum* can also be seen in the so-called *prytaneum* at Butrint.[41] This was clearly a building of significance in the early years of the colony. An inscription set with lead letters recording Cn. Domitius Eros, a freedman of Cn. Domitius Ahenobarbus (father of L. Domitius Ahenobarbus) was reused within the pavement close to the building, but is likely to originate from it.[42] Melfi argues convincingly that this building housed the Augustan portrait group from Butrint, citing parallels from elsewhere in Greece. It is thus striking that the only example of reticulate masonry in the town appears in this building.

As well as the use of *opus reticulatum*, a second point to note on the Actium monument lies in the inscription, which departs from most of the epigraphy from Nikopolis by being solely in Latin.

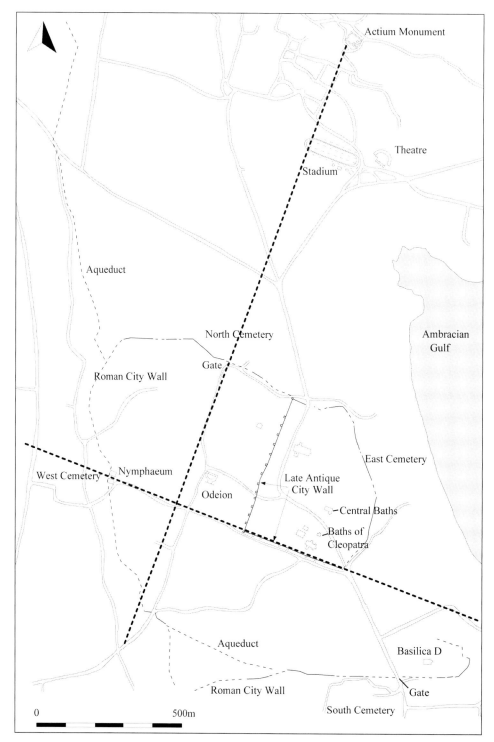

Figure 7.4. Nikopolis (W. Bowden mainly after Pierrepont-White 1986–97). The dashed lines indicate the probable cardo maximus *and* decumanus maximus.

Imp · Caesa]r · Div[i · Iuli ·]f · vict[oriam · consecutus · bell]o · quod · pro [·r]e[·]p[u]blic[a] · ges[si]t · in · hac · region[e · cons]ul [· quintum · i]mperat[or · se] ptimum · pace [·] parta · terra [· marique · Nep]tuno [· et ·Ma] rt[i · c]astra [· ex ·] quibu[s · ad · hostem · in]seq[uendum egr]essu[s ·est · navalibus · spoli]is [· exorna]ta · c[onsacravit

("Imperator Caesar, son of the Divine Julius, following the victory in the war which he waged on behalf of the *res publica* in this region, when he was consul for the fifth time and *imperator* for the seventh time, after peace had been secured on land and sea, consecrated to Neptune and Mars the camp from which he set forth to attack the enemy, now ornamented with naval spoils").[43]

Lange argues that Murray and Petsas's reconstruction is very problematic, with the last part based on the description of Suetonius.[44] He argues that the subject and wording of the inscription (which does not mention the enemy by name) indicate that Augustus himself had a direct role in its composition and that the intended audience was Roman, describing the Actium *tropaeum* as "a Roman monument for Romans, built onsite and thus of course also given a Greek context".[45] The inscription dates to between 30 BCE and 27 BCE, with 29 BCE considered the most likely date.[46] This early date means that there may be no direct connection between the monument and the foundation of the city, or at least that they were not initially conceived as a unified concept. Certainly the inscription gives no indication of any connection with the city foundation, and it appears that the inscription was not primarily intended to be read by the city's population as otherwise it would have been in Greek or bilingual.

The layout of the city certainly acknowledges the monument, with the *cardo maximus* seemingly aligned on it, with a major tomb-lined street leaving the north gate and running towards the monument and sanctuary area.[47] If the street grid does recognise the presence of the monument this would also suggest that the monument predates the formal laying out of the city, although whether by months or years is unknown.

Ultimately, interpretations of the Actium monument should acknowledge that it would have held different meanings for different audiences and that these meanings would have changed over time. It was a multi-layered monument emphasising triumph in a civil war that many of Nikopolis's future inhabitants would only have been dimly aware of, and at the same time part of a religious complex dedicated to Apollo (who paradoxically was not mentioned on the monument's inscription). How it was viewed by the city's inhabitants can only be imagined, but there is no need to envisage a single response to it on the part of either Greeks or Romans.

The built environment of the city and its cults would in fact have acted as a constant reminder to the city's inhabitants of their former towns. As well as transferring the populations of the synoecised towns, the new city was adorned with statues and architectural elements taken from other sites.[48] The latter included squared limestone blocks reused in the facing on the gates on the city wall together with numerous architectural terracottas, mainly of the 5th and 4th centuries BCE, which are readily paralleled at Leucas and Ambracia.[49] As well as the transfer of the cult of Apollo from Actium itself, other cults at

Nikopolis had also been transferred from settlements involved in the synoecism. These included cults of Apollo from Leucas and Ambracia, together with other statues from Aetolia and Acarnania.[50] It is interesting to consider whether these cults and cult images remained the focus of identities based around the earlier communities transferred to the new city.

One important public building missing from Nikopolis is an amphitheatre, which might be expected if the town was conceived in part as a destination for veteran soldiers. An amphitheatre was certainly a feature of Augustus's other Nikopolis, which lay to the east of Alexandria, where it was apparently detrimental to Alexandria's traditional cults.[51] Closer to Actian Nikopolis, the colony at Patrae was given an amphitheatre by Domitian to celebrate the centenary of the colony. According to Welch, amphitheatres were implicitly associated with a Roman civic identity, which she advances as an explanation for the presence of the amphitheatre at Corinth.[52] The absence of such a building from Nikopolis, however, is fully in accordance with the suggestion that the city's urban elite is derived from pre-existing local elites, who would have probably shared the negative feelings of Greece's intellectual upper class towards amphitheatres which were viewed as having a polluting effect on cities and their sanctuaries. Interestingly there is no physical evidence for an amphitheatre at Butrint, although the 10th-century text of Bishop Arsenios of Corfu describes the martyrdom of St Therinus in a theatre at the town during the Decian persecution of CE 251.[53] The existing theatre has no facility for animal spectacles, although Arsenios's story may have simply taken Butrint as the setting for a standard tale of martyrdom.

The urban plan

When the suburb on the Vrina Plain at Butrint was first identified through geophysical survey, it was thought to represent a planned gridded extension to the town that could be associated with the colony, a pleasing theory that unfortunately had to be abandoned when excavations stubbornly refused to yield any material earlier than the later part of the 1st century CE.[54] The excavations within the town thus far have not revealed any new streets that can be definitely associated with the foundation of the colony, although as noted above, the public areas of the town saw some alterations that probably date to the foundation of the colony.[55]

At Nikopolis, of course, an entire new gridded street plan was apparently laid out, although the street grid as reasonably reconstructed by Zachos remains almost entirely hypothetical with the exception of the streets excavated to the west of Basilica B and to the east of the villa of Manius Antoninus, together with two short sections of the proposed *decumanus maximus* and *cardo maximus* respectively.[56] The gates of the town in particular remain stubbornly asymmetrical in relation to the gridded plan, as does the plan of the wall circuit (generally thought to be Augustan in date, with 2nd-century additions) which wholly defies explanation. The scale of the enclosed area is breathtaking, with the (incomplete) perimeter of the wall circuit measuring more than 5 km. The purpose of the wall was presumably to create a symbolic boundary and a sense of identity for the town, rather than anything defensive.[57] The extent to which it was ever densely occupied is open to question. Excavations around the 6th-century Basilica A close to the *decumanus maximus* revealed little in the way of underlying stratigraphy, although as Malcrino notes, one of the few structures revealed was a wall in *opus reticulatum* which it is tempting to associate with the early laying out of plots within the town.[58]

Water supply

The conspicuous consumption of water for baths and fountains was an important aspect of Roman civic identity, and bathing establishments formed one of the most visible monuments within the Roman city. Nikopolis was no exception to this and the city acquired three substantial bath complexes (the Central Baths, the Baths of Cleopatra and the Proasteion Baths), of which the latter two have been suggested to partly date to the Augustan period.[59] To supply the baths, the city was furnished with a major aqueduct, which ran from the springs of the Louros River some 40 km away.[60]

A similar facility was created at Butrint, despite the town having plentiful springs around the base of the acropolis. The Butrint aqueduct probably ran from Murcia some 12 km away and an arcaded structure probably representing the aqueduct appears on the coins of the colony under both Augustus and Nero. The aqueduct necessitated the construction of the bridge across the Vivari Channel that linked the peninsula of Butrint to the Vrina Plain. While this connection already existed (evidenced by the major gateway in the Hellenistic wall circuit at the point where the bridge later reached the town) served presumably by private boats and ferries, the presence of the bridge would have wholly changed the relationship between Butrint and the land and

settlements to the south. The isolation of the peninsula lent itself to the rise of the earlier settlement and sanctuary site, which suddenly became connected to its hinterland in an unprecedented way.[61]

This connection between Butrint and the land to the south was an essential aspect of the colony. It not only brought water to the town via the aqueduct, thereby supplying the baths and fountains that were an essential aspect of Roman civic life, but more importantly connected the political heart of the colony to the agricultural land that formed the basis of power for the new local elite.

The creation of water supplies (and associated drainage systems) would have played a vital role in changing the urban identity of Butrint and creating the urban identity of Nikopolis, with baths and fountains creating an urban Roman *habitus*. The ostentatious nature of the water supply, which signalled mastery over natural resources, gave out a clear message to the inhabitants of both settlements, as well as providing an amenity that would presumably have been viewed positively by them.

Changes in the landscape

Whatever the nature of political elites at Butrint and Nikopolis, it was land rather than statues that ultimately mattered to the region's inhabitants both old and new. While arguably the erection of inscriptions and the division of land were both different aspects of an overall process of development, the changes within Butrint's political centre could not have happened without the fundamental changes in landownership that accompanied the foundation of the colony. Equally, the built city of Nikopolis was only one aspect of a fundamental reorganisation of the entire social and economic basis of the region, other signs of which can be readily discerned in the landscape.

At Butrint recent work has detected the traces of two major programmes of centuriation on the Vrina Plain to the south of the colony (Fig. 7.5).[62] One followed a grid based on a 20 × 20 *actus* division, while a second on the same alignment was divisible by 12 and 16 *actus*. The 20 × 20 *actus* system was that which was used at Nikopolis and can be reasonably assumed to contemporary with the Augustan foundation (see below).[63] It therefore seems reasonable to date the 20 × 20 *actus* grid at Butrint to the same period. The 16 × 12 *actus* grid is more difficult to date. Three successive 16 × 12 (or 24) grids are known from Corinth, which Romano dates respectively to a reorganisation associated with

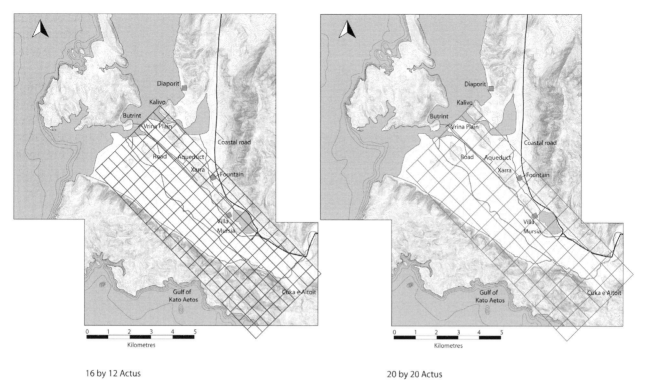

16 by 12 Actus   20 by 20 Actus

Figure 7.5. Centuriation schemes at Butrint (Butrint Foundation).

the *lex agraria* of 111 BCE, the foundation of the Caesarean colony in 44 BCE and the refounding of the colony under Vespasian.[64] None of these is readily applicable to Butrint, as the putative Caesarean colony was seemingly not established prior to its ratification under Augustus. There is also no evidence of a Flavian refoundation although the archaeology suggests significant expansion in the latter part of the 1st century CE. A similar programme has been noted in the area of Phoinike to the north east of Butrint, and it is possible that the territory of Phoinike was also included in the land divided for the Augustan colony.[65]

This land division was fundamental in effectively restructuring the social and political hierarchy of Butrint. It is notable that none of the families known from Butrint's manumission inscriptions appear in the epigraphic record from the town after the foundation of the colony. The only family that appear to have survived in a position of power are the Pomponii, presumably because of their familial relationship to Agrippa, the son in law of the *princeps*.

At Nikopolis too, the foundation of the Roman settlement seems to have had a far reaching effect upon the landscape although, as I have described elsewhere, the synoecism, together with the brutal actions of Aemilius Paullus in 167 BCE, have tended to be treated as unproblematic explanations of

archaeologically detectable change in Epirus.[66] The abandonment of many of the fortified Hellenistic hill-top sites is invariably associated with one of these events.[67] While it would be foolish to deny their possible effects, we must be wary of seeking or expecting destruction and abandonment. Indeed, more recent work in the region suggests that the destruction of 167 BCE was not as comprehensive as previously thought.[68] Equally the effects of the synoecism on settlement patterns, while undoubtedly dramatic are probably rather more complex than previously thought. Indeed, Petropoulos argues that the desertion of Aetolia and Acarnania increasingly appears to be a myth.[69] At Arta (Ambracia), for example, recent excavation has demonstrated that life in the town continued into the 4th century CE.[70] This is not surprising as the drainage and centuriation on the plain of Arta created land that was hardly going to be farmed by people commuting daily from Nikopolis some 30 km to the southwest.

The landscape around Nikopolis itself was subject to a major programme of land division on a 20×20 *actus* grid that followed the alignment of the street grid of the city (Fig. 7.6), and it is reasonable to suggest that this land division was contemporary with the foundation of the city.[71] This centuriation might give some support to the idea of a colony at Nikopolis, although equally the synoecism is likely to

Figure 7.6. Centuriation around Nikopolis (after Doukellis 1988).

have involved a similar programme of land division. The fundamental aims of any act of land division and distribution are to dismantle existing power structures and create new ones that reward supporters and penalise or appease opponents, while creating easily taxable units of land.

The synoecism involved towns and territories at some considerable distance from Nikopolis, and at least some of these territories underwent similar programmes of land division. As noted above, the plain of Arta was divided into a similar 20 × 20 *actus* grid.[72] Was this land distributed among the inhabitants of Ambracia, or was it (as seems more likely) given to new landlords in Nikopolis who subsequently rented it back to those who continued to live in the reduced settlement of Ambracia? It is not impossible that future epigraphic discoveries may shed some light on this, but it seems a fundamental issue if we are trying to understand questions of identity in new communities. The wholesale redistribution of land among the synoecised population (if they were the beneficiaries rather than colonists) must have diminished any sense of identity with a previous community.

Populations and cemetery evidence

The archaeological evidence relating to the incoming populations themselves is frustratingly limited at both sites No residential building has been found at Butrint that actually dates to this period, although as noted above in most parts of the site it has proved impossible to reach levels of the Augustan period. Nonetheless, away from the public heart of the city finds of the Augustan period are very limited, with little showing up even as residual finds. Of the 8 coins from the period 44 BCE–CE 14 found in the recent excavations, 6 come from the villa of Diaporit.[73] This obviously in part reflects the fact that it was possibly to reach levels of the appropriate period at Diaporit (although most were residual finds in later contexts). Nonetheless even at Diaporit only a single deposit was found dating to the latter half of the 1st century BCE, suggesting that occupation of the site in this period was not extensive.

Perhaps the clearest evidence of an immigrant population at Butrint may come from the cemetery evidence, where there is significant evidence of cremation burial, which is otherwise rare in Greece during the imperial period.[74] The Italian Mission at Butrint found a number of cremation groups within the cemetery on Mount Sotirës to the west of the town, while more recently a substantial cremation tomb has been documented on the Vrina Plain. Further probable examples can be seen in the marshes along the Vivari Channel approaching the site from the Corfu Strait and on the lakeshore on the north side of the site.[75] Flämig points to further examples of cremation burials from Epirus, including a very substantial tomb from Nikopolis, positioned in front of the south east gate, together with other Italic traits in the funerary architecture of the region.[76] Further *columbaria,* apparently dating to the 1st century CE, were revealed in more recent excavations in the north cemetery.[77] The fact that cremation failed to become an established part of funerary practice in Greece, suggests that these relatively isolated examples of the practice do represent individuals from the Italian peninsula or their descendants maintaining the practice. Whether this was intended in part as a deliberate statement of a different identity is impossible to say, but the cremation ritual will presumably have appeared as an alien practice to the Greek inhabitants of Butrint and Nikopolis.

Conclusion

It is clear that the evidence for a colony at Nikopolis is debatable, given the differences apparent between it and other contemporary Augustan colonies such as Butrint and Patras, particularly in terms of epigraphy and numismatic data. Lange presents the arguments for and against the colony at Nikopolis, but the evidence is ultimately inconclusive.[78] However, whether or not there was ever a colony at Nikopolis, the similarities between Butrint and Nikopolis are marked, particularly in terms of the fundamental reorganisations of landownership apparent at both sites.

In this sense the insistence of many commentators on the "Greekness" of Nikopolis seems rather reductive, and slightly perverse given the manner of its foundation. It appears redolent of the 19th- and 20th-century ethos that remains strong in classical studies in which Greece is seen as untainted by the years of Roman domination.[79]

The Roman colonists at Butrint, and the synoecised settlers at Nikopolis, were part of an overall political process involving a fundamental restructuring of localised power structures, although it is clear that there were myriad variations in the ways in which this was achieved in Greece.[80] We shouldn't lose overall sight of this process through artificial separation of colonies and non colonies, or Greeks and Romans.

Finally, the fundamental, and perhaps slightly depressing conclusion, is that most of our currently available evidence in north-west Greece is basically ill-suited to addressing questions about the reality of the colonial experience for both colonists and colonised or for those who were forcibly or voluntarily transferred from one place to another. The evidence outlined in this paper merely gives tantalising hints about the ways in which very small sections of the population wished to portray themselves usually in formal circumstances (*e.g.* in epigraphy or in death).

Although they were doubtless of great interest to a small circle of participants, it is likely that many people took little notice of statues of distant political leaders and their wives and relations, or inscriptions in a language that would have been unfamiliar to many. While we are interested in the machinations of the Julio-Claudians and Augustus's use of Trojan imagery, because of the way that study of the Roman past has developed in the 19th and 20th centuries, it is questionable whether these things would have been the subject of widespread discussion on the streets of Butrint and Nikopolis. While not wishing to draw an overly facile comparison, it is worth considering how few people in the UK would be able to name their local councillors or their representatives to the European Parliament, notwithstanding the influence that such representatives arguably have on their lives or local environment.

There remains a need for an archaeology of the colonists and colonised which actively seeks to move away from the sorts of evidence that have been discussed in this paper, as ultimately this evidence is a by-product of a Classical archaeological tradition based on an art-historical discipline framed within narrative political history. As such, the chances of such evidence being suited to understanding the lives of the inhabitants and the ways in which they viewed themselves and each other are very limited. Personal identity entails choices in house design, clothing, personal adornment, diet, food preparation and many other areas, but extensive domestic contexts of the late 1st century BCE–1st century CE have not thus far been excavated at either Butrint or Nikopolis. Without excavation of such areas, the chances of advancing this field of study seem slim, although systematic study of the excavated cemetery assemblages and skeletal evidence from Nikopolis should be a priority for the excavators.

In conclusion, therefore, future work on the Julio-Claudian foundations in Epirus and elsewhere needs to widen its remit from understanding the aspirations, achievements and ideologies of the ruling dynasty and the associated political class, to an explicit focus on the lives of those Romans and natives who still remain largely invisible.

Bibliography

Alcock, S. 1993. *Graecia Capta. The Landscapes of Roman Greece* (Cambridge).

Baccin, A. and V. Ziino 1940. "Nicopoli d'Epiro," *Palladio* 4, 1–17.

Bergemann, J. 1998. *Die Römische Kolonie von Butrint und die Romanisierung Griechenlands* (Munich).

Bescoby, D. 2007. "Geoarchaeological investigation at Roman Butrint", in R. Hodges and I. Hansen (eds), *Roman Butrint: an Assessment* (Oxford) 95–118.

Bowden, W. 2003. *Epirus Vetus: the Archaeology of a Late Antique Province* (London).

Bowden, W. 2007. "Butrint and Nicopolis: urban planning and the "Romanization" of Greece and Epirus", in R. Hodges and I. Hansen (eds), *Roman Butrint: an Assessment* (Oxford) 189–209.

Bowden, W. 2009. "Thesprotia in the context of Roman and late antique Epirus", in B. Forsen (ed.), *Thesprotia Expedition I. Towards a Regional History*, (Papers and Monographs of the Finnish Institute at Athens XV) (Helsinki) 167–84

Cabanes, P. and F. Drini (eds) 2007. Corpus des inscriptions grecques d'Illyrie méridionale et d'Épire. Vol. 2, pt 2, Inscriptions de Bouthrôtos (Athens).

Çondi, Dh. and D. Hernandez 2008. "The Roman forum at Butrint (Epirus) and its development from Hellenistic to mediaeval times", *JRA* 21, 275–92.

Crowson, A., and O. Gilkes 2007. "The archaeology of the Vrina Plain: an assessment", in R. Hodges and I. Hansen (eds), *Roman Butrint: an Assessment* (Oxford) 119–64.

Deniaux, E. 2007. "La structure politique de la colonie romaine de Buthrotum", in R. Hodges and I. Hansen (eds), *Roman Butrint: an Assessment* (Oxford) 33–9.

Doukellis, P. N. 1988. "Cadastres romains en Grèce; traces d'un réseau rural à Actia Nicopolis," *Dialogues d'histoire anciennes* 14, 159–66.

Doukellis, P. N. 1990. "Ένα δίκτυο αγροτικόν όριον στην πεδιάδα της Άρτασ," *Meletemata* 10, 269–86.

Doukellis, P. N., J-J. Dufaure and E. Fouache 1995. "Le contexte géomorphologique et historique de l'aqueduc de Nicopolis," *BCH* 119, 209–33.

Faklari, I. 2007. Αναθηματική επιγραφή του Γυμνασίου της Νικόπολης, in K. Zachos (ed.) *Nicopolis B. Proceedings of the Second International Nicopolis Symposium (11–15 September 2002* (Preveza) 563–69.

Flämig, C. 2007. "Nicopolis and the grave architecture in Epirus in Imperial times", in K. Zachos (ed.) *Nicopolis B. Proceedings of the Second International Nicopolis Symposium (11–15 September 2002* (Preveza) 325–31.

Forsen, B. (ed.) 2009. *Thesprotia Expedition I. Towards a Regional History*, (Papers and Monographs of the Finnish Institute at Athens XV) (Helsinki).

Georgiou, A. 2007. Βόρεια νεκρόπολη της Νικόπολης. Οργάνωση και ταφική αρχιτεκτονική, in K. Zachos (ed.) *Nicopolis B. Proceedings of the Second International Nicopolis Symposium (11–15 September 2002* (Preveza) 307–23.

Giorgi, E. 2002. "Ricerche e ricognizioni nel territorio," in S. De Maria and S. Gjongecaj (eds) *Phoinike I: rapporto preliminare sulla campagna di scavi e ricerche 2000* (Florence) 121–31.

Giorgi, E. 2003. "Ricerche e ricognizioni nel territorio," in S. De Maria and S. Gjongecaj (eds) *Phoinike II: rapporto preliminare sulla campagna di scavi e ricerche 2001* (Florence) 91–8.

Gravani, K. 2001. "Archaeological evidence from Cassope. The local workshops of mould-made bowls", in J. Isager (ed.), *Foundation and Destruction. Nikopolis and Northwestern Greece: the Archaeological Evidence for the City Destructions, the Foundation of Nikopolis and the Synoecism*, (Athens) 117–47.

Gravani, K. 2007. Ανασκαφικές μαρτυρίες για το συνοικισμό στη Νικόπολη, in K. Zachos (ed.) *Nicopolis B. Proceedings of the Second International Nicopolis Symposium (11–15 September 2002* (Preveza) 101–22.

Hammond, N. G. L. 1967. *Epirus. The Geography, the Ancient Remains, the History and the Topography of Epirus and Adjacent Areas* (Oxford).

Hansen, I. L. 2007. "The Trojan connection: Butrint and Rome", in R. Hodges and I. L. Hansen (eds), *Roman Butrint: an Assessment* (Oxford) 44–61.

Hodges, R., W. Bowden, O. Gilkes and K. Lako, 2004. "Introduction", in R. Hodges, W. Bowden and K. Lako (eds) *Byzantine Butrint. Excavations and Surveys 1994–99* (Oxford) 1–19.

Hodges, R., W. Bowden, and K. Lako, (eds) 2004. *Byzantine Butrint. Excavations and Surveys 1994–99* (Oxford)

Hodges, R. and I. L. Hansen (eds) 2007. *Roman Butrint: an Assessment* (Oxford).

Hodges, R. and I. L. Hansen 2007. "Introduction", in R. Hodges and I. L. Hansen (eds), *Roman Butrint: an Assessment* (Oxford) 1–16.

Karatzeni, V. 2001. "Epirus in the Roman period", in J. Isager (ed.), *Foundation and Destruction. Nikopolis and*

Northwestern Greece: the Archaeological Evidence for the City Destructions, the Foundation of Nikopolis and the Synoecism (Athens) 163–79.

Katsadima, J. 2007. "Disjecta membra. Δείγματα πήλινων αρχιτεκτονικών από τη Νικόπολη", in K. Zachos (ed.) *Nicopolis B. Proceedings of the Second International Nicopolis Symposium (11–15 September 2002* (Preveza) 87–100.

Lange, C. 2009. Res Publica Constituta: *Actium, Apollo and the accomplishment of the Triumviral assignment* (Leiden).

Malcrino, C. 2007. "Il Monumento di Ottaviano a Nicopoli e l'opera reticolata in Grecia: diffusione, caratteristiche, significato", in K. Zachos (ed.) *Nicopolis B. Proceedings of the Second International Nicopolis Symposium (11–15 September 2002* (Preveza) 371–91.

Melfi, M. 2007. "The sanctuary of Asclepius", in R. Hodges and I. L. Hansen (eds), *Roman Butrint: an Assessment* (Oxford) 17–32.

Moorhead, S., S. Gjongecaj and R. Abdy, 2007. "Coins from the excavations at Butrint, Diaporit and the Vrina Plain", in R. Hodges and I. L. Hansen (eds), *Roman Butrint: an Assessment* (Oxford) 78–94.

Murray, W. M and P. M. Petsas 1989. *Octavian's Campsite Memorial for the Actian war*, (Transactions of the American Philosophical Society, 79.4) (Philadelphia)

Patterson, J. 2007. "Appendix: a dedication to Minerva Augusta from Butrint", in R. Hodges and I. L. Hansen (eds), *Roman Butrint: an Assessment* (Oxford) 40–43.

Petropoulos, M. 2007. Νικόπολης–Πάτρα μέσω Αιτωλοακαρνανίας, in K. Zachos (ed.) *Nicopolis B. Proceedings of the Second International Nicopolis Symposium (11–15 September 2002* (Preveza) 175–211.

Pierrepont White, W. 1986–87. "Plans of Nicopolis in the archives of the Scuola Archeologica Italiana di Atene," *Annuario della Scuola Archeologica di Atene* 64–5, 295–325.

Purcell, N. 1987. "The Nicopolitan synoecism and Roman urban policy," in E. Chrysos (ed.), *Nicopolis I. Proceedings of the First International Symposium on Nicopolis (2–29 September 1984)* (Preveza) 71–90.

Riginos, G. 2007. Η Ρομαιοκρατία στα δυτικά παράλια της Ηπείρου με βάση τα πρόσφατα αρχαιολογικά δεδομένα από τη Θεσπρωτία, in K. Zachos (ed.) *Nicopolis B. Proceedings of the Second International Nicopolis Symposium (11–15 September 2002* (Preveza) 163–73.

Rizakis, A. D. 1990. "Cadastres et espace rural dans la nord-ouest du Péloponnèse," *Dialogues d'histoire anciennes* 16, 259–80.

Rizakis, A. D. 1997. "Roman colonies in the province of Achaia: territories, land and population," in S. Alcock (ed.) *The Early Roman Empire in the East* (Oxford) 15–36.

Romano, D. G. 2000. "A tale of two cities: Roman colonies at Corinth", in E. Fentress (ed.) *Romanization and the City: Creation, Transformations, and Failures* (Journal of Roman Archaeology Suppl. Series 38) (Portsmouth, R. I.) 83–104.

Romano, D. G. 2003. "City planning, centuriation, and land division in Roman Corinth", in C. K. Williams II and N. Bookidis (eds) *Corinth XX. Corinth, the centenary 1896–1996* (Athens) 279–301.

Samsaris, D. K. 1994. Η Ρωμαική Αποκία της Φωτικής στη Ξεσπρωτία της Ηπείρου, (Ioannina).

Schwandner, E.-L. 2001. "Kassope, the city in whose territory Nikopolis was founded", in J. Isager (ed.), *Foundation and Destruction. Nikopolis and Northwestern Greece: the Archaeological Evidence for the City Destructions, the Foundation of Nikopolis and the Synoecism* (Athens) 109–17.

Sear, F. 2003. "The theatre at Butrint: parallels and function", in O. J. Gilkes (ed.), *The Theatre at Butrint. Luigi Maria Ugolini's Excavations at Butrint 1928–1932 (Albania Antica IV)* (British School at Athens Supplementary Volume 35) (London) 181–94.

Sorinen, E. 2009. "Some notes on inscriptions of Roman date from Thesprotia", in B. Forsen (ed.), *Thesprotia Expedition I. Towards a Regional History* (Papers and Monographs of the Finnish Institute at Athens XV) (Helsinki) 185–96.

Tzouvara-Souli, C. 2001. "The cults of Apollo in northwestern Greece," in J. Isager (ed.), *Foundation and Destruction. Nikopolis and Northwestern Greece: the Archaeological Evidence for the City Destructions, the Foundation of Nikopolis and the Synoecism* (Athens) 233–55.

Ugolini, L. M., 1937. *Butrinto: il mito d'enea gli scavi* (Rome).

Welch, K. 1999. "Negotiating Roman Spectacle Architecture in the Greek World: Athens and Corinth," in B. Bergmann and C. Kondoleon (eds), *The Art of Ancient Spectacle* (Washington D.C) 125–45.

Zachos, K. 2001. *Το Μνημείο του Οκταβιανού Αυγούστου στι Νικόπολη. Το τρόπαιο της ναυμαχίας του Ακτίου* (Athens).

Zachos, K. 2003. "The *tropaeum* of the sea-battle of Actium at Nikopolis: interim report", *JRA* 16, 65–92.

Zachos, K. 2007. Η οχύρωση και η πολεοδομική οργάνωση της ρωμαϊκής Νικόπολις. Νεότερα στοιχεία και παρατηρήσεις, in K. Zachos (ed.) *Nicopolis B. Proceedings of the Second International Nicopolis Symposium (11–15 September 2002* (Preveza) 273–98.

Zachos, K., D. Kalpakis, H. Kappa and T. Kyrkou, 2008. *Nicopolis. Revealing the City of Augustus' Victory* (Athens).

Notes

1. Cabanes and Drini 2007.
2. Strabo, *Geog.* 7.7.5.
3. Polybius xxx, 16; Liv. xiv, 34; Plut. *Aemil.* 29.
4. Strabo vii, 327.
5. Cicero, *Att.* 1.5, 2.6; Varro, *Rust.* 2.1.1–2, 2.2.1.
6. Deniaux 2007, 33.
7. Hodges and Hansen 2007, 6.
8. Hansen 2007.
9. Pliny *N.H.*4.5 (trans. Rackham 1942); Tacitus *Ann.*6.5.10; *Ann.*2.53; Lange 2009, 100.
10. Purcell 1987.
11. Lange 2009, 100–102.
12. Rizakis 1990, 271–2.
13. Samsaris 1994; Sironen 2009.
14. Bowden 2009; Forsen 2009.
15. Hammond 1967, 693 *contra* this identification.
16. Hodges *et al.* 2004.
17. Hodges, Bowden and Lako 2004; Hansen and Hodges 2007.
18. Bowden 2003 with references.
19. Baccin and Ziino 1940.
20. Pierrepont-White 1986–7.
21. See papers in Zachos (ed.) 2007; Zachos *et al.* 2008.
22. Bowden 2007.
23. Bowden 2007; Çondi and Hernandez 2008.
24. Çondi and Hernandez 2008, 285.
25. Patterson 2007, 41–2.
26. Sear 2003, 183.
27. Deniaux 2007, 34.
28. Edward Bispham in Crowson and Gilkes 2007, 156–8.

29. Hansen 2007, 55.
30. translated Sorinen 2009, 192.
31. Sorinen 2009, 190–1.
32. Hansen 2007 and *this volume*.
33. Rizakis 1997, 25
34. Bowden 2007, 193.
35. Strabo, *Geog.* 7.7.6.
36. Faklari 2007.
37. Faklari 2007, 564–65.
38. Zachos 2001; 2003; 2007; Lange 2009.
39. Malcrino 2007.
40. Malcrino 2007, 381.
41. Bowden 2007, 203
42. Deniaux 2007, 35; Melfi 2007, 27
43. Reconstruction and translation by Murray and Petsas 1989, 76 and 86. A recently discovered part of the inscription indicates that the name of Mars appeared before that of Neptune rather than after (as in Suetonius) (Zachos 2003, 76).
44. Suet.*Aug*.18.2; Lange 2007, 167–9.
45. Lange 2009, 117.
46. Lange 2009, 110–11.
47. Bowden 2007, 190. See also Zachos 2007 on the street plan of Nikopolis.
48. Katsadima 2007.
49. Zachos 2007, 295 (walls); Katsadima 2007 (terracottas).
50. Paus. 7.6; Tzouvara-Souli 2001.
51. Strabo 17. 1. 10; Purcell 1987, 76–7.
52. Welch 1999, 138.
53. Ugolini 1937, 92.
54. Crowson and Gilkes 2007, 121.
55. Bowden 2007.
56. Zachos 2007.
57. Bowden 2007, 195.
58. Malcrino 2007, 381.
59. Bergemann 1998, 98–100.
60. Doukellis, Dufaure and Fouache 1995.
61. The barrier of the Vivari Channel can still be keenly felt at moments when the existing cable ferry breaks down. It was also used as a checkpoint by the isolationist communist government who maintained the Butrint peninsula as a militarised zone to prevent people escaping to Greece.
62. Bescoby 2007.
63. Doukellis 1988.
64. Romano 2000; Romano 2003.
65. Giorgi 2002; 2003.
66. Bowden 2009. For an example see Gravani 2007.
67. For example by Schwander 2001 and Gravani 2001 for Kassope.
68. Riginos 2007
69. Petropoulos 2007.
70. Karatzeni 2001.
71. Doukellis 1988.
72. Doukellis 1990.
73. Moorhead *et al.* 2007.
74. Flämig 2007, 328.
75. Crowson and Gilkes 2007, 149–51.
76. Flämig 2007.
77. Georgiou 2007, 321; Zachos *et al.* 2008, 109–19.
78. Lange 2009.
79. Alcock 1993, 2.
80. Rizakis 1997, 22.

8. Colonia Iulia Nobilis Cnosus, the first 100 years: the evidence of Italian sigillata stamps

Martha W. Baldwin Bowsky

The historical sources are relatively silent about the first one hundred years after the foundation of Knossos,[1] but the material record is not. This study focuses on one specific element of material culture, stamped Italian fine wares, in order to gauge the Knossian response to becoming a Roman colony. The history of this particular industry – active between the mid-1st century BCE and the mid-2nd century of our era – coincides nicely with the century after the colony's foundation soon after 27 BCE.[2] These fine wares, like language choice, give voice to an otherwise silent century, during which residents of the colony set the table like Romans, even if they did not speak Latin at the dinner table.[3]

The presence of Italian sigillata in the Greek East is the result not of cultural diffusion or colonial domination but of "self-Romanization," as local elite tastes converged with Roman ones and local elites negotiated their own integration into the Roman world.[4] The diffusion of Italian sigillata in the Greek East is cited as one manifestation of such a hybrid culture and at the same time a way for individuals and communities to express, communicate, and demonstrate their position in the provincial landscape.[5] Among Romanists in the post-colonial era this phenomenon is no longer read as straightforward evidence of the mass adoption of one material element of Roman civilization.[6] Ceramic evidence – traditionally a standard index for tracing "Romanization" – can now be located in the context of involvement in a wider economic system, heralded by the presence of imported pottery and other goods.[7]

The Italian sigillata stamps known from Crete can provide evidence for colonial identity, particularly for the way colonists and other residents of Knossos might behave like Romans in material culture. Tablewares are not monumental expressions of identity but small finds and therefore an aspect of material culture that was easier and more affordable to adopt than architecture or town planning. A concentration of Romans at Knossos, consequent to the founding of the colony, might create an increased demand for imported Italian fine wares and at the same time explain why no early Augustan stamps are known from the colony. There is onomastic evidence, in fact, that some of the colonists of Knossos came to the new "little Rome" from elsewhere on the island.[8]

Material evidence suggests that reallocation of the exploitable resources of the colony – some of it owned by the city of Capua and producing an annual income that did not stay in Crete – still supported a colonial elite, including men who appear to have been wealthy landowners who maintained villas in the countryside or even at Herakleion.[9] At Karnari on the eastern border of the Capuan lands, an inscription records a territorial arbitration between Capua and a local land owner, Plotius Plebeius.[10] At Archanes, on the other side of Mt. Iuktas from Karnari, an inscription found in second use names another Plotius, Corinthos, as a doctor in a dedication to Zeus Soter.[11] More recently another inscription from Karnari records the name of M. Claudius Thettaliskos, whose slave may have made his dedication to the Kouretes as protectors of pastoral interests.[12] Thettaliskos may have owned the land from which a Cretan plane tree was taken to his suburban villa in Italy.[13] On the western border of the Capuan lands at Asites and Ag. Myron (ancient Rhaukos), two ceramic waterpipes – likely from a system constructed to provide drinking water, possibly to a villa – bear the name of Var(r)o.[14] At the Knossian port of Herakleion, six mosaics adorned a Roman villa whose owner has yet to be identified.[15]

We should examine the Knossian corpus of stamped fragments – and those from Gortyn and other locations in Crete – so as to address a series of fundamental questions about continuity and change in the material record of Knossos and Crete. We will survey briefly (1) where stamped Italian sigillata has been found in significant quantities; (2) when the attested potters were active and therefore when their wares were likely imported; (3) whence this pottery made its way to the island; (4) how these imported goods might have made their way there and what that contributes to our knowledge of distribution patterns. We will then discuss in greater detail a fifth question: why Knossians and other Cretans imported Italian wares to supplement their own local and regional production.[16]

Adopting this approach enables us to address a number of theories about colonization, symbiosis, and identity. We can showcase a way in which Knossos was just one type of city in the socio-political map of Roman Crete and yet a particular one, a colony whose exploitable resources and early foundation date might serve as predictors of Romanization. We can also document the role the colony played in the regional context, alongside Gortyn (identified by Guarducci as the *caput provinciae)*[17] and amid other centers in the realigned civic landscape of the island. Identification of the production centers for Italian sigillata imported to Knossos and Crete, and the multiple routes by which these wares might have made their way to the island, give concrete expression to the symbiotic relationship between the Empire and its colony. We can finally illustrate Knossos' ability both to present a *simulacrum Romae* and also to retain and return to her particular identity as an Aegean city.

Where: Italian sigillata stamps at Knossos and elsewhere on Crete

Kenrick's new edition of the *Corpus Vasorum Arretinorum* includes 34 Cretan stamps, to which we will add another 23: 11 from Knossian and seven from Gortynian publications not included in his edition; one each from Khamalevri, Viannos, and Kommos; and two from unknown locations in Crete.[18] Kenrick was rightly puzzled about the absence of Gortynian stamps from the material available to him.[19] Eiring also noted the lack of published material from Gortyn,[20] a situation now being remedied by the publication of excavations undertaken by the Italian School of Archaeology at Athens. Adding seven stamps from Gortyn will not bring the city up to the level of Knossos as a known importer of Italian sigillata, but will begin to redress the absence of Gortyn from the study of these finewares on the island. In the coming discussion

potters will be identified by the number that appears in the first column of Table 8.1 a–b.

The Italian sigillata stamps from Knossos are the first assemblage from Crete that has been systematically published. Despite the fact that Roman Knossos has been rather randomly excavated, either for rescue purposes or to reveal Minoan levels,[21] it has yielded a respectable assemblage of stamped fragments. One of the wells dug during rescue excavations connected with the building of the present Sanatorium yielded two stamped fragments,[22] while a well and fill layers of the Villa Dionysus produced five more,[23] and excavations undertaken in preparation for the building of the Stratigraphical Museum added another six.[24] Excavations undertaken to reveal the Unexplored Mansion more than tripled the number of Italian sigillata stamps discovered at Knossos, from 13 to 45.[25] Most recently a rescue excavation brought to light another stamped fragment from a local pottery workshop and kiln at Bougada Metochi.[26]

The corpus of Italian sigillata stamps found elsewhere on Crete is distressingly limited (Fig. 8.1). From Gortyn only seven stamps have been published to date, beginning with one stamp in *Inscriptiones Creticae,* and now including stamps from the Odeion and so-called Praetorium complex, and from excavations connected with the laying of new telephone cables in 1978 and 1979.[27] Single stamps from Khamalevri and Viannos were shown to or seen by Hood, Warren, and Cadogan during their 1962 tour of Crete.[28] Systematic excavation at Kommos produced another Italian sigillata stamp.[29] Stamps of unknown provenance were seen by Holwerda and Guarducci in museums in Leiden and Chania, respectively.[30]

By adding to the Cretan corpus the 23 stamps documented above we can increase the number of stamps published from Crete dramatically (72.3%). Given the small number of Italian sigillata stamps from Crete, each and every increase will yield an admittedly high percentage. We can also introduce the names of eleven new potters and second Camurius and Gellius stamps to the Knossian corpus, and add the names of eight new potters and an additional stamp of L. Rasinius Pisanus to the Cretan corpus. We can thus begin to answer the call issued by Poblome and Talloen to put together a case-study at the level of a community like *Colonia Iulia Nobilis Cnosus*, a region like central Crete, or eventually the whole island.[31]

The presence of Italian sigillata at Knossos and elsewhere on Crete was a result of Roman manipulation of the Cretan landscape of cities and realignment of transit and communication corridors, *e.g.*, in the center of the island.[32] It also serves to take

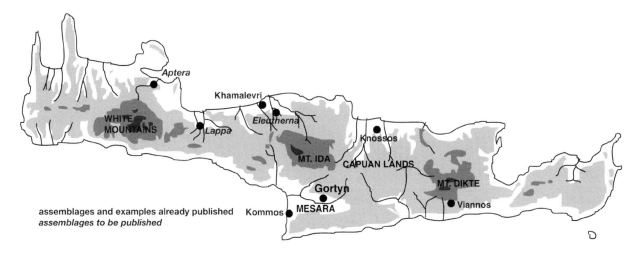

Figure 8.1 Map showing location of Italian Sigillata on Crete

the colony out of its solitary status and set it into a regional context, together with Gortyn and cities of other statuses on the island.[33] Changes in the civic landscape of Crete might in fact be investigated by the distribution of Italian sigillata as much as the Roman road that connected Gortyn with Knossos, western and eastern Crete.[34] Once Italian sigillata reached the island, it would have been hawked from port to port and inland via rivers and road systems, such as the Roman road which ran between Knossos to Gortyn.[35] Italian sigillata would have come to Knossos even if it had not become a Roman colony.[36] The apparent concentration of Italian sigillata at Knossos, and its relative scarcity at Gortyn, is an artefact of archaeological history and publication, not an ancient preference for different civic types. What is needed is the excavation and publication of small finds from domestic contexts like the Unexplored Mansion at Knossos, or a Hellenistic-Roman house discovered at the free city of Lappa.[37] Italian sigillata has also been discovered in domestic and public contexts at Eleutherna, in public contexts at Aptera, and in a possibly domestic context at the Knossian port of Herakleion.[38]

What distinguishes Knossos from other cities in Roman Crete is its position and role within the center of an island that was reorganized and realigned from Augustus onward. Such reorganization involved people as well as land, a diaspora of Romans already present on the island – particularly at Gortyn – to be gathered into the new colony.[39] It further entailed a reallocation of some of the exploitable resources of the new colony, in the form of the so-called Capuan lands which created a commercial outpost for agricultural opportunities.[40] There is to date no evidence of centuriation in the Knossian countryside,

despite Harrison's theoretical model of change in the rural landscape of Roman Knossos.[41] These lands now belonged to the Italian city of Capua, and could be leased out to their former owners, the Knossians, to produce an annual income of 1,200,000 sesterces.[42] Central Crete was effectively realigned along a north-south axis – from *Colonia Iulia Nobilis Cnosus* south to the Capuan lands and Gortyn in the Mesara plain – to formalize and stabilize a corridor important to communications and trade.[43] At the same time two different sea routes might be secured,[44] one linking Crete with the Greek peninsula and the other linking Crete with Africa. Knossos lay on the north coast of Crete and so could have been accessible via a west-east route passing north of the island, or by a north-south route that linked Achaia and Crete.[45] A north-south route linked Alexandria with eastern Crete,[46] while another north-south route linked western Crete with Cyrenaica.[47]

When: reorganization and civic status

Eiring concluded that the earliest examples of Italian sigillata found at the Roman colony were late Augustan, despite the historical and epigraphical sources which detail the formal founding of the Roman colony – and the arrival of colonists – near the end of the early Augustan period, soon after 27 BCE. Rather, quantities of Italian sigillata increased at Knossos under Tiberius, but these fine wares were not important until the reign of Claudius and culminated under Nero.[48] The apparent lag of a half-century between colonization and a significant influx of Italian sigillata led Eiring to suggest that colonists did not bring Italian sigillata to the colony but rather that Knossos participated in the general

Table 8.1a. Italian Sigillata stamps at Knossos. **Bold** = stamps not in OCK.

Number	Name (40 potters)	Provenance	Reference (45 stamps)	Type[1]	Date	Production
1	Amar(antus)	North House	Sackett 144 Y17[2]	OCK 83	CE 1+	Pisa?
2	Sex. Annius	S-East House	Sackett (Supra n.2), 144 Y19	OCK 183	20 BCE-CE 10	Arezzo
3	C. Arvius	S-West House	Sackett (Supra n.2), 144 Y16	OCK 254	15 BCE-CE 15+	Arezzo
4	Ateius (5)	North House	Sackett (Supra n.2), 144 Y10	OCK 270	15 BCE-CE 30	Arezzo/Pisa/Lyon
5	**Cn. Ateius (1)**	**Strat Museum**	**AR 1987–88, 91**	**OCK 274**	**Augustan?**	**Arezzo/Pisa**
6	Cn. Ateius Euhodus	S-West House	Sackett (Supra n.2), 144 Y14	OCK 292	5 BCE-CE 25	Pisa
7	Avillius	North House	Sackett (Supra n.2), 144 Y8	OCK 371	20 BCE-CE 40	unknown
8	Bassus (1)	North House	Sackett (Supra n.2), 144 Y23	OCK 435	10 BCE-CE 10	Po Valley
9	Calidius (Strigo)	North House	Sackett (Supra n.2), 144 Y24	OCK 487	15 BCE-CE 5	Arezzo
10	Camurius	North House / Strat Museum	Sackett (Supra n.2), 146 Y50; **AR 1987–88, 91**	OCK 514	CE 30–70	Arezzo
11	Chrestus (2)	North House	Sackett (Supra n.2), 144 Y1	OCK 553	15 BCE–CE 15+	unknown
12	Cornelius (2)	North House	Sackett (Supra n.2), 144 Y7	OCK 612	CE 10–50+	Arezzo
13	**P. Cornelius (1)**	**Strat Museum**	**AR 1987–88, 90**	**OCK 623**	**5 BCE-CE 40**	**Arezzo**
14	P. Cornelius (2)	S-East House (?)	Sackett (Supra n.2), 144 Y3	OCK 624	5 BCE-CE 40	Arezzo
15	Crestus (1)	North House	Sackett (Supra n.2), 144 Y4 and 145 Y30	OCK 698	10 BCE-CE 30	Pisa/Lyon
16	**Ennius**	**V Dionysos**	**Hayes, 132 no. 203[3]**	**OCK 761**	**CE 1+**	**Puteoli**
17	**C. Gavius Symmacus**	**Sanatorium Well**	**Hayes, 264 no. 16[4]**	**OCK 875**	**10 BCE-CE 10**	**Arezzo?**
18	Gellius	HD Frescoes / Bougada Metochi	Sackett (Supra n.2), 144 Y5; **Bannou, 897 no. 22[5]**	OCK 878	CE 10–50	Arezzo?
19	L. Gellius	S-West House	Sackett (Supra n.2), 145 Y36	OCK 879	15 BCE-CE 50	Arezzo?
20	M. Iulius	S-West House	Sackett (Supra n.2), 145 Y28	OCK 998	10 BCE-CE 10	Puteoli
21	Manneius	East House S-East House	Sackett (Supra n.2), 144 Y2 and 145 Y32	OCK 1099	CE 30–70	Arezzo
22	**C. Murrius**	**Strat Museum**	**AR 1987–88, 91**	**OCK 1203**	**CE 1–30+**	**Arezzo**
23	N. Naevius Hilarus	S-West House	Sackett (Supra n.2), 198 C1.1	OCK 1250	CE 1+?	Puteoli
24	(M. Perennius) Bargathes (1)	S-West House	Sackett (Supra n.2), 145 Y39	OCK 1404	CE 1–30	Arezzo
25	**(M. Perennius) Tigranus (2)**	**V Dionysos**	**Hayes (Supra n.3), 138 no. 206**	**OCK 1412**	**10 BCE-CE 10**	**Arezzo**
26	**L. Ple. Amar.**	**V Dionysos**	**Hayes (Supra n.3), 132 no. 205**	**OCK 1477**	**1st half of 1st c**	**Pisa?**
27	Rasinius (2)	HD Frescoes	Sackett (Supra n.2), 145 Y46	OCK 1623	15 BCE–CE 40	Arezzo
28	C. Rasinius	HD Frescoes	Sackett (Supra n.2), 145 Y33	OCK 1686	CE 15+	unknown
29	L. Rasinius Pisanus	S-West House	Sackett (Supra n.2), 145 1992 and 145 Y25	OCK 1690	CE 50–120	Pisa
30	T. Rufrenus sl. Rufio	North House	Sackett (Supra n.2), 145 Y31	OCK 1732	15–5 BCE	Arezzo?
31	M. S. Pu(dens?)	East House / North House	Sackett (Supra n.2), 144 Y9 and 144 Y18	OCK 1760	CE 50–70	Po Valley
32	**C. Sentius**	**Strat Museum**	**AR 1987–88,91**	**OCK 1861**	**20 BCE-CE20**	**Etruria?**
33	**Serenus(2)**	**V Dionysos**	**Hayes (Supra n.3), 132 no. 204**	**OCK 1878**	**10 BCE-CE10**	**Puteoli**
34	**Sertorius**	**Sanatorium Well**	**Hayes (Supra n.4), 264 no. 11**	**OCK 1909**	**CE 1–30**	**Arezzo**
35	**A. Sestius Dama**	**Strat Museum**	**AR 1987–88, 91**	**OCK 1947**	**20–1 BCE**	**Arezzo?**
36	Statilia sl. Canopus	HD Frescoes	Sackett (Supra n.2), 144 Y21	OCK 1991	20–1 BCE	unknown
37	L. Su. M.	S-East House	Sackett (Supra n.2), 145 Y27	OCK 1999	2nd half of 1st c	Pisa
38	L. Umbricius sl. Felix	North House	Sackett (Supra n.2), 144 Y20	OCK 2457	20–1 BCE	unknown
39	L. Umbricius H	HD Frescoes	Sackett (Supra n.2), 144 Y4	OCK 2470	CE 50+	Torrita di Siena
40	**Zoilus(1)**	**V Dionysos**	**Hayes (Supra n.3), 138 no. 207**	**OCK 2543**	**5 BCE+**	**Pisa**

1. Oxé, A., H. Comfort and P. Kenrick 2000. *Corpus vasorum Arretinorum: a catalogue of the signatures, shapes and chronology of Italian sigillata* (2nd edn., Bonn).
2. Sackett, L. H. 1992. *Knossos: from Greek city to Roman colony* (Oxford).
3. Hayes, J. W. 1983. "The Villa Dionysos Excavations, Knossos: the pottery," *ABSA* 78, 97–169.
4. Hayes, J. W. 1971. "Four Early Roman Groups from Knossos," *ABSA* 66, 249–75.
5. Ε. Μπάνου 2004. «Η ελληνορωμαϊκή Κνωσός μετά τις ανασκαφές των ετών 1996–1998· στοιχέια απο την κεραμική και τοπογραφία,» in *Creta romana e protobizantina, Atti del Congresso Internazionale (Iraklion, 23–30 settembre 2000)*, vol. III.1 (Padua) 879–907

Table 8.1b. Italian Sigillata stamps in Crete, beyond Knossos. **Bold** = *stamps not in OCK.*

Number	Name (12 potters)	Provenance	Reference (12 stamps)	Ock Type	Date	Production
41	C. An(nius)	Gortyn (Chandax 1979)	Rizzo,186 no. 292[6]	OCK 128 if plain ware	15 BCE-CE 5	Arezzo
42	Ate(i)us	Crete	Holwerda 40 no. 511[7]	in planta pedis → OCK 268	5 BCE-CE25	Pisa
43	Camurius	Khamalevri	Hood, Warren and Cadogan, 62 and n.15[8]	OCK 514	CE30-70	Arezzo
44	P. Clodius Proculus	Gortyn (Odeion)	I.Cret. IV 542; Chaniotis and Preuss, 195 no. 8[9]	OCK 592	CE40-100	Arezzo
45	Crestus	Viannos	Hood, Warren and Cadogan (Supra n.7), 87 and n.42	OCK 698	10BCE-CE30	Pisa/Lyon
46	C. Gavi Homullus	unknown location in western Crete	I.Cret. II,xxx 18	OCK 872	uncertain	uncertain
47	Sex. Murrius Festus	Gortyn (Odeion)	A. Di Vita, pers. comm.	OCK 1212	60-150	Pisa
48	Sex. M(urrius) P(isanus)	Gortyn (Praetorium)	Rizzo, 38 no. 1; Magnelli 2001, 631 no. 6[10]	OCK 1213	CE 60-150	Pisa
49	C.P. P(isanus)	Gortyn (Odeion)	A. Di Vita, pers. comm.	OCK 1342	CE50-100+	Pisa
50	L. Pomponius? Pis(anus)	Gortyn (Praetorium)	Rizzo (Supra n.9), 38 no. 2, citing OC 1365	OCK 1503	BCE15+	Arezzo
51	L. Rasinius Pisanus	Kommos, Temple C	Shaw and Shaw 132 no. 99[11]	OCK 1690	CE50-120	Pisa
52	L. Rast(icanus) Pre...?	Gortyn (Chandax 1979)	Rizzo (Supra n.5), 188-89 no. 323	OCK 1694	Flavian?	central Italy?

6.   Rizzo, M. A. 2004. "Ceramica sigillata," in Di Vita A. (ed.), *Gortina VI: scavi 1979–1982* (Padua) 184–98.
7.   Holwerda, J. H. 1936. *Het laat-grieksche en romeinsche Gebruiksaardewerk uit het Middellandsche-zee-gebied in het Rijksmuseum van Oudheden te Leiden* ('S-Gravenhage).
8.   Hood, S., P. Warren and G. Cadogan. 1964. "Travels in Crete, 1962," *ABSA* 59, 50–99.
9.   Chaniotis, A. and G. Preuss. 1990. "Neue fragmente des Preisedikts von Diokletian und weitere lateinische Inschriften aus Kreta," *ZPE* 80, 189–202.
10. Rizzo, M.A. 2001. "Terra sigillata italica," in Di Vita, A. (ed.), *Gortina V: Lo scavo del Pretorio (1989–1995)*, vol. V.3 (Padua) 36–8; Magnelli, A. 2001. "Iscrizioni," in *ibid.*, 626–54.
11. Shaw, J. W. and M. C. Shaw (eds), 2000. *Kommos IV: The Greek Sanctuary* (Princeton and Oxford).

vogue of importing Italian sigillata to the eastern Mediterranean.[49] Eiring based his chronological analysis on knowledge of the unstamped as well as stamped fragments of Italian sigillata and the archaeological contexts in which they were found. He notes, however, that there has been no excavation in the public center of the Hellenistic and Roman city.[50] He calls specific attention to the rarity of stratified contexts, especially in the Augustan period, whether at Knossos or elsewhere.[51]

The stamped fragments may tell a more nuanced story and allow us to date the production of the majority of these stamps to the middle as well as late Augustan period (Table 8.2).[52] A significantly smaller group of Italian sigillata stamps found at Knossos date to the Tiberian-Claudian and post-Claudian periods, and only one so-called late potter is attested there.[53] From Gortyn, the seven stamps published to date fall into three different periods, the mid-Augustan, the mid-1st century, and the period after

50.[54] Such percentages are, however, skewed by the small number of stamps published from Gortyn.

In order to construct a baseline for future studies of Italian sigillata on Crete, it is useful to tabulate the chronology of Italian sigillata stamps published from Crete. The majority of the datable stamps still belong to the Augustan period, particularly the mid-Augustan period.[55] The evidence of the stamps continues to show a significant decrease during the Tiberian-Claudian period and in the late period of Italian sigillata production, after CE 50.[56]

The century after 27 BCE is also a period during which Augustan sigillata stamps at Knossos and elsewhere on Crete may be explained by the historical circumstances under which the island was reorganized and cities accorded their various statuses. The trigger event that led to the foundation of a colony at Knossos was the need for land after the civil wars between Octavian and Antony. The Capuan lands between Knossos and Gortyn were *agri vectigales*

Table 8.2. Chronology of Italian sigillata stamps on Crete.

Period	Knossos #	Gortyn #	other locations in Crete	all #	all %
mid-Augustan	20	2	1	23	40.4
late Augustan	10	0	1	11	19.3
Augustan?	1	0	0	1	1.8
Tiberian-Claudian	9	1	1	11	19.3
after 50	5	4	1	10	17.5
uncertain	0	0	1	1	1.8
Total	45	7	5	57	

or *vectigalia* assigned to Capua in compensation for the Italian city's territorial loss in the settlement of Octavian's veterans.[57] Knossos was not a veteran colony but a civilian one that may have included some veterans.[58] Land was needed not only for Romans already present in Crete but for populations displaced in the wake of Octavian's settlements in the Italian peninsula.[59] The *deductio* at Knossos was a relatively early one and that – together with the possession of exploitable resources and patronage – should further predict Romanization at the only colony on the island.[60] At Gortyn and Italian Formiae there is archaeological and epigraphic evidence for a change in triumviral loyalties and the concomitant patronage of L. Munatius Plancus.[61] M. Nonius Balbus, proconsul of Creta-Cyrenae around 25 BCE, may have been responsible for the reorganization of Crete, to judge from the fact that he was honored at Herculaneum by the *commune Cretensium, Colonia Iulia Cnosus,* and the *Gortyniei.*[62]

Poblome and Talloen's study of Italian sigillata in the eastern Mediterranean – to which only 5% of the *OCK* entries can be traced[63] – provides a template against which we can measure this enlarged Cretan corpus: a noticeable, substantial increase during the Augustan period and a peak at the end of the Augustan period and during the Tiberian, with important quantities still exported in Neronian times, before a steady decline that made Italian sigillata a sporadic phenomenon by the end of the Flavian period.[64]

The chronological profile we have already identified at Knossos and Gortyn renders these two cities somewhat different participants in the Italian sigillata market of the Greek East. The Augustan-Claudian evidence suggests that Knossos was more like the Roman colony at Corinth than such cities as Argos, Olympia, and Athens, the island of Cyprus, or Alexandria.[65] At Corinth Italian sigillata became the dominant fine ware in the late Augustan to early Tiberian period, and reached a remarkably high level in the Tiberian-Claudian period.[66] These sites are

not, however, equally excavated or published, with the result that there is likely to be a considerably archaeological bias in our evidence, one that favors Corinth, Argos, Olympia, or Athens, over Cyprus, Alexandria, or Knossos.

Gortyn – where two mid-Augustan stamps have been published but the remainder of the record is relatively late – may have been more like other Greek cities, despite its status as a presumed administrative seat. At Athens no Italian sigillata has been found in deposits before the turn of the century.[67] Italian sigillata appeared on the island of Cyprus only at the beginning of the 1st century, and Alexandria began to import Italian sigillata in the Tiberian period.[68] Argos and Olympia participated in the same current of trade that supplied Corinth, only with a delayed beginning.[69] Italian sigillata only became dominant at Argos in the second quarter of the 1st century.[70]

We should also compare the chronological pattern for the island as a whole with that available for Cyrenaica, the other half of the double province (Table 8.3).[71] At Berenike – which practically constitutes the Cyrenaican corpus – Eiring reports that Italian sigillata was imported in the later 1st century BCE or at the turn of the century, gained momentum under Tiberius, and continued to be acquired throughout the 1st century.[72] By converting numbers of stamps to percentages we can more accurately compare the Cretan and Cyrenaican markets, without the distorting effect of archaeological history. Increasing the Cretan corpus to 57 stamps rather than 34 at least gives the island nearly half the record of Cyrenaica.

Despite the presence of two very early stamps found in Cyrenaica, the dates given in *OCK* for potters who supplied the province of Cyrenaica suggest that Italian potters supplied Crete somewhat more in the mid-Augustan period and even more in the late Augustan period.[73] This may well be due to the presence of a Roman colony at Knossos and the presumed provincial capital at Gortyn. Cyrenaica, on the other hand, preserves more Italian sigillata stamps in the Tiberian-Claudian period.[74] Between

Table 8.3. Chronology of Italian Sigillata stamps in Crete and Cyrenaica.

Period	Crete #	Crete %	Cyrenaica # (OCK Potters Supplying Cyrene)[1]	Cyrenaica %
early Augustan			2	1.7
mid-Augustan	23	40.4	45	37.8
late Augustan	11	19.3	14	11.8
Augustan?	1	1.8	1	0.8
Tiberian-Claudian	11	19.3	34	28.6
after CE50	10	17.5	21	17.6
uncertain	1	1.8	2	1.7
Total	57		119	

1. Oxé, A., Comfort, H. and Kenrick, P. 2000. *Corpus Vasorum Arretinorum: a catalogue of the signatures, shapes and chronology of Italian sigillata* (2nd ed.) (Bonn).

50 and 150 the two halves of the province appear to have been equally supplied by Italian potters.[75]

Whence: the Italian side of a symbiotic relationship

Until now, the profile of potters and therefore production sites supplying Crete was that for just one city, Knossos. By adding stamps of Knossos and other Cretan sites not included in Kenrick's edition we can begin to establish a new profile with which to compare future assemblages (Table 8.4). The ultimate question is whether this process will not only increase the total number of published stamps but also affect the provenance profile for the Italian sigillata imported to the island.

The provenance of the stamps discovered at Knossos and elsewhere on Crete can be analyzed according to the development of the Italian sigillata industry. Table 8.4 is arranged accordingly, and not in alphabetical order as in the search results available from the *OCK* CD-ROM.[76] The percentage increases for Knossian stamps from the Po Valley, Puteoli, and Pisa may not matter much on the scale of the Empire, but the introduction of stamps that are or may be from Etruria and central Italy are noteworthy 1st century phenomena. West-east trade mechanisms rarely brought to Crete Etruscan imports, despite their tendency to follow a grain route returning to Rome from Alexandria via Cyprus, the southern coasts of Asia Minor, Crete, and Sicily.[77] In the Augustan-Flavian period central Italian stamps appear on vessels produced for Rome and Latium, Umbria, northern Italy and western provinces including North Africa, but are also found in Achaia rather than cities along the grain route running to or from Alexandria.[78] It is intriguing to note that the central Italian workshop at Vasanello was owned by an Ancharius, whose nomen is attested once or twice

at Knossos.[79] These stamps constitute evidence for the Italian side of the symbiotic relationship between the Empire and its colonies. As a group, they attest to an active trade relationship between Knossos and Italian production centers of the 1st century. This phenomenon is contemporary with the development of Eastern Sigillata B, produced in the last decades of the 1st century BCE and the first half of the 1st century, as an eastern offshoot of one or more genuine Arretine factories.[80]

In her study of the Italian sigillata from Ephesos Zabehlicky-Scheffenegger estimated that the typical profile for the Greek East – *i.e.*, Achaia, Egypt, and Asia – consists of about 30% from Arezzo, 10% from Arezzo/Pisa/Lyon/Padana, and larger quantities from Puteoli, central Italy, and Pisa.[81] These figures are based on a range of percentages, presented in Table 8.5 together with the profiles of production sites supplying various provinces in the Greek East. Corinth, Antioch, Alexandria, and probably Ephesos served as the main eastern markets for workshops that primarily targetted the Mediterranean.[82] This study will now address a market on the island of Crete, possibly supplied by two redistribution centers at Knossos and Gortyn.

We have already seen that the current corpus of stamps from Crete suggests a slightly higher proportion of pottery from Arezzo and a significant quantity from Puteoli, central Italy and Pisa. What distinguishes Crete from the typical profile for the Greek East is the larger proportion of stamps that can be traced to workshops active at Arezzo/Pisa/Lyon/Padana, and the small but interesting proportion from Etruria. Comparison with the profile of Crete's provincial partner Cyrenaica is again instructive in that it reveals a profile that, at first sight, suggests that Cyrenaica might have participated in a different current of trade than that which supplied Crete. While percentages can be affected by the total number of

Table 8.4. Provenance of Italian Sigillata stamps on Crete. **Bold** = *regional subtotals.*

Production Center	OCK[1] #	OCK %	Knossos #	Knossos %	Gortyn #	other locations in Crete	all #	all %
Arezzo	**11**	**32.4**	**15**	**33.3**	**3**	**1**	**19**	**33.3**
Arezzo?	4	11.8	6	13.3	0	0	6	10.5
Arezzo/Pisa	1	2.9	1	2.2	0	0	1	1.8
Arezzo/Pisa/ Lyon	1	2.9	1	2.2	0	0	1	1.8
Pisa/Lyon	2	5.9	2	4.4	0	1	3	5.3
Po Valley	3	8.8	3	6.7	0	0	3	5.3
Arezzo or ArezzoPisa/Lyon/ Po Valley	**11**	**32.3**	**13**	**28.9**	**0**	**1**	**16**	**28.1**
Puteoli	3	8.8	4	8.9	0	0	4	7.0
central Italy?	0	0	0	0	1	0	1	1.8
Pisa	3	8.8	4	8.9	3	2	10	17.5
Pisa?	1	2.9	2	4.4	0	0	2	3.5
Puteoli/central Italy/Pisa	**7**	**20.5**	**10**	**22.2**	**4**	**2**	**16**	**28.1**
Torrita di Siena	1	2.9	1	2.2	0	0	1	1.8
Etruria?	0	0	1	2.2	0	0	1	1.8
Etruria	**1**	**2.9**	**2**	**4.4**	**0**	**0**	**2**	**3.5**
uncertain	5	14.7	5	11.1	0	1	6	10.5
Total	34		45		7	5	57	

1. Oxé, A., Comfort, H. and Kenrick, P. 2000. *Corpus vasorum Arretinorum: a catalogue of the signatures, shapes and chronology of Italian sigillata* (2nd edn., Bonn).

stamps, they can still indicate a province's relative position in the scheme of things.

From the profiles of potters who supplied the two halves of the province, Crete appears to have been more typical of the Greek East than Cyrenaica. Poblome argues that Knossos participated in an Aegean pattern of importing Eastern Sigillatae more than Italian sigillata, while Gortyn may have imported more Italian sigillata than Eastern Sigillatae because it lay along the route of the *annona*.[83] Eiring suggested that the trade pattern bringing Italian sigillata to Berenike was quite different from that which supplied Crete, the other half of the province.[84] It would be tempting to conclude that Knossos and therefore central Crete lay along one east-west shipping route between Italy and the East, while Cyrenaica lay along another, but the situation may not be so simple.

Crete lay at a crossroads in the Mediterranean, along an east-west route from Egypt and the Greek East to Rome and a north-south route that linked Cyrenaica and Egypt with the Aegean.[85] The *annona* route bypassed Crete on the way to Alexandria, but on the return voyage the island was the last landfall before an open-sea route to Malta.[86] The import as well as export activities of Cretan cities in the Roman period were fundamentally linked to their function as trans-shipment points along sea routes that reached the island from Egypt, the Levant, and southwestern Anatolia.[87] From Rhodes the route ran west along the south shore of Crete.[88]

How: the Cretan side of a symbiotic relationship

Lund and Poblome separately provide a framework within which Italian sigillata might be transported to Crete, not as a profit-producing luxury product but as a commonly available product shipped together with other commodities.[89] Unlike Delos and Corinth – both places with a strong western connection in the Hellenistic period – Crete did not lie directly on a shipping route between Italy and the East.[90] Nor was there a strong military presence there, as in Macedonia.[91] Yet like Berenike, Crete had strong ties with Campania, so that Puteoli might have been a chief port reached from there.[92] Puteoli and Alexandria were also the chief ports at either end of the *annona* route, which passed south of the island of Crete.

Goods such as Italian sigillata should have been collected at regional and intermediary ports like Puteoli and Ostia, then passed on to similar ones such as Corinth or Alexandria.[93] Sicily was a major trans-shipment point, from which one route ran east to Corinth, another southeast to Alexandria, and a third south to Carthage and then east to Berenike and Alexandria. Potters attested on Sicily will not

Table 8.5. Provenance of Italian Sigillata stamps in the Greek East.[1] **Bold** = *regional subtotals*

Production Center	Crete % (Table 3)	Cyrene %	Eypgt %	Achaia %	Macedonia %	Asia %	Cyprus %	Cilicia %	Syria-Phoenike %	Judaea %	Arabia %
Arezzo	**33.3**	**14.8**	**30.0**	**30.8**	**28.6**	**32.1**	**15.9**	**26.3**	**37.8**	**63.0**	**14.3**
Arezzo?	10.5	4.7	6.9	9.7	35.7	13.2	4.5	15.8	11.1	3.7	9.5
Arezzo/Pisa	1.8	0.8	0.3								
Arezzo/Pisa/Lyon	1.8	1.6	6.6	0.8			1.9	2.3	2.2	3.7	9.5
Arezzo/Lyon					7.1						
Pisa/Lyon	5.3	5.0	1.6						4.4		
Lyon?				0.2							
Arezzo/Po Valley				0.5		1.9			4.4		
Lyon/Po Valley										3.7	
Po Valley	5.3		0.9	1.5		0.9					
Faenza				0.1							
Arezzo or Arezzo/Pisa/ Lyon/Po Valley	**28.1**	**12.1**	**16.3**	**12.8**	**42.8**	**17.9**	**6.8**	**15.8**	**22.1**	**11.1**	**19.0**
Puteoli	7.0	4.7	12.8	1.7		6.6			2.2	7.4	42.9
Puteoli?		0.8	2.8	0.1							
Campania?									4.4		
central Italy	1.8	2.3	3.4	23.3		2.8	2.3	5.4	8.9		
central Italy?		1.6	4.4	4.4		1.9			2.2		
Pisa	17.5	32.0	8.8	5.2		12.3	63.6	21.1	2.2	11.1	9.5
Pisa?	3.5	6.3	3.8	0.8		0.9	2.3				4.8
Puteoli/central Italy/Pisa	**28.1**	**47.7**	**33.0**	**35.5**		**24.5**	**68.2**	**26.5**	**19.9**	**18.5**	**57.2**
Torrita di Siena	1.8			0.3		0.9		5.3			
Vasanello				0.1							
Etruria?	1.8		1.6	0.6		2.8	2.3				9.5
Etruria/Lyon			0.3	0.5							
Etruria	**3.5**		**1.9**	**1.5**		**3.7**	**2.3**	**5.3**			**9.5**
uncertain	10.5	25.0	15.9	19.2	28.6	21.7	6.8	26.3	20.0	7.4	

1. Crete: Table 8.3. Other columns: Oxé, A., Comfort, H. and P. Kenrick 2000. *Corpus vasorum Arretinorum: a catalogue of the signatures, shapes and chronology of Italian sigillata* (2nd edn., Bonn) CD-ROM: Summaries of Potters Supplying Cyrene, Egypt, Achaia, Macedonia, Asia, Cyprus, Cilicia, Syria-Phoenike, Judaea, Arabia.

be counted in the calculations below, as they could participate in overlapping distribution patterns. While the evidence of comparable stamps is too scanty to be statistically significant, it can still permit some historical conclusions about trends and probabilities. Table 8.6 has been constructed so as to tabulate the number of stamps – comparable to those found on Crete – that are attested at Italian ports, on Sicily, along two southern routes that led to Egypt, and along another northern route that led to Greece and beyond.

Crete could have been supplied by some of the same potters who shipped Arretine, Pisan, and central Italian sigillata from Ostia to Patras, and Corinth, if not also the Ephesos/Smyrna region, and Antioch or the Black Sea.[94] If we compare the potters' stamps preserved on Crete with those at Ostia, Corinth, in the region of Smyrna and Ephesos, and at Antioch or on the Black Sea, we can account for 77.2% of the stamps found on the island.[95]

Crete could also have been supplied by some of the same potters who took advantage of the major grain route that ran from Puteoli to Sicily and on to Alexandria then eastward only to return via Crete, and carried Puteolan as well as Campanian and the so-called "Campanian Orange" *sigillata*.[96] If we compare the potters' stamps preserved on Crete with those at Puteoli and in Egypt, we can account for 68.4% of the stamps attested on the island.[97]

Crete could at the same time have been supplied by many of the same potters who took advantage of a grain route that ran from Sicily to Carthage and along the southern shore of the Mediterranean to Berenike, on the way to Alexandria.[98] If we compare the potters' stamps preserved on Crete with those from Carthage and Berenike, we can account for 82.5% of the stamps attested on the island.[99] The evidence in favor of this route is further strengthened by the fact that Egypt – also the destination of the Carthage-Berenike route – preserves 28 potters' stamps comparable with those found on Crete and also at Carthage and in Cyrenaica.[100]

It is not necessary to choose any one of these routes over the other. Rather the distribution of potters' stamps shows that in the Roman period Crete was well-situated within a larger, more complex trade pattern. The cumulative evidence may still, however, favor (1) a supply route via Sicily, Carthage, Berenike, and Alexandria, over (2) the route that connected Ostia with Corinth, the Smyrna/Ephesos region, Antioch, or the Black Sea, or (3) the route that linked Puteoli with Alexandria, the eastern Mediterranean and Crete on the way back to Italy. It would be tempting to suggest that Gortyn was a center of redistribution for the island, given her position along the south coast and along a Roman road that ran north to Knossos. The evidence thus far available, however, favors Knossos, where the large number of single stamps, mostly from different workshops in the mid-Augustan period is comparable with the situation at the colony of Corinth, despite the fact that Corinth has been far more systematically excavated and published than Knossos.[101] There could even have been two centers of redistribution, one at Knossos and another Gortyn, to judge from the fact that no potters' stamps are currently attested at both cities.

The Italian sigillata stamps known from Crete now provide evidence for the Cretan side of the symbiotic relationship between colonies or provinces and the Empire. There are local reasons that a ship might sail to Knossos or Gortyn, and so bring Italian sigillata to the north and south coasts of the island. Knossos was not only a Roman colony, but one with a port at Herakleion, which began to flourish in the early-mid 1st century of our era.[102] The Capuan lands may not preserve traces of centuriation, but modern Herakleion may retain traces of an unusual circular grid pattern.[103] At Herakleion there was a mid-1st to mid-2nd century amphora production facility and at least one Roman villa that has yielded stamped fragments of Italian sigillata.[104]

Of the potters attested on Crete, three seem – on the basis of the evidence currently available – to belong to entirely different distribution patterns, due to military action along the Rhine and Danube river frontiers which in turn determined the location of their workshops within the Italian peninsula.[105] These three stamps appear to belong to a distribution pattern that developed as Arretine potters migrated to the Po Valley in order to take advantage of northern and western markets.[106] Workshops whose markets were primarily Mediterranean – northeast Spain, southern Gaul, the northern Adriatic and occasionally North Africa – are rarely attested on stamps found north of the Alps.[107] How and why these stamps came to be present in Crete must remain a mystery, unless they hint at the presence of veterans at Gortyn as well as Knossos.

Why: identity and Romanization/normalization

In the context of a pre-industrial agricultural economy and society like that of the Greek East, it is important to evaluate local production in order to understand why the tableware landscape should change in a community or region like Crete.[108] The Hellenistic pottery of Knossos consisted of imitations of international shapes and such notable local forms as the cylindrical cup, produced at least until Augustan times.[109] Strictly local shapes continued at Knossos during the Roman period, as did the habit of copying international shapes, with the result that 35% of the 1st century pottery at Knossos remained local in production.[110] The Hellenistic pottery of Gortyn is more difficult to profile but recent publications may suggest some characteristics of the local tableware landscape during the period when Italian sigillata was on the market. Local black-glazed production stopped during the 1st century BCE.[111] Dull brown-red glazed wares and local products inspired by Eastern Sigillata A are well-documented at Gortyn as well as on Crete in the last third of the 1st century.[112]

In the Greek East – with its own respectable ceramic tradition – the advent of Italian sigillata has been credited to a number of phenomena. At the colony and administrative center of Corinth, Slane sees the earliest wares – particularly large platters – as personal possessions and a mark of Roman status, and then as a sign of recovery from the disastrous impact of the civil wars on the East.[113] In the context of recovery, imported ceramics could fill the gap between local production – which might not increase in productivity – and growing demand as Roman status became increasingly desirable or accessible.[114] Members of Italian communities – *e.g. mercatores, coloni,* and a rising sub-elite class in *civitates* along the Mediterranean coasts – responded to social pressure and a desire for Italian-style artefacts, coupled with sheer availability and affordability, by buying Italian sigillata.[115]

In the particular case of Knossos we need to ask whether the Italian sigillata preserved there reflects the Campanian connections of the colony or the general vogue of importing Italian sigillata into the eastern Mediterranean.[116] It would appear that sub-regional patterns – the annona routes, particularly from Carthage or Puteoli to Alexandria – are the better explanation for the amount of Puteolan pottery at Knossos, not a specific Campanian link. The amount of pottery produced in and imported from Puteoli to Knossos is indeed high, far above the percentage attested at Corinth, Achaia, or Syria-Phoenike. But Puteolan sigillata was even more frequently imported to Cyrene, Asia and Judaea and particularly to Egypt. It is surprising then that Gortyn – which should have received Puteolan sigillata along

Table 8.6a. Distribution Patterns for Stamps Attested at Knossos.

Knossos	Ostia	Puteoli	Sicily	Carthage	Berenike	Egypt	Corinth	Smyrna, Ephesos region	Antioch	Black Sea
Amar(antus) 83, possibly = Cn. Ateius Amarantus 281	Amarantus 83		Cn. Ateius Amarantus 281	Cn. Ateius Amarantus 281	Cn. Ateius Amarantus 281	Cn. Ateius Amarantus 281	Cn. Ateius Amarantus 281			
Sex. Annius 183	Sex. Annius 183		Sex. Annius 183	Sex. Annius 183		Sex. Annius 183	Sex. Annius 183		Sex. Annius 183	
C. Arvius 254		C. Arvius 254	C. Arvius 254	C. Arvius 254		C. Arvius 254	C. Arvius 254			
Ateius 270	Ateius 270	Ateius 270	Ateius 270	Ateius 270	Ateius 270	Ateius 270				
Cn. Ateius 274					Cn. Ateius 274					
Cn. Ateius Euhodus 292			Cn. Ateius Euhodus 292	Cn. Ateius Euihodus 292	Cn. Ateius Euhodus 292	Cn. Ateius Euhodus 292		Cn. Ateius Euhodus 292		
Avillius 371	Avillius 371		Avillius 371	Avillius 371	Avillius 371	Avillius 371	Avillius 371		Avillius 371	
Bassus 435										
Calidius (Strigo) 487						Calidius (Strigo) 487	Calidius (Strigo) 487			
Camurius 514 (twice)	Camurius 514		Camurius 514	Camurius 514	Camurius 514	Camurius 514	Camurius 514	Camurius 514		Camurius 514
Chrestus 553				Chrestus 553		Chrestus 553				
Cornelius 612	Cornelius 612		Cornelius 612	Cornelius 612			Cornelius 612			
P. Cornelius 623			P. Cornelius 623			P. Cornelius 623	P. Cornelius 623			
P. Cornelius 624		P. Cornelius 624	P. Cornelius 624	P. Cornelius 624		P. Cornelius 624	P. Cornelius 624			P. Cornelius 624
Crestus 698 (twice)	Crestus 698		Crestus 698	Crestus 698	Crestus 698	Crestus 698	Crestus 698		Crestus 698	
Ennius 761		Ennius 761				Ennius 761				
C. Gavius Summacus 875			C. Gavius Summacus 875	C. Gavius Summacus 875						
Gellius 878 (twice)	Gellius 878		Gellius 878	Gellius 878		Gellius 878	Gellius 878	Gellius 878	Gellius 878	Gellius 878
L. Gellius 879	L. Gellius 879		L. Gellius 879	L. Gellius 879	L. Gellius 879	L. Gellius 879	L. Gellius 879			
M. Iulius 998		M. Iulius 998				M. Iulius 998				
Manneius 1099 (twice)				Manneius 1099						
C. Murrius 1203			C. Murrius 1203	C. Murrius 1203		C. Murrius 1203	C. Murrius 1203			
N. Naevius Hilarus 1250		N. Naevius Hilarus 1250	N. Naevius Hilarus 1250	N. Naevius Hilarus 1250	N. Naevius Hilarus 1250			N. Naevius Hilarus 1250		
M. Perennius Bargathes 1404	M. Perennius Bargathes 1404	M. Perennius Bargathes 1404					M. Perennius Bargathes 1404			
(M. Perennius) Tigranus 1412			(M. Perennius) Tigranus 1412		(M. Perennius) Tigranus 1412	(M. Perennius) Tigranus 1412				
L. Ple. Amar. 1477				L. Ple. Amar 1477		L. Ple. Amar. 1477				
Rasinius 1623	Rasinius 1623		Rasinius 1623	Rasinius 1623	Rasinius 1623	Rasinius 1623	Rasinius 1623	Rasinius 1623	Rasinius 1623	
C. Rasinius 1686			C. Rasinius 1686	C. Rasinius 1686		C. Rasinius 1686	C. Rasinius 1686			
L. Rasinius Pisanus 1690 (twice)	L. Rasinius Pisanus 1690	L. Rasinius Pisanus 1690	L. Rasinius Pisanus 1690	L. Rasinius Pisanus 1690	L. Rasinius Pisanus 1690		L. Rasinius Pisanus 1690	L. Rasinius Pisanus 1690		
T. Rufrenus sl. Rufio 1732 → T. Rufrenus Rufio 1735			T. Rufrenus Rufio 1735	T. Rufrenus Rufio 1735	T. Rufrenus Rufio 1735	T. Rufrenus Rufio 1735	T. Rufrenus Rufio 1735			
M. S. Pu(dens) 1760 (twice)										

1. Numbers after potters' names refer to the *OCK* type given in Oxé, A., Comfort, H. and P. Kenrick 2000. *Corpus vasorum Arretinorum: a catalogue of the signatures, shapes and chronology of Italian sigillata* (2nd edn., Bonn).

Table 8.6a. continued.

Knossos	Ostia	Puteoli	Sicily	Carthage	Berenike	Egypt	Corinth	Smyrna, Ephesos region	Antioch	Black Sea
C. Sentius 1861	C. Sentius 1861		C. Sentius 1861	C. Sentius 1861		C. Sentius 1861	C. Sentius 1861	C. Sentius 1861		
Serenus 1878		Serenus 1878		Serenus 1878		Serenus 1878	Serenus 1878			
Sertorius 1909				Sertorius 1909		Sertorius 1909				
A. Sestius Dama 1947, surely A. Sestius with slaves 1928–46			A. Sestius sl. Arci[---] 1932	A. Sestius Dama sl. Hilarus 1952 A. Sestius sl. Arci[---] 1932	A. Sestius sl. Priamus 1942	A. Sestius Dama sl. Hilarus 1951			A. Sestius Dama 1947	
Statilia sl. Canopus 1991				Statilia sl. Canopus 1991						
L. Su. M. 1999	L. Su. M. 1999			L. Su. M. 1999						
L. Umbricius sl. Felix 2457, cf. L. Umbricius with slaves 2453–68			L. Umbricius sl. Hospes 2459 L. Umbricius sl. Philargurus 2462	L. Umbricius sl. Apollo 2459 L. Umbricius sl. Rufio 2464	L. Umbricius sl. Archebus 2455		L. Umbricius sl. Rufio 2464			L. Umbricius sl. Felix 2457, cf. L. Umbricius with slaves 2453–68
L. Umbricius H 2470	L. Umbricius H 2470			L. Umbricius H 2470			L. Umbricius H 2470	L. Umbricius H 2470?		L. Umbricius H 2470
Zoilus 2543	Zoilus 2543			Zoilus 2543						Zoilus 2543

Table 8.6b. Distribution Patterns for stamps Attested beyond Knossos.

Gortyn and other locations on Crete	Ostia	Puteoli	Sicily	Carthage	Berenice, Cyrene	Egypt	Corinth	Ephesos, Smyrna region	Antioch	Black Sea
C. Annius 128			C. Annius 128							
Ateius 268	Ateius 268		Ateius 268	Ateius 268	Ateius 268	Ateius 268	Ateius 268			
Camurius 514	Camurius 514		Camurius 514	Camurius 514	Camurius 514	Camurius 514	Camurius 514	Camurius 514		Camurius 514
P. Clodius Proculus 592	P. Clodius Proculus 592			P. Clodius Proculus 592	P. Clodius Proculus 592	P. Clodius Proculus 592	P. Clodius Proculus 592	P. Clodius Proculus 592		
Crestus 698	Crestus 698		Crestus 698	Crestus 698	Crestus 698	Crestus 698	Crestus 698		Crestus 698	
C. Gavi Homullus 872			C. Gavius 868 C. Gavius 869			C. Gavi Menolaos 873	C. Gavius 869			
Sex. Murrius Festus 1212	Sex. Murrius Festus 1212	Sex. Murrius Festus 1212	Sex. Murrius Festus 1212	Sex. Murrius Festus 1212	Sex. Murrius Festus 1212		Sex. Murrius Festus 1212			
Sex. M. P. 1213	Sex. M.P. 1213	Sex. M.P. 1213	Sex. M. P. 1213	Sex. M. P. 1213	Sex. M. P. 1213		Sex. M.P. 1213	Sex. M.P. 1213		
C. P. P. 1342	C.P.P. 1342		C. P. P. 1342	C. P. P. 1342	C. P. P. 1342		C.P.P. 1342			
L. Pomponius? Pis(anus) 1503							L. Pomponius? Pis. 1503			
L. Rasinius Pisanus 1690	L. Rasinius Pisanus 1690		L. Rasinius Pisanus 1690	L. Rasinius Pisanus 1690	L. Rasinius Pisanus 1690		L. Rasinius Pisanus 1690	L. Rasinius Pisanus 1690		
L. Rast. Pre. 1694				L. Rast. Pre 1694			L. Rast. Pre. 1694	L. Rast. Pre. 1694		

Table 8.6c. Distribution Patterns for Stamps Attested on Crete.

Crete	Ostia-Corinth-Smyrna/Ephesos-Antioch-Black Sea	Puteoli-Egypt	Carthage-Cyrenaica	Carthage-Cyrenaica-Egypt
Knossos	33/45	32/45	38/45	24
Gortyn and elsewhere	11/12	7/12	9/12	4
Total	44/57 (77.2%)	39/57 (68.4%)	47/57 (82.5%)	28

the same annona route – preserves no stamps that can be traced to Campania.

We are now in a position to consider whether the importation of Italian sigillata to Knossos constitutes evidence for a new identity for Knossos and Knossians. At Knossos as elsewhere in the Greek East, Italian sigillata was not the only imported fineware but one that enjoyed a period of popularity alongside regionally produced tablewares, particularly Eastern Sigillata B. Poblome emphasizes the importance of regional patterns, in which Eastern Sigillata B dominated Aegean markets.[117] In the Augustan period Eastern Sigillata A and Cypriot Sigillata are represented at Knossos: Eastern Sigillata common and belonging mostly to a period between 25 BCE and 25; Cypriot sigillata in relatively small quantities imported in declining numbers through the remainder of the 1st century.[118] The mid-late Augustan period appears to have been pivotal in the changing balance between eastern and Italian sigillatae at Knossos.[119] Even as Italian Sigillata was imported at Knossos, Eastern Sigillata B was introduced in the early 1st century and gained popularity throughout that century at the final expense of Italian sigillata, which all but disappeared by the 2nd century.[120] Across time at Knossos Italian sigillata is estimated to have been less significant than eastern sigillatae.[121]

In order to set Knossos into the broader context of central Crete, we should consider the evidence provided by field surveys in the Knossos-Gortyn corridor. The Capuan lands between Knossos and Gortyn have not been surveyed at all, and La Torre's survey of the northern territory of Gortyn – extending to Prinias – was not a field survey but a campaign to identify structures.[122] The territory of western and southern territory of Gortyn has, however, been the focus of four surveys: the Kommos region, the Western Mesara, the coastal area between the Ayiofarango and Chrisostomos, and the lower Ayiofarango Valley. The Kommos survey found several sherds of Arretine ware on the acropolis of ancient Metallon (Roman Metellum), the latest of which was of 1st-century date, and a single sherd at Ayios Stephanos.[123] In the early Roman period, the population of the Kommos region had continued to centralize at Vigles and at Metallon, whose acropolis preserves several sherds of Arretine Ware on its central ridge, where two cisterns have been found, as well as remains of at least one kiln that produced Hellenistic commercial amphoras, in whose vicinity a rim fragment from an Eastern Sigillata A dish, and two sherds of Arretine Ware were found.[124] A survey of the Western Mesara found an impressive rise in imported pottery – including Eastern Sigillata A,

Arretine, and Italian Terra Sigillata but apparently not Eastern Sigillata B – as overseas contacts expanded during the early Roman period.[125] Arretine wares, Italian terra sigillata, and Northern Italian wares were found (1) up the Koutsoulitis tributary of the Ieropotamos River; (2) above the Ieropotamos delta on Phaistos hill; (3) in the foothills south of Phaistos, near Ag. Ioannis and Kamilari; and (4) in the southern foothills near Sivas.[126] The coastal area between the Ayiofarango and Chrisostomos included the site of ancient Lasaia, the summit of whose acropolis yielded eight sherds of 1st century Arretine, and a nearby farmstead that yielded two sherds of terra sigillata not identified as Arretine, Italian, or Eastern.[127] Survey of the lower Ayiofarango Valley – where a cult of Asklpeios was removed in favor of the Asklepieion at Lebena – found a single sherd of 1st century Arretine at Ag. Kyriaki and at Gaviliana a single piece of 1st/2nd century sigillata not identified as Arretine, Italian, or Eastern.[128]

Despite predictors of Romanization such as the possession of exploitable resources and an early foundation date for the colony at Knossos, the evolving mix of tablewares there suggests that over the long term Knossos experienced not so much Romanization as normalization, a return to the status quo ante after a century of development by fits and starts. Knossos was both a *simulacrum Romae* in its houses as well as cemeteries and public spaces and also an Aegean city in its taste for regionally-produced fine wares and preference for the Greek language.[129] Gortyn, by comparison has been characterized as a city where Italian sigillata – unstamped more than stamped – was more significant that eastern sigillatae but we must still be aware that the numbers are low and need to be treated with caution.[130] The evidence of field surveys in the territory of Gortyn – presented above – may, however, lend weight to this hypothesis.

At both Knossos and Gortyn access to Italian sigillata along west-east trade routes may well have combined with economic recovery and population growth to increase demand for Italian tablewares. Even if the colonists at Knossos did not bring their tablewares with them, they appear to have soon imported Italian sigillata to fill a need not met by local or regional producers. At the same time the Italian community of *negotiatores* resident at Gortyn in the wake of the fall of Delos was joined by administrative personnel in a presumed *caput provinciae* that became a magnet city for the Italianate population of Roman Crete.[131] Involvement in wider economic systems – the *annona* and the Cretan wine trade – brought Knossos and Gortyn into direct contact with the Italian west and set Italian finewares on their tables.

Bibliography

Abadie-Reynal, C. 2004. "Les modalités d'importation de la sigillée italique à Argos," in *Early Italian Sigillata,* 59–66.

Alcock, S. E. 1997. "The Problem of Romanization, the Power of Athens," in M. C. Hoff and S. I. Rotroff (eds), *The Romanization of Athens* (Oxford) 1–7.

Baldwin Bowsky, M. W. 1994. "Cretan Connections: The Transformation of Hierapytna," *Cretan Studies* 4, 1–44.

Baldwin Bowsky, M. W. 1999. "The Business of Being Roman: the prosopographical evidence," in A. Chaniotis (ed.), *From Minoan Farmers to Roman Traders: Sidelights on the Economy of Ancient Crete* (Stuttgart) 305–47.

Baldwin Bowsky, M. W. 2002a. "Colonia Iulia Nobilis Cnosus (Creta), in *Proceedings of the 11th International Congress of Classical Studies, Kavala 24–30 August 1999* (Athens) B 75–89.

Baldwin Bowsky, M. W. 2002b. "Reasons to Reorganize: Antony, Augustus and central Crete," in E. Dabrowa (ed.), *Tradition and Innovation in the Ancient World* (Electrum VI, Krakow) 25–65.

Baldwin Bowsky, M. W. 2004. "Of Two Tongues: Acculturation at Roman Knossos," in G. Salmeri, A. Raggi, A. Baroni (eds), *Colonie romane nel mondo greco* (Rome) 94–150.

Baldwin Bowsky, M. W. 2006. "From Capital to Colony: Five New Inscriptions from Roman Crete," *ABSA* 101, 385–426.

Baldwin Bowsky, M. W. 2009. "Setting the Table at Roman Eleutherna: Italian sigillata stamps from Sector I," in P. G. Themetis (ed.), *Ancient Eleutheria. Section I, I* (Athens) 155–96.

Baldwin Bowsky, M. W. forthcoming a. "All in the Family: Forming Social and Economic Networks in Roman Crete," in N. Vogeikioff-Brogan and K. Glowacki (eds), *STEGA: the archaeology of houses and households in ancient Crete* (Princeton).

Baldwin Bowsky, M. W. forthcoming b. "Apteraian Renaissance: the evidence of the Italian sigillata stamps."

Baldwin Bowsky, M. and E. Gavrilaki forthcoming. "Klio's Clay: inscribed *instrumenta domestica* from Lappa (Crete)."

E. Μπάνου 2004. "Η ελληνορωμαϊκή Κνωσός μετά τις ανασκαφές των ετών 1996–1998· στοιχεία απο την κεραμική και τοπογραφία," in *Creta romana e protobizantina, Atti del Congresso Internazionale (Iraklion, 23–30 settembre 2000)* (Padua) 879–907.

Blackman, D. and K. Branigan 1975. "An Archaeological survey on the South Coast of Crete, between the Ayiofarango and Chrisostomos," *ABSA* 70, 17–36.

Blackman, D. and K. Branigan 1977. "An Archaeological Survey of the Lower Catchment of the Ayio Farango Valley," *ABSA* 77, 13–84.

Burnett, A., M. Amandry, and P. P. Ripollès 1992. *Roman Provincial Coinage, Volume 1. From the Death of Caesar to the death of Vitellius (44 BC–AD 69)* (London and Paris) 229.

Chaniotis, A. and G. Preuss 1990. "Neue fragmente des Preisedikts von Diokletian und weitere lateinische Inschriften aus Kreta," *ZPE* 80, 189–202.

De Tommaso, G. 2001. "Ceramica a vernice nera," in *Gortina V,* V.3, 2–17.

De Tomasso, G. 2001. "Ceramica a pareti sottili," in *Gortina V,* V.3, 21–4.

De Caro, S. 1992–3. "Vino di Cnosso dei Campani: un nuovo documento epigrafico per la storia del vino cretese in età romana," *ASAA* 70–1, 307–12.

Dialogues in Roman Imperialism = Mattingly, D. J. (ed.). 1997.

Dialogues in Roman Imperialism: Power, discourse, and discrepant experience in the Roman Empire (Portsmouth).

Early Italian Sigillata = Poblome, J., P. Talloen, R. Brulet and M. Waelkens (eds) 2004. *Early Italian Sigillata: The chronological framework and trade patterns* (Leuven-Paris-Dudley).

Eiring, J. 2000. "Knossos at the turn of the millennium: *Romanitas* and Pottery," *Rei Cretariae Romanae Fautorum Acta* 26, 197–203.

Eiring, L. J. 2001. "The Hellenistic period," in J. N. Coldstream, L. J. Eiring and G. Forster (eds), *Knossos Pottery Handbook: Greek and Roman* (London) 91–135.

Eiring, J. 2004. "The earliest Italian sigillata at Knossos," in *Early Italian Sigillata,* 71–2.

Elaigne, S. 2004. "L'apport italique sigillées en Egypt au début du Haut-Empire: le cas d'Alexandrie et de Coptos," in *Early Italian Sigillata,* 133–44.

Forster, G. 2001. "The Roman Period," in J. N. Coldstream, L. J. Eiring and G. Forster (eds), *Knossos Pottery Handbook: Greek and Roman* (London) 137–67.

Gasperini, L. 1995. "Formiana Epigraphica," *Miscellanea Greca e Romana* XIX (Rome) 281–306.

Gortina V = Di Vita, A. (ed.), 2000–1. *Gortina V: Lo scavo del Pretorio (1989–1995)* (Padua).

Haggis, D. C. 1996. "The port of Tholos in eastern Crete and the role of a Roman *Horreum* along the Egyptian 'Corn Route'," *OJA* 15, 183–209

W. S. Hanson. 1997. "Forces of change and methods of control," in *Dialogues in Roman Imperialism,* 67–80.

Harrison, G. W. M. 1993. *The Romans and Crete* (Amsterdam).

Hayes, J. W. 1971. "Four Early Roman Groups from Knossos," *ABSA* 66, 249–75.

Hayes, J. W. 1983. "The Villa Dionysos Excavations, Knossos: the pottery," *ABSA* 78, 97–169.

Hayes, J. W. 1985. "Sigillate orientali," in *Enciclopedia dell'arte antica e classica. Atlante delle forme ceramiche,* II. *Céramica fine romana nel bacino mediterraneo (Tardo Ellenismo e Primo Impero)* (Rome) 1–96.

Hingely, R. 1997. "Resistance and domination: social change in Roman Britain," in *Dialogues in Roman Imperialism,* 81–100.

Holwerda, J. H. 1936. *Het laat-grieksche en romeinsche Gebruiksaardewerk uit het Middellandsche-zee-gebied in het Rijksmuseum van Oudheden te Leiden,* 'S-Gravenhage.

Hood, S., P. Warren and G. Cadogan 1964. "Travels in Crete, 1962," *ABSA* 59, 50–99.

Hope Simpson, R. 1995. "The Archaeological Survey of the Kommos Area," in J. C. Shaw and M. C. Shaw (eds), *Kommos I, The Kommos Region and Houses of the Minoan Town: Part 1, The Kommos Region, Ecology, and Minoan Industries* (Princeton) 325–402.

Ιωαννίδου-Καρέτσου, Α. 2008. *Ηράκλειο· η άγνωστη ιστιορία της αρχαίας πόλης* (Ηράκλειο).

Kenrick, P. M. 2004. "Signatures on Italian sigillata: a new perspective," in *Early Italian Sigillata,* 253–61.

La Torre, G. F. 1988–9. "Contributo preliminare alla conoscenza del territorio de Gortina," *ASAA* 66–7, 278–322.

Lund, J. 2004. "Italian-Made Fine Wares and Cooking Wares in the Eastern Mediterranean Before the Time of Augustus," in *Early Italian Sigillata,* 3–15.

Magnelli, A. 2001. "Iscrizioni," in *Gortina V,* V.3, 626–54.

Malfitana, D. 2004a. "The Importation of Stamped Italian Sigillata to Cyprus," in *Early Italian Sigillata,* 109–15.

Malfitana, D. 2004b. "Italian Sigillata Imported in Sicily: the Evidence of Stamps," in *Early Italian Sigillata,* 309–36.

Marangou-Lerat, A. 1995. *Le vin et les amphores de Crète: de l'époque classique à l'époque impériale* (Athens).

Μαρκουλάκη, Σ. 2008. "Τα ψηφιδωτά δάπεδα του Ηρακλείου και το περιβάλλον τους," in Ιωαννίδου-Καρέτσου, Α., *Ηράκλειο· η άγνωστη ιστιορία της αρχαίας πόλης* (Ηράκλειο) 107–47.

Martin, A. 2004. "Italian Sigillata in the East. Olympia: A Case Study," in *Early Italian Sigillata, 67–70*.

Mattingly, D. J. 1997 "Introduction: dialogues of power and experience in the Roman Empire," in *Dialogues in Roman Imperialism, 7–24*.

Menchelli, S. 2004. "Ateian Sigillata and Import-Export Activities in North Etruria," in *Early Italian Sigillata, 271–7*.

OCK = Oxé, A., H. Comfort, and P. Kenrick. 2000. *Corpus vasorum Arretinorum: a catalogue of the signatures, shapes and chronology of Italian sigillata,* 2nd ed. (Bonn).

Olcese, G. 2004. "Italian terra sigillata in Rome and the Rome area: production, distribution and laboratory analysis," in *Early Italian Sigillata, 279–98*.

Oxé, A., H. Comfort and P. Kenrick 2000. *Corpus Vasorum Arretinorum: a catalogue of the signatures, shapes and chronology of Italian sigillata* (2nd ed.) (Bonn).

Pagano, M. 2004. "Rapporti fra la Campania e Creta in epoca romana," in *Creta romana e protobizantina, Atti del congresso internazionale (Iraklion, 23–30 settembre 2000)* (Padua) I 29–32.

Papadopoulos, J. 1999. "La ceramica," in Allegro, N. and M. Ricciardi (eds), *Gortina IV. Le fortificazioni di età ellenistica* (Padua) 194–241.

Poblome, J. 2004. "Italian sigillata in the eastern Mediterranean," in *Early Italian Sigillata, 17–30*.

Poblome, J. and R. Brulet 2005. "Production mechanisms of sigillata manufactories. When East meets West," in M. B. Briese and L. E. Vaag (eds), *Trade Relations in the Eastern Mediterranean from the Late Hellenistic Period to Late Antiquity: The Ceramic Evidence* (Halicarnassian Studies vol. III, Odense) 27–36.

Poblome, J. and P. Talloen 2004. "The eastern Roman empire," in *Early Italian Sigillata, xii–xiv*.

Purcell, N. 2007. "*Ubicumque vicit Romanus habitat:* Coloniae and other communities of Roman citizens in the provinces" (paper, St. Andrews).

Rackham, O. and J. Moody 1996. *The making of the Cretan landscape* (Manchester and New York).

Rigsby, K. J. 1976. "Cnossus and Capua," *TAPA* 106, 313–30.

Rizzo, M. A. 2001. "Terra sigillata italica," in *Gortina V,* V.3, 36–8.

Rizzo, M. A. 2009 "Ceramica sigillata," in A. Di Vita (ed.), *Gortina VI: scavi 1979–1982* (Padua) 184–98.

Robinson H. S. 1959. *Pottery of the Roman Period: Chronology* (Athenian Agora V, Princeton).

Roques, D. 1999. "Ports et campagnes de Cyrène: d'Apollonia à Phycous," in A. Laronde and J.-J. Maffre (eds), *Cités, ports et campagnes de la Cyrénaïque gréco-romaine* (Paris) 187–95.

Sackett, L. H. 1992. *Knossos: from Greek city to Roman colony* (Oxford).

Shaw, J. W. and M. C. Shaw (eds) 2000. *Kommos IV: The Greek Sanctuary* (Princeton and Oxford).

Slane, K. W. 1989. "Corinthian Ceramic Imports: the Changing Patterns of Provincial Trade in the First and Second Centuries A.D.," in S. Walker and A. Cameron (eds), *The Greek Renaissance in the Roman Empire* (London) 219–25.

Slane, K. W. 2004. "Corinth: Italian Sigillata and Other Italian Imports to the Early Colony," in *Early Italian Sigillata, 31–42*.

Watkins, T. H. 1997. *L. Munatius Plancus: Serving and Surviving in the Roman Revolution* (Illinois Classical Studies, Supplement 7, Atlanta).

Watrous, L. V., *et al.* 1993. "A Survey of the Western Mesara Plain in Crete: Preliminary Report of the 1984, 1986, and 1987 Field Seasons," *Hesperia* 62, 191–248.

Watrous, L. V., D. Hadzi-Vallianou and H. Blitzer 2004. *The Plain of Phaistos: Cycles of Social Complexity in the Mesara Region of Crete* (Los Angeles).

Zabehlicky-Scheffenegger, S. 2004. "Italische Sigillata in Ephesos," in *Early Italian Sigillata, 73–80*.

Notes

1. Dio 49.14.5; Velleius 2.81.2; Strabo 10.4.9; Philostratus *VA* 4.34.2.
2. Soon after 27 BCE: Forster, G. 2001. "The Roman Period," in Coldstream, J. N., L. J. Eiring and G. Forster, (eds), *Knossos Pottery Handbook: Greek and Roman* (London), 137–67, esp. 137; Burnett, A., M. Amandry and P. P. Ripollès 1992. *Roman Provincial Coinage, Volume I, From the death of Caesar to the death of Vitellius (44 BC–AD 69)* (London and Paris), 229. Around 25 BCE: Eiring, J. 2004. "The earliest Italian sigillata at Knossos," in Poblome, J., P. Talloen, R. Brulet and M. Waelkens (eds), *Early Italian Sigillata* (Leuven, Paris and Dudley), 71–2, esp. 71.
3. Baldwin Bowsky, M. W. 2004. "Of Two Tongues: Acculturation at Roman Knossos," in Salmeri, G., A. Raggi and A. Baroni (eds), *Colonie romane nel mondo greco* (Rome), 94–150.
4. Poblome, J. and P. Talloen 2004. "The eastern Roman Empire," in *Early Italian Sigillata* (Supra n.2), xii–xiii. Compare Mattingly, D. J. 1997. "Introduction: dialogues of power and experience in the Roman Empire," in Mattingly, D. J. (ed.), *Dialogues in Roman Imperialism: Power, discourse, and discrepant experience in the Roman Empire* (Portsmouth) 7–24, esp. 9–10; Hanson, W. S. 1997. "Forces of change and methods of control," in *ibid.*, 7–80, esp. 67 for self-Romanization by negotiation/convergence.
5. Poblome and Talloen (Supra n.4), xiii.
6. Mattingly (Supra n.4), 17–8; R. Hingely, "Resistance and domination: social change in Roman Britain," in *ibid.*, 81–100, esp. 81 and 83–4.
7. Alcock, S. E. 1997. "The Problem of Romanization, the Power of Athens," in Hoff, M. C. and S. I. Rotroff (eds), *The Romanization of Athens* (Oxford), 1–7, esp. 2 and 4.
8. Baldwin Bowsky, M. W. 2002b. "Reasons to Reorganize: Antony, Augustus and central Crete," in Dabrowa, E. (ed.), *Tradition and Innovation in the Ancient World* (Krakow), 25–65, esp. 40.
9. Baldwin Bowsky (Supra n.3), 115; Marangou-Lerat, A. 1995. *Le vin et les amphores de Crète: de l'époque classique à l'époque impériale* (Athens), 44; Ιωαννίδου-Καρέτσου, Α. 2008. *Ηράκλειο· ηάγνωστη ιστορία της αρχαίας πόλη* (Ηράκλειο), 91–2.
10. *AE* 1969/70.635; Rigsby, K. J. 1976. "Cnossus and Capua," *TAPA* 106, 313–30.
11. *I.Cret.* I,viii 17, found in the church of the Panagia at Archanes but probably not from Knossos as Guarducci had supposed.
12. *Kr.Est.* 2 (1988) 321; *Arch.Delt.* 42 (1987) 530; to be published by Ch. Kritzas.
13. Pliny *NH* 12.12; De Caro, S. 1992–3. "Vino di Cnosso dei Campani: un nuovo documento epigrafico per la storia del

vino cretese in età romana," *ASAA* 70–1, 307–12, esp. 312.

14. *Kr.Chr.* 11 (1957) 339 = *SEG* XXIII 531 (Asites); *I.Cret.* I,xviii 4 (Rhaukos); Ch. Kritzas, pers. comm.

15. Μαρκουλάκη, Σ. 2008. "Τα ψηφιδωτά δάπεδα του Ηρακλείου και το περιβάλλον τους," in Ιωαννίδου-Καρέτσου (Supra n.9), 107–47, esp. 141–3.

16. Compare Poblome, J. 2004. "Italian sigillata in the eastern Mediterranean," in *Early Italian Sigillata.* (Supra n.2), 17–30, esp. 17, 23.

17. *I.Cret.* IV, *praef. hist.* 27.

18. Oxé, A., H. Comfort and P. Kenrick 2000. *Corpus vasorum Arretinorum: a catalogue of the signatures, shapes and chronology of Italian sigillata* (2nd edn, Bonn), CD-ROM: Summary of Potters Supplying Creta.

19. *OCK* (Supra n.18), 38.

20. Eiring, J. 2000. "Knossos at the turn of the millennium: *Romanitas* and Pottery," *Rei Cretariae Romanae Fautorum Acta* 26, 197–203, esp. 201.

21. Eiring (Supra, n.20), 197.

22. Hayes, J. W. 1971. "Four Early Roman Groups from Knossos," *ABSA* 66, 249–75, esp. 264 nos 11 and 16. See Table 8.1a, nos 17, 34.

23. Hayes, J.W. 1983. "The Villa Dionysos Excavations, Knossos: the pottery," *ABSA* 78, 97–169, esp. 132 no. 203–5, 138 no. 206–7. See Table 8.1a, nos 16, 25–6, 33, 40.

24. *AR* 1987–8, 90–1. See Table 8.1a: 5, 10, 13, 22, 32, 35.

25. Sackett, L. H. 1992. *Knossos: from Greek city to Roman colony* (Oxford), 144 Y1–5, 7–8, 10–1, 14, 16–7, 19–21, 23–4; 145 Y25, 27–8, 31–3, 36, 39, 40, 46; 146 Y50; 198 C1.1. See Table 8.1a: 1–4, 6–12, 14–5, 18–21, 23–4, 27–31, 36–9.

26. E. Μπάνου. 2004. "Η ελληνορωμαϊκή Κνωσός μετά τις ανασκαφές των ετών 1996–1998· στοιχέια απο την κεραμική και τοπογραφία," in Liviadotti, M. and I. Simiakaki (eds), *Creta romana e protobizantina, Atti del Congresso Internazionale (Iraklion, 23–30 settembre 2000)*, vol. III.1 (Padua) 879–907, esp. 897 no. 22. See Table 8.1a: 18.

27. *I.Cret.* IV 542 = Chaniotis, A. and G. Preuss. 1990. "Neue fragmente des Preisedikts von Diokletian und weitere lateinische Inschriften aus Kreta," *ZPE* 80, 189–202, esp. 195 no. 8. Odeion: Di Vita, A., pers. comm. So-called Praetorium complex: Rizzo, M.A. 2001. "Terra sigillata italica," in Di Vita, A. (ed.), *Gortina V: Lo scavo del Pretorio (1989–1995)*, vol. V.3 (Padua) 36–8, esp. 38 nos 1–2; Magnelli, A. 2001. "Iscrizioni," in *ibid.*, 626–54. esp. 631 no. 6. Telephone cables: Rizzo, M. A. 2004. "Ceramica sigillata," in Di Vita, A. (ed.), *Gortina VI: scavi 1979–1982* (Padua) 184–98, esp. 186 no. 292. See Table 8.1b: 41, 44, 47–50, 52.

28. Hood, S., P. Warren and G. Cadogan. 1964. "Travels in Crete, 1962," *ABSA* 59, 50, esp. 62 and n.15 (Khamalevri), 87 and n.42 (Viannos). See Table 8.1b: 43, 45.

29. Shaw, J. W. and M. C. Shaw (eds), 2000. *Kommos IV: The Greek Sanctuary* (Princeton and Oxford), 132 no. 99. See Table 8.1b: 51.

30. Holwerda, J. H. 1936. *Het laat-grieksche en romeinsche Gebruiksaardewerk uit het Middellandsche-zee-gebied in het Rijksmuseum van Oudheden te Leiden* ('S-Gravenhage), esp. 511; *I.Cret.* II,xxx 18. See Table 8.1b: 42, 46.

31. Poblome and Talloen (Supra n.4), xii–xiii.

32. Realignment of transit and communication corridors in the center of the island rather than reward for Gortyn and punishment for Knossos, in the wake of the civil wars: Baldwin Bowsky, M. W. 2002a. "Colonia Iulia Nobilis Cnosus (Creta)" in *Proceedings of the 11th International Congress of Classical Studies, Kavala 24–30 August 1999*, vol. B (Athens) 75–89; Baldwin Bowsky (Supra n.8), esp. 27–8.

33. Purcell, N. 2007. "*Ubicumque vicit Romanus habitat:* Coloniae and other communities of Roman citizens in the provinces" (paper, St. Andrews, 2007).

34. De Georgi, A., this volume.

35. Menchelli, S. 2004. "Ateian Sigillata and Import-Export Activities in North Etruria," in *Early Italian Sigillata* (Supra n.2), 271–7, esp. 276.

36. Purcell, N. 2007. (Supra n.33).

37. Sackett (Supra n.25); Baldwin Bowsky, M. W. and E. Gavrilaki forthcoming. "Klio's Clay: inscribed *instrumenta domestica* from Lappa (Crete)."

38. Baldwin Bowsky, M. W. 2009. "Setting the Table at Roman Eleutherna: Italian sigillata stamps fro Sector I," in P. G. Themelis (ed.), *Ancient Eluetheria, Section I, I* (Athens) 155–96; Baldwin Bowsky, M. W. forthcoming 2. "Apteraian Renaissance I: the evidence of the Italian sigillata stamps". Ιωαννίδου-Καρέτσου (Supra n.9), 91–92.

39. Baldwin Bowsky (Supra n.8), esp. 40–2; Baldwin Bowsky, M. W. forthcoming 1. "All in the Family: Forming Social and Economic Networks in Roman Crete," in Vogeikoff-Brogan, N. and K. Glowacki (eds), *STEGA: the archaeology of houses and households in ancient Crete* (Princeton).

40. Baldwin Bowsky (Supra n.32), esp. 80–1.

41. Harrison, G. W. M. 1993. *The Romans and Crete* (Amsterdam), 67–77.

42. Dio 49.14.5; Velleius 2.81.2.

43. Baldwin Bowsky (Supra n.32), 80.

44. Purcell, (Supra n.33).

45. West-east route passing north of the island: Slane, K. W. 2004. "Corinth: Italian Sigillata and Other Italian Imports to the Early Colony," in *Early Italian Sigillata* (Supra n.2), 31–42, esp. 4, 41; Abadie-Reynal, C. 2004. "Les modalités d'importation de la sigillée italique à Argos," in *Early Italian Sigillata* (Supra n.2), 59–66, esp. 63 for Ostia-Patras-Corinth. North-south route linking Achaia and Crete: Strabo 10.4.5; Pliny, *NH* 4.60.

46. Strabo 10.4.5.

47. Pliny, *NH* 4.58, 60; Strabo 10.4.5; Roques, D. 1999. "Ports et campagnes de Cyrène: d'Apollonia à Phycous," in Laronde, A. and J.-J. Maffre (eds), *Cités, ports et campagnes de la Cyrénaïque gréco-romaine* (Paris), 187–95.

48. Eiring (Supra n.20), 198; Eiring (Supra n.2), 71.

49. Eiring (Supra n.2), 71.

50. Eiring (Supra n.20), 197.

51. Eiring (Supra n.20), 201.

52. Middle to late Augustan 68.9% (Table 8.2). Compare Slane, K. W. 1989. "Corinthian Ceramic Imports: the Changing Patterns of Provincial Trade in the First and Second Centuries A.D.," in Walker, S. and A. Cameron (eds), *The Greek Renaissance in the Roman Empire* (London), 219–25, esp. 222.

53. Tiberian-Claudian 20%, post-Claudian 8.9% (Table 8.2). Late potter: L. Rasinius Pisanus (Table 8.1a: 29).

54. Mid-Augustan 28.6%, mid-1st century 14.3%, after 50 57.1% (Table 8.2).

55. Augustan period 61.5%, mid-Augustan period 40.5% (Table 8.2).

56. Tiberian-Claudian 19.3%, after 50 17.5% (Table 8.2).
57. Dio 49.14.5; Baldwin Bowsky (Supra n.32), 75–6.
58. Baldwin Bowsky (Supra n.3), 101.
59. Baldwin Bowsky (Supra n.8), 30.
60. Purcell (Supra n. 33).
61. *AE* 1995.278; Gasperini, L. 1995. "Formiana Epigraphica," in *Miscellanea Greca e Romana XIX* (Rome), 281–306, esp. 298–306; Watkins, T. H. 1997. *L. Munatius Plancus: Serving and Surviving in the Roman Revolution* (Atlanta), 105–8; Baldwin Bowsky (Supra n.8), 32–6.
62. *PIR²* N 129; *CIL* X 1425–34; Pagano, M. 2004. "Rapporti fra la Campania e Creta in epoca romana," in *Creta romana e protobizantina* (Supra n.26) 29–32.
63. Poblome and Talloen (Supra n.4), xiv.
64. Poblome (Supra n.16), 25; compare Eiring (Supra n.20), 201.
65. *Pace* Eiring (Supra n.20), 200.
66. Slane (Supra n.52), 222; Eiring (Supra n.20), 200; Slane (Supra n.45), 40–1.
67. Eiring (Supra n.20), 200, citing Robinson, H. S. 1959. "Pottery of the Roman Period: Chronology," *The Athenian Agora V* (Princeton), 11–2 nos. F1–15.
68. Malfitana, D. 2004a. "The Importation of Stamped Italian Sigillata to Cyprus," in *Early Italian Sigillata* (Supra n.2), 109–15, esp. 112; Elaigne, S. 2004. "L'apport italique sigillées en Egypt au début du Haut-Empire: le cas d'Alexandrie et de Coptos," in *Early Italian Sigillata* (Supra n.2), 133–44, esp. 135–6.
69. Abadie-Reynal (Supra n.45), 65; Martin, A. 2004. "Italian Sigillata in the East. Olympia: A Case Study," in *Early Italian Sigillata* (Supra n.2), 67–70, esp. 69.
70. Abadie-Reynal (Supra n.45), 63; Eiring (Supra n.20), 199.
71. Table 8.3 includes 72 potters from Berenike (named on 112 stamps, 95.7% of the Cyrenaican corpus); four potters from Cyrene, including the sanctuary of Demeter and Persephone (named on 5 stamps, 4.3% of the corpus); and one from an unknown location in Cyrenaica (named on one stamp, 0.9% of the corpus) (*OCK* (Supra n.18): CD-ROM: Summary of Potters Supplying Cyrene; Stamps Listed from Berenice, Cyrenaica, Cyrene.
72. Eiring (Supra n.20), 199.
73. Crete 61.5%, Cyrenaica 50.4% (Table 8.3).
74. Crete 19.3%, Cyrenaica 28.6% (Table 8.3).
75. Crete 17.5%, Cyrenaica 17.6% (Table 8.3).
76. Compare the arrangement in Zabehlicky-Scheffenegger, S. 2004. "Italische Sigillata in Ephesos," in *Early Italian Sigillata* (Supra n.2), 73–80, esp. 79.
77. See Menchelli (Supra n.35), 274 for the rarity of Etrurian stamps on Crete.
78. Olcese, G. 2004, "Italian terra sigillata in Rome and the Rome area: production, distribution and laboratory analysis," in *Early Italian Sigillata* (Supra n.2), 279–98, esp. 280, 282, 295. Compare Kenrick, P. M. 2004. "Signatures on Italian sigillata: a new perspective," in *Early Italian Sigillata* (Supra n.2), 253–61, esp. 254. See Zabehlicky-Scheffenegger (Supra n.76), 78, for the remark that no stamps from central Italy are known from Crete while 23% of the stamps found in Achaia are central Italian. Compare Table 8.5 for calculated percentages from Achaia (27.7%), Syria/Phoenike (11.1%), Egypt (7.8%), Cilicia (5.4%), Asia (4.7%), Cyrenaica (3.9%), Cyprus (2.3%), and now Crete (1.8%).
79. *I.Cret.* I,viii 21 (Nonia Ancharia); Baldwin Bowsky, M. W. 2006. "From Capital to Colony: Five New Inscriptions from Roman Crete," *ABSA* 101, 385–426, esp. 393–6 no. 2.
80. Hayes, J. W. 1985. "Sigillate orientali," in *Enciclopedia dell'arte antica e classica. Atlante delle forme ceramiche,* II. *Céramica fine romana nel bacino mediterraneo (Tardo Ellenismo e Primo Impero)* (Rome), 1–96, esp. 49; Zahbelicky-Scheffenegger (Supra n.76), 222–3 and 227; Poblome, J. and R. Brulet. 2005. "Production mechanisms of sigillata manufactories. When East meets West," in Briese, M. B. and L. E. Vaag (eds), *Trade Relations in the Eastern Mediterranean from the Late Hellenistic Period to Late Antiquity: The Ceramic Evidence* (Odense), 27–36, esp. 34.
81. Zabehlicky-Scheffenegger (Supra n.76), 78.
82. Slane (Supra n.45), 35–6.
83. Poblome (Supra n.16), 23.
84. Eiring (Supra n.20), 199.
85. Haggis, D. C. 1996. "The port of Tholos in eastern Crete and the role of a Roman *horreum* along the Egyptian 'corn route'," *Oxford Journal of Archaeology* 15, 183–209, esp. 203; Baldwin Bowsky, M. W. 1994. "Cretan Connections: The Transformation of Hierapytna," Cretan Studies 4, 1–44, esp. 7.
86. Haggis (Supra n.85), 204.
87. Haggis (Supra n.85), esp. 201; Baldwin Bowsky (Supra n.85), esp. 7–9.
88. Haggis (Supra, n.85), 204.
89. Lund, J. 2004. "Italian-Made Fine Wares and Cooking Wares in the Eastern Mediterranean Before the Time of Augustus," in *Early Italian Sigillata* (Supra n.2), 3–15, esp. 11, for the "piggy-back theory"; Poblome (Supra n.16), 28–9.
90. Lund (Supra n.89), 11; Slane (Supra n.45), 35–6.
91. Eiring (Supra n.2), 71.
92. Slane (Supra n.52), 224.
93. Slane (Supra n.52), 224.
94. Slane (Supra n.45), 4, 41; Malfitana, D. 2004b. "Italian Sigillata Imported in Sicily: the Evidence of Stamps," in *Early Italian Sigillata* (Supra n.2), 309–36, esp. 315 for Ostia carrying Arretine, Pisan and central Italian sigillata; Abadie-Reynal (Supra n.45), 63 for Ostia-Patras-Corinth; Menchelli (Supra n.35), 271 for Ostia to Ephesos and 274 for a grain route that ran from Corinth to Smyrna and Ephesos before the Black Sea.
95. Table 8.6a–b: Ostia, Corinth, the region of Smyrna and Ephsesos, Antioch, the Black Sea; tabulated in Table 8.6c.
96. Slane (Supra n.45), 4, 36 on Alexandria as a major market; Malfitana (Supra n.94), 315 on Puteolan, Campanian, and Campanian Orange *sigillata.*
97. Table 8.6a–b: Puteoli, Egypt; tabulated in Table 8.6c.
98. Menchelli (Supra n.35), 274.
99. Table 8.6a–b: Carthage, Berenike; tabulated in Table 8.6c.
100. Table 8.6a–b: Carthage, Berenike, Egypt; tabulated in Table 8.6c.
101. Slane (Supra n.45), 32.
102. Marangou-Lerat (Supra n.9), 44.
103. Rackham, O. and J. Moody. 1996. *The making of the Cretan landscape* (Manchester and New York), 92.
104. Marangou-Lerat (Supra n.9), 44; *Arch.Delt.* 51 (1996) 622; Ιωαννίδου-Καρέτσου (Supra n.9), 91–2.
105. Table 8.1b: 41; Table 8.1a: 8, 31.
106. *OCK* (Supra n.18), 32 and 37–8.
107. Slane (Supra n.45), 32 and 36.
108. Poblome and Talloen (Supra n.4), xiii.

109. Eiring (Supra n.20), 197; Eiring, L. J. 2001. "The Hellenistic period," in *Knossos Pottery Handbook: Greek and Roman* (Supra n.2), 91–135, esp. 93.

110. Eiring (Supra n.20), 197.

111. De Tommaso, G. 2001. "Ceramica a vernice nera," in *Gortina V: Lo scavo del Pretorio (1989–1995)* (Supra n.27), 2–17, esp. 4–5; De Tommaso, G. 2001. "Ceramica a pareti sottili," in *ibid.*, 21–4, esp. 23.

112. Papadopoulos, J. 1999. "La ceramica," in Allegro, N. and M. Ricciardi (eds), *Gortina IV. Le fortificazioni di età ellenistica* (Padua), 194–241, esp. 194–5, 198–9.

113. Slane (Supra n.45), 40–1.

114. Slane (Supra n.45), 41; Poblome (Supra n.16), 29.

115. Menchelli (Supra n.35), 276.

116. Forster (Supra n.2), esp.141; Eiring (Supra n.2), 71–2.

117. Poblome (Supra n.16), 23.

118. Forster (Supra n.2), 139–40.

119. Eiring (Supra n.2), 71.

120. Forster (Supra n.2), 143.

121. Poblome (Supra n.16), 18 and 22.

122. La Torre, G. F. 1988–9. "Contributo preliminare alla conoscenza del territorio de Gortina," *ASAA* 66–7, 278–322.

123. Hope Simpson, R. 1995. "The Archaeological Survey of the Kommos Area," in Shaw, J. C. and M. C. Shaw (eds), *Kommos I, The Kommos Region and Houses of the Minoan Town: Part 1, The Kommos Region, Ecology, and Minoan Industries* (Princeton), 325–402, esp. 337 (acropolis of ancient Metallon), 347 and 383–4 K38–1 (Ayios Stephanos NW).

124. Hope Simpson (Supra n.123), 329 and 336–7, plate 7.50.

125. Watrous, L. V., *et al.* 1993. "A Survey of the Western Mesara Plain in Crete: Preliminary Report of the 1984, 1986, and 1987 Field Seasons," *Hesperia* 62, 191–248, esp. 203.

126. Watrous, L. V. and D. Hadzi-Vallianou 2004. "Appendix D: Register of Archaeological Sites," in Watrous, L. V., D. Hadzi-Vallianou and H. Blitzer, *The Plain of Phaistos: Cycles of Social Complexity in the Mesara Region of Crete* (Los Angeles), 530 site 27 and 537 site 86; 527–8 site 6, 536 sites 77 and 79; 532 site 44, 538 sites 96 and 97; 535 sites 70 and 2; 531 sites 32 and 33, 538 sites 91 and 94.

127. Blackman, D. J. and Branigan, K. 1975. "An Archaeological survey on the South Coast of Crete, between the Ayiofarango and Chrisostomos," *ABSA* 70, 17–36, esp. 27–8 and 31. See *SEG* L 932 for the Asklepieion at Ayiofarango as a sanctuary in Gortynian territory.

128. Blackman, D and K. Branigan 1977. "An Archaeological Survey of the Lower Catchment of the Ayio Farango Valley," *ABSA* 77, 13–84, esp. 74.

129. A. Gellius, *NA* 16. 13.8–9; Baldwin Bowsky (Supra n.3), esp. 138–41.

130. Poblome (Supra n.16), 23.

131. Baldwin Bowsky, M.W. 1999. "The Business of Being Roman: the prosopographical evidence," in A. Chaniotis (ed.), *From Minoan Farmers to Roman Traders: Sidelights on the Economy of Ancient Crete* (Stuttgart), 305–47, esp. 330.

9. Colonial Space and the City: Augustus' geopolitics in Pisidia

Andrea U. De Giorgi

From its introduction in the early republic to the Severan foundations of the 3rd century CE in the East, the Roman *colonia* was a reflection of Rome's militaristic views and political pressures.[1] Exploited for centuries, albeit in episodic fashion, the founding of colonies reached a new height in the aftermath of the civil wars of the late Republic when Julius Caesar and Augustus created foci that occupied key coastal sites and inland districts linking Italy to the Greek East. Augustus, especially, promoted a vast, ambitious program that mobilized and relocated thousands of Roman citizens east and west, from Emerita in Lusitania to Berythus in Syria. More than creating *propugnacula*[2] these plans were designed to promote the visibility of Rome and extend her administrative infrastructure. In practice, however, the realization of a colony was grounded into the pursuing of one or more of the following strategies, notably:

1. Resolving efficiently the discharge of veterans, particularly after the civil wars
2. Transferring indigent elements of the population
3. Establishing a Roman enclave in a newly acquired territory
4. Incorporating individuals and communities from nearby territories into the organization of the colony.
5. Providing new recruits for the legions

The foundation of Lystra in Lycaonia which sanctioned Roman presence in a hostile Lycaonian region and that of Patras, where the relocation of veterans led to a re-configuration of the social matrix in northern Achaia illustrate but two of a colony's schemes. Local political factors and historical vicissitudes, however, led to other solutions. The Augustan settlements of *coloni* within existing communities in Galatia and Pamphylia[3] and the foundation of Actium with a substantial population from the surrounding region[4] remind us of the dangers of conceptualizing a "blueprint" of a Roman colony.

In this respect, the Augustan foundations in Southern Galatia, a group of twelve cities implemented by Augustus at the end of the civil war are no exception. Fully-fledged colonies were established at Antiochia, Comama, Olbasa, Parlais, Lystra, Iconium and Ninica while settlements of coloni were appended to Apollonia, Neapolis, Isaura and Attaleia.[5] Nevertheless, their structural asymmetries and individual foundation strategies present a surprising variety of which the two most striking examples are the cities of Antioch[6] and Parlais.[7] The former became the home of a new class of senators within just a few generations; the latter was an isolated and elusive creation on the shores of Lake Eğirdir.

These two foci are paradigms of the colonization process in southern Galatia that is still far from being understood. Nevertheless it can be argued that in them and at Cremna[8] and Comama[9] we may see examples of extensively inhabited districts that were occupied by the Romans for no military purpose but rather to incorporate near-by polities and communities into the colonial administrative framework. Put simply, this paper addresses the territorial impact of the colonies and the results of the insertion of Roman enclaves in the mesh of Greek cities and polities of south Galatia. The analysis is twofold: firstly, the investigation of the urban nucleus and of *territoria* on the one hand enables us to formulate hypotheses about the creation of a "colonial space" and its impact on pre-existing socio-political frameworks; secondly, how the agencies involved in the making of the colony exploited and eventually redesigned this space is a problem that this paper will bring into focus.

At issue is the title of *colonia* and its wider significance, especially when tested against the universe of Greek cities that surrounded the Augustan

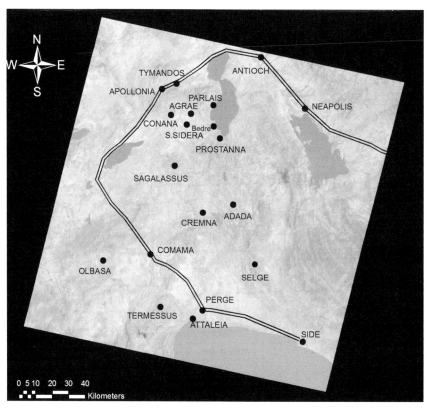

Figure 9.1. Roman colonies and colonial settlements in Pisidia.

foundations. As Barbara Levick argued,[10] these cities' performance as *coloniae* had a finite limit. What benefits and advantages, if any, the title *colonia* carried for these Galatian cities in the 2nd century CE remains to be determined. Antioch's membership to a *symmachia* against Rome's eastern threats from the time of the Severans onwards, crystallized by the *Socia Romanorum* title,[11] may have served to reinforce the notion of loyalty but had no effects on the political profile of the city at that point in history. Although obscured by Roman urban forms and visual culture, the Greek and indigenous substrata of these communities never ceased to exist and re-claimed primacy the moment southern Galatia was pacified and was no longer Rome's eastern frontier. This problem is central in this paper: of interest are the effects that the superimposition of Roman legal and administrative frameworks had on a Greek territory. The archaeological and epigraphical evidence available for four of the colonies, namely Antioch, Cremna, Comama and Parlais, will serve to illustrate these points. Situated in the mountainous district of Pisidia, these foundations display a spatial concentration that is in sharp contrast with the pattern of dispersal presented by Iconium or north Galatian Germa. The termination of dynastic struggles and

resistance, reconfiguration of local powers, and considerable land resources, plausibly accounted for the unity of purpose that underlies the foundation of these colonies.

At this juncture, however, a description of the territory where this system of colonies developed, Pisidia, is in order.

The "Land of the Pisidians" only became an administrative district under Diocletian.[12] It is a topographically complex and mountainous region that loosely corresponds to the modern Turkish provinces of Burdur and Isparta, between Antalya on the coast and the great lakes to the north (Fig. 9.1).[13] Four lakes frame the northern part of the region: from west to east, these are Lake Anava (Burdur), Lake Limnae (Eğirdir), Lake Koralis (Beyşehir), and Lake Trogitis (Suğla), the last demarcating the easternmost border between Pisidia and Isauria. Pisidia is watered by two main rivers: the Cestrus (Aksu) and the Eurymedon (Koca Çay). Massive mountain chains from the Taurus cut through the territory from north to south. An abundance of plain land especially along the western and eastern shores of Eğirdir Lake is one of the region's most distinct characters.

Rugged terrain, formidable heights, and scattered

patches of very fertile land are thus the hallmarks of this region. Nevertheless human settlement was not slow to develop here; a dense network of villages and communities may have populated the region during the 2nd and 1st millennia BCE.[14] While the 6th and 5th centuries BCE are also represented in the Pisidian archaeological record,[15] it was during the Hellenistic period[16] that a number of Pisidian cities rose to prominence, possibly on account of Macedonian re-foundations:[17] Selge, Termessos, and Sagalassos, are but a few of those mentioned in the sources.[18] The excellent reputation of these cities was not matched by that of their inhabitants, however, and it is a matter of record or external perception that the Pisidians were perfectly trained and loyal mercenaries abroad, but brigands of the worst kind at home.[19]

Piecemeal, and often contradictory, reports about the region come from Arrian, Strabo (using Artemidoros of Ephesos), and Pliny, among others.[20] These authors provide views of ethnicities, cities, and geography for us that are often inconsistent as well as anachronistic. Strabo's catalogue of Pisidian cities, for instance, is far from complete.[21] To make matters worse, there is no narrative account of the circumstances that led to the implementation of a colonial system in Southern Galatia under Augustus. Even Pliny, whose accounts of colonization are meticulous, fails to mention the Pisidian foundations and cites only Antioch.[22] His silence has not prevented historians from proposing interpretational frameworks for these events,[23] and it is now the consensus[24] that the pacification of Galatia in the aftermath of Amyntas' death and the bequest of his kingdom to Rome was driven by two primary concerns:

1. the subjugation of unruly Pisidian tribes, chiefly the Homonadeis
2. the creation of Roman enclaves in a territory that knew little of the Roman world.

Seen in these terms, one may safely infer that the Augustan Pisidian scheme fits the Geopolitik of veteran settlement that was carried out between 30 and 14 BCE described in the text of the *Res Gestae*. The text of the *Res Gestae*, however, also brings a series of problems about the Pisidian colonies into focus. Augustus, although he does not name them, mentions having founded colonies in Pisidia. Six cities are conventionally added to this group:[25] Antioch, Cremna, Comama, Olbasa, Lystra, and Parlais. However, the limits of Pisidia in antiquity are beyond our grasp. Nor does the intersection with the districts of Milyas to the west and Lycaonia to the east facilitate the identification of these Pisidian colonies. Nevertheless, it could be inferred that with

the exception of Olbasa (located in Cibyratis) and Lystra (in Lycaonia) the other four cities form a discrete group of foundations that may be identified as "Pisidian." Inserted in a complicated, yet discrete landscape shielded by the Taurus Mountains and gravitating around the region of the great Lakes, these colonies attest to Roman penetration during the last decades of the 1st c. BCE. Their titles, *Colonia Caesarea, Colonia Iulia Augusta Cremnena, Colonia Iulia Augusta Prima Fida Comama, and Iulia Augusta Colonia Parlais*,[26] appearing on coins and inscriptions, leave no doubt about the agencies behind the foundations.

While other colonies were settled east of Pisidia at Ninica and Iconium[27] and in northern Galatia at Germa, an area hitherto marginally urbanized,[28] and it is known that contemporary veteran settlements were also situated within Pisidia and further south, the location and dates of the Pisidian colonies invite speculations.

The two main *termini* for the establishment of the colonies were the installation of the Via Sebaste and the war against the Homonadeis conducted by P. Sulpicius Quirinus between 6 BCE and CE 4,[29] which granted him the *ornamenta triumphalia*.[30] The earliest date that can be assigned to the milestones of the Via Sebaste is 6 BCE, under the legate Cornutus Aquila.[31] However, the first of the colonial foundations, Antioch, is firmly dated to the year 25 BCE. It is highly unlikely that twenty years would have elapsed between the founding of the colony at Antioch and those of the other colonies. Secondly, the Via Sebaste served only two of the colonies in question, Comama and Antioch, and the colonial settlements at Apollonia and Neapolis. In this context, the Via Sebaste functioned as a continental artery for traffic; in combination with other pre-existing routes it created a *trait d'union* between the Pisidian highlands and the west of Asia, Pamphylia and thence western Cilicia.[32]

At any event, its construction was independent of the war against the Homonadeis and, more importantly, was unrelated to the colonization processes that were underway in southern Galatia during the late 20's BCE. The other arteries serving these communities consisted in the main of a series of roads running north to south that skirted the area around the lakes, and their true extent is unknown.[33]

I now turn to the analysis of the individual cities, and investigate the agencies involved in their settlement solutions. The district around Lake Eğirdir, in particular, offers some interesting points to illustrate the problems that this paper addresses. While dispersal is apparently the signature of veteran settlement in Galatia, as the example of Germa proves, in Pisidia the tight knit installation of four colonies (Antioch, Cremna, Comama and Parlais) in a region punctuated by Pisidian cities and former Attalid and Seleucid colonies suggests that a precise strategy was at work. Incorporation of pre-existing polities and reduction of the latter to the status of *komai* were in all likelihood two desiderata in the mapping out of the colonization plan, something which the modality of Antioch's foundation illustrates well.

Antioch merits special consideration. Arguably a "handbook" illustration of Roman-colony making, Antioch is chief among the veteran settlements and the best known on account of its archaeological evidence and rich body of inscriptions. The main station on the Via Sebaste, or *caput viarum*, the city is situated northeast of Lake Eğridir, on the rolling hills that stem from the Sultan Dağ massif, thus enjoying the economic benefits of a vast, fertile plan. In modern Yalvaç, Antioch's successor, still lingers the thriving agricultural tradition of her illustrious predecessor. Itself a 3rd c. BCE Seleucid colony of Magnesians,[34] the city's vast and fertile territory watered by the Anthius river had previously been only marginally exploited. No trace of the Hellenistic city plan that the Augustan colony superseded was found in the archaeological investigations conducted at the site by Kelsey and Ramsay of the University of Michigan in 1924 and later by Taşlıalan in the early 90's.[35] No other Augustan colony could compete with Antioch in terms of ambition. While all Roman colonies were to function according to the legal and administrative systems of Rome, Antioch was also designed to replicate the social and urban configuration of the capital; the introduction of *vici* and tribes illustrate the lofty aims of the colony. Although the procedures attendant on its *deductio* were not as drastic as those under Caesar in Greece and Pontus,[36] the commencement of Roman operations brought the imposition of Roman law and order. As early as 25 BCE, Roman commissioners confiscated the land belonging to the sanctuary of *Mên Askaênos* to the southeast of the settlement and appropriated the assets of the temple's estates, which were to be allotted among the veterans.[37] The outcome was the acquisition of a territory that encompassed some 540 sq miles checkered with estates owned by Roman citizens situated in Antioch's *chora*.[38] This configuration offered ample opportunities to the considerable number of colonists who participated in the foundation, apparently on the order of some 5,000 families, which came primarily from central Italy.[39] Whether these measures also have secured land for those pre-existing communities dislocated

by the establishment of the colony is hard to infer.[40] The archaeological record from the Antioch's vast territory is silent as to the modality of settlement that populated the region before the installation of the colony. The scattered evidence of *Türsteine* may hint to the lingering of a local Phrygian traditions,[41] yet the very nature of these finds, typically removed from their original contexts hampers any definite conclusion. Nor is the epigraphical record able to inform any of the negotiations that must have taken place upon the founding of the colony.

While this is purely conjectural, the overall nature of the evidence suggests that the superimposition of a colony involved responses ranging from coercion to acceptance. The case of the Salassi in the territory of Augusta Praetoria in northwestern Italy[42] and of Patras in Greece[43] illustrate the process well. It can nevertheless be inferred that the scheme at work in Antioch might be similar to that employed at the colony of Orange, where the best land was confiscated for the benefit of the colonists, with the remainder at the disposal of the local population.[44] At Orange, this led to a juridical, social, and spatial divorce between *coloni* and *incolae*, a distinction present in the famous decree of the governor of Galatia, Lucius Antistius Rusticus, in CE 92, that aimed to resolve Antioch's pending food crisis.[45] Whether the obligations prescribed there for the *incolae* of Antioch were also matched by honors and more practically, by access to civic appointments is difficult to say.

The territory of the colony at Antioch became a mosaic of land-holdings and estates. The abundant gravestones with Latin inscriptions dating to the Julio-Claudian period found scattered for miles outside the city indicate the scale of Antioch's colonization and reflect the aspirations and struggles of the colonists who came from the poorest districts of central Italy or were veterans of the 5th and 7th legions.[46] But changes were not limited to the city's territory. This systematic exploitation of the rural districts went hand in hand with the architectural elaboration of an urban milieu that would celebrate and justify the Roman presence in the heart of Galatia. Antioch was drastically re-configured in order to accommodate the new arrivals, and witnessed a frenzy of building activity, a common procedure in the implementation of a colony, as also seen, for example, at Alexandria Troas.[47] To that end, a new city plan replicating Rome in design and in spirit was probably introduced in Antioch as early as the first decades of the 1st century CE (Fig. 9.2).

Thanks to the largesse of donors, the city's two main axes, while still acknowledging their Hellenistic origins, were re-designated the *Plateia Augusta* and *Tiberia*,[48] but the city's urban reconfiguration culminated with the construction of the sanctuary of Augustus, begun about 2 BCE, while the *princeps* was still alive. Its design and decoration have been amply discussed by scholars,[49] but it is still worthwhile to look at some of its key features and how they served to create a miniature Rome and a new civic identity.

At Antioch, a combination of steps and free standing arch at the end of an east-west axis functioned as propylon and led to a large open space framed by two porticos with an exedra in the rear. Once a subject of debate,[50] it is now accepted that the arch was a triple one, with engaged Corinthian columns and decorated with reliefs on the exterior illustrating Augustus' provincial triumphs. Amidst symbols of these were also representations of kneeling Pisidian captives,[51] visually reminiscent of the kneeling Parthian type, an iconography that was particularly en vogue in Augustan Rome as demonstrated recently by Brian Rose.[52] On the interiors were inscribed in columns the *Res Gestae*, (as were the consular and triumphal fasti on the triple arch of Augustus in the Roman Forum), some fragments of which were recovered by Ramsay in the 1930s.[53] He also recovered some fragments of the architrave inscription which mentions Augustus as *Pater Patriae*, commemorates his 13th consulship, the 22nd year of his *tribunicia potestas* and 14th triumph to furnish the date of 2 BCE for the beginning of construction of the complex.

In the center of this area stood a small (26 m × 15 m) prostyle temple dedicated to Augustus, now heavily weathered, and of uncertain plan because the arrangement of the columns in the *pronaos* may be read in a variety of ways (Figs 9.3–4).[54] Be that as it may, its architectural decoration in Corinthian style consisted of lavish friezes with garlands and buchrania and luxuriant acanthus plants above the architraves. While this type of artistic idiom finds abundant parallels both in the east and west at such sites as Aphrodisias, Pola, Nîmes, and Merida,[55] some of the features adopted by the planners of the sanctuary make it distinctive.

The sequence *steps, arch and temple* with the visual corollary of the *Res Gestae* created an environment where visual and textual media converged in a celebration of the *Princeps*' achievements (Fig. 9.3). This architectural program, culminating in the small temple framed by the great exedra, is heavy with Augustan symbolism and in its overall design may be linked to one of Augustus' key monuments in the city of Rome. The two great exedrae of Augustus' forum in Rome[56] provided a model for

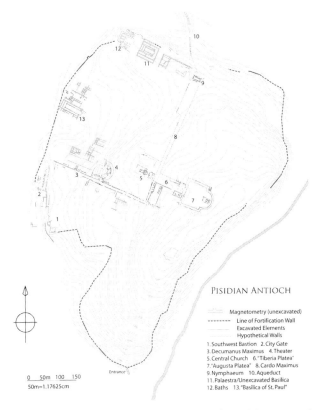

PISIDIAN ANTIOCH

—··—··— Magnetometry (unexcavated)
--------- Line of Fortification Wall
——— Excavated Elements
Hypothetical Walls
1. Southwest Bastion 2. City Gate
3. Decumanus Maximus 4. Theater
5. Central Church 6. "Tiberia Platea"
7. "Augusta Platea" 8. Cardo Maximus
9. Nymphaeum 10. Aqueduct
11. Palaestra/Unexcavated Basilica
12. Baths 13. "Basilica of St. Paul"

0   50m 100   150
50m=1.17625cm

Figure 9.2. Antioch's City plan (Kelsey Museum of Archaeology).

Antioch's planners; their *porticus*, however, were by no means comparable to those of Augustus' forum, with grandiose Corinthian columns, *lesene*, potent impressive cariatids and reliefs of Juppiter Amon.[57] Nor were the statues of the *summi viri* and gods to be found in Antioch. Nevertheless, in its modesty it appropriated and re-interpreted the exedra scheme and brought to fruition the notion of closed, discrete space that realized in the Forum of Augustus and in the Roman forum as well, where the temple of *Divus Iulius* closed the eastern end of the square. Antioch's planners, moreover, were able to exploit the dark limestone outcroppings in which the exedra was cut so as to create a backdrop reminiscent of the tufa perimeter wall of the Forum of Augustus, thereby enhancing the connection between the two complexes. The building program at Antioch reached beyond the limits of the Augustan sanctuary to other sectors of the city; an inscription attests to the donation by the *aedile* Caius Paepius of an *Ara Pacis Augustae* in the early 1st c. CE, probably located in the eastern sector of the city.[58]

All in all, this presentation of the Augustan age to engage the viewer may also have served to diminish any possible malaise attendant for those now living in this remote corner of Galatia, but it should not be

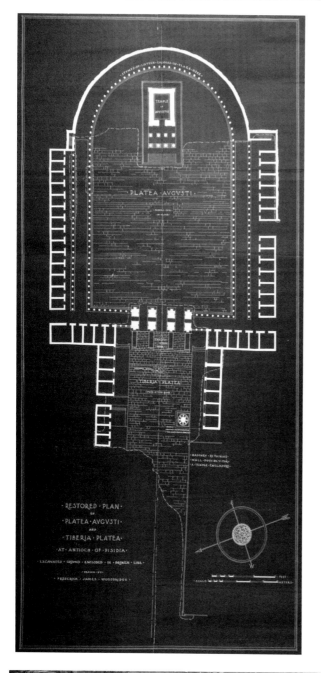

forgotten that only a minority of Antioch's inhabitants were familiar with Augustan Rome and in a position to appreciate allusions to it. Still the creation of this simulacrum of Rome in the heart of Galatia was not limited to the cosmetics of visual culture. On the contrary, there was also in play serious patronage of the highest order; members of the Julio-Claudian family as well as consuls figure among the local magistrates of Antioch as early as the first decade of the 1st century CE, thus confirming the serious investments and the aspirations that converged in the foundation of this colony. There are examples of prominent citizens of Antioch, members of a new landed aristocracy, serving as prefects of the colony on behalf of Sulpicius Quirinus, Cn. Domitius Athenobarbus (the father of Nero), the elder Drusus and others.[59] The parabola of the Flavonii, Anicii, and Caristani,[60] who were promoted overseas from southern Etruria as others were promoted to Rome and, like them, achieved senatorial dignity and consular rank within a few generations is noteworthy and shows the prominence Antioch had attained by the 2nd c. CE.[61] While these forms of imperial patronage appear in other contexts, the extent of their implementation in Antioch, so soon after the foundation of the colony, is particularly striking. This haste suggests that the city, in conjunction with the provincial capital Ancyra, was expected to become a secondary administrative and, for a short time, military center for the southern half of the province.[62] Certainly Antioch could not have done so on its own. At the time it was a town of a few thousand inhabitants, of which the first two generations of settlers consisted chiefly of aging veterans who had more interest in political careers than in the military. Still it attracted individuals from nearby communities and cities, who were eager to

Figure 9.3 (above). Antioch: Temple of Augustus. The Plan (Kelsey Museum of Archaeology).

Figure 9.4 (left). Antioch: Temple of Augustus from northeast.

secure the opportunities citizenship in the colony could provide.[63] Tax exemptions and the exactions of tolls in the territory, as at Alexandria Troas, may be but some of the benefits that the colonial citizenship would provide.[64] It needs to be underscored, however, that colonies could not bestow *civitas* Romana on anybody; the prerogative was restricted first to the senate and then to the emperor. It was through the mechanisms of the *adlectio*, an administrative device attested to in Spain and Africa that new Roman citizens were also presented with colonial citizenship, and thus enjoyed the tax exemptions, full ownership of land, and lastly, prestige that the *Ius Italicum* carried.[65] The example of Dio of Prusa's acquisition of citizenship in the Roman colony of Apamea in Bithynia under the Flavians, as described in his own words in Oration 41, may reflect these legal and administrative frameworks.[66] While their technicalities lie beyond the scope of this paper, it may be inferred that Apamea's acceptance of Dio's petition, marked the beginning of his dialogue with the Roman authorities that would not have been possible otherwise. [67]

Antioch's new constituents of Greek and Phrygian origins may have followed this trend. The example of Titus Flavius Salgurius under the Flavians is representative.[68] As the *praenomen* and the *gentilician* suggest, he received citizenship under the Flavians and was enrolled in the tribe of the original colonists, the Sergia; what needs to be stressed is that Salgurius is neither a Greek nor a Roman name, but that of a local of likely Phrygian descent. Nor was Salgurius an exception; the case of Syneros, former freedman of St. Anicius,[69] suggests that the addition of new citizens to the body of original constituents was a common procedure in the social landscape of Antioch.[70]

This introduction of new citizens to the colonial matrix might have been the result of an institutional scheme designed to strengthen a colonial identity that presumably was losing its raison d'être. An issue of Antioch's mint under Vespasian, with the symbols of the legions V and VII that had contributed to the foundation of the colony 90 years earlier, was not mere *amarcord*. The commemoration of that event probably had a dual significance: on the one hand, it may have celebrated the city and its legacy, while on the other, it augured the beginning of a new phase, one in which the addition of Greek and local notables to its citizenry would reinforce the role of Antioch as a center of Romanitas in the heart of Galatia.

The reinvigoration of Antioch's social matrix under the Flavians may have ensured continuity for a community that was losing its central strategic importance on account of the addition of the province

of Cappadocia, but, contrary to its expectations, it also marked the beginning of the city's *re-hellenization*. The colony's momentum by the end of the 2nd c. CE had begun to dwindle: its language, symbols and administrative schemes were in all likelihood seen as a mannerism at odds with the customs and the cultural traditions of the Greek Pisidia. Bilingualism, in particular, informs this trend, as attested by epitaphs in both Latin and Greek.[71] More to the point, three indices are particularly relevant:

1. the sanctuary of *Mên*, de-legitimized by the *agrimensores*, never went out of use;[72] the epigraphical record, after the decades of decline, shows intense activity in the early 2nd c. and beyond, with citizens of Italian origin, carrying the *tria nomina,* making dedications to the local deity in Greek.[73]
2. Latin inscriptions in general begin to be scarce around the mid 2nd c. and practically disappear by the end of the century[74]
3. Magistracies like those of the Irenarch or Gymnsiarch, hitherto absent from the fixed scheme of Roman public appointments, began to appear around the end of the 2nd c.[75]

Altogether, these factors indicate the trajectory that the city was to adopt in the 2nd c. CE. To what extent the grand sanctuary of Augustus could still rally the masses at Antioch we don't know. It is likely, however, that the city gradually lost its imperial patronage in spite of the number of senators and consuls that it had produced. The archaeological record suggests that, with the exception of an arch built under Hadrian, no other major building program was to be carried out in Antioch.[76] From having been the main focus of Roman interest in southern Galatia Antioch became one of the many graeco-roman cities of Asia Minor; what kind of privileges the city retained, and in what form, is difficult to estimate. 3rd c. CE coinage in particular, elucidates some of the mechanisms of Antioch's social re-configuration. Alongside the title *Socia Romanorum*, which renewed the city's allegiance to Rome, the Severan issues presented also a reiteration of the iconography of the god *Mên*, thus signaling the wholesale adoption of the Phrygian god. Ironically, the bust of the god had already appeared on issues of that had preceded the founding of the colony in 25 BCE.[77]

At this juncture, the question that must be addressed is, to what extent Antioch is representative of the system of colonies that were installed in the same years in Galatia. While it could be inferred that each of the colonies was the product of very specific political

Figure 9.5. Cremna: the Baths.

pressures, and economic interests, it is nonetheless true that they share some common denominators. The scale and grandiosity of the colony at Antioch should not deceive us, as some of its mechanisms were replicated, *mutatis mutandis*, at some of the other Pisidian colonies. The incorporation of pre-existing, nearby communities in the colony framework is the most visible of these dynamics. The paucity of the archaeological record, however, makes the analysis particularly arduous, with the exception of Cremna, where salvage excavations and one architectural/epigraphical survey offer important evidence about the shape of the city.

One of the most spectacular classical sites in Asia Minor, and known for its dramatic revolt against Rome in the 3rd century,[78] Cremna was a formidable fortress perched on top of a cliff that commanded a 360 degree vista over southern Galatia. Location was thus Cremna's fundamental asset and there was perhaps a strategic need for the Romans to control this town in the campaigns of the 20's, yet it was hardly garrisoned and held by veterans, let alone regular soldiers. It is not easy to determine the socio-political profile of Cremna, or how this developed in the aftermath of the colony's foundation, and whether the same degree of social mobility that we have observed at Antioch was at work. Nor does the archaeological record provide any information

about building activities carried out in the city under Augustus. Steven Mitchell's comprehensive survey of the city failed to identify a single structure datable to the 1st c. CE, on account of the poor state of the ruins and illicit digging. The Hellenistic Doric agora, the columned street and the Hadrianic forum, basilica and baths are in fact the only structures the layout of which could be safely reconstructed. The baths, which were excavated in the 1970s by Jale Inan[79] are of interest as they yielded a staggering cache of sculpture that can be dated to the time of Hadrian (Fig. 9.5). The original spirit of the colony, however, is not to be found in this collection of gods, goddesses, and nymphs that are now on display at the Museum of Burdur;[80] it was assembled probably during the 3rd c. CE, as the reused bases prove.[81] The original setting for this group must be situated somewhere in the forum, perhaps in the basilica, and may have reproduced similar solutions adopted at nearby Sagalassos. They do nevertheless illustrate the building programs carried out at Cremna in the reign of Hadrian and the Antonine period when a series of sanctuaries may also have been built.[82]

Some symmetries with Colonia Caesarea may also be discussed here. First, the imperially sponsored building programs dating to the Antonine period,[83] albeit later and less ambitious than those at Antioch, were probably designed to reinforce the colonial

Figure 9.6. Comama: view of the mound from east.

identity of this Roman community at a time when Cremna had become an ethnic hybrid loosely bound together by the Roman constitution.[84] The presence of new citizens at the time of Trajan,[85] might be in accord with this. Second, the dedicatory inscriptions for Hadrian's forum and basilica set up by the local notable C. Fabricius Longus mentioned at least twice the building of an exedra. This may not coincide with a late antique addition to the eastern end of the basilica as argued by Balance,[86] but might rather consist of a detached, porticoed area for the accommodation of statues.[87] Whether this space was architecturally reminiscent of the exedra at Antioch cannot be known.

While the lack of archaeological and epigraphical evidence frustrates the study of the colony in the Augustan period, some hypotheses can be advanced about its territory during the 1st c. CE. As the limited scale of the foundation at Cremna suggests, it did not replicate Antioch. Nevertheless, some negotiations with towns and polities in the vicinity made possible the consolidation of Cremna's position and the acquisition of lands. Outside its limits the city displayed a tendency to incorporate pre-existing communities within its territorial boundaries; the fate of the town of Keraia is an excellent case in point. Located to the west of Cremna and recorded numismatically in a series of joint issues with Cremna,[88] the Keraia community disappears abruptly from the numismatic and epigraphic record by the mid 1st century CE.[89]

It is difficult to say how this came about, but it seems evident that in this case the Roman community

at Cremna employed a device typical of the political landscape of Asia Minor, namely the *sympoliteia*,[90] to forge a unity of polities that was later resolved in the territorial annexation of Keraia. These maneuvers don't make leaders at Cremna politically adroit or with a bent for local customs. Rather, we should consider these strategies as part of the Roman modus operandi in Asia Minor since the early 2nd century after the battle of Apamea, as their involvement in the *sumpoliteia* between Miletos and Pidasa attests.[91] It is thus likely that access to land resources produced solutions of this sort, as attested also at Apamea Myrlea with the absorbtion of the community of Triglia into the colonial framework.[92]

Nondescript, and located at the center of a narrow plain between the modern villages of Ürkütlü and Garipce, to the south of Sagalassus, an area that would later be crossed by the Via Sebaste, modern-day Comama looks like nothing more than a low-profile, middle-sized mound; even the trained eye has difficulty recognizing the presence of an ancient city (Fig. 9.6.). To judge by the relatively small corpus of inscriptions that provide us with a few names of the leading families it is evident, however, that a small colony planted its roots here and minted coins until the mid 3rd c. CE. Boasting to be Η ΠΡΩΤΗ ΚΑΙ ΠΙΣΤΗ ΚΟΜΑΜΕΩΝ ΚΟΛΩΝΙΑ and yet governed by *demos* and *boulé*[93] the settlement plausibly underwent the same social adaptations that the other colonies experienced in the 2nd c. CE. As demonstrated by Barbara Levick, the Severan inscription of L. Paccia Valeria Saturnina displays a corruption of the Latin text that suggests the move of this community into the universe of Greek poleis in Pisidia.[94] While it is impossible to construct a narrative of Comama's social history, it is nevertheless interesting to note that the colony had also secured its territory by incorporating adjacent pre-existing communities such as Cretopolis into itself. The loss of most of the land and the transfer of some of Cretopolis' families to Comama brought about the economic demise of the community.

The inscription of an unknown chief magistrate at Comama who provided a cash distribution in his hometown Cretopolis illustrates how colonies increased their holdings by attracting well-off constituents from near-by communities to themselves.[95] In the case of Comama, however, this incorporation of coterminous communities may have also occurred under the auspices of the *Commune Myliadum*, a league including Comama and at least four other towns known at the time of Cicero.[96] How this intersected with the *Ius coloniae* and its legal framework is unclear. It nevertheless invites a more thorough analysis of the colony's social matrix.

An inscription of 5 BCE (Aug. 19th trib.pot) from the Sebasteion at Kozluca, 5 km North of Comama, refers to Romans settled in the area, those located at Comama and in the surrounding region of Mylias,[97] as πραγματευόμενοι that is businessmen.[98] Had they been veterans, the Greek would have been οὐετερανοὶ. To put it simply, Comama was another colony that served clearly as no bulwark of *Romanitas* in south Galatia but consisted, more realistically, of farmers and *negotiatores* who took advantage of the economic opportunities offered by this well connected and fertile corner of western Pisidia.[99] The picture that emerges is thus one of complex negotiations between preexisting polities and contingents of Romans, one in which the latter appear not exclusively based in the colonial milieu.

The inscription's use of the term κατοικοῦντες, in particular, is of interest for two reasons. First, it shows a highly dynamic landscape, by no means a barbarous, mountainous backwater, but rather a region where economic interests led to the converging of various communities, chiefly Greeks, Phrygians, Romans and Thracians as soon as the military operations in the region were completed.[100] Second, it uses a designation that is common for Roman citizens conducting business and living in poleis of the region. The case of Romans κατοικοῦντες at Apollonia, Apamea, Neapolis, Isaura and Attaleia was amply described by Mitchell and needs not to be discussed here.[101] Whether these mixed settlements preceded or followed the foundation of the colonies is hard to say, but this problem becomes central when

one enters the district of Colonia Parlais, the one colony that apparently defied all strategic, political, and economic calculations. Its location on the rocky western shores of lake Eğirdir still posits questions as to the rationale of its foundation.

"The smallest and most insignificant of the colonies".[102] Pausanias' remarks on Panopeus, a town of insignificant size,[103] warn us that scale and grandiosity do not necessarily go hand in hand with the concept of urban functionality as it was understood in classical antiquity. Likewise, the expectation that Roman colonies must necessarily showcase elements of Roman urbanism might be not met, as the case of Parlais and also Comama suggest.[104] Parlais was finally located by Louis Robert on the western shore of lake Eğridir under the modern town of Barla (Fig. 9.1).[105] Ramsay, in his quest for ancient Parlais, had completely dismissed the possibility of Barla on the grounds that it needed to be near Beyşehir and because, as he stated, "colonists at Barla would be cut off from the world and utterly useless."[106]

Unfortunately for Ramsay, Barla *was* the site of ancient Parlais. But he was certainly right to point out the apparent absurdity of founding a settlement on the rocky slopes of Lake Eğridir's western shore. Today, the modern town has completely obliterated the ancient settlement and only traces of walls to the north of the village, including the Byzantine church of Hagios Theodoros, indicate the presence of ancient structures. While some contend that Parlais was already showing signs of failure within a few generations,[107] it now appears that the city had produced coinage before the arrival of the Romans and continued to mint coins, albeit infrequently, until the Severan period.[108] At that time, it vanishes from the historical record for more than two centuries until it reappears represented by its bishop at the Council of Constantinople in the late 4th century CE.[109]

Parlais occupied a small pocket of land measuring a total of 8.5 km² that, although of good quality, could hardly sustain a population of a few hundred individuals. Furthermore, the Attalid foundation of Prostanna, located 14 km to the south of Parlais, is a city of particular interest.[110] Prostanna thrived until the 7th century CE and apparently posed a severe limitation to the expansion and the economic growth of Parlais, for it blocked access to the corridor south of the lake that led to Attaleia and thence to the Pamphylian plain. In the 1940s Louis Robert located boundary markers at the village of Bedre that established Parlais' sovereignty to the north and Prostanna's to the south.[111] Thus knowing the location of these urban centers the partial extent of their territories can be hypothesised, as in Fig. 9.1.

Was the shortage of land, the isolation, and the apparently small number of colonists the result of dilettanti at work in Parlais' city planning, or are we simply missing a part of the story? While no guesses can be made about its shape or organization, some apposite hypotheses about its territory can be made, especially in regard to its relations with the pre-existing communities situated within its environs.

As there was a finite limit beyond which the colony could not expand, and the resources of this territory were limited, Parlais' rationale must be rather sought in the colony's relations to the lake and the western and northwestern plain districts behind the Barla massif. That the city served as port and that the lake represented a fundamental component of the local economy shouldn't surprise us. Two elements in particular support this hypothesis. First, satellite imagery suggests the presence of submerged structures that might be part of a small harbor. Second, the visual culture of the region, namely pre-Roman coins with the legend ΠΑΡΛΑΙΤΕΩΝ and representations of ships[112] may confirm the role of Parlais as a port. Also noteworthy is a small funerary relief recorded by B. Pace's survey in 1915; crudely rendered in vernacular style it nevertheless depicts scenes of fishing from boats that were clearly a signature of life in Roman Parlais.[113]

More importantly, however, it can be argued that Parlais was a bridgehead from which contingents of Romans could access the heavily urbanized districts of the Senirkent Ovası and the Gönen Ovası, where a network of towns and polities, namely Tymandos,[114] Conana, Agrae and Seleucia Sidera were to become extensions of the colonial settlement. While the usual formula of κατοικοῦντες appears in the epigraphical record of the 2nd and early 3rd centuries pertaining to these communities end especially to Conana,[115] also of interest is the small community of Agrae where a building in honor of Augustus was probably erected during the principate of Tiberius, as attested by an inscription embedded in the masonry of the Ertokuş Medresesi in Atabey (Fig. 9.7).[116] Conana however, not only counted Roman citizens among its constituents, but also served as a recruiting ground for Roman legions. As early as 19 BCE three of her citizens served in Legio VII in Pannonia;[117] whether this was the result of Parlais' influence on nearby communities is a suggestive possibility. Be that as it may, a colony the size of Parlais had neither the numbers nor the resources to influence a region that, although remote, was densely urbanized and relied on a delicate balance among its various polities. Nevertheless, the changes that colonia Parlais brought about with the cooptation of several

Figure 9.7 Atabey, Ertokuş Medresesi.

communities into a Roman framework were in all likelihood what the Romans had intended. Whether the administrative, political and social configurations of the colony underwent the same changes as the other foundations in the late 2nd cannot be determined.

In conclusion, in spite of the historical uncertainty that looms large over the foundation of the Augustan colonies in Pisidia, we are now in a position to observe some important patterns and differences in the way that the program was carried out. Clearly, scale mattered. Not all colonies in the east were Corinth or Antioch; in Pisidia the hierarchical configuration of the colonization scheme is particularly evident. The disparity among the colonies is macroscopic: I need not repeat that the strategies and investments that flowed into Antioch's foundation were unmatched. Political, military and religious considerations coalesced in the planning of the city and contributed to the realization of a truly Roman milieu in the heart of Galatia. It may be that the other colonies set out with similar aspirations; their sizes, the nature of their populations and their locations led, however, to markedly different results. Common denominators, in summary, bring them together:

1. The disappearance of Latin, occurring in the mid/late 2nd c. CE, a factor in striking contrast with contemporary contexts in Sicily for example, where colonies had proactively contributed to the wholesale adoption of Latin.
2. The attraction of local religious cults and their rituals.
3. Finally, their expansionistic nature and drive to reshape their landscapes and to incorporate within their boundaries communities, polities, and whatever else that could be exploited.

Some of the colonies did so on a grand scale; others not. Nevertheless, they were all part of the larger scheme that aimed to fundamentally change the socio-political matrix of southern Galatia. In this sense, the Via Sebaste, with its awkward trajectory that, when it eventually came, benefited some of these colonies, is perhaps the most visible example of the altered landscape resulting from the application of Augustus' geo-political plan for Pisidia.

Bibliography

Arena G. 2005. *Città di Panfilia e Pisidia sotto il dominio romano* (Catania).

Arundell, F. V. J. 1834. *Discoveries in Asia Minor, including a description of several ancient cities, and especially Antioch of Pisidia* (London).

Balance, M. H. 1959. "The Site of Prostanna", *Anatolian Studies* 9, 125–129.

Balty, J. C. 1960. *Études sur la Maison Carrée de Nîmes* (Bruxelles).

Baroni, A. 2004. "La colonia ed il Governatore", in G. Salmieri, A. Raggi and A. Baroni (eds) *Colonie Romane nel Mondo Greco*, (Roma) 9–54.

Bean, G. 1959. "Notes and Inscriptions from Pisidia", *Anatolian Studies* 9, 67–117.

Belke, K. and N. Mersich 1990. "Phrygien und Pisidien", *Tabula Imperii Byzantini* 7 (Wien).

Blickenberg, C. 1941. *Lindos. Fouilles de l'Acropole 1902–1914. Inscriptions II* (Berlin).

Brandt, H. 1995. "Parlais: Eine römische Kolonie in Pisidien", *Epigraphica Anatolica* 24, 56–60.

Buckler, W. H. *et al.* (eds) 1936. Monuments and Documents from Eastern Asia and Western Galatia. *Monumenta Asiae Minoris Antiqua*, vol. 4 (Manchester).

Buckler, W. H. and W. M. Calder 1939. Monuments and Documents from Phrygia and Caria. *Monumenta Asiae Minoris Antiqua*, vol. 6 (Manchester).

Byrne, A. and G. Labarre 2006. *Nouvelles Inscritions d'Antioche de Pisidie*. Bonn.

Calder, W. M. 1912. "Colonia Caesareia Antiocheia", *JRS* 2, 79–109.

Cheesman, G. L. 1913. "The family of the Caristani at Antioch in Pisidia", *JRS* 3, 253–266.

Christol, M. *et al.* 2001. "L'empereur Claude, le chevalier C. Caristanus Fronto Caesianus Iullus et le culte imperial à Antioche de Pisidie", *Tyche* 16, 1–20.

Christol, M. and T. Drew Bear (2004). "Caracalla et son medicine à Antioche de Pisidie", in S. Colvin (ed.) *The Greco-Roman East. Politics, Culture, Society* (Cambridge) 85–118.

Collas-Heddeland, E. 2002. "Une famille bilingue d'Antioche", in T. Drew Bear, M. Taşlıalan and C. M. Thomas (eds) Actes du Ier Congrès International sur Antioche de Pisidie. Lyon, 169–175.

Corsten, T. 1987. *Die Inschriften von Apameia (Bithynien) und Pylai* (Bonn).

Cronin, H. S. 1904. "First Report of a Journey in Pisidia, Lycaonia and Pamphylia, Part III, *JHS* 24, 121–122.

Cumont, F. and J. G. C. Anderson 1912. "Three New Inscriptions from Pontus and Pisidia", *JRS* 2, 233–236.

Darrouzès, G. 1981. *Notitiae, episcopatuum ecclesiae constantino-politanae*, Institut français d' études byzantines, (Paris 1981).

Davies, G. 2000. "Cremna in Pisidia: a Re-Appraisal of the Siege Works", *Anatolian Studies* 50, 151–158.

Degrassi, A. 1948. "Quattuorviri in colonie romane e in municipi retti da duoviri", *Atti della Accademia Nazionale dei Lincei Serie VIII* 2, 281–349.

De Giorgi, A., B. Hürmüzlu and P. Iversen 2009. "New research in Northwestern Pisidia: Ancient Konane (Conana) and its Territory." *Colloquium Anatolicum* 8, 235–256.

De La Barrera, J. L. 2000. *La decoración arquitectónica de los foros de Augusta Emerita*. (Roma).

De Planhol, X. 1958, *De la plaine pamphylienne aux lacs pisidiens* (Paris).

Drew Bear, T. and M. Taşlıalan 2002. *Actes du Ier congrès international sur Antioche Pisidie* (Paris).

Fernoux, H. L. 2004. *Notables et élites des cités de Bithynie aux époques hellénistique et romaine* (Dijon).

Fischer, G. 1996. *Das Romische Pola* (Munchen).

French, D. 1992. "Roads in Pisidia", in E. Schwertheim (ed.) *Forschungen in Pisidia* (Bonn) 167–75.

Gauthier, P. 2001. "Les Pidaséns entrent en sympolitie avec les Milésiens: la procedure et les modalités institutionnelles", in A. Bresson and R. Descat, *Les cités d'Asie Mineure occidentale au 2e siècle a.c.* (Bordeaux) 117–127.

Hall, A. S. 1986. "R.E.C.A.M. Notes and Studies No.9: The Milyadeis and Their Territory", *Anatolian Studies* 36, 137–157.

Hatzfeld, J. 1919. *Les Trafiquants italiens dans l'Orient hellénistique* (Paris).

Hoet-van Cauwenberghe, C. 2002. "Statius Anicius, Decurion d'Antioche", in T. Drew Bear, M. Taşlıalan and C. M. Thomas (eds) *Actes du Ier Congrès International sur Antioche de Pisidie*. Lyon, 153–167.

Horsley, G. H. R. 1987. "The Inscriptions from the So-Called 'Libray' at Cremna", *Anatolian Studies* 37, 49–80.

Horsley, G. H. R. and S. Mitchell, 2000. *The Inscriptions of Central Pisidia* (Bonn).

Hürmüzlü, B. 2007. "Pisidia Bölgesi'nde Ele Geçen Anthemion Tipi Steller", *Colloquium Anatolicum* 6, 97–114.

Jones, A. H. M. 1971. *Cities of the Eastern Roman Provinces* (Oxford).

Inan, J. 1970. "Kremna kazısı raporu", *Türk Arkeoloji Dergisi* (1970), II, 51–97.

Kosmetatou, E. 2005. "Macedonians in Pisidia", *Historia* 54, 2005, 216–221.

Krzyzanowska, A. 1970. *Monnaies coloniales d'Antioche de Pisidie* (Warschau).

Labarre, G. *et al.* 2005. "Parlais et Prostanna: sites et territories", *Anatolica Antiqua* 13, 223–257.

Laffi, U. 2004. "La colonia augustea di Alessandria di Troade", in G. Salmeri, A. Raggi and A. Baroni (eds) *Colonie Romane nel Mondo Greco* (Roma) 151–164.

Lane, E. N. 1971–1978. *Corpus Monumentorum Religionis Dei Menis*, vol 1–4 (Leiden).

La Rocca E. *et al.* 1995. *I luoghi del consenso imperiale. Il Foro di Augusto. Il Foro di Traiano. Introduzione storico-topografica*. Roma.

Levick, B. 1958. "Two Pisidian Colonial Families", *JRS* 48, 74–78.

Levick, B. 1967. *Roman Colonies in Southern Asia Minor* (Oxford).

Levick, B. 1968. "Antiocheia", *RE Suppl.* 11, 49–61.

Levick, B. 1970a. "Dedications to Mên Askaênos", *Anatolian Studies* 20, 37–50.

Levick, B. 1970b. "Parlais", *RE Suppl.* 12, 990–1006.

Lenski, N. 1999. "Assimilation and Revolt in the Territory of Isauria, from the 1st Century BC to the 6th Century AD", *The Journal of the Economic and Social History of the Orient*, 42, no.4, 413–465.

Mitchell, S. 1976a. "Legio VII and the Garrison of Augustan Galatia", The Classical Quarterly 26, n. 2, 298–308.

Mitchell, S. 1976b. "Requisitioned Transport in the Roman Empire", *JRS* 66, 106–131.

Mitchell, S. 1979. "Iconium and Ninica. Two Double Communities in Roman Asia Minor", *Historia* 28, 409–438.

Mitchell, S. 1991. "The Hellenization of Pisidia", *Mediterranean Archaeology* 4, 120–145.

Mitchell, S. 1993. *Anatolia. Land, Men and Gods in Asia Minor* (Oxford).

Mitchell, S. 1994. "Three Cities in Pisidia", *Anatolian Studies* 44, 129–148.

Mitchell, S. 1995. *Cremna in Pisidia. An Ancient City in Peace and in War* (London).

Mitchell, S. and M. Waelkens 1987. "Sagalassus and Cremna 1986", *Anatolian Studies* 37, 37–47.

Mitchell, S. and Waelkens, M. 1988. "Cremna and Sagalassus 1988", *Anatolian Studies* 38, 53–65.

Mitchell, S. and Waelkens, M. 1998. *Pisidian Antioch: the Site and its Monuments* (London).

Nollé, J. 1995. "Colonia und social der Römer. Ein neuer Vorschlag zur Auflösung der Buchstaben SR auf den Münzen von Antiocheia bei Pisidien", in C. Schubert-K. Brodersen (ed.) *Rom und der griechische Osten. Festschrift für Hatto H. Schmitt* (Stuttgart) 350–369.

Owens, E. J. 1991. "The Kremna Aqueduct and Water Supply in Roman Cities", *Greece and Rome* 38, 41–58.

Pace, B. 1921. "La zona costiera da Adalia a Side", *Annuario della Regia Scuola Archeologica di Atene e delle Missioni Italiane in Oriente* 3, 29–71.

Pavan, G. 2000. *Il tempio d'Augusto di Pola. Istituto giuliano di storia, cultura e documentazione* (Trieste).

Picagnol, A. 1962. "Les documents cadastraux de la colonie romaine d'Orange", 16e *Suppl. à Gallia* (Paris).

Raggi, A. 2004. "Cittadinanza coloniaria e cittadinanza romana", in G. Salmieri, A. Raggi and A. Baroni (eds) *Colonie Romane nel Mondo Greco* (Roma) 55–68.

Ramsay, W. M. 1888. "Antiquities of Southern Phrygia and the Border-Lands", *AJA* 4, 263–283.

Ramsay, W. M. 1907. *The Cities of St. Paul* (London).

Ramsay, W. M. 1916. "Colonia Caesarea (Pisidian Antioch) in the Augustan Age", *JRS* 6, 83–134.

Ramsay, W. M. 1924. "Studies in the Roman Province Galatia. VI. Some Inscriptions of Colonia Caesarea Antiochea", *JRS* 14, 172–205.

Ramsay, W. M. 1962. *The Historical Geography of Asia Minor* (Amsterdam).

Ramsay, W. M. 1975. *The Cities and Bishoprics of Phygia* (New York).

Reger, G. 2004. "Sympoliteiai in Hellenistic Asia Minor", in S. Colvin (ed.) *The Greco-Roman East. Politics, Culture, Society* (Cambridge) 145–180.

Ricl, M. 1997. *The Inscriptions of Alexandria Troas* (Bonn).

Rizakis, A. D. 1998. "Incolae-Paroikoi: populations and communautés dependants dans les cites et les colonies romaines d'orient", *Revue des Études Anciennes* 100, 599–617.

Robert, L. 1938. *Études épigraphiques et philologiques* (Paris).

Robert, L. 1949. "Sur une monnaie de Synnada TPOΦEYΣ", *Hellenica* 7, 74–81.

Robert, L. 1962. *Villes d'Asie Mineure* (Paris).

Rose, C. B. 2005. "The Parthians in Augustan Rome", *AJA* 109, 21–75.

Roussel, P. and M. Launey 1937. *Inscriptions de Délos* (Paris).

Saffrey, H. D. 1988. "Un Nouveau Duovir à Antioche de Pisidie", *Anatolian Studies* 38, 67–69.

Salmieri G. 2000. "Dio, Rome, and the Civic Life of Asia Minor", in S. Swain (ed.) *Dio Chrysostom: Politics, Letters and Philosophy* (Oxford), 53–91.

Salmieri, G., A. Raggi and A. Baroni (eds) 2004. *Colonie Romane nel Mondo Greco* (Roma).

Settis, S. 1973. "'Esedra' e 'ninfeo' nella terminologia architettonica del mondo romano. Dall'età repubblicana alla tarda antichità", *Aufstieg und Niedergang der Römischen Welt*, I, 4, (Berlin 1973) 661–745.

Shaw, B. 1990. "Bandit Highlands and Lowland Peace: the Mountains of Isauria-Cilicia. (Continued)", *Journal of the Economic and Social History of the Orient* 33, 237–270.

Smith, R. R. R. 1987. "The Imperial Reliefs from the Sebasteion at Aphrodisias", *JRS* 77, 88–138.

Spanu, M. 2002. "Considerazioni sulle plateae di Antiochia", in T. Drew Bear and M. Taşlialan 2002. *Actes du Ier congrès international sur Antioche Pisidie* (Paris) 349–358.

Sterrett, J. R. S. 1888. The Wolfe Expedition to Asia Minor, *Papers of the American School of Classical Studies at Athens* 2 (Boston).

Syme, R. 1995. *Anatolica. Studies in Strabo* (A. R. Birley ed.) (Oxford).

Taşlialan, M. 1991. *The Journeys of St Paul to Antioch* (Istanbul).

Ungaro, L. *et al.* 1995. *I luoghi del consenso imperiale. Il Foro di Augusto. Il Foro di Traiano.* Roma

von Aulock, H. 1970. "Kleinasiatische Münzstätten VI–VII", *Jahrbuck für Numismatik und Geldeschichte* 20, 151–159.

von Aulock, H. 1972. "Die römische Kolonie Lystra und ihre Münzen", *Historia* 2, 509–518.

von Aulock, H. 1973. "Kleinasiatische Münzstätten", *Jahrbuch für Numismatik und Geldgeschichte* 23, 7–18.

von Aulock, H. 1977. "Münzen und Städte Pisidiens. Teil 1", *IstMitt Beiheft* 19 (Tübingen).

von Aulock, H. 1979. "Münzen und Städte Pisidiens. Teil 2", *IstMitt Beiheft* 22 (Tübingen).

von Lankoroski, K. G. 1890–1892 Städte Pamphyliens und Pisidiens I (Vienna).

Waelkens, M. 1986. Die kleinasiatischen Türsteine. Typologische und epigraphische Unterschungen der kleinasiatischen Grabreliefs mit Scheintür. Mainz.

Ward Perkins, J. B. and M. H. Balance 1958. "The Caesareum at Cyrene and the Basilica at Cremna, with a note on the inscriptions of the Caesareum by J. M. Reynolds", *Papers of the British School at Rome* 26, 137–194.

Zanker, P. 1988. *The Power of Images in the Age of Augustus.* Ann Arbor.

Notes

1. Kornemann 1919.
2. Cic. *Agr.* 2.73.
3. Namely: Apollonia, Attaleia, Neapolis, Isaura. See also Mitchell 1993, 77.
4. Pau 7,18,7.

5. Mitchell 1993, 77.
6. A selected bibliography on Antioch (Colonia Caesarea): Mitchell and Waelkens 1998; Mitchell 1993; B. Levick 19687; Levick 1968; Arundell 1834; Calder 1912; Sterrett 1888; Syme 1995; Taşlıalan 1991; Drew Bear and Taşlıalan 2002. Inscriptions: Cheesman 1913; Cumont and Anderson 1912; Ramsay 1916; Ramsay 1924; Levick 1970a; Byrne and Labarre 2006. On Antioch's coins: Krzyzanowska 1970.
7. On Parlais (Iulia Augusta Colonia Parlais): Levick 1970b; Levick 1967; Mitchell 1993, 77; Robert 1938, 265–285; Brandt 1995; Pace 1921, 45–54; Darrouzès 1981; Belke and Mersich 1990, 356; Labarre *et al.* 2005. On Parlais' coins: von Aulock 1973; von Aulock 1977, 44–45.
8. On Cremna (Colonia Iulia Augusta Cremnena): Mitchell 1995; Mitchell and Waelkens 1987; Mitchell and Waelkens 1988; Owens 1991; B. Levick 1967; Robert 1962; von Lankoroski 1890–1892; R. Syme, 1995, 225–241; Mitchell 1994; Sterrett 1888, 319–326. On Cremna's coins: von Aulock 1979, 36–40
9. On Comana (Colonia Iulia Augusta Prima Fida Comama): Levick 1967; Levick 1958, 77–78; The coins: H. Von aulock 1970, 151–159
10. Strabo 12.6.5.; Syme 1995, 204–224.
11. Nollé 1995, 350–369.
12. For an historical overview of the region see Arena 2005.
13. For a comprehensive description of this territory see de Planhol 1958.
14. The site of Hacilar is perhaps the most obvious indication that pre-classical Pisidia still needs to be thoroughly investigated. See De Giorgi 2009.
15. Hürmüzlü 2007.
16. Mitchell 1991.
17. Kosmetatou 2005.
18. Arrian, *Anab.* I 28, 1; Strabo, 12, 7, 2. See also Syme 1995, 181–182 on Strabo and Artemidoros' problematic geography of Pisidia.
19. Xen. *Hell.* 3. 1, 13; Arrian, *Anab.* I, 27, 5–28; Strabo, 12, 7, 1–3. See especially R. Syme 1994, 214.
20. Strabo's list of Pisidian cities is particularly valuable, see 12, 7, 2; Arrian, *Anab.* I, 24,5; Pliny, *NH* v147; Livy, 38, 12, 8–18, 10 is also of interest, as his description of Cn. Manlius Vulso's campaign of 189 BCE includes the names of several pisidian towns and polities (to be integrated with Polybius 21, 35, 5.)
21. Strabo, 12, 7.2..
22. Syme 1995, 225.
23. For a concise description of the Augustan colonization policy in Galatia, see S. Mitchell 1993, 86–91.
24. Mitchell 1993, 73.
25. Levick 1967.
26. Syme 1995, 238. See also Ramsay 1916, 84.
27. Mitchell 1979.
28. Among these Attaleia and Apollonia, see S. Mitchell 1976b, 117. On the contemporary foundations in north Galatia, namely Tavium, Ancyra, Pessinus and colonia Germa see Mitchell 1993, 86–91.
29. Strabo, 14, 5, 6. Dio, 28. 2.
30. Various unsystematic sources, namely Strabo and Pliny, converge on this matter: for their discussion see Syme 1995, 204–241.
31. *ILS* 5828;14185.
32. Mitchell 1993, 76–79.

33. French 1992. See also Mitchell on Cremna and her roads, Mitchell 1995, 5–6.
34. Strabo, 12.8.14; *Die Inschriften von Magnesia* n.61.
35. *Supra*, n.6
36. Rizakis 1998, 609.
37. Strabo 12. 8. 14.
38. Mitchell and Waelkens 1998, 3. It is worth mentioning that the territory' size of other great city of the region, Sagalassos, was probably of comparable scale, as attested by the land controversy with Tymbrianissos (Bean, 1959, no. 30 X/Y) and the famous decree of Sextus Sotidius Strabo Libuscidianus governor of Galatia in the Tiberian period on transport abuses in the territory of the city. For these matters see Mitchell 1976.
39. Levick 1967, 60–67.
40. The *Corpus Agrimensorum Romanorum* suggests that the initial operation in establishing any Roman colony, was the division of the land on the basis of quality and accessibility, see Frontin 1–4.
41. Waelkens 1986.
42. Rizakis1998, 609.
43. Pausanias, 7, 18.7.
44. Picagnol 1962.
45. Baroni 2004, 9–54.
46. Mitchell 1976, 298–308.
47. Ricl 1997, 66–67. On Alexandria Troas accommodating an Augustan foundation see Laffi 2004 151–164.
48. Spanu 2002, 349–353.
49. Mitchell and Waelkens 1998, 113–173.
50. Mitchell and Waelkens 1998.
51. In all likelihood symbolizing the pacification of the region after Quirinus's campaigns, see Syme 1995, 229–230.
52. Rose 2005.
53. Ramsay 1916, 108–129.
54. Mitchell and Waelkens 1998, 135–136.
55. On the Sebasteion at Aphrodisias: Smith 1987; Pola: Pavan 2000, Fischer 1996; the *Maison Carrée* at Nimes: Balty 1960; Merida: De La Barrera 2000.
56. Zanker 1988.
57. La Rocca *et al.* 1995; Ungaro *et al.* 1995.
58. Ramsay 1924, n.2 p.177.
59. See Cheesman1913, 255–256; Pace, 1921, 57.
60. Levick1958; Cheesman 1913; Christol *et al.* 2001.
61. Although L. Sergius Paullus is traditionally referred to as the first Antiochian senator at the time of Claudius and thus the first out of the Pisidian colonies, the case of Rutilius Propinquus must be accurately weighted, as it would situate the first non-Antiochian Pisidian senator at the time of Hadrian. See Horsley and Mitchell 2000, 58–59.
62. Mitchell 1993, 77–79.
63. See the case of the Pomponian family who received citizenship from the *legatus* of Galatia Pomponius Bassus (AD 95–100). Ramsay 1916, 90.
64. On Alexandria Troas and the *Lex Portoria*, see Ricl 1997, 225.
65. Raggi 2004, 55–68
66. Dio, 41, 6.
67. Salmieri 2000, 53–91.
68. Christol-Drew Bear 2004, 85–118.
69. Hoet-Cauwenberghe 2002, 153–175
70. Ramsay 1924, 199–200.
71. Collas-Heddeland 2002, 169–175.
72. Ramsay 1916, 94.

73. Lane1971–1978; Levick 1970, 37–50.
74. Ramsay 1916, 106; Christol and Drew Bear 2004, 85–118.
75. Calder1912, 81–84; Saffrey, 1988. An Irenarch in Conana: Bean1960, 51 n.100; Iconium, *ILS* 9414
76. Mitchell and Waelkens 1998, 11.
77. Krzyzanowska 1970, 19.
78. On Cremna's siege and its archaeological record: Zosimus, *The New History*, I.69–70; Mitchell 1995, 177–218; Lenski 1999; Shaw 2000; Davies 2000.
79. Inan 1970.
80. On the statues and their inscriptions see Horsley 1987.
81. On the re-use of bases and their market, see Blickenberg 1941, n. 49z.30.44.
82. Mitchell 1995, 79–109.
83. Mitchell 1995, 108–118.
84. The colony's coinage also may substantiate this point; two issues of Marcus Aurelius and Commodus respectively celebrates the rhetoric of Augustus demarcating the city's territory with a pair of oxen, see Von aulock 1979, n. 1091 and 1121.
85. Horsley and Mitchell 2000, pp. 55–57.
86. J. B. Ward Perkins and M. H. Balance 1958, 167–186.
87. On *exedrae* in classical antiquity: Settis 1973.
88. von Aulock 1979, 106 (types 887–891); se also Robert 1962, 63.
89. Horsley and Mitchell 2000, 94.
90. Reger 2004.
91. Fernoux 2004, 179.
92. Cortsen 1987, 48–49; Fernoux 2004.
93. *CIL* III 6866.
94. *CIL* III 6887; Levick 1958, 78.
95. See Steven Mitchell on a unknown Cretopolis notable accessing the duovirate at Comama: Mitchell 1994, 132–136.
96. Jones 1971,143. Cicero, *Verrines* I, 95, refers to a Commune Milyadum in connection with exactions of grain carried out by Verres when he was *quaestor* to C. Dolabella in the Province of Cilicia in 80–79.
97. On Mylias: Hall 1986.
98. *SEG* 36:1207.
99. Hall 1986, 152–154. For the presence of *negotiatores* in Pisidia, see Hatzfeld 1919.
100. The assumption is that the Via Sebaste's milestones dated to the year 6 BCE may sanction the pacification of south Galatia.
101. Mitchell 1976 requisitioned JRS 1976, 117; Mitchell 1979, 411; see also Buckler and Calder 1939, 180–183, two Apamean instances in which the κατοικοῦντες ʻΡωμαῖοι figure prominently alongside the city's councils.
102. Levick 1967, 54.
103. Pau.10.4.1.
104. Brandt 1995, 57.
105. Robert 1938, 265–285. See also L. Robert 1949 on the base for a prominent colony's δύανδρα, referred to as κτίστην τῆς κολονείας.
106. Ramsay1890, 390–391.
107. Syme 1995, 226.
108. von Aulock 1977, 44–45.
109. Darrouzès 1981, 9.
110. On Prostanna dedicating at Delos in 113 BCE see Roussel and Launey, 1937, n.1603.
111. *CRAI* 1949, 402.
112. von Aulock 1973, 12 (types 5 and 6)
113. Pace 1921, 45–54.
114. Buckler *et al.* 1993, 82–94, see particularly n. 236, (=*CIL* 3, 6866) the famous petition with which the community at Tymandos appeals to the authorities ...*ut ius et dignitatem civitatis preaceptio nostro consequantur*. On new fieldwork and epigraphical documents from Tymandos see De Giorgi and Hürmüzlü 2009.
115. Conana: *SEG* 2:744, *IGR* 3.325.
116. *MbBerlin* 1879:314; *CIL*. 3, 6869.
117. Mitchell 1976, 304.

10. Catastrophe and Aftermath

Greg Woolf

Colonization stands at the convergence of three great historical processes characteristic of Roman antiquity: large scale redistribution of property; the relocation of entire populations; and the ongoing urbanization of the ancient world. Yet colonization was never more than one component of any one of these processes, and perhaps not always the most significant element. Understanding its significance requires a little contextualization.

Redistribution first. Property acquired as spear-won land in civil war or external conquests, or through confiscation of the property of political enemies was treated by the Roman state in a variety of ways. A quantity was let out for rent (*vectigalia*), much was redistributed through sale, and some was given as a reward to partisans of various kinds, among them allied cities and kings, members of the urban plebs and veteran soldiers, not all of them citizens. Some land in the provinces was also acquired by entrepreneurs, often exploiting the indebtedness of many of Rome's subjects. The resulting part of land ownership might be complex. Part of the territory of the colony of Knossos was in fact owned by the city of Capua, itself another colony.[1]

Second, relocation. Colonial settlements did typically move a few thousand individuals and provide them with new homes. But populations were also moved by enslavement and warfare, conquered tribes were occasionally resettled *en masse* in the frontier zones, and provincial populations were gathered up in forced synoecisms, or else expelled to make space for colonists. Not all settlement was managed through formal colonization. Some citizens were settled in what we term *viritane* schemes, dispersed that is the countryside or around smaller settlements anchored on roads. Versions of this can be found from Gracchan Italy to the Wetterau in early imperial Germany. Besides, state organised mobility

accounted for only part of the movements of peoples in this period.[2] A special parallel and sometimes precursor to colonisations were the communities of Italians living within local settlements around the Mediterranean. The trading colony archaeologically attested on the Magdalensburg in Austria, the Italians massacred in Cirta in the Numidian War or in Asian cities on the command of Mithridates in Asia or during anti-Roman risings in Gaul during Caesar's campaigns, and the merchants based on the site of Lyon long before it was a Roman colony were all part of a much wider distribution.[3] Associations (*conventus*) of Roman citizens are well attested epigraphically in provincial cities during the early Empire: many perhaps were simply the latest avatar of older settlements.

Lastly, urbanization. Urban systems had been emerging throughout the iron age Mediterranean in tandem with the growth of states and markets. The processes proceeded through a complex combination of mutually reinforcing pressures. Roman administrative convenience was one stimulus. The division of regions into city states happened when Rome dismantled Hellenistic kingdoms in Sicily, Macedon and Pontus, and again when some ready made system of government was required in tribal regions of Spain, Gaul or central Anatolia. Certain kinds of taxation accelerated the process and drew local systems into larger hierarchies.[4] New ideologies of the good life probably played a part too. Colonization was just part of a much more complex story.

Why single out colonization, then, for special attention? Successive generations of modern writers have done so, because they encountered in ancient texts the notion that colonization was a long-lasting Roman institution and one that was in some senses central to the reproduction of the Roman people.

Ideologically this was clearly true, even if social and economic analysis indicates the story was more complex. Ancient formulations, once again, have set our agenda. So a preliminary question is why the prominence of colonization in ancient testimony, relative that is to other kinds of settlements, other forms of dispossession and other patterns of city foundation and urban growth?

During the Republic, the creation of a new colony – unlike some of the other kinds of action mentioned above – required a formal decision made through the organs of the Roman state. Effectively this meant a debate in the senate. Once the decision had been made, founders (*deductores*) were appointed – often military commanders connected with the operations through which the land in question had been acquired – and a roster of settlers was gathered. All this, and perhaps some of the rituals associated with foundation, was liable to be recorded in the *acta senatus*. No formal governmental bureau kept records of *coloniae*, no magistrate had special responsibility for them, nor were there Roman officials permanently or even regularly dispatched to them. Occasional censorial building is recorded in republican-period *coloniae* in Italy, and they were subject to the levy. But the anecdote of the senatorial mission that discovered that a number of recent foundations had been quietly abandoned shows how far colonies might be left to themselves. For these reasons, the formal creation of a colony left more of a mark in historical writing, than did its subsequent history.

Even less systematically recorded were decisions made by commanders on the ground to reward former soldiers (Roman, Italian and non-Italian allied alike) with land and or recognise their communities in some way. That sort of informal analogue to colonization was certainly common enough in mid-Republican Spain and Gaul: to the case of Medellín, an army camp based by a Lusitanian hillfort that came to become a *colonia* in the forties, can be compared the Pompeian foundation of Saint-Bertrand-de-Comminges in 72 BCE in the aftermath of the Sertorian war.[5] Similar processes perhaps explain some of the complex institutional arrangements attested in eastern foundations like Nicopolis, Dyme and Patras.[6] Most of our knowledge of such *ad hoc* arrangements derives from anecdotal references. It is inconceivable that many parallel cases were not left unrecorded, and they are thus under-represented in our accounts of the impact of Roman imperialism on landholding and human settlement.

What Roman antiquarians could mine from official records and histories based on them were the notices of formal *deductiones* of new *coloniae*.

At a later date certain administrative records were generated that listed provincial communities by their formal status. None of these have survived, but a number were used by Pliny the Elder.[7] Records of this kind must have made possible the first reflective and synoptic accounts of colonization by ancient scholars. We have, for example, the list compiled by Velleius Paterculus into which he wove "the various extensions of the citizenship and the growth of the Roman name through granting to others a share in its privileges".[8] The earliest strata of the *Libri Coloniarum* which in their final version date from the 4th century CE, emanated from similar synoptic accounts.[9] Then there are the various passages which reveal attempts to establish the norms – legal, ritual, architectural – of colonial settlement. Vitruvius' account of how land was divided up and the basic framework of a city was laid out, and Gellius' much quoted description of *coloniae* as miniatures of Rome come into this category. Further products of this sort of reflection can be gathered from legal texts and scattered references in other works such as Servius' commentary on the *Aeneid*.[10] Perhaps discussions of this kind fed into the creation of increasingly standardized colonial laws of which that of Urso is the only surviving provincial exemplar.[11] The inscription, set up in the Flavian period, records a Caesarian statute that already included archaic or archaizing elements such as the reference to a *tumultus Gallicus*.

When Mommsen set the study of colonial statuses on a modern footing, then, he was already able to draw on normalizing accounts of this kind from antiquity. Modern historians have made successive attempts to taxonomise colonies by period, by function and by legal status and to define their common institutional features.[12] There have even been attempts to establish an archaeological template for a colony, based on the excavations at Cosa, Alba Fucens and a few other sites.[13] To be fair, virtually every account of Roman colonization stresses the diversity of sites formally designated as colonial.[14] Indeed, taxonomies of different kinds could be viewed as attempts to capture this diversity, within a generalizing and normalizing discourse. Yet in many respects the differences among *coloniae* were at least as great as those between *coloniae* and other cities in their vicinity.[15] One of the major advances in the archaeological investigation of *coloniae* in recent years has been the move from examining individual communities to the study of entire landscapes.[16] Yet this analytical move absolutely requires that the foundations themselves be set within complex patterns of land-holding and occupation, whether reconstructed from ancient texts like those through which the territory of Merida may be examined, or inscriptions like the Orange and Medellín documents, or else modern maps generated by aerial photography and surface survey. The major sites designated as *coloniae* have to take their place alongside a whole range of settlement types, as well as infrastructure and remodelling of the landscape of different kinds. The writings of the *agrimensores* make very clear how complex a job this might be.[17]

The existing scholarly literature on colonization is of enormous value. Yet for the reasons I have given it is worth being a little sceptical of the category. Roman antiquarians were in general concerned to anchor current practices in the deep past, about which they often had little reliable information. This was especially true of writers like Gellius. Even more seriously, in the increasingly chaotic political conditions of the last century of the Republic it was almost routine to represent institutional innovations in traditionalist terms. What the Gracchi and their successors attempted to do with the land was a new solution to a new problem: dressing it up as a renewal of the kinds of colonization that took place in Italy in the 3rd and early 2nd century was purely political tactics. Something similar applies to the settlements and redistributions initiated by Sulla, Pompey, Caesar, Antony and Octavian: civil war and the need to demobilise huge armies of landless veterans were new problems. Evicting and dispossessing Roman citizens and allies was a new as well as a disruptive solution. The language and ritual of colonization provided political camouflage. For reasons of this kind, we should be very careful before representing colonization as a traditional Roman practice, rather than as set of terms applied in different periods to different modes of exercising power over land and people.[18]

Consider for example the stereotypical view of colonies as new urban foundations on greenfield sites that emerges if we combine rituals of ploughing, attested from Cato and on numerous coins, with the Vitruvian prescriptions for surveying, the modern idea of a standard colonial *lex* and notions such as that all *coloniae* had three-bayed *capitolia* at their centres. Paper after paper gathered in this volume shows how few *coloniae* ever conformed to this pattern. Even in the Po Valley and southern France, areas where there was little developed urbanism before the arrival of Roman settlers, it is common to find earlier settlements incorporated in some sense into the new settlement.[19] Entremont was in some sense a predecessor to Aquae Sextiae (Aix-en-Provence), the colony at Nîmes made use of an Iron Age monument, the Tour Magne, in its circuit and so on. Roman Bononia (Bologna) had Gallic and perhaps Etruscan antecedents. Many more colonial foundations consisted simply of inserting new property owners into existing civic communities. The recipient community might be a Greek city like Butrint, an Italian one like Pompeii or even (rather often in fact) an existing Roman *colonia* like Cordoba.[20] Cases like Paestum, that was at various stages Greek *polis*, Lucanian city and Roman *colonia* and which accumulated monuments, burial rights and other material culture from all three, remind us of the potential complexities.[21] A recurrent theme in this volume, illustrated from Lusitania to Anatolia, is the increased signs of the integration of pre-foundation settlements and populations into the new order.

One response to a scepticism about colonization as a long-lasting Roman institution would be to conduct a Foucauldian archaeology of the term, stripping away the layers of meaning it accreted over time. This is not the place for such a project, but some broad shifts in connotation are evident even on a casual survey. Colonization is commonly held to end in the Severan periods, although the status remained important for some cities for much longer, the Edict of Caracalla notwithstanding. During the 2nd century CE we might note a variety of ideological uses, among them Hadrian's appropriation of Jerusalem as Colonia Aelia Capitolina and the accusation that Commodus was planning to rename Rome Colonia Commodiana.[22] This is also the period of the antiquarian speculations of Gellius and Hadrian, which responded to the high value which some provincial communities evidently placed on securing the title of *colonia* for their cities.[23] That being part of a colony mattered beyond the elite is demonstrated by the widespread use of abbreviations that flag the colonial status of an individual's *origo*, acronyms like CCAA for Cologne, CUT for Nijmegen and CIAE for Emerita. *Colonia*, then, in the last stages of its life, was all about relative status in the hierarchy of cities. Competition for the title – which generally also linked a city to a particular member of the imperial house with titles such as Colonia Ulpia Traiana, Colonia Iulia Genetiva – might be compared to the competition for neokorates among the cities of Asia Minor.[24]

References to colonization in the writings of the late Republic and early Empire, on the other hand, are less often about civic status and more often associated with violence and civil strife.[25] The terms clearly had the military connotations that Cicero tried to conjure up with his phrase *propugnacula imperii*, although perhaps his effort shows that the connection with Roman expansion, the renewal of the citizen army and the defence of conquered land against external enemies was by his day not always the first connotation that came to mind.[26] All the same Livy and Velleius generally attribute particular foundations to military motives. It is still common enough to read that colonies were first and foremost military outposts. That may well have been true in some cases. The geo-strategic argument seems strong for some southern Anatolian foundations, and the *Libri Coloniarum* associate a number of Sullan settlements in central Italy with civic fortification.[27] Yet the foundations in Epirus and Achaia, and indeed in the Greek east in general, are difficult to fit into this model.[28] It is even more difficult to work out exactly how these colonists were intended to operate militarily. From Sulla onwards, there was a clear *immediate* use for stationing military veterans of the civil war within reach of the capital. Yet even in Pompeii, the Sullani were not based on a garrison or common defensible quarter from which they could dominate their home town. How long were veteran communities really militarily viable? The monumental arches provided for veteran colonies in the south of Gaul might have reminded settlers (and their neighbours) of the nature of their title to the land.[29] Yet for how long were ageing veterans still a force to be reckoned with? There is no sense that *coloniae* in the provinces were organised to provide additional troops like the Seleucid colonies based across their Empire, nor that they were regularly subject to the levy like republican *coloniae* in Italy.[30] Individual recruits to the legions certainly were often drawn from provincial *coloniae* in the 1st century CE. But this was a function of where eligible citizens were located, and they seem in any case to have been replaced by more local recruits over time.[31] One possible conclusion to draw from this is that the military associations of *coloniae* were, in the triumviral period and later, largely ideological. The paucity of testimony means that it is not easy to excavate even earlier connotations of *colonia*.[32] It is suggestive, however, that the etymology of *colonus* most obviously connotes farmer not soldier, those who inhabit and cultivate a particular place.[33] New emphases did not wholly displace older ones of course, and the antiquarian scholars and commentators of the middle and late Empire were particularly interested in etymological investigations of this sort.

The fact that the language of colonization always denotes farming and landholding returns us to my opening observation that the core value of colonization in most periods of Roman history that we can observe,

is the redistribution of property, and the movement of people from one city to another. Economically the impact of these changes was fundamental. Put in Marxist terms, the two main factors of production in a pre-industrial economy like that of Rome were labour and land. Colonization schemes reallocated both. To the extent that commerce also mattered, Roman colonies were often located on key nodes in exchange systems, sites like Narbonne, Corinth and Patras. Unsurprisingly, most of these prime locations were already occupied. Expropriation of economic resources by force resulted in the reallocation of wealth *and the means of generating it* to those favoured by the imperial power (or those who controlled it at that moment). It is less clear how often the new owners changed the way wealth was produced.

In economic terms too, it is necessary to treat each period separately. The colonization schemes mostly treated in this volume seem rarely to have been transformative, as far as the economy was concerned. In most cases the arrival of new owners seems not to have changed the way that land was farmed. The history of Roman agriculture can, naturally, be correlated with the history of Roman imperial expansion. But in so far as this involved the growth of new markets it was consumption led, rather than driven by innovations in production. New techniques, breeds and cultigens did spread, but the impact was greatest in areas where colonization in the formal sense is least easy to demonstrate: the dissemination of irrigation techniques in arid zones, the spread of arboriculture in Europe north of the Alps and new means of processing and distributing fish products are cases in point.

Few Roman colonies were created outside the Mediterranean before the 1st century CE. Earlier colonization schemes mostly targeted territory that was as similar as possible to that familiar to the settlers. If the standard maps of Sullan, Caesarian, Triumviral and Augustan *coloniae* are examined,[34] clear patterns emerge. On the Italian peninsula the greatest concentrations are in Campania, in the Po Valley and along the northern Adriatic coast. The less fertile Mezzogiorno, especially Puglia, suffered few colonizations and those that took place, like the two colonizations of Tarentum, were in favoured sites. Outside Italy the preferred locations were the alluvial plains of the lower Rhône and the Guadalqivir; other coastal plains in Mediterranean France, Spain and around Carthage, and the Atlantic sites in Lusitania and Mauretania and around Carthage. To these can be added the prime locations in Sicily and Epirus[35] and also those in Macedonia. The match to the best agricultural territory in the Mediterranean basin is not perfect. Somehow the great river valleys of western Asia Minor were not colonized south of Alexandria Troas and only Beirut and Heliopolis had *coloniae* before the death of Augustus. The southern Anatolian colonies are unusual in being located so far inland. But in general terms the impact of this period of colonization was to appropriate territory with climates and landscapes most like those of Italy. The modern parallels are obvious.[36] Subsequent colonization schemes targeted different, mostly non-Mediterranean, landscapes, the frontier zones of the Rhineland and the Danube valleys, the continental interiors of the Balkans, the Magreb and the Roman Near East. The rate of settlement was slower too, and the means of expropriation and settlement quite different. But their stories demand separate treatment.

Almost all the colonies discussed in this volume were created in this period that began with the conclusion of the Sullan civil war and ended during the principate of Augustus. The revolutionary scale of this mass settlement was appreciated in antiquity. Augustus himself claimed to have settled more than 300,000 veterans either in *coloniae* or back in their *municipia* and to have given them land or money as a reward for military service.[37] Naturally he does not draw attention to the number of losers in this redistribution. Sulla had given land to some 80,000 soldiers – all in Italy – and Caesar some 50,000. Between the foundation of Narbonne in 118 and the end of Augustus' reign just over one hundred provincial communities had received Roman colonists, some on more than one occasion. Between 30 and 40 Italian communities had had the same experience in Augustus' reign, adding to maybe 20 odd in the dictatorship of Sulla.[38]

The detailed case studies gathered here show how the circumstances of the various foundations had marked resemblances. The two Iberian examples – Cordoba and Merida with Medellín – show how projects of settlement and redistribution were imposed on top of earlier schemes. The palimpsest landscapes of southern Gaul with their multiple overlapping cadastrations would tell a similar story.[39] The same violent disruption to existing regimes of ownership recurs in Sicily and Epirus, Crete and southern Asia Minor. Occasionally the actual mechanics of negotiation and implantation come into focus. Butrint offers a spectacular example of how local and imperial politics intersected to plan, prevent and then implement the colony, and then to shape its first few years. Merida allows us to watch the land surveyors at work. These are variations in the quality of evidence more than in the experiences of colonial

implantation. However much we might wish to recover discrepant experiences, the strong impression is that the mechanisms of colonial settlement varied little from one location to another. This should not surprise given the rapidity with which it took place, and the small group of people responsible for all these schemes.

Each moment of Roman colonization had its own character. Even those accounts – like those of Velleius or Salmon or Laffi – that represent colonization as a single long story, take care to emphasise the discontinuities. Occasionally the temporary cessations are seen as what needs explaining, as if emitting colonies was a somehow natural process for Rome, one that was perhaps even dangerous to interrupt for fear of bottling up social tensions at home. Yet the reality was that each moment of colonization was different in origin, aim and mechanism. This makes it important to explore the historical context of each movement. That with which these essays are concerned occurred during a period characterised by accelerating territorial expansion and by civil war. Most of Rome's eventual Empire was acquired between the 80 BCE and 10 CE, with expansion fastest in the sixties and fifties, and again in the twenties and teens BCE. The civil wars were most ferocious in the eighties and seventies, and the forties and thirties. The Augustan autocracy put a temporary stop to conquest and civil war. The greatest period of Roman settlement overseas is to be set firmly in the context of these various conflicts, with the seventies, the forties, and the twenties the key decades for colonization.[40] Dressing up blatantly partisan redistributions of land as colonization in the traditional style allowed Sulla, Caesar and Augustus to represent their acts as a resumption of the redistribution of Italian *ager publicus* to Roman citizens that took place after the Gallic and Hannibalic Wars. Revolution was again expressed as traditionalism.

Roman colonization was one component of these wider convulsions of the Mediterranean world. Those convulsions need to be seen against a background not of static systems but rather one of changes operating on different periodicities. Consider mobility. It is now widely accepted that from early in the last millennium BCE (if not earlier), the Mediterranean world was characterised by a background level of mobility of various kinds.[41] Superimposed on this sort of human 'Brownian motion', there were, during the last few centuries BCE, some structured patterns of movement that were the indirect consequence of Empire-building. Most of these have to be inferred rather than demonstrated, but they included movement of slaves from the peripheries of the Empire to its centre, and the movement of individuals from country to towns and from smaller to larger towns. The growth and maintenance of large urban populations in the major cities is inconceivable without such flows, given the certainty that their death rates exceeded birth rates.[42] Mass colonization represents a sudden intervention superimposed on these background patterns and secular trends. This kind of sudden change is appropriately described as catastrophic, hence my title.

Our knowledge of the catastrophe of late Republican colonization derives mainly from historical sources. Only very occasionally, as in the case of Cicero's correspondence on Butrint, we can observe the human experience of this.[43] But mostly we are reduced to saying, as in the case of Sicily, that by such and such a date a group of *coloniae* had appeared. It is now clear that only rarely did this mean the construction of new cities. As a result, the physical changes are difficult to detect. Corinth is one of the best and most intensively studied cases, yet even there questions remain about the exact nature of the colonial foundation on the ground.[44] The same applies to the sites of Lyon and Paestum.[45] The sense of a time lag between historically attested foundations and the first archaeological traces suggested the original title of the conference. But if archaeology and epigraphy are only rarely able to spot the moment of foundation, they have more powerful tools for studying changes in the longer term. The papers in this volume show how in onomastics and ceramics, in sociolinguistics and architecture, the aftermath of the colonization catastrophe can be pieced together.

What are the main conclusions to emerge? Perhaps the most important is that however similar the initial foundations, cities which had experienced colonization almost immediately started to develop on quite different trajectories. If colonization was a global catastrophe, then, the experiences of its aftermath (and for some of recovery) were very various and, if one wishes, discrepant. That colonies founded at the same time in the same region had different fates has long been realised. To the discussions here gathered on Lusitanian, Sicilian, Pisidian and Epirote clusters can be compared other studies of regional groups that also reveal the divergent fates of sister-foundations.[46] This is apparent whatever criterion we adopt, from the continued use of Latin epigraphy to that of *terra sigillata*.

What made some colonies succeed relative to others? A number of explanations are offered in different papers. Emerita out-competed its neighbour *coloniae* because of the new functions it acquired almost immediately in Roman provincial administration. Lyon and Nyon would offer a parallel case, as would Carthage and Utica. Butrint's success was owed to a mixture of patronage and the combination or good luck and adroit diplomacy that inserted itself into the new foundation myths of Rome. Corinth, first despised, became prominent through the cults to which it was heir and which it deliberately developed. Knossos was the beneficiary of trade routes. All of these explanations are plausible. Yet none have much to do with the colonial status of the cities concerned. Other, non-colonial, cities benefited from cult and a mythic connection to Rome: Aphrodisias is the obvious example. Not all governors were based in Roman colonies:[47] Ephesos, Antioch on the Orontes and Alexandria all show that centrality in governmental systems could benefit any city. Patronage must often have helped, but Butrint had contacts before the imposition of its first colony. The only conclusion possible is that colonial status alone was not a key determinant of future success. Medellín and Nyon remained small provincial towns, while other, non-colonial, cities thrived.

The idea, floated in respect of Knossos, that in the generations following the implantation of settlers we are observing a process of normalization, is an attractive one. Onomastics and public epigraphy in Greek lands – Sicily as well as the east – certainly suggested pressures to conform to the cultural standards of Greek *poleis*, but also that these operated on a slow timescale. The title *colonia* retained its high status, but over time the disparity between the cities with that title and those that were most successful must have become more and more apparent. Perhaps such perceptions provided one reason for colonial 'promotions' of centres like Lepcis that had not been subjected to the imposition of settlers or the confiscation of part of its land. One way to understand this is that secular trends reasserted themselves after the catastrophic disruption of the dying Republic. Market systems, pilgrimage routes, trade networks and governmental structures had for the most part emerged organically. By this I mean that urban networks develop as a consequence of their implication in wider patterns of activity, systems of dominance, geographical and political contexts. Cities in general succeed or fail largely on the basis of what role they play in such systems.[48]

Colonization changed little of this, simply allowing a different group to benefit from these processes. Colonization brought new owners but not usually any new capital, nor new technologies that would enable it to sustain that prestige. There is no sign that *coloni* managed their land any differently than did its previous owners. Nor do Roman emperors seem to have favoured *coloniae* over other kinds of city.

Catastrophic change is a sudden interruption. Some kinds of catastrophes can derail existing trends and change the rules of the game completely. Major extinction events are often viewed in these terms. The Roman colonization of last century BCE was not like that, however devastating it must have seemed at the time to the inhabitants of old cities like Butrint and Syracuse, or even new ones like Medellín and Cordoba. Rather, when the dust settled, the ancient Mediterranean worked in much the same way it always had done. A hundred years of solitude restored something like the pre-colonisation urban order, and the main legacy of that catastrophic scattering was a new vocabulary to express gradations of honour among cities that, by the early 3rd century, were all of them Roman.

Acknowledgements

These comments respond not only to the papers gathered here, generally refered to here by author's name followed by '*this volume*', but also to other papers presented at the conference held at St Andrews, and to the exceptionally lively and informative discussion around the table on that occasion. An important part of my argument on periodisation owes a good deal to Nicholas Purcell's insightful closing remarks. Naturally, what I have made of all this is my responsibility and no-one else's. I am also grateful to the Max Weber College of the University of Erfurt where these remarks were written during my tenure of a Visiting Fellowship as part of DFG funded research group.

Bibliography

Ando, C. 2007. "Exporting Roman Religion." In *Companion to Roman Religion*, J. Rüpke (ed.),(Oxford) 429–45.

Bispham, E. 2006. "Coloniam deducere: how Roman was Roman colonization during the Middle Republic." In *Greek and Roman Colonization. Origins, ideologies and interactions*, G. Bradley and J.-P. Wilson (eds), (Swansea) 73–160.

Boatwright, M. T. 2000. *Hadrian and the Cities of the Roman Empire* (Princeton).

Bradley, G., and J.-P. Wilson (eds) 2006. *Greek and Roman Colonization. Origins, ideologies and interactions* (Swansea).

Brunt, P. A. 1971. *Italian Manpower 225 B.C.–A.D. 14* (Oxford).

Brunt, P. A. 1974. "Conscription and volunteering in the Roman imperial army." *Scripta Classica Israelica* 1, 90–115.

Burrell, B. 2004. *Neokoroi. Greek cities and Roman emperors*, Cincinnati Classical Studies (Leiden and Boston).

Campbell, B. 1996. "Shaping the Rural Environment. Surveyors in ancient Rome." *Journal of Roman Studies* 86, 74–99.

Càssola, F. 1991. "La colonizzazione romana della Transpadana." In *Die Stadt in Oberitalien und in den nordwestlichen*

Provinzen des Römischen Reiches, W. Eck and H. Galsterer (eds) (Mainz), 17–44.

Chouquer, G. and F. Favory (eds) 1980. *Contribution à la recherche des cadastres antiques*, Annales littéraires de l'Université de Besançon (Paris).

Christol, M. 1999. "La municipalisation de la Gaule Narbonnaise." In *Cités, municipes, colonies. Le processus d'urbanization en Gaule et en Germanie sous le Haut Empire*, M. Dondin-Payre and M.-T. Raepsart-Charlier (eds) (Paris), 1–27.

Christol, M. 2006. "Interventions agraires et territoire colonial. Remarques sur le cadastre B d' Orange." In *Autour des Libri Coloniarum. Colonisation et colonies dans le monde romain. Actes du colloque International (Besançon, 16–18 octobre 2003)*, A. Gonzales and J.-Y. Guillamin (eds) (Besançon), 83–92.

Clavel-Lévêque, M. (ed.) 1989. *Puzzle gaulois. Les gaules en mémoire, textes, histoire*, Annales littéraires de Besançon (Paris).

Crawford, M. H. 2006. "From Poseidonia to Paestum via the Lucanians." In *Greek and Roman Colonization. Origins, ideologies and interactions*, G. Bradley and J.-P. Wilson (eds) (Swansea), 59–72.

Crosby, A. W. 1986. *Ecological Imperialism. The biological expansion of Europe, 900–1900*, Studies in environment and history (Cambridge).

Dondin-Payre, M., and M.-T. Raepsart-Charlier (eds) 1999. *Cités, municipes, colonies. Le processus d'urbanization en Gaule et en Germanie sous le Haut Empire* (Paris).

Fentress, E. (ed.) 2000. *Romanization and the City. Creations, transformations and failures*, in J. H. Humphrey (ed.), Journal of Roman Archaeology Supplementary Series.

Forni, G. 1953. *Il reclutamento delle legioni da Augusto a Diocleziano*, Pavia. Università. Facoltà di lettere e filosofia (Milan).

Freyberger, B. 1999. *Südgallien in 1. Jahrhundert v. Chr. Phasen, Konsequenzen und Grenzen römischer Eroberung (125–27/22 v. Chr.)*. Vol. 11, Geographica historica (Stuttgart).

Galsterer, H. 1976. *Herrschaft und Verwaltung im republikanischen Italien. Die Beziehungen Roms zu den italischen Gemeinden vom Latinerfrieden 338 vor Chr. bis zum Bundesgenossenkrieg 91 v. Chr.* Vol. 68, Münchener Beiträge zur Papyrusforschung und antiken Rechtsgeschichte (Munich).

Galsterer, H. 1991. "Römische Kolonisation im Rheinland", in *Die Stadt in Oberitalien und in den nordwestlichen Provinzen des Römischen Reiches*, W. Eck and H. Galsterer (eds) (Mainz), 9–16.

Gonzales, A. and Guillamin, J.-Y. (eds) 2006. *Autour des Libri Coloniarum. Colonisation et colonies dans le monde romain. Actes du colloque International (Besançon, 16–18 octobre 2003)*, Institut de Sciences et technique de l'Antiquité (Besançon).

Goudineau, C. (ed.) 1989. *Aux origines de Lyon*, Documents d'archéologie en Rhône-Alpes (Lyon).

Haensch, R. 1997. *Capita Provinciarum. Statthaltersitze und Provinzialverwaltung in der römischen Kaiserzeit*, Kölner Forschungen (Mainz).

Hermon, E. 2006. "La lex Cornelia Agraria dans le Liber Coloniarum I." In *Autour des Libri Coloniarum. Colonisation et colonies dans le monde romain. Actes du colloque International (Besançon, 16–18 octobre 2003)*, in A. Gonzales and J.-Y. Guillamin (eds) (Besançon), 31–45.

Herzig, H. E. 2006. "Novum genus hominum: Phänomene der Migratione im römischen Heer." In *"Troianer sind wir gewesen" Migrationen in der antiken Welt. Stuttgarter*

Kolloquium zur Historischen Geographie des Altertums, 8 2002 E. Olshausen and H. Sonnabend (eds) (Stuttgart), 325–8.

Hopkins, K. 1978. *Conquerors and Slaves. Sociological Studies in Roman History I*. Cambridge: Cambridge University Press.

Hopkins, K. 1978. "Economic Growth and Towns in Classical Antiquity." In *Towns in Societies. Essays in economic history and historical sociology*, P. Abrams and E. A. Wrigley (eds) (Cambridge), 35–77.

Horden, P. and N. Purcell 2000. *The Corrupting Sea. A study of Mediterranean history* (Oxford).

Hurst, H. (ed.) 1999. *The Coloniae of Roman Britain. New studies and a review. Papers of the conference held at Gloucester on 5–6 July, 1997*. J. H. Humphrey (ed.), Journal of Roman Archaeology Supplementary Series.

Hurst, H. and S. Owen (eds) 2005. *Ancient Colonizations. Analogy, similarity and difference* (London).

Jones, R. F. J. 1987. "A false start? The Roman urbanisation of western Europe." *World Archaeology* 19, no. 1, 47–58.

Keppie, L. J. F. 1983. *Colonisation and Veteran Settlement in Italy 47–14 BC* (London).

Laffi, U. 2007. *Colonie e municipi nello stato romano*, Storia e Letteratura. Raccolta di studi e testi.

Leveau, P., P. Sillières and J.-P. Vallat 1993. *Campagnes de la Méditerranée Romaine: Occident*. A. Schnapp and P. Vidal-Naquet (eds) (Rome), Bibliothèque d'Archéologie.

Levick, B. 1967. *Roman Colonies in Southern Asia Minor* (Oxford).

Mackie, N. K. "Augustan Colonies in Mauretania." *Historia. Zeitschrift für Alte Geschichte* 32, no. 3 (1983): 332–58.

Mann, J. C. 1983. *Legionary Recruitment and Veteran Settlement throughout the Principate*, University of London Institute of Archaeology Occasional Publications (London).

Millar, F. 1990. "The Roman coloniae of the Near East: a study of cultural relations." In *Roman Eastern Policy and Other Studies in Roman History. Proceedings of a Colloquium at Tvärminne 2–3 October 1987*, H. Solin and M. Kajava (eds) (Helsinki), 7–58.

Moatti, C. 2001. "Les archives du census: le contrôle des hommes." *Melanges de l'École française à Rome* 113, no. 2, 559–764.

Moatti, C. (ed.) 2004. *La mobilité des personnes en Méditerranée de l'antiquité à l'époque moderne. Procédures de contrôle et documents d'identification*. Collection de l'Ecole française de Rome (Rome).

Moatti, C. and Kaiser, W. (eds) 2007. *Gens de passage en Méditerranée de l'Antiquité à l'époque moderne. Procédures de contrôle et d'identification*, Collection L'atelier méditerranéen (Paris).

Patterson, J. R. 2006. "Colonization and historiography. The Roman Republic." In *Greek and Roman Colonization. Origins, ideologies and interactions*, G. Bradley and J.-P. Wilson (eds) (Swansea), 189–212.

Purcell, N. 1987. "The Nicopolitan Synoecism and Roman urban policy." In *Nicopolis I. Proceedings of the first international symposium on Nicopolis 23rd–29th September 1984*, E. K. Chrysos (ed.) (Preveza), 71–90.

Purcell, N. 1990. "The creation of provincial landscape. The Roman impact on Cisalpine Gaul." In *The Early Roman Empire in the West*, T. Blagg and M. Millett (eds) (Oxford), 7–29.

Richardson, J. S. 1986. *Hispaniae. Spain and the development of Roman imperialism* (Cambridge).

Purcell, N. 2005. "Romans in the Roman World." In *Cambridge Companion to the Age of Augustus*, K. Galinsky (ed.) (New York), 85–105.

Rizakis, A. D. 1997. "Roman colonies in the province of Achaia: territories, land and population." In *The Early Roman Empire in the East*, S. E Alcock (ed.) (Oxford), 15–36.

Romano, D. 2000. "A tale of two cities: Roman colonies at Corinth." In *Romanization and the City. Creations, transformations and failures*, E. Fentress (ed.) (Portsmouth, Rhode Island), 83–104.

Rüpke, J. 2006. "Urban religion and imperial expansion: priesthoods in the Lex Ursonensis", in *The Impact of Imperial Rome on Religions, Ritual and Religious Life in the Roman Empire*, L. de Blois, P. Funke and J. Hahn (eds) (Leiden and Boston), 11–23.

Salmeri, G., A. Raggi and A. Baroni (eds) 2004. *Colonie Romane nel mondo greco*, Minima Epigraphica et Papyrologica – Supplementa (Rome).

Salmon, E. T. 1969. *Roman Colonization under the Republic* (London).

Scheidel, W. 2004. "Human mobility in Roman Italy I: the free population." *Journal of Roman Studies* 94, 1–26.

Scheidel, W. 2005. "Human mobility in Roman Italy II: the slave population." *Journal of Roman Studies* 95, 64–79.

Shaw, B. D. 1981. "The Elder Pliny's African Geography." *Historia. Zeitschrift für Alte Geschichte* 30, no. 4, 421–71.

Silberberg-Pierce, S. 1986. "The many faces of the Pax Augusta: images of war and peace in Rome and Gallia Narbonensis." *Art History* 9, 306–24.

Sweetman, R. J. 2007. "Roman Knossos. The nature of a globalized city." *American Journal of Archaeology* 111, no. 1, 61–81.

Trimble, J. 2001. "Rethinking 'Romanization' in early imperial Greece: Butrint, Corinth and Nicopolis." *Journal of Roman Archaeology* 14, 625–28

Vittinghof, F. 1952. *Römische Kolonisation und Bürgerrechtspolitik unter Caesar und Augustus* (Mainz).

Wierschowski, L. 2001. *Fremde in Gallien – "Gallier" in der Fremde: die epigraphisch bezeugte Mobilität in, von und nach Gallien vom 1. bis 3. Jh. n. Chr.: (Texte-Übersetzungen-Kommentare)*. Vol. 159, Historia Einzelschriften (Stuttgart).

Woolf, G. 1997. "The Roman urbanization of the east", in *The Early Roman Empire in the East*, S. E. Alcock (ed.) (Oxford), 1–14.

Notes

1. Baldwin Bowsky *this volume.*
2. For recent approaches to this phenomenon, see C. Moatti, ed., *La mobilité des personnes en Méditerranée de l'antiquité à l'époque moderne. Procédures de contrôle et documents d'identification* Collection de l'Ecole française de Rome (2004), C. Moatti and W. Kaiser, eds, *Gens de passage en Méditerranée de l'Antiquité à l'époque moderne. Procédures de contrôle et d'identification*, Collection L'atelier méditerranéen (2007), C. Moatti, "Les archives du census: le contrôle des hommes," *Melanges de l'École française à Rome* 113, no. 2 (2001), W. Scheidel, "Human mobility in Roman Italy I: the free population," *Journal of Roman Studies* 94 (2004), W. Scheidel, "Human mobility in Roman Italy II: the slave population," *Journal of Roman Studies* 95 (2005), L. Wierschowski, *Fremde in Gallien – "Gallier" in der Fremde: die epigraphisch bezeugte Mobilität in, von und nach Gallien vom 1. bis 3.*

Jh. n. Chr.: (Texte-Übersetzungen-Kommentare). vol. 159, Historia Einzelschriften (2001).

3. N. Purcell, "Romans in the Roman World," in *Cambridge Companion to the Age of Augustus*, ed. K. Galinsky (2005).

4. K. Hopkins, "Economic Growth and Towns in Classical Antiquity," in *Towns in Societies. Essays in economic history and historical sociology*, ed. P. Abrams and E. A Wrigley, *Past and Present Publications* (1978), G. Woolf, "The Roman urbanization of the east," in *The Early Roman Empire in the East*, ed. S. E. Alcock (1997), R. F. J. Jones, "A false start? The Roman urbanisation of western Europe," *World Archaeology* 19, no. 1 (1987).

5. On Medellin, see Edmondson *this volume*. On other kind of informal settlement in the context of peripheral imperialism, such as the 'hybrid' settlements at Carteia and Gracchuris, see J. S. Richardson, *Hispaniae. Spain and the development of Roman imperialism* (1986), H. E. Herzig, "Novum genus hominum: Phänomene der Migratione im römischen Heer," in *"Troianer sind wir gewesen" Migrationen in der antiken Welt. Stuttgarter Kolloquium zur Historischen Geographie des Altertums, 8 2002*, ed. E. Olshausen and H. Sonnabend, *Geographica Historica* (2006).

6. On the complex status of Nicopolis see Bowden *this volume* and also N. Purcell, "The Nicopolitan Synoecism and Roman urban policy," in *Nicopolis I. Proceedings of the first international symposium on Nicopolis 23rd–29th September 1984*, ed. Euangelos K. Chrysos (1987).

7. On Spain B. D. Shaw, "The Elder Pliny's African Geography," *Historia. Zeitschrift für Alte Geschichte* 30, no. 4 (1981). On Africa, appendix 14 of P. A. Brunt, *Italian Manpower 225 BC–AD 14* (1971). Reconstruction of such documents are essential to N. K. Mackie, "Augustan Colonies in Mauretania," *Historia. Zeitschrift für Alte Geschichte* 32, no. 3 (1983).

8. Velleius 1.14–15. A conscious desire to minimise the differences between the colonization ventures of different periods seems revealed by the lack of mention of differences of status, while a consciousness that this homogenisation had its limits is revealed by the self-conscious exclusion of 'military colonies' from the lists.

9. On which see A. Gonzales and J.-Y. Guillamin, eds, *Autour des Libri Coloniarum. Colonisation et colonies dans le monde romain. Actes du colloque International (Besançon, 16–18 octobre 2003)*, Institut de Sciences et technique de l'Antiquité (2006).

10. Servius ad Virg *Aeneid* 1. 12 defining the term (stressing the contrast with a *secessio* as a movement of the people that took place without the consent of the home city), and 7.755 city Cato the Elder on ploughing the boundary. On this and on colonial ritual in general, C. Ando, "Exporting Roman Religion," in *Companion to Roman Religion*, ed. J. Rüpke (2007). On the cults of *coloniae*, and their differences from Rome, J. Rüpke, "Urban religion and imperial expansion: priesthoods in the Lex Ursonensis," in *The Impact of Imperial Rome on Religions, Ritual and Religious Life in the Roman Empire*, ed. L. de Blois, P. Funke, and J. Hahn (2006).

11. Vitruvius *On architecture* Book 1. 4–7 dealing with the foundations of cities in general although much clearly relates primarily to colonization. Aulus Gellius *Attic Nights* 16.13.8–9 for the characterisation of colonies as 'small images and imitations of the Roman people'. On the extent to which modern discussions rely on this passage see Ando, "Exporting Roman Religion," 431–6, E. Bispham, "Coloniam deducere: how Roman was Roman colonization during the Middle Republic," in *Greek and Roman Colonization. Origins, ideologies and interactions*, ed. G. Bradley and J.-P. Wilson (2006).

12. Most recently U. Laffi, *Colonie e municipi nello stato romano*, Storia e Letteratura. Raccolta di studi e testi (2007), M. Dondin-Payre and M.-T. Raepsart-Charlier, eds, *Cités, municipes, colonies. Le processus d'urbanization en Gaule et en Germanie sous le Haut Empire* (1999). For a deft discussion of how the category *colonia* has been reified and normalised, see Bispham, "Coloniam deducere: how Roman was Roman colonization during the Middle Republic."

13. On archaeological blueprints of colonization a range of views are presented in E. Fentress, ed., *Romanization and the City. Creations, transformations and failures*, Journal of Roman Archaeology Supplementary Series (Journal of Roman Archaeology, 2000). Fentress' own successive reassessments of the archaeology of Cosa have demolished a number of myths.

14. The best general accounts are H. Galsterer's entry in *Der Neue Pauly* sv. coloniae and E. T. Salmon, *Roman Colonization under the Republic* (1969), Fr. Vittinghof, *Römische Kolonisation und Bürgerrechtspolitik unter Caesar und Augustus* (1952). Two useful recent collections of essays are provided by G. Bradley and J.-P. Wilson, eds, *Greek and Roman Colonization. Origins, ideologies and interactions* (2006), H. Hurst and S. Owen, eds, *Ancient Colonizations. Analogy, similarity and difference* (2005).

15. See Baldwin Bowsky *this volume*.

16. *E.g.* N. Purcell, "The creation of provincial landscape. The Roman impact on Cisalpine Gaul," in *The Early Roman Empire in the West*, ed. T. Blagg and M. Millett (1990), G. Chouquer and F. Favory, eds, *Contribution à la recherche des cadastres antiques*, Annales littéraires de l'Université de Besançon (1980), A. D. Rizakis, "Roman colonies in the province of Achaia: territories, land and population," in *The Early Roman Empire in the East*, ed. S. E Alcock, *Oxbow Monographs* (1997).

17. B. Campbell, "Shaping the Rural Environment. Surveyors in ancient Rome," *Journal of Roman Studies* 86 (1996).

18. Bispham, "Coloniam deducere: how Roman was Roman colonization during the Middle Republic."

19. On the settlement of the Po Valley, F. Càssola, "La colonizzazione romana della Transpadana," in *Die Stadt in Oberitalien und in den nordwestlichen Provinzen des Römischen Reiches*, ed. Werner Eck and Hartmut Galsterer, *Kölner Forschungen* (1991), Purcell, "The creation of provincial landscape. The Roman impact on Cisalpine Gaul." For southern Gaul, see M. Clavel-Lévêque, ed., *Puzzle gaulois. Les gaules en mémoire, textes, histoire*, Annales littéraires de Besançon (1989), M. Christol, "La municipalisation de la Gaule Narbonnaise," in *Cités, municipes, colonies. Le processus d'urbanization en Gaule et en Germanie sous le Haut Empire*, ed. M. Dondin-Payre and M.-T. Raepsart-Charlier (1999), M. Christol, "Interventions agraires et territoire colonial. Remarques sur le cadastre B d' Orange," in *Autour des Libri Coloniarum. Colonisation et colonies dans le monde romain. Actes du colloque International (Besançon, 16–18 octobre 2003)*, ed. A. Gonzales and J.-Y. Guillamin, *Institut de Sciences et technique de l'Antiquité* (Besançon: Presses Universitaires de Franche-Comté, 2006), B. Freyberger, *Südgallien*

in 1. Jahrhundert v. Chr. Phasen, Konsequenzen und Grenzen römischer Eroberung (125–27/22 v. Chr.), vol. 11, Geographica historica (1999). From a different perspective, P. Leveau, P. Sillières, and J.-P. Vallat, *Campagnes de la Méditerranée Romaine: Occident*, ed. A. Schnapp and P. Vidal-Naquet, Bibliothèque d'Archéologie (1993).

20. Jiménez and Carillo *this volume*. Among many other examples of multiple colonizations the cases of Cosa, Capua and Corinth are well known.

21. M. H. Crawford, "From Poseidonia to Paestum via the Lucanians," in *Greek and Roman Colonization. Origins, ideologies and interactions*, ed. G. Bradley and J.-P. Wilson (2006).

22. Dio *Roman History* 69.12 on Jerusalem, *Epitome* 73.15 on Rome and also *Historia Augusta Life of Commodus* 8.6.

23. Gellius Attic Nights 16.13 with discussion in chapter 3 of M. T. Boatwright, *Hadrian and the Cities of the Roman Empire* (2000).

24. On which B. Burrell, *Neokoroi. Greek cities and Roman emperors*, Cincinnati Classical Studies. New Series (2004). A less close parallel are the first century foundations incorporating the element Caesar-, Augusto- and the like.

25. J. R. Patterson, "Colonization and historiography. The Roman Republic," in *Greek and Roman Colonization. Origins, ideologies and interactions*, ed. G. Bradley and J.-P. Wilson (2006).

26. Cicero *On the Agrarian Law* 2.27 in a reference to ancestral practice, compare *On behalf of Fonteius* 1 applied to Narbonne.

27. On Anatolia see De Giorgi *this volume* and B. Levick, *Roman Colonies in Southern Asia Minor* (1967). On the Sulla colonies *muro deductae* E. Hermon, "La lex Cornelia Agraria dans le Liber Coloniarum I," in *Autour des Libri Coloniarum. Colonisation et colonies dans le monde romain. Actes du colloque International (Besançon, 16–18 octobre 2003)*, ed. A. Gonzales and J.-Y. Guillamin, *Institut de Sciences et technique de l'Antiquité* (2006).

28. F. Millar, "The Roman coloniae of the Near East: a study of cultural relations," in *Roman Eastern Policy and Other Studies in Roman History. Proceedings of a Colloquium at Tvärminne 2–3 October 1987*, ed. H. Solin and M. Kajava, *Commentationes Humanarum Litterarum* (1990), Rizakis, "Roman colonies in the province of Achaia: territories, land and population", G. Salmeri, A. Raggi, and A. Baroni, eds, *Colonie Romane nel mondo greco*, Minima Epigraphica et Papyrologica – Supplementa (2004).

29. S. Silberberg-Pierce, "The many faces of the Pax Augusta: images of war and peace in Rome and Gallia Narbonensis," *Art History* 9 (1986).

30. The colonial charter of Urso refers to levies in emergencies. Presumably inhabitants of colonies were subject to the same processes of levy and recruitment as other provincial communities, on which P. A. Brunt, "Conscription and volunteering in the Roman imperial army," *Scripta Classica Israelica* 1 (1974).

31. J. C. Mann, *Legionary Recruitment and Veteran Settlement throughout the Principate*, University of London Institute of Archaeology Occasional Publications (1983), Giovanni Forni, *Il reclutamento delle legioni da Augusto a Diocleziano*, Pavia. Università. Facoltà di lettere e filosofia. Pubblicazioni (1953). For the late Republican prequel see L. J. F. Keppie, *Colonisation and Veteran Settlement in Italy 47–14 BC* (1983).

32. Ando, "Exporting Roman Religion" points out that only in rare periods do literary and archaeological evidence about colonization coincide.

33. Servius *On the Aeneid* 1.12 "colonia dicta est a colendo".

34. Conveniently gathered by H. Galsterer in his *Neue Pauly* entry s.v. coloniae. The basis are the lists provided by E. Kornemann in the *Realencyclopädie* 4, 510–88, the maps are drawn from there and Hartmut Galsterer, *Herrschaft und Verwaltung im republikanischen Italien. Die Beziehungen Roms zu den italischen Gemeinden vom Latinerfrieden 338 vor Chr. bis zum Bundesgenossenkrieg 91 v. Chr*, vol. 68, Münchener Beiträge zur Papyrusforschung und antiken Rechtsgeschichte (1976), Vittinghof, *Römische Kolonisation und Bürgerrechtspolitik unter Caesar und Augustus*, Salmon, *Roman Colonization under the Republic*, Keppie, *Colonisation and Veteran Settlement in Italy 47–14 BC*. For alternative lists of coloniae see Brunt, *Italian Manpower 225 BC–AD 14*, appendices 15 and 17.

35. Korhonen *this volume*, Bowden *this volume*

36. Compare the distinction made between the experience of settlers in the temperate 'Neo-Europes' and those in the tropics by A. W. Crosby, *Ecological Imperialism. The biological expansion of Europe, 900–1900*, Studies in environment and history (1986).

37. *Res Gestae* 3.

38. For all these calculations, conducted with exemplary caution, see Brunt, *Italian Manpower 225 BC–AD 14*, especially chapters 15 and 19 and appendices 15 and 17.

39. See note 20 above.

40. Brunt, *Italian Manpower 225 BC–AD 14*.

41. P. Horden and N. Purcell, *The Corrupting Sea. A study of Mediterranean history* (2000), 377–400.

42. The most lucid account remains that in chapter 1 of K. Hopkins, *Conquerors and Slaves. Sociological Studies in Roman History I* (1978). See also Brunt, *Italian Manpower 225 BC–AD 14* and the works cited in note 3 above.

43. Hansen *this volume*

44. Scotton *this volume*. D. Romano, "A tale of two cities: Roman colonies at Corinth," in *Romanization and the City. Creations, transformations and failures*, ed. E. Fentress, *Journal of Roman Archaeology Supplementary Series* (2000).

45. C. Goudineau, ed., *Aux origines de Lyon*, Documents d'archéologie en Rhône-Alpes (1989), Crawford, "From Poseidonia to Paestum via the Lucanians."

46. *E.g.* Levick, *Roman Colonies in Southern Asia Minor*, Rizakis, "Roman colonies in the province of Achaia: territories, land and population", H. Hurst, ed., *The Coloniae of Roman Britain. New studies and a review. Papers of the conference held at Gloucester on 5–6 July, 1997*, Journal of Roman Archaeology Supplementary Series (1999), J. Trimble, "Rethinking "Romanization' in early imperial Greece: Butrint, Corinth and Nicopolis," *Journal of Roman Archaeology* 14 (2001), Mackie, "Augustan Colonies in Mauretania", H. Galsterer, "Römische Kolonisation im Rheinland," in *Die Stadt in Oberitalien und in den nordwestlichen Provinzen des Römischen Reiches*, ed. W. Eck and H. Galsterer, *Kölner Forschungen* (1991).

47. For a full survey R. Haensch, *Capita Provinciarum. Statthaltersitze und Provinzialverwaltung in der römischen Kaiserzeit*, Kölner Forschungen (1997).

48. R. J. Sweetman, "Roman Knossos. The nature of a globalized city," *American Journal of Archaeology* 111, no. 1 (2007).